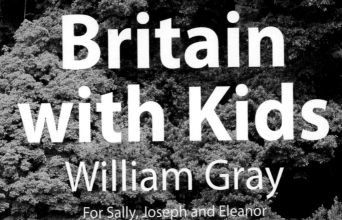

Britain
with Kids
William Gray

For Sally, Joseph and Eleanor

Green Loch cycle trail, Glenmore, Cairngorms. Previous page: canoeing on Ullswater, Lake District.

Not going on holiday in Britain this year? Poor you. Never mind, though, I'm sure you'll have a great time and everything, but do you realise what you're missing? Family holidays in Britain are riding a new wave of popularity. And it's not simply due to the strength of the euro, the credit crunch or concerns over the costs of flying further afield.

The fact is there's never been a more varied, enticing or exciting range of things to do or places to stay. Not only is Britain beautiful and diverse, with beaches and national parks to rival the world's finest, but its family attractions – from castles to woodland adventure parks – are some of the best you'll find anywhere.

Britain with Kids is a celebration of all these things and much more. It aims to inform and inspire; highlighting accommodation and local food that won't cost the earth, as well as trumpeting the best child-friendly activities, back-to-nature escapades and big days out – many of which are free. So, don't let your family holidays languish like seaweed on a sluggish tide, coming and going with barely a ripple of excitement. Explore Britain with your kids and give family holidays a fresh surge of adventure.

Award-winning writer and photographer **William Gray** is also the author of Footprint's *Travel with Kids*, voted Guidebook of the Year 2008 by the British Guild of Travel Writers.

BeWILDerwood, Norfolk.

About the book

Britain with Kids is a bit like an RNLI beach lifeguard – good looking and useful to have around. It will happily grace a coffee table for winter evening perusal, just as it can slip into a coat pocket or the glovebox of your car for on-the-spot holiday reference. On this page you'll find background information on getting the most out of the book, plus some important safety information.

Beach safety

The 'FLAGS' code by the RNLI (rnli.org.uk/beachlifeguards) is a handy checklist for staying safe at the beach:

F Find the red and yellow flags and swim between them.

L Look at the safety signs.

A Ask a lifeguard for advice.

G Get a friend to swim with you.

S Stick your hand in the air and shout for help if you get into difficulty.

Family favourites

Some family holiday operators have a presence in several parts of Britain. Five of the most special are highlighted in *Family favourites* (pages 12-23), but it's also worth checking out the following well established and deservedly popular options:

Butlins T0845-070 4734, butlins.com.
Haven T0871-468 0499, haven.com.
Pontins T0844-576 5943, pontins.com.

Family rates

Unless otherwise specified, family rates quoted in *Britain with Kids* are for two adults and two children. If you have more than two children it's always worth checking if there are special deals for larger families.

Members' perks

Throughout *Britain with Kids*, boxes highlight properties, nature reserves and attractions that are free to members of English Heritage, The National Trust and The Royal Society for the Protection of Birds (RSPB). Family membership of these charities represents excellent value for money when travelling in Britain, and also helps to support conservation work.

English Heritage T0870-333 1182, english-heritage.org.uk. Annual membership £41.50/adult, including up to six children (under 19).

The National Trust T0844-800 1895, nationaltrust.org.uk. Annual family membership £82 (two adults and their children under 18, free for under 5s). Direct debit rate of £61.50 is available for first year's membership.

The RSPB T01767-693680, rspb.org.uk. For family membership (two adults and all children under 19) you can choose how much to give, although £5/month is suggested.

Blue Flag awards

These are given for one season only and are subject to change.

Overseas travellers

See page 310 for travel advice and other useful information.

Tourist Boards

Details for local and regional tourist boards are given in relevant chapters.

Britain visitbritain.co.uk.
England enjoyengland.com.
Wales visitwales.com.
Scotland visitscotland.com.

Contents

8   **Top 10**

12   **Family favourites**
14   Feather Down Farm Days
16   Center Parcs
18   Forest Holidays
20   Luxury Family Hotels
22   Boating Holidays

24   **Kids' stuff**

28   **Southeast England**
32   London
34   Sussex
46   Isle of Wight
64   New Forest

68   **Southwest England**
72   Isles of Scilly
74   Jurassic Coast
88   Devon
118   Cornwall

150 **Central & East England**
154   Cotswolds
156   Forest of Dean

168   National Forest
174   North Norfolk

190 **North England**
194   Peak District
196   Yorkshire
214   Lake District
230   Northumberland

238 **Wales**
242   Pembrokeshire
260   Gower Peninsula
268   Snowdonia

282 **Scotland**
286   Glasgow & Edinburgh
288   The Cairngorms
302   Isle of Mull

310   Information for
        Overseas travellers
311   Index

A rough
diamond in
the Lizard's
crown,
Kynance
Cove is the
stuff of
childhood
fantasy.

Beach beauties

Bantham South Devon 97
Barafundle Pembrokeshire 246
Fidden Bay Isle of Mull 308
Holkham Bay Norfolk 178
Kynance Cove Cornwall 128
Newton Haven Northumberland 231
Rhossili Gower Peninsula 265
Whistling Sands Llŷn Peninsula 273
Whitesand Bay Cornwall 126
Woolacombe Sands North Devon 95

Cool rides

Camel Trail Cornwall 132
Cardi Bach Pembrokeshire 250
Cornish Camels 132
Doone Valley Trekking Exmoor 100
Family Cycle Trail Forest of Dean 158
Llama trekking Forest of Dean 160
Mawddach Trail Snowdonia 275
Loch Morlich Cairngorms 292
Seven Sisters Park Sussex 39
Tarka Trail North Devon 99

Perfect pitches

Bracelands Forest of Dean 164
Cloud Farm Exmoor 108
Compton Farm Isle of Wight 59
Hook's House Farm Yorkshire 208
Low Wray Lake District 224
Pencarnan Farm Pembrokeshire 254
Sheilings Isle of Mull 304
South Penquite Farm Bodmin 140
Three Cliffs Gower Peninsula 262
Ty'n yr Onnen Snowdonia 278

Fish & chips

Audrey's Bridlington 211
Bardsley's Brighton 44
The Esplanade Lynmouth 116
Fishermen's Pier Tobermory 308
Harbour Lights Falmouth 148
Magpie Café Whitby 211
Mary Jane's Cromer 188
The Mermaid Barmouth 280

Something's Cooking Letterston 257
Stein's Padstow 148

Wild & wonderful

Bempton Cliffs gannets 206
Bolderwood fallow deer 65
Cairngorm reindeer 296
Cornwall basking sharks 122
Devon Badger Watch 101
Kimmeridge Bay snorkel trail 76
Mull eagles, otters and whales 307
Skomer Island puffins 248
Symonds Yat peregrines 159
Titchwell Marsh bird life 177

Free attractions

Beechenhurst Forest of Dean 158
Donkey Sanctuary Devon 76
Highland Folk Museum Scotland 290
Lake District Visitor Centre 218
The Moors Centre Yorkshire 199
National Railway Museum York 198
Natural History Museum London 32
Ranworth Broad Norfolk 177
Welsh Wildlife Centre 245
Wembury Marine Centre Devon 90

Local scoff

The Balloon Tree Yorkshire 211
Carruan Farm Cornwall 146
Clootie Dumplings Cairngorms 300
Cookies Crab Shop Norfolk 188
The Garlic Farm Isle of Wight 61
Glasshouse Café Pembrokeshire 257
Grasmere Gingerbread The Lakes 227
The Quay Café Devon 114
The Sea Shanty Devon 86
Shepherd's Forest of Dean 166

Crumbly but cool

Bamburgh Castle Northumberland 234
Bodiam Castle Sussex 40
Caernarfon Castle Snowdonia 276
Carisbrooke Castle Isle of Wight 54
Castell Henllys Pembrokeshire 252

Top 10

Kids will be like squirrels on steroids the moment they scurry inside the Discovery Centre at Conkers.

Fountains Abbey Yorkshire 206
St Michael's Mount Cornwall 136
Tintagel Castle Cornwall 136
Tintern Abbey Forest of Dean 163
Tower of London 32

Big days out
Abbotsbury Swannery Dorset 82
Alton Towers Staffordshire 155
Chessington Surrey 27
Conkers National Forest 169
Eden Project Cornwall 135
Isles of Scilly 72
London 32
Longleat Wiltshire 73
Lundy Island Devon 103
Robin Hill Park Isle of Wight 55

Boats & trains
Blakeney Point cruises Norfolk 185
Bluebell Railway Sussex 40
Cairn Gorm Mountain Railway 295
Ilfracombe Princess North Devon 98
North York Moors Railway 206
St Mary's Boatmen Isles of Scilly 72
SeaLife Surveys Isle of Mull 308
Snowdon Mountain Railway 276
South Devon Railway 103
Swanage Railway 83

Not-so-boring museums
Dinosaur Isle Isle of Wight 54
Eureka! Yorkshire 204
Future World Cornwall 134
Jorvik Viking Centre York 205
Kelvingrove Glasgow 286
Murton Park Yorkshire 207
Nat. Maritime Museum Cornwall 135
Our Dynamic Earth Edinburgh 287
Roald Dahl Museum Bucks 26
Science Museum London 32

Big thrills & spills
Canoeing River Wye 161
Coasteering Pembrokeshire 251

Kumali coaster Flamingo Land 205
Mountain biking Cairngorms 292
Ramsey Island RIB rides 249
Surfing Devon, Cornwall & The Gower
Tree climbing Isle of Wight 52
UK Sailing Academy Isle of Wight 53
Via Ferrata Lake District 221
White-water rafting Snowdonia 274

Zoos & aquariums
Amazon World Isle of Wight 56
Aquarium of the Lakes 222
Cotswold Wildlife Park 154
The Deep Yorkshire 204
Howletts Kent 26
London Zoo 32
Monkey World Dorset 82
Nat. Marine Aquarium Devon 102
Nat. Seal Sanctuary Cornwall 138
Weymouth Sea Life 83

Woodland adventures
Be WILDerwood Norfolk 182
Coed y Brenin Snowdonia 271
Cornish Tipi Holidays 145
Dalby Forest Yorkshire 203
Go Ape Various locations
Kelling Heath Norfolk 187
National Forest 168
Parkhurst Forest Isle of Wight 48
Puzzlewood Forest of Dean 162
Whinlatter Forest Lake District 218

Rites of childhood
Catch crabs off a harbour wall.
Slurp hot choc after a day's surfing.
Scoff fish and chips on the seafront.
Hunt for fossils and rock-pool critters.
Paddle a kayak to a secret cove.
Pitch a tent somewhere special.
Pedal a bike along a forest trail.
Roast marshmallows on a campfire.
Spot a dolphin on a boat trip.
Storm a castle's ramparts.

Top 10

14 Feather Down Farm Days

16 Center Parcs

18 Forest Holidays

20 Luxury Family Hotels

22 Boating Holidays

Feather Down Farm Days

Safari chic with wellies on, Feather Down Farm tents lead the herd when it comes to luxury camping. Lift the flap on these canvas creations and you step into a snug den complete with wood stove, oil lanterns, three bedrooms (including a secret cubbyhole for kids) and everything you need for a relaxing holiday at one of 20-plus working farms across Britain.

Each Feather Down Farm has a clay oven for baking potatoes or pizzas, and an honesty shop stocked with local produce. A few even have field spas or the option of renting a private chicken coop. But no matter how you embellish individual sites, the winning formula remains the same: cool camping plus effortless immersion in farm life.

A typical day starts with children hurrying outside in pyjamas and wellies to collect chicken eggs while you grind fresh coffee beans and clunk the kettle on top of the stove. Breakfast is always late – it will take the kids at least an hour to check on their favourite ponies, lambs and puppies. With your car parked out of sight (and mind) in the farmyard, and with no electricity to bring radio, television or computer games crashing into your consciousness, time at a Feather Down Farm ebbs and flows to a calming, rural rhythm.

Later in the day, the farmer may need a hand milking the cows or goats. You might plan a picnic or cycle ride (all farms offer bike rental), play hide and seek, build a den, ride a pony or simply squander a happy hour or two watching swallows flitting to and from their nests in an old barn.

At meal times, cooking becomes a family affair and a chance to indulge in the often-neglected pleasures of a good old chat, while bedtime stories are infused with the magical glow of candlelight.

T01420-80804, featherdown.co.uk. Apr-Nov, £395-795/ wk, £245-545/weekend, £195-495/midweek (Mon-Fri). Locations include Cornwall, Cumbria, Devon, Dorset, East Lothian, Essex, Hampshire, Herefordshire, Kent, Lancashire, Leicestershire, Lincolnshire, Somerset, Suffolk, Wales, West Sussex and Wiltshire.

Center Parcs

People who say Center Parcs is like Marmite (you either love it or hate it) obviously don't have kids themselves. From a child's point of view there is nothing not to like at one of these action-packed woodland villages where boredom – like your car – is left at the entrance and promptly forgotten.

The transition from the real world to a Center Parcs one requires three things: bicycle, swim gear and stale bread. There are at least nine million bicycles in every Center Parcs (it's how everyone gets around on the traffic-free woodland lanes), while the fabulous Subtropical Swimming Paradise – imagine The Eden Project with water chutes, wild rapid rides and a wave machine – will become a daily fixture in your itinerary. The bread, meanwhile, is for the ducks and geese that will be waiting outside your patio doors every morning to be fed.

Activities at Center Parcs are based largely on the three W's – woodland, water and wildlife. You can choose from over a hundred things to do for all ages, from tree trekking, falconry, quad biking and archery to canoeing, sailing, fishing and scuba diving. There's more than a nod towards conservation, too, with birdwatching, nature trails and ranger activities, while indoors you can sign up for dance and craft classes, ten-pin bowling, plus an Olympian range of sports.

It sounds exhausting, but it's actually quite revitalizing. You can easily clock up a normal year's worth of cycling during a week at Center Parcs, but the effort is rewarded by comfortable self-catering accommodation which features a growing number of lodges, some with their own games room and sauna. Each village also has an excellent range of restaurants for eating out, while the Aqua Sana Spa provides a stylish retreat for saddle-sore grown-ups in need of pampering.

T08448-267723, centerparcs.co.uk. Year round, from £249/week for a two-bedroom comfort villa (sleeps four). Center Parcs are located at Whinfell Forest, Cumbria; Sherwood Forest, Nottinghamshire; Elveden Forest, Suffolk and Longleat Forest, Wiltshire.

Forest Holidays

A partnership between the Forestry Commisson and The Camping & Caravanning Club, you might expect Forest Holidays to know a thing or two about running campsites in some of Britain's most beautiful woodland locations. But its select group of cabin sites in Cornwall, Yorkshire and Scotland might come as a surprise.

Branching out into cabin holidays has come as easily to Forest Holidays as falling off a log. Not only has it infused wild forests with home comforts, but it has done so in such a way as to preserve, or even enhance, the elemental thrill of sleeping deep in the woods. You'll hear tawny owls hooting – but from the comfort of your private verandah, a wood stove glowing in the lounge behind you. And chances are, your best sightings of squirrels and woodpeckers will be in the treetops directly above your open-air hot tub.

Each cabin is carefully sited so that you feel an intimate part of the woodland. Double-storey windows flood open-plan living areas with tree-dappled sunlight. Kitchens come with all the mod cons, most cabins have barbeques, flatscreen TVs and DVD players, while a few have an en-suite treehouse attached by an adventurer's bridge. You'll even find a Wii games console in Golden Oak cabins, but don't fret – children get ample opportunity to live in the real world thanks to ranger-led activities that include night-vision wildlife watching and forest survival skills. You can book them at the Forest Retreat, an information hub at the heart of each site where you can also buy local food and arrange activities such as mountain biking, canoeing and pony trekking.

T0845-130 8223, forestholidays.co.uk. Year round, from £209-891/wk for an Evergreen Cabin (sleeping 4-6) to £845-1975/wk for a Golden Oak Cabin (sleeping 8 with attached treehouse). Mid-week and weekend breaks from £104. Cabins are located at Deer Park, Cornwall; Keldy and Cropton, North Yorkshire, plus Argyll, Cairngorm and Strathyre, Scotland. See individual chapters for campsites in the Forest of Dean, New Forest, Yorkshire and Norfolk.

Luxury Family Hotels

It could be absolutely ghastly – little Mia running amok in the hotel lobby, shattering *l'ambience* and drawing disdainful glances from the concierge...

Going posh with kids only works when you find a luxurious hotel devoid of pretentiousness, where staff are able to engage with life forms lower than navel height and where the term 'child friendly' doesn't in fact mean 'child friendly but we'd really rather not, thank you awfully.'

Does such a place exist? Yes. In fact, there's a whole chain of them (if you'll excuse the crude expression) called Luxury Family Hotels. Each one is a stylish, character property set in a stunning location – from the Jacobean Woolley Grange in 14 acres of Wiltshire countryside to Suffolk's Ickworth Manor in 1800 acres of National Trust parkland. Cornwall's Fowey Hall, Dorset's Moonfleet Manor (see page 79) and The Elms in Worcestershire complete the absolutely fabulous five.

But let's drop the airs and graces. There's no denying that these hotels are upmarket and unique, offer indulgent spa treatments, a gorgeous array of suites and interconnecting rooms, superb cuisine and quaffable wine lists. What sets them apart from your average Hilton, though, is that adults and children are given equal importance.

You might expect facilities like swimming pools, trampolines, table football and playstations, but it's the human touches that add real value – baby sitting or baby listening, for example, or OFSTED-registered dens with qualified nannies organising games and activities, or staff that simply go out of their way to make sure your children are happy.

As all parents know (particularly if they have babies or toddlers), one of the the biggest luxuries in life is a having a happy, contented child. And if that means splashing out on a fancy hotel where you can spend time together as a couple as well as a family, it's got to be a price worth paying.

T01761-240124, luxuryfamilyhotels.com. Year round, from £160 dinner, bed and breakfast per room for two adults (children stay free when sharing with parents).

Boating Holidays

'Believe me, my young friend, there is nothing – absolutely nothing – half so much worth doing as simply messing about in boats.'

Of course, Ratty was absolutey right when he shared this nugget of wisdom with Mole in *The Wind in the Willows*. Moments later their boat struck the bank, but that didn't dent their enthusiasm for a jolly day out on the river.

You're bound to have the odd scrape or gunwale-grabbing moment if you take your kids on a boating holiday – safety obviously has to be paramount – but there's no denying the simple pleasures or sense of adventure that accompanies a journey by narrowboat or cruiser. Think it's all a bit too fuddy-duddy? Try telling that to children who love the idea of nesting in cosy cabins, taking turns at the helm, working lock gates, feeding swans, spotting kingfishers and tying up for riverside picnics. The leisurely pace of a boating holiday also makes it one of the best opportunities busy families will ever get to simply wind down, share a good book or simply chat. And don't imagine you'll be cramped or skimping on comforts. Most boats are cleverly equipped with kitchens, bathrooms and saloons, with many boasting mod-cons like flat-screen televisions.

Where to get afloat? The simple answer is 'Somewhere near you.' Britain's waterways range from the Norfolk Broads to Scotland's Caledonian Canal – with an intriguing tangle of canals and rivers stretching between Basingstoke and Skipton. Short breaks are available for testing the water, or you could embark on a two-week odyssey, perhaps sharing an eight-berth cruiser with another family.

Hoseasons, T0844-499 0088, hoseasons.co.uk/uk-boating. Hundreds of options are available. For a four- to six-berth cruiser on the Norfolk Broads, allow around £500-1000/wk depending on time of year. An eight-berth boat from Moonfleet Marine, Stalham, costs around £900-1750/wk. The four-berth *Brymar* narrowboat (pictured) from Clifton Cruisers, Rugby, costs around £750-1200/wk, while the eight-berth *Abbeydale* costs around £910-1500/wk.

Dig for glory
Make the perfect sandcastle

1 Location is crucial. Site your castle near a stream so it's easy to divert water into the moat. Also, make sure the sand is neither too dry nor too sticky.

2 A moat without a boat is no fun at all. Create a harbour on one side of your castle, using a piece of driftwood as a gate. Periodic dredging will be required.

3 Using a spade, carve steps and terraces on the flanks of the castle. Add pebbles and shells for windows and seagull feathers for medieval banners.

4 Don't overlook your outer defences. At least one tide-restraining wall will be required outside your moat. This should feature crenellations or 'dribble sand' towers.

5 Main access should always be via a bridge with pebble parapets (or a drawbridge using flat driftwood). Cobbles make ideal stepping stones across the moat.

6 Special features can include jetties to outlying towers and lighthouses, or tunnels scooped by hand through sturdy bastions of the main castle.

Harry spotter

You don't need a broomstick or magic wand to visit several of the places featured in the Harry Potter movies. Platform 9¾, the mystifying departure point for the Hogwarts Express, was filmed at London's King's Cross Station. Harry and his fellow wannabe-wizards disembark at Hogsmeade Station which is none other than Goathland in the Yorkshire Moors (page 206), while Glenfinnan Viaduct (page 297) featured in a spectacular action sequence in the *Chamber of Secrets*. The interior of Hogwarts School is based on several locations, including Lacock Abbey in Wiltshire, Gloucester Cathedral, Oxford University's Bodleian Library and the Great Hall at Christ Church – also in Oxford. In Northumberland, meanwhile, Alnwick Castle (page 237) will always be remembered for the setting for broomstick lessons and Quidditch matches.

Boredom busters

Car bingo Give players a sheet of paper and ask them to write down 25 different numbers between one and 99. The person in the front passenger seat calls out the last one or two digits from the licence plates of passing cars. The winner is the first to cross off all their numbers and shout "Bingo!"

Licence to thrill Make up phrases based on the letters of licence plates. For example, 234 IFS 00 could be 'Ice-cream for Sally', 'Ian fancies Susan' or 'I feel sick!'

Buzz words Pick a word, then turn on the radio or play a story CD and try to be the first to shout "buzz" when the word is mentioned.

Good read
10 children's classics set in Britain

Early years
Katie Morag's Island Stories
by Mairi Hedderwick (Red Fox)
A small Hebridean community seen through the eyes of a child. Katie Morag always seems to be in some sort of bother, but her family and the friendly islanders manage to keep her out of serious trouble.

Winnie-the-Pooh
by AA Milne (Egmont)
The original collection of stories about the world's most famous bear, including old favourites, such as when Piglet meets a Heffalump and Eeyore loses his tail. Hundred Acre Wood and the antics of Pooh, Piglet, Tigger and Christopher Robin are brought to life by EH Shepard's simple, but delightful illustrations.

Ages 6-12
The Wind in the Willows
by Kenneth Grahame (Egmont)
"Believe me, my young friend, there is nothing – absolutely nothing – half so much worth doing as simply messing about in boats."

Swallows and Amazons
by Arthur Ransome (Red Fox)
Camping on a 'castaway' island, fishing, swimming, sailing and exploring – all without an adult in sight. A childhood dream come true?

The Railway Children
by E Nesbit (Oxford)
When their father is falsely imprisoned for espionage, Bobbie, Peter, Phyllis and their mother are forced to abandon their fancy London lifestyle and move to the country where they pass the time waving at trains, befriending local characters, like Perks the station porter, and slowly devising a plan to prove their father's innocence.

Five go off in a Caravan
by Enid Blyton (Hodder)
"I DO love the beginning of the summer hols," said Julian. "They always seem to stretch out for ages and ages." A jolly super tale from The Famous Five series, but what adventure will Julian, Dick, Anne, George and Timmy find this time?

Teens
A Kestrel for a Knave
by Barry Hines (Penguin)
Life is tough for Billy Casper, a disillusioned teenager growing up in Yorkshire. But when he finds Kes, his pet kestrel, he discovers a new passion in life.

Cider With Rosie
by Laurie Lee (Vintage Classics)
A vivid and lyrical memoir of a childhood spent in rural bliss in a remote Cotswold village – before electricity or cars changed the world.

Watership Down
by Richard Adams (Puffin)
Fiver senses something terrible is about to happen to the warren, so he persuades his brother Hazel and a brave band of fellow bunnies to set out on a long and perilous journey in search of a new home. An epic and compelling tale about courage and survival against the odds.

Tarka the Otter
by Henry Williamson (Penguin Classics)
Timeless and simply beautiful, this classic tale of an otter living in the Devonshire countryside skilfully evokes life in the wild as seen through Tarka's own eyes. An exquisite portrait, rich in description, empathy and emotion.

Seaside safari

Join an organised rock-pool ramble or set off on your own, equipped with a good guidebook, such as *Seashore* (Dorling Kindersley, 2008). Remember to check tide times to ensure that you do not become trapped by the rising tide. Wear shoes with good grip, take care to disturb animals and plants as little as possible – particularly when looking under rocks – and leave creatures where you find them. Find out more about the Seashore Code from the Marine Conservation Society (mcsuk.org).

Barnacle *rock pool*	◯
Beadlet anemone *rocky shore/rock pool*	◯
Blue-rayed limpet *rock pool*	◯
Brown shrimp *sandy shore/rock pool*	◯
Common cockle *sandy shore*	◯
Common blenny or shanny *rock pool*	◯
Common goby *sandy shore/rock pool*	◯
Common limpet *rock pool*	◯
Common mussel *rock pool*	◯
Common periwinkle *rock pool*	◯
Common ragworm *sandy shore*	◯
Common starfish *rocky shore*	◯
Dog whelk *rock pool*	◯
Flat periwinkle *rock pool*	◯
Green sea urchin *rock pool*	◯
Hermit crab *rock pool*	◯
Painted top shell *rock pool*	◯
Razor shell *sandy shore*	◯
Rock goby *rock pool*	◯
Shore crab *rock pool*	◯
Snakelocks anemone *rock pool*	◯
Velvet swimming crab *rock pool*	◯

If you like Roald Dahl books

You'll love the **Roald Dahl Museum** (Great Missenden, T01494-892192, roalddahlmuseum.org, year round, Tue-Sun, £6/adult, £4/child (5-18), £19/family). Two fun and interactive galleries reveal the fascinating story of the phizz-whizzingly brilliant writer, while the Story Centre inspires you to dress up, get arty and put pencil to paper to create your own masterpiece. And even more scrumdiddlyumptious is that you get a free Story Ideas Book, just like Roald Dahl's, to scribble down your ideas.

If you like CBBC's Roar

You'll love **Howletts & Port Lympne Wild Animal Parks** (Kent, T01227-721286 for Howletts, T01303-264647 for Port Lympne, totallywild.net, year round, daily from 1000, £14.95/adult, £11.95/child (4-16), £48/family). The filming location for the children's television series, these outstanding wildlife conservation parks work with the Aspinall Foundation to breed rare and endangered animals for return to the wild. So far, they've managed to release Przewalski's horses, black rhinos, Sumatran rhinos, Cape buffalos, ocelots, pythons and gorillas to safe, protected areas in their homelands.

You can witness conservation-in-action by visiting the parks where you'll get spine-tingling views of tigers, gorillas, clouded leopards, Barbary lions, monkeys, tapirs, Iberian wolves, macaques, rhinos and many other threatened species from around the world. Don't miss the black rhino breeding sanctuary, Britain's largest herd of African elephants or the Walking with Lemurs enclosure.

At Port Lympne you can even go on safari – an expert ranger driving you across grasslands roamed by giraffe, black rhino, zebra, wildebeest, ostrich and antelope. And for the ultimate safari experience outside of Africa, Livingstone Safari Lodge (minimum age 9) offers overnight accommodation overlooking Kent's very own mini-Serengeti!

See you at Howletts!

Thrill rides
37 good reasons to have a growth spurt

The park	The ride	The thrill	The catch Min height
Alton Towers Staffordshire T0871-222 9950 altontowers.com	Nemesis	Experience G-forces greater than a space shuttle take-off.	140 cm/55 in
	Oblivion	More bonkers than a bungee – plunge 200 ft into the abyss.	140 cm/55 in
	Air	Float, swoop, soar, dive and feel like you're flying.	140 cm/55 in
	Rita	She's the Queen of Speed, reaching 60 mph in 2.5 seconds.	140 cm/55 in
	Ripsaw	Spinning is to be expected, but watch out for the water jets.	140 cm/55 in
	Submission	Wild contraption that spins and rotates in all directions.	120 cm/47 in
Blackpool Pleasure Beach T0871-222 1234 blackpoolpleasure beach.com	Pepsi Max Big One	World's tallest (236-ft) and fastest (87-mph) coaster.	132 cm/52 in
	Infusion	Suspended coaster, five loops, plus water features.	132 cm/52 in
	Ice Blast	Get catapulted at 80 mph up a vertical 210-ft tower.	132 cm/52 in
	Bling	Imagine being strapped to a Catherine wheel...	122 cm/48 in
	Grand National	Twin track racing wooden coaster.	117 cm/46 in
	Big Dipper	Classic coaster with five big drops and dips.	117 cm/46 in
	Avalanche	Britain's only bobsled coaster, reaching speeds of 50 mph.	112 cm/44 in
Chessington World of Adventures Surrey T0870-999 0045 chessington.co.uk	Rameses Revenge	Monster-machine lowers you head first over water fountains.	140 cm/55 in
	Rattlesnake	Spinning, twisting, dipping, bone-rattling ride.	140 cm/55 in
	Dragon's Fury	A fiery family spinning rollercoaster.	120 cm/47 in
	Billy's Whizzer	Dennis the Menace-inspired spinning thing. You will get wet.	120 cm/47 in
	Tomb Blaster	Battle with mummies to beat the curse of the tomb.	110 cm/43 in
	Vampire	Fly over Transylvanian treetops on a bloodcurdling coaster.	110 cm/43 in
Drayton Manor Staffordshire T0844-472 1950 draytonmanor.co.uk	Apocalypse	The world's first stand-up tower drop (175 ft at 4 Gs).	140 cm/55 in
	Shockwave	Europe's only stand-up rollercoaster.	140 cm/55 in
	G Force	Vertical ascent of 75 ft followed by loops at over 45 mph.	130 cm/51 in
	Maelstrom	Stomach-churning, outward-facing gyro-swing.	130 cm/51 in
	Stormforce 10	Plunge backwards down a 30-ft water drop.	120 cm/47 in
	Pandemonium	Swing through 360 degrees, experiencing a force of 3.8 Gs.	120 cm/47 in
Flamingo Land	See page 205.		
Legoland Windsor T0871-222 2001 legoland.co.uk	Viking Splash	Surge downstream in a fantasy Viking World.	110 cm/43 in
	Jungle Coaster	Legoland's fastest (37 mph) with a hair-raising 52-ft drop.	110 cm/43 in
	The Dragon	Twist and turn through the depths of a castle.	100 cm/39 in
	Pirate Falls	Mild but wild, swashbuckling water-splash ride.	100 cm/39 in
Thorpe Park Surrey T0870-444 4466 thorpepark.com	Saw	The world's first ever horror movie-themed rollercoaster.	140 cm/55 in
	Samurai	Relentless, spinning stomach-churner with forces of 5 Gs.	140 cm/55 in
	Stealth	0-80 mph in less than two seconds, and heights of 200 ft.	140 cm/55 in
	Colossus	Swirl and corkscrew around a thundering steel track.	140 cm/55 in
	Detonator	Get fired to ground level from a height of 100 ft at 45 mph.	130 cm/51 in
	Rush	Swing back and forth to 75 ft at over 50 mph, topping 4 Gs.	130 cm/51 in
	Tidal Wave	Climb to 85 ft then get soaked splashing down to earth.	120 cm/47 in

Fishing nets and floats,
Steephill Cove, Isle of Wight.

Contents

30 Map

32 London
33 Portsmouth
33 Thanet Coast

34 Sussex Coast
36 Fun & free
38 Best beaches
39 Action stations
40 Big days out
42 Sleeping
44 Eating
45 Essentials

46 Isle of Wight
48 Fun & free
50 Best beaches
52 Action stations
54 Big days out
58 Sleeping
60 Eating
63 Essentials

64 The New Forest

Southeast England

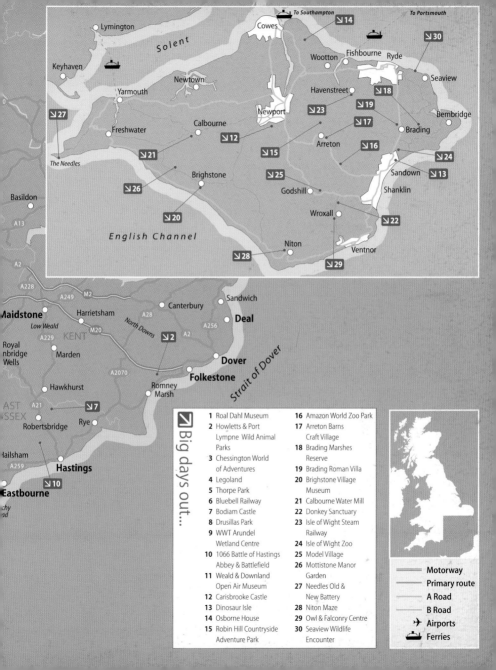

Lymington
Cowes
To Southampton
↘ 14
To Portsmouth
↘ 30
Solent
Keyhaven
Wootton
Fishbourne
Ryde
Seaview
Yarmouth
Newtown
Havenstreet
↘ 18
Bembridge
↘ 27
Newport
↘ 23
↘ 19
Brading
Calbourne
↘ 17
Freshwater
↘ 12
Arreton
The Needles
↘ 21
↘ 15
↘ 16
↘ 24
Sandown
↘ 13
↘ 26
Brighstone
↘ 25
Shanklin
Basildon
↘ 20
Godshill
A13
Wroxall
↘ 22
A2
English Channel
Niton
Ventnor
↘ 28
↘ 29

A228
A249
M2
Sandwich
Maidstone
Harrietsham
Canterbury
Low Weald
A28
North Downs
Deal
KENT
M20
A256
A2
Royal
A229
Marden
↘ 2
Dover
nbridge
A2070
Folkestone
Wells
Hawkhurst
Romney
Marsh
Strait of Dover
AST
A21
↘ 7
SSEX
Robertsbridge
Rye
Hailsham
A259
Hastings
↘ 10
Eastbourne

Big days out...

1 Roal Dahl Museum
2 Howletts & Port Lympne Wild Animal Parks
3 Chessington World of Adventures
4 Legoland
5 Thorpe Park
6 Bluebell Railway
7 Bodiam Castle
8 Drusillas Park
9 WWT Arundel Wetland Centre
10 1066 Battle of Hastings Abbey & Battlefield
11 Weald & Downland Open Air Museum
12 Carisbrooke Castle
13 Dinosaur Isle
14 Osborne House
15 Robin Hill Countryside Adventure Park

16 Amazon World Zoo Park
17 Arreton Barns Craft Village
18 Brading Marshes Reserve
19 Brading Roman Villa
20 Brighstone Village Museum
21 Calbourne Water Mill
22 Donkey Sanctuary
23 Isle of Wight Steam Railway
24 Isle of Wight Zoo
25 Model Village
26 Mottistone Manor Garden
27 Needles Old & New Battery
28 Niton Maze
29 Owl & Falconry Centre
30 Seaview Wildlife Encounter

── Motorway
── Primary route
── A Road
── B Road
✈ Airports
⛴ Ferries

London top 10

The London Eye
ba-londoneye.com
A fun, 30-minute ride and the best way for kids to grasp the scale of the capital and pinpoint landmarks, from the Houses of Parliament to Wembley Stadium.

The London Aquarium
londonaquarium.co.uk
A watery world of rushing streams, coral reefs, mangrove swamps and teeming rockpools, plus the aquarium's highlight is a huge Pacific tank prowled by sharks.

London Dungeon thedungeons.com
Torture, plague and the Great Fire of London – it's all here in gory detail, plus thrill rides like Extremis: Drop Ride to Doom, a simulated hanging for anyone over 120 cm tall.

The National Gallery nationalgallery.org.uk
Talks, workshops and trails are available for families at this fabulous (and free) collection of art.

British Museum thebritishmuseum.ac.uk
Children's trails at this free museum range from Ancient Egyptian quests to hunting for dragons. Don't miss the Egyptian mummies in Rooms 62-63.

Greenwich greenwich.gov.uk
Take a boat trip from central London to reach this World Heritage Site where the National Maritime Museum and Royal Observatory (nmm.ac.uk) has seafaring treasures and a spectacular planetarium.

Natural History Museum nhm.ac.uk
A skeleton of Diplodocus has long reigned supreme in the Central Hall of this magnificent (and free)

museum, but kids usually get more of a buzz from the new-fangled animatronic T-Rex in the dinosaur gallery. Other highlights include the Mammal Hall and the new Darwin Centre.

Science Museum sciencemuseum.org.uk
London's best museum for hands-on fiddling and twiddling, the Science Museum has play zones targeting different age groups, as well as motion simulators, science shows and an IMAX cinema.

London Zoo londonzoo.co.uk
Gorilla Kingdom is home to a troop of western lowland gorillas, while the Clore Rainforest Lookout recreates a little piece of Amazon jungle. The new Animal Adventure gets kids scurrying around at treetop level and underground to experience different habitats and learn about conservation.
And no visit is complete without riding on the top of a double-decker bus, brass-rubbing at St Martin-in-the-Fields, strolling through St James's Park, ogling the toys at Hamleys and waving to the Queen at Buckingham Palace.
>> visitlondon.com

Portsmouth

Portsmouth Historic Dockyard (historicdockyard. co.uk) is not only home to three of the most important warships ever built – HMS Victory, HMS Warrior 1860 and the Mary Rose – but it also boasts the Royal Naval Museum and Action Stations where you can find out what it's like to fly a helicopter or go into battle with the Royal Marines. Also on a military theme, **The D-Day Museum** (ddaymuseum.co.uk) uses a walk-through air-raid shelter, command room, crashed glider and landing craft to evoke war-time Britain. For more peaceful waters, head to **The Blue Reef Aquarium** (bluereefaquarium.co.uk) with its otter family, cuttlefish nursery and underwater tunnel. Pack your swim gear if it's warm – the aquarium's outdoor Blue Reef Beach Club has a sandy beach, fountains and water cannons. Another good warm-weather option, Southsea's seafront has a pebble beach, playgrounds, funfair and plenty of space to fly a kite. To really get on a high, though, you need to visit Portsmouth's **Spinnaker Tower** (spinnakertower.co.uk) – the city's shining white beacon rises 170 m tall and offers dizzying views from the glass-floored observation deck. Back on ground level, **Gunwharf Quays** (gunwharf-quays.com) has an 11-screen cinema, a bowling complex and a year-round programme of music and street theatre.
>> visitportsmouth.co.uk

Thanet Coast

The **Thanet Coast Project** (thanetcoast.org.uk) was established in 2002 to raise awareness of the unique coastline of northeast Kent. Beyond the traditional seaside towns of Margate, Broadstairs and Ramsgate, this geologically-rich shore of chalk stacks, arches, sandy bays and reefs is a haven for marine life and an internationally important wintering ground for birds. You can make a date with nature by joining one of the project's regular events and activities – many are free and include fossil hunting with the Rock Doc, cycle rides to Pegwell Bay, rock-pool rambles, orchid-spotting walks, beach cleans and a chance to try activities such as scuba diving and surfing. Several boat operators offer trips to see seals hauled out on the sandbanks off the Thanet Coast, including **Horizon Sea Safaris** (horizonseasafaris.co.uk), **Sandwich River Bus** (sandwichriverbus.co.uk), **Seasearcher Boat Trips** (seasearcher.co.uk) and **Wildlife Sailing** (wildlifesailing. com). For surfing lessons sign up with **Joss Bay Surf School** (jossbay.co.uk).
>> visitthanet.co.uk

South Bank highlights – The London Eye and London Aquarium.

Main photo: Bodiam Castle. Right: a handful of slipper limpets scooped up at West Wittering; ring-tailed lemur at Drusillas; flotsam seahorse at Seven Sisters Country Park.

Sussex

It's not everyday that Britain gets a new national park. Following its designation in 2009, the South Downs National Park rubs shoulders with other treasured landscapes like the Lake District and Snowdonia. And about time too. The coast and countryside of Sussex deserve the recognition.

To give neighbouring Hampshire fair credit, the South Downs National Park actually extends across the border as far west as Winchester. But it's only in Sussex that the new protected area dabbles its toes in the sea – and for many family holidays it's the sea that makes Sussex special.

The chalk cliffs of Beachy Head and The Seven Sisters are a fitting finale to the national park. At Hope Gap children can scour rock pools for speckled strawberry anemones or explore the Cuckmere Valley by bicycle or canoe. Head a short distance east or west, however, and wild pebbly beaches give way to the tidy proms of seaside resorts like **Eastbourne** and **Seaford**.

Sussex has a 'chameleon coast' – it changes its mood and appearance often. You could spend the morning sprinting across the vast, rippled tidal flats at **Wittering Sands** and the afternoon whooping it up at Harbour Park fairground in **Littlehampton**. Fossil sharks' teeth litter the sands at **Bracklesham Bay**, while real sharks cruise the Sea Life centre in **Brighton**. From donkey rides on **Camber Sands** to thrill rides on Brighton Pier; from sailing lessons in **Hove** to boat trips bound for Beachy Head, the Sussex coast is a natural magnet for families on holiday.

Don't overlook the Sussex countryside though. The South Downs and High Weald are prime territory for walking, cycling and horse riding, while Ashdown Forest is a must for fans of Winnie-the-Pooh. For the ultimate nostalgia rush, combine a game of Pooh Sticks near **Hartfield** with a steam-train ride on the Bluebell Railway between **Sheffield Park** and **Kingscote**. Other honeypots include **Arundel** (with its castle and wetland centre) and **Alfriston** (with its tea rooms and nearby Drusillas Park). East Sussex is also 1066 Battle Country, where the pretty village of **Battle** often echoes with war cries from children wielding wooden spears fresh from the battleground centre.

You must

- Walk with ring-tailed lemurs at Drusillas Park.

- Lay siege to mighty Bodiam Castle.

- Hunt for fossils at Bracklesham Bay.

- Play Pooh Sticks in Ashdown Forest (aka the '100 Acre Wood').

- Run wild on West Wittering beach.

- Feed the nene geese at Arundel Wetland Centre.

- Walk, canoe or cycle to Cuckmere Haven.

- Ride a steam train on the Bluebell Railway.

Out & about Sussex

Fun & free

Find a fossil shark's tooth

Bracklesham Bay, on the West Sussex coast, is one of Britain's most prolific and satisfying fossil-hunting beaches. All you need to do is pigeon-step along the sands at low tide, keeping your eyes peeled for sharks' teeth, rays' teeth and various fossil shells. Try to time your expedition to follow a spring tide after waves have scoured the fossil bed and washed the 40-million-year-old treasures onto the beach. Don't be tempted to venture onto the fossil-bearing, but dangerously soft muds and clays. If you want to join a fossil hunt with an expert, contact Chichester District Museum (T01243-784683, chichester.gov.uk).

Play Pooh Sticks

It's been replaced a couple of times (most recently in 1999 with a £15,000 grant from Walt Disney), but Pooh Sticks Bridge still spans a stream in the Ashdown Forest near Hartfield – the village where AA Milne wrote Winnie-the-Pooh in the 1920s. Best take your own sticks, though – they can be pretty scarce at this most popular of Pooh pilgrimage sites. Leaflets describing walks to the bridge are available from the Ashdown Forest Centre (Wych Cross, Forest Row, T01342-823583, ashdownforest.org) and Pooh Corner (pooh-country.co.uk), a shop on Hartfield's High Street that's crammed with Pooh memorabilia. Equip yourself with a map (and a little imagination) and you can also track down the North Pole, Eeyore's Sad and Gloomy Place, Roo's Sandpit and other Pooh spots. Just watch out for the Heffalump Trap as you approach Lone Pine from the Enchanted Place.

See the light

The Beachy Head Countryside Centre (T01323-737273, beachyhead.org) has a free exhibition focussing on the wildlife and history of the area, including a fascinating insight into how the lighthouse was built. The buggy-friendly Peace Path walk provides good views of the famous red-and-white-striped beacon.

Walk this way

One of Britain's National Trails (nationaltrail.co.uk), the South Downs Way runs 100 miles from Winchester to Eastbourne, undulating across beautiful countryside – much of which was declared a national park in March 2009.

In addition to the visitor centres at Beachy Head (left) and Seven Sisters Country Park (right), one of the best places for families to access the trail is from Duncton, near Petworth.

Watch the birdies

With circular trails across the Arun Valley, an excellent visitor centre, café and shop, children's events, Explorer Backpacks and an adventure playground, the RSPB Pulborough Brooks Reserve (T01798-875851, rspb.org.uk) is free to members, as is the WWT Arundel Wetland Centre (see page 41). Other good birdwatching sites in Sussex include the Pevensey Levels and Pagham Harbour.

Lying adjacent to Pulborough Brooks Reserve, Wiggonholt Common (mid-way between Pulborough and Storrington on the A283) is an area of open woodland where kids can play hide-and-seek, build dens and generally mess around.

Wander in the woods

In a region best known for its chalk downland, Friston Forest (forestry.gov.uk) provides 'leaf relief' with its network of walking and cycling trails weaving beneath a shady canopy of beech trees. The forest can be accessed from the Seven Sisters Country Park (see right). Bike hire is available from the Cuckmere Cycle Company (page 39).

Walk to the chalk

Hard luck kids, you have to walk if you want to see the famous chalk cliffs of The Seven Sisters. The good news is that it's one of the best family strolls in Britain. Pick up a free Seashore Safari leaflet from the visitor centre (see box), then set off on the mile-long track which follows the Cuckmere River through Seven Sisters Country Park. You can also cycle or canoe (see page 39) – either way, listen out for skylarks singing overhead and keep your eyes peeled for herons hunched over the riverbank. There are also Second World War pillboxes to explore, as well as three large concrete pillars, known as dragon's teeth, which were placed here to stop enemy tanks. Once you reach the beach, it's time for a picnic on the shingle – and an obligatory stone-throwing contest – before using your Seashore Safari leaflet to comb the strandline or delve in rock pools, depending on the tide. And, oh yes, don't forget to gaze up at those mighty cliffs of chalk. Walk back the same way, or take the high route over the downs.

Walking towards the visitor centre.

Seven Sisters Country Park
Off the A259 between Eastbourne and Seaford, T01323-870280, sevensisters.org.uk. Visitor centre open Apr-Oct, daily 1030-1630; Nov-Mar, Sat-Sun 1100-1600. Buses from Brighton, Seaford and Eastbourne stop at the park entrance. Car parking costs £2.50 for up to 2 hours, £3.50 for over 2 hours.
Pop into the visitor centre for information on local walks, bird sightings and displays on the changing shape of the Cuckmere Valley and Sussex coast. There's also a nature table crammed with strandline treasures, a sea horse sculpture made from debris washed up at Cuckmere Haven (see page 35) and a mammoth tusk found at Seaford Head.

Out & about Sussex

Best beaches

The two best sandy beaches in Sussex are Camber Sands and West Wittering (see below). The coastline is dominated by a chain of resorts with excellent facilities and a healthy stash of Blue Flag awards. From east to west, these include:

Hastings Divided into zones to help prevent children from getting lost, Pelham Beach lies next to the pier and has a prom bristling with amusements, restaurants and hotels.

Bexhill A popular spot for sailing and kitesurfing, Bexhill has a mainly shingle beach with a wide prom and beach huts.

Eastbourne Stretching from the pier to the Martello Tower, the resort's Blue Flag beach (shingle/sand) is backed by a stunning promenade with elegant hotels, an art deco bandstand and the famous Floral Carpet Gardens.

Brighton & Hove Two stretches of beach consistently scoop Blue Flag awards at this iconic resort – Hove Lawns and West Beach (between the piers). Safe swimming areas are dotted along the mainly pebbly stretch of coast, and there's also a lido at Saltdean. Brighton's seafront attractions are legendary, ranging from the aquarium at Sea Life Brighton (sealifeeurope.com) to Brighton Pier (brightonpier.co.uk) with its arcades and funfair.

Littlehampton Low tide reveals a huge expanse of sand at the Blue-Flag Coastguards Beach which has a Kids Care scheme (colour-coded wristbands linked to beach zones), a prom with grassy picnic areas and the excellent Harbour Park amusements (harbourpark.com).

Bognor Regis Another Kids Care programme operates at Bognor where the seafront has everything from crazy golf and amusement arcades to gardens and miniature trains. This seasoned family resort is also home to Butlins (see page 43).

Camber Sands

There's no shortage of holiday parks at Camber, but when the tide goes out at this stunning beach near Rye, a sandy wilderness emerges where you can walk for miles across rippled flats without seeing another footprint. There are shallow pools to paddle in, streams to dam and sand dunes to explore. Beach activities include horse riding, kitesurfing, windsurfing and donkey riding.

West Wittering

One of the finest stretches of sand on the Sussex coast, West Wittering has something for everyone. Shell-seekers can sift the strandline for slipper limpets and razor shells, while kite-flyers should find plenty of air-space at low tide when vast sand flats, dimpled by shallow lagoons, are exposed. To windsurf or kitesurf you need to be a member of the local club (near the car park entrance) Beyond the designated zone for watersports, however, there's a lifeguard-patrolled Blue Flag area where most families stake out their windbreaks. It's also where you'll find the Beach Café (summer 0900-1800, winter 1000-1600), a great snack shack with sandwiches from £3.95 and a good range of beach gear. Behind the café, large grassy areas are perfect for ball games. Swimming is dangerous at the far end of the beach where it peters out at East Head – a sand spit that provides nesting habitat for skylarks, curlews and ringed plovers. It's a wonderful spot for a picnic – especially in the dunes from where you get views across yacht-flecked Chichester Harbour.

Action stations

Beach sports
Yellowave Beach Sports
Brighton, T01273-672222,
yellowave.co.uk. Mar-Sep, daily from
1000, Oct-Feb, Mon-Fri from 1100,
Sat-Sun from 1000. Kids' club drop-in
session £3.50/child. Minimum age 6.
Qualified coaches put kids
through their paces with beach
sports, including soccer, tag
rugby and volleyball. Holiday
sessions are available for
Grommetts (6-9) and Juniors
(10-15), while adults can join in
the fun with ultimate frisbee,
handball and other beach
games. There's also a café and a
play area for younger children.

Boat trips
Allchorn Pleasure Boats
Eastbourne, T01323-410606,
allchornpleasureboats.co.uk. May-
Oct, daily. £9/adult, £5.50/child (5-
14), £1/child (under 5), £24/family.
Cruises (lasting 45 minutes) to
Beachy Head and its famous
red-and-white lighthouse.

Cycling
Cuckmere Cycle Company
Seven Sisters Country park, nr
Seaford, T01323-870310, cuckmere-
cycle.co.uk. Year round, daily 1000-
1800. Bikes from £8/2 hrs to £20/day;
family packages £35-75.
As well as the surfaced track to
Cuckmere Haven (see page 37),
this bike-hire centre has direct
access to Friston Forest (page
36) where the Family Cycle Trail

Top to bottom: Beach huts at West
Wittering; Brighton Pier; stream-jumping
and sandcastles at Camber Sands.

provides a relatively flat, hour-
long pedal along forest roads.

Future Cycles
Forest Row, T01342-822847,
futurecycles.org. Year round, Mon-
Sat from 0900, Sun from 1000. Bikes
from £10/half-day to £18/day, trailers
£7.50-10; family packages £35-60.
Located a few minutes from the
12-mile, traffic free Forest Way in
the Ashdown Forest.

Watersports
Lagoon Watersports
Hove, T01273-424842,
hovelagoon.co.uk. Apr-Oct, daily.
Hove Lagoon is an ideal location
for kids to learn windsurfing and
dinghy sailing, with RYA Youth
Sailing Level 1 courses (two half-
days) on offer from around £110
(minimum age 6).

Seven Sisters Canoe Centre
Seven Sisters Country park, nr
Seaford, T01323-491289. Year round,
daily from 0900. Canoeing classes
£15/person, based on 8 people.
Paddle down the Cuckmere
in a kayak or Canadian canoe.
Canoe hire is usually available for
prebooked groups only.

Southwater Watersports
Southwater Country Park, nr
Horsham, T01403-734424,
southwatersports.co.uk. Taster
sessions (2 hrs) from £40, canoe hire
£10/half-hour.
Sailing and windsurfing courses
available during holidays, along
with canoe and kayak hire.

Out & about Sussex

Bluebell Railway

Sheffield Park Station, T01825-720800, timetable T01825-720825, bluebell-railway.co.uk. Year round, return tickets (Sheffield Park–Horsted Keynes–Kingscote) £12/adult, £6/child (3-16), £33/family. Light years from the manic A27, the Bluebell Line winds slowly through unspoilt Wealden countryside, the train's soporific clickety-clack broken only by occasional shrill whistles as the magnificent *Sir Archibald Sinclair* approaches a bridge or station. The carriages are proper old-fashioned ones, divided into compartments so kids can imagine they're Harry Potter on the Hogwarts Express when they tire of spotting bluebells (late Apr-May). Sheffield Park Station has a museum, restaurant and shop, and organises children's activities in August. A mile from the station, Sheffield Park Garden (nationaltrust.org.uk) is a fine spot for a lakeside walk.

Bodiam Castle

Nr Robertsbridge, T01580-830196, nationaltrust.org.uk. Feb-Oct, daily 1030-1800, Nov-Dec, Wed-Sun 1030-1600 (last entry to castle 1 hr before closing), £5.80/adult, £2.90/child (5-17), £14.50/family. Bodiam (see page 34) is just as castles should be. Walk around the edge of the moat, scheming

over how best to lay siege to the medieval fort, then take the easy option across the footbridge, cowering as you pass through the gatehouse with its original wooden portcullis. Inside the castle, stairways corkscrew through bulbous towers, leading to battlements with wonderful views. Repel invaders (or at the very least take imaginary pot-shots at families picnicking on the grassy banks), then turn your attention to the children's quiz. Bodiam Bat Packs are also available to help families with young children discover what it's like to travel back in time.

Drusillas Park

Alfriston, T01323-874100, drusillas.co.uk. Year round, daily from 1000, £10.80-13.80/person, £41.20-53.20/family (children under 2 free). This could well be Britain's best small zoo. It doesn't need big, charismatic species to keep kids rapt. Instead, it combines critters like lemurs, meerkats, fennec foxes, otters, tamarins and penguins with inspired interpretation. Right from the start, kids are hooked on Zoolympics where they're challenged with wild feats, such as jumping as high as a serval cat or matching the 115-decibel scream of a ruffed lemur (thankfully from inside an old telephone box). Lots of push-button, flap-lifting displays and a well-planned Zoo Route maintain interest levels all the way to the fabulous walk-through ring-tailed lemur enclosure. Then, suddenly, you emerge into a huge adventure playground with zip wires, climbing nets, slides, cafés, shops, a

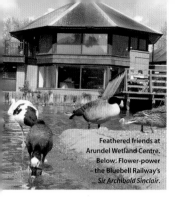

Feathered friends at Arundel Wetland Centre. Below: Flower-power – the Bluebell Railway's *Sir Archibald Sinclair*.

Thomas the Tank Engine train ride and a few cheeky extras, like gold-panning and jungle golf.

WWT Arundel Wetland Centre

T01903-883355, wwt.org.uk. Year round, daily from 0930, £8.95/adult, £4.50/child (4-16), £23.95/family, free to members (see page 36).
Feed the ducks (or Hawaiian nene geese) and learn about conservation at the same time. A 65-acre mosaic of lagoons, pools and reedbeds, this water-wonderland in the Arun Valley is home to dozens of rare species of wildfowl from around the world. But it's native treasures – minibeasts squirming in a pond-dipping net, a water vole poking its head out from the reeds, a fluffy raft of mallard ducklings – that leave the most lasting impressions. Don't miss the boat safaris, the Peter Scott Hide or the excellent visitor centre and café. Just before Arundel Wetland Centre, you pass a lovely park beneath Arundel Castle (arundelcastle. org). Rowing boats can be hired on nearby Swanbourne Lake.

More family favourites

1066 Battle of Hastings Abbey & Battlefield

Battle, T01424-775705, english-heritage.org.uk. Year round, daily from 1000, £6.70/adult, £3.40/child (5-15), £16/family.
Prepare for battle at the dramatic introductory film, get hands-on with weapons used in 1066, then arm yourself with an audio tour to explore the actual battleground and the ruins of William the Conqueror's abbey.

Weald & Downland Open Air Museum

Singleton, T01243-811348, wealddown.co.uk. Feb-Dec, daily from 1030, £8.95/adult, £4.70/child, £24.25/family.
Six centuries of rural life tucked into the Sussex Downs, this living museum has restored buildings and traditional crafts.

Also recommended
Bentley Wildfowl & Motor Museum Halland, nr Lewes, T01825-840573, bentley.org.uk.

Blackberry Farm
Whitesmith, nr Lewes, T01825-872912, blackberry-farm.co.uk.

Herstmonceux Castle
Hailsham, T01323-833816, herstmonceux-castle.com.

Wilderness Wood
Hadlow Down, nr Uckfield, T01825-830509, wildernesswood.co.uk.

Rain check

Arts & crafts
• The Painting Pottery Café, Brighton, T01273-628952, paintingpotterycafe.co.uk.

Cinemas
• Curzon, Eastbourne, T01323-731441.
• Odeon, Hastings, T0871-224 4007.
• Odeon, Brighton, T0871-224 4007.
• Picturedrome, Bognor Regis, T01243-823138.
• Windmill, Littlehampton, T01903-722224.

Indoor play
• Flying Fortress, Ford, nr Arundel, T01903-733550, flying-fortress.co.uk.
• Monkey Bizness, Lewes, T08458-739645, monkey-bizness.co.uk.
• Westows Play & Football, Hove, T01273-711944, westows.com.

Indoor swimming pools
• Butlins, Bognor Regis (day visitors), T01243-822445, butlins.com.
• King Alfred Leisure Centre, Hove, T01273-290290, kingalfredleisure.co.uk.
• Sovereign Centre, Eastbourne, T01323-738822, sovereigncentre.org.

Members' perks

Family membership (see page 5) entitles you to free entry to:

English Heritage
• 1066 Battle of Hastings Abbey & Battlefield, Battle.

National Trust
• Bodiam Castle, Robertsbridge.
• Sheffield Park Garden.

RSPB
• Pulborough Brooks Reserve.

Sleeping Sussex

Pick of the pitches

Bay View Park

Pevensey Bay, T01323-768688,
bay-view.co.uk. Year round, £14.50-
17/pitch (2 people), plus £2.50/extra
adult, £2/extra child (5-16). Holiday
homes (6 berth) from £194/wk.

A grassy 6-acre site at the end
of a private road, Bay View Park
is yards from the beach and has
a choice of touring pitches and
holiday homes, a well-stocked
shop and a children's play area.

Cobbs Hill Farm

Bexhill-on-Sea, T01424 -213460,
cobbshillfarm.co.uk. Apr-Oct, £9.50-
13.50/pitch (2 people), plus £2/extra
person, £1/extra child (under 5).

Just 3 miles from the beach at
Bexhill, this small, friendly site has
an adventure playground and a
mini-menagerie of farm animals.

Honeybridge Park

Dial Post, T01403-710923,
honeybridgepark.co.uk. Year round,
£8-13/pitch, plus £3-6/adult, £2.50/
child (5-14).

Nestled in beautiful countryside
on the edge of the South
Downs, Honeybridge Park has
first-rate facilities, including a
large adventure playground.

Wapsbourne Manor Farm

Sheffield Park, T01825-723414,
wowo.co.uk. Year round, £8/adult,
£4/child (3-16). Yurts from £85/night.

For kids, Wapsbourne (or Wowo
as regulars call it) is a scraped
knees, smoke-in-your-eyes
kind of camping adventure.
It's about getting dizzy on
the rope swing (and muddy
when you fall off), making
dens in the woods, playing
hide-and-seek, climbing trees,
exploring streams and roasting
marshmallows around the
campfire. Number of pitches?
Who knows? Who cares? Just
find a spot that takes your fancy
in the soft, clover-covered fields
on this 150-acre site where, to
complete the Famous Five-style
idyll, you can even hear the
whistle of the nearby Bluebell
Railway (see page 40). Facilities
are fairly basic – toilets and hot
showers in portacabins, plus
some composting toilets in
strategic locations. A couple
of yurts up the comfort stakes
slightly, but the real luxury of
this atmospheric campsite is the
daily delivery round of firewood
(£5/crate) straight to your tent.
Budding musicians get to camp
for free on Friday nights – but
only if they hold an 'open fire' so
that anyone can hum along.

Wicks Farm Holiday Park

West Wittering, T01243-513116,
wicksfarm.co.uk. Mar-Oct, £15-24.50/
pitch (4 people).

A 40-pitch site with a David
Bellamy Conservation Award for
its eco-credentials, Wicks Farm
also has a winning location
– just 1.5 miles from the sandy
beach at West Wittering (page
38). The farm's holiday park (with
73 caravans) is for owners only.

Also recommended

Horam Manor Touring Park

Nr Heathfield, T01435-813662,
horam-manor.co.uk.

Cool & quirky

Safari Britain

Firle, T07780-871996,
safaribritain.com. May-Sep,
weekends £140/adult, £70/child
(including activities); weekdays
£30/adult, £20/child (activities
not included). Exclusive bookings
(up to 16 people) from £1400/
weekend, £2300/week.

Herds of wildebeest streaming
across the South Downs? Not
quite. This is a homegrown safari
where local guides help you track
minibeasts like bats, insects and
rabbits – the latter destined for
the pot as you learn how to prepare
soups and stews from wild plants
and animals. Kids can get expert
tips on den-building, make bows
and arrows and join nature treasure
hunts. Base camp is a cluster of six
bell tents and a sumptuous yurt
furnished with sofas, rugs, cushions,
and a wood-burning stove. There's
a sawdust eco loo and a hot-water
shower tucked into an ancient
beech tree. Everything is provided
except food, which can be pre-
ordered from the local farm shop.
Another wild and wonderful option
is **Sussex Tipis (Broad Oak, nr Rye,
T01424-713868, sussextipis.co.uk)**.

Best of the rest

Butlins
Bognor Regis, T0845-070 4734, butlins.com. Year round, check website for latest offers.
Butlins is the Marmite of seaside resorts. Whether you love it or hate it, however, there's no denying the family appeal of this self-contained holiday village, with its plethora of activities, live entertainment and places to eat. Accommodation ranges from basic self-catering apartments to the luxurious new, 200-room Ocean Hotel where parents can take refuge in the spa. Kids meanwhile can go bonkers with Bob the Builder and Barney the Dinosaur, take a dip at the huge, indoor Splash waterpark or a spin on the new Junior Driving School. Other recent additions include adventure golf, archery, bungee trampolines and a high ropes course.

If Butlins sounds a little brash, a more relaxed budget option is the **Littlehampton Youth Hostel** (T0870-770 6114, yha. org.uk, £13.95/adult, £10.50/child). It's right by the harbour next to the Look & Sea Visitor Centre (lookandsea.co.uk) and a great little café. The hostel makes a stab at a nautical theme (room names on fake bits of driftwood etc) and the ensuite family rooms are small but clean. Other hostels can be found at Alfriston and Arundel.

Flackley Ash Hotel
Peasmarsh, nr Rye, T01797-230651, flackleyashhotel.co.uk. Year round, from £120/room (children under 14 free when sharing with parents).
Luxurious country hotel with indoor swimming pool and spa, family suites and fine cuisine.

Riverdale House
Alfriston, T01323-871038, riverdalehouse.co.uk. Year round, B&B £85-140/room.
A rather special B&B, Riverdale has views across the Cuckmere Valley and is just a short walk from cutesy Alfriston. Childcare facilities are second to none, with family suites, a babysitting service, baby-feeding gear, a playroom (with DVD library, freeview and Wii) and bikes to borrow for exploring the nearby Cuckoo Trail.

Seattle Hotel
Brighton Marina, T01273-679799, hotelseattlebrighton.com. Year round, B&B from around £150/room (children stay free when sharing).
A contemporary hotel on Brighton's vibrant waterfront, the Seattle welcomes kids with a special pack containing a streetwise guide to the city. Rooms are spacious, with king-size bed, WiFi and Sky TV. A children's menu and baby-listening service are available, while the marina is a good spot for crabbing. The Thistle (T0871-376 9041, thistle.com) is another good family option in Brighton.

Holiday parks

Camber Sands
Camber, T0871-664 9719, park-resorts.com.

Coghurst Hall
Hastings, T0845-815 9780, parkholidaysuk.com.

Crowhurst Park
Battle, T01424-773344, crowhurstpark.co.uk.

Frenchman's Beach
Rye, T0844-826 2633, hoseasons.co.uk.

West Sands
Selsey, T01243-606080, bunnleisure.co.uk.
The biggest and busiest of a trio of resorts that also includes Green Lawns and White Horse.

Winchelsea Sands
Rye, T0845-815 9740, parkholidaysuk.com.

Cottage agents

Best of Brighton and Sussex Cottages
T01273-308779, bestofbrighton.co.uk.

Fairhaven Holiday Cottages
T01208-821255, fairhaven-holidays.co.uk.

Garden of England Cottages
T01892-510117, gardenofenglandcottages.co.uk.

Hideaways Cottages
T01747-828170, hideaways.co.uk.

Mulberry Cottages
T01233-813087, mulberrycottages.com.

Eating Sussex

Local goodies

Heaven Farm

Furners Green, nr Sheffield Park Station, T01825-790226, heavenfarm.co.uk. Farm shop year round, daily 1000-1700; museum Apr-Oct 1100-1700; nature trail Mar-Oct 1100-1700; tea room Feb-Nov from 1000.

An organic farm shop is just one facet of Heaven Farm, where an atmospheric little museum takes you back in time, up to 180 years, to demonstrate how farming has changed in the Sussex Weald. There are also farm tours and nature trails, a craft shop, campsite and tea room.

Middle Farm

Firle, nr Lewes, T01323-811324, middlefarm.com. Year round, daily, 0930-1730.

The perfect place to provision a gourmet picnic, Middle Farm offers a sumptuous spread of organic food, from local Sussex mayonnaise to freshly baked pasties. The farm makes 20 varieties of sausages and stocks 50 different British cheeses. You can buy cakes and scones at the bakery, seasonal fruit and veg, plus local ice cream. And as if the farm shop wasn't enough to put a rumble in your tummy, there are regular farmers' markets (Sun 1000-1400) throughout the year, as well as a restaurant serving light lunches and Sussex cream teas in a sunny courtyard. The farm itself, meanwhile, is open to visitors (£3/person, under 3s free) and features a playground, play barn, nature trail, picnic area, plus a chance to meet the animals and watch the cows being milked.

Roundstone Pick Your Own

Ferring, nr Worthing, T01903 770670. Jun-Oct, daily 0900-1700.

Fruit picking, tractor rides, picnic area and farm shop.

Quick & simple

The Beach House

West Wittering, T01243-514800, beachhse.co.uk. Tue-Sun (high season), Fri & Sat (low season).

Snack menu with baguettes from £5.50, plus excellent seafood dishes (fish and chips £9.95) served on a verandah.

Market days

Arundel Town Square, 3rd Sat.
Battle Battle Abbey Green, 3rd Sat.
Firle Middle Farm, 4th Sun.
Hove George St, 4th Sat.
Hastings Robertson St, 2nd/4th Thu.
Heathfield Co-op car park, 3rd Sat.
Rye Strand Quay, Wed.

Fish & chips

Try **Bardsley's** (Baker St, Brighton), **Chandlers** (Station Rd, Bosham), **Kettle o'Fish** (Wish St, Rye), **Maggie's** (Rock-a-Nore Rd, Hastings) and **The Real Fish & Chips Company** (Upper Brighton Rd, Worthing).

RSPB Pulborough Brooks

Wiggonholt, T01798-875851, rspb.org.uk. Year round.

Serving snacks and lunches using local produce, the tea room at Pulborough Brooks overlooks the nature reserve.

Scoop & Crumb

East St, Brighton, T01273-202563. Year round, daily.

Retro-style café renowned for its open sandwiches and freshly made ice creams, sorbets and shakes. Flavours include sherry trifle and plum crumble.

Also recommended
Grub Café

East Grinstead, T01342-313139, grubonline.co.uk. Mon-Sat from 0900.

Trendy café-bar serving good quality local food.

Momma Cherri's Soul Food

Little East St, Brighton, T01273-325305, mommacherri.co.uk. Year round, daily.

Taste of the American Deep South, with jerk chicken, mash, veg and gravy from £12.50.

Posh nosh

The Hungry Monk

Jevington, T01323-482178, hungrymonk.co.uk. Daily from 1845; lunch, Tue-Sun from 1200.

The birthplace of 'banoffi' pie, this cosy restaurant is located in a 14th-century former monks' abode and offers a two-course lunch menu from £18.95.

Essentials Sussex

Getting there
By train Southern Railway (southernrailway.com) operates services from London to several destinations in Sussex, with fast trains from Victoria Station to Brighton taking only 50 minutes. Thameslink services (thameslinkprogramme.co.uk) run from London King's Cross and London Bridge to Brighton, while Southeastern (southeasternrailway.co.uk) runs trains between London and Battle, Hastings and Rye.
By coach National Express (T0871-781 8181, nationalexpress.com) serves towns along the Sussex coast, plus several destinations inland, including Arundel, Hailsham and Horsham.

Getting around
By bus Several companies operate bus services in Sussex, including Brighton & Hove (buses.co.uk), Compass (compass-travel.co.uk) and Stagecoach (stagecoachbus.com). One of the most useful services for visitors is the Cuckmere Valley Rambler (cuckmerebus.freeuk.com) which runs an hourly weekend circular service from Berwick station via Drusillas Park, Alfriston, Seaford and the Seven Sisters Country Park. Family tickets cost from £11.

Maps
Choose sheets 121-124 and 134-135 from the Ordnance Survey Explorer series, or Landranger maps 197 (Chichester & South Downs), 198 (Brighton & Lewes) and 199 (Eastbourne & Hastings).

Tourist Information Centres
Useful websites include visitsussex.org, enjoysussex.info, sussexbythesea.com and visitbrighton.com. TICs are generally open Mon-Sat 1000-1700, Sun 1000-1600, and include the following:
Arundel River Rd, T01903-882268.
Battle & Bexhill High St, T01424-773721.
Bognor Regis Belmont St, T01243-823140.
Brighton Pavilion Buildings, T09067-112255.
Burgess Hill Church Walk, T01444-238202.
Chichester South St, T01243-775888.
Eastbourne Cornfield Rd, T01323-411400.
Hastings Queens Square, T01424-781111.
Horsham The Causeway, T01403-211661.
Lewes High St, T01273-483448.
Littlehampton Look and Sea Ctr, Surrey St, T01903-721866.
Midhurst North St, T01730-817322.
Petworth The Old Bakery, T01798-343523.
Seaford Church St, T01323-897426.
Worthing Chapel Rd, T01903-221066.

Hospital
Eastbourne District General Kings Drive, T01323-417400.
Royal Sussex County Eastern Rd, Brighton, T01273-696955.

Pharmacies
Arundel Lloyds, High St.
Battle Day Lewis, High St.
Bognor Regis Boots, London Rd.
Brighton Asda, Brighton Marina.
Chichester Lloyds, High St.
Eastbourne Asda, Pevensey Bay Rd.
Hastings Lloyds, High St.
Lewes H Baker, High St.
Littlehampton Boots, High St.
Seaford Boots, Broad St.
Worthing Boots, Goring Rd.

Supermarkets
Bognor Regis Morrisons, Tesco.
Brighton Asda, Marks & Spencer, Sainsbury's, Tesco, Waitrose.
Chichester Budgens, Somerfield, Tesco, Waitrose.
Eastbourne Asda, Sainsbury's Tesco, Waitrose.
Hastings Morrisons.
Lewes Tesco, Waitrose.
Littlehampton Sainsbury's, Somerfield, Tesco.
Worthing Sainsbury's, Somerfield.

Other shops
Baby supplies Hastings Baby Shop, Queens Rd.
Camping supplies Millets, Western Rd, Brighton.
Toys & beach gear Sussex Toy Ctr, High St, Hailsham.

Environmental groups
Sussex Wildlife Trust, T01273-492630, sussexwt.org.uk.

Major Events
May Brighton Festival, brightonfestival.org.
Jul Lions Festival, Worthing.

Visit while you can. At the current rate of erosion, most of the island will have been washed up on the south coast of England in 10,000 years time.

Hunt for dinosaurs

Local experts lead two-hour fossil-hunting walks at Brook Bay. You'll find fossil wood, sponges, shells and, if you're lucky, sea urchins preserved in flint. Don't be fooled by Carparkosaurus – you might think you've found armour plating from a Polacanthus, but it's probably just asphalt from the eroding clifftop. What you're really looking for are black fragments of dinosaur bone – easily confused with petrified wood, they won't leave a charcoal-like streak if rubbed against flint. At Hanover Point you can literally walk with Iguanodons – or at least admire their giant, three-toed footprint casts (right) that litter the beach at low tide. Fossil walks are organised by Dinosaur Isle (see page 54) and cost £4/adult, £2.40/child or £12.50/family. The Dinosaur Farm Museum near Brighstone (T01983-740844, dinosaur-farm.co.uk) also offers fossil-hunting trips.

Compton Bay.

Isle of Wight

Old fashioned and just a bit uncool. If that's your impression of the Isle of Wight, think again. This grand dame of British seaside resorts might have Victorian heritage, but recent years have seen it evolve into a hotspot for outdoor sports, fossil hunting and back-to-nature family holidays.

The Isle of Wight's oldest town, **Yarmouth** retains a distinctly medieval layout with its tangle of streets and market square. Yarmouth Castle bears testament to Henry VIII's coastal defence programme, while the town's 19th century timber pier is still used for boat trips to Hurst Castle. Keen birdwatchers, meanwhile, are lured to the Yar Estuary – best appreciated from the cycle track that follows an old railway line to **Freshwater**.

Strike out across Tennyson Down and you'll reach The Needles, the Isle of Wight's famous trio of chalk pinnacles, but don't overlook the beaches in this western extremity of the island. They may not have the golden-sand reputation of those in East Wight, but they are often less crowded and have unique drawcards, such as Alum Bay's coloured cliffs or Brook Bay's fossils.

From Freshwater Bay, the A3055 undulates along the south coast, skirting St Catherine's Point before continuing on to **Ventnor**, **Shanklin** and **Sandown**. Divert inland at Brook, however, and you'll find the antithesis to these busy seaside resorts. Narrow lanes burrow through secluded Brighstone Forest before straddling open downland and descending to Calbourne. It's equally unspoilt around Shalfleet and Newtown where you'll find opportunities for woodland walks and boat trips on the estuary.

Lying at the hub of the island's web of inland roads, **Newport** can feel gridlocked at times – but it's worth enduring the traffic to visit Carisbrooke Castle and the weekly farmers' market. North of the Isle of Wight's 'capital', **Cowes** also has a buzz, thanks to its lively yachting scene. Things are more serene at nearby Osborne House, the former home of Queen Victoria.

More interested in shaking off its Victorian past, **Ryde** has developed a thriving entertainment scene, with everything from trendy cafés to an ice-skating rink. Quieter seaside resorts, such as **Bembridge**, can be found further along the coast, while Amazon World Zoo Park, Brading Roman Villa and the Robin Hill Country Park top the list of inland attractions for families in the east of the island.

You must

- Fly a kite on the downs.

- Spot a red squirrel in Parkhurst Forest.

- Search for dinosaur footprints at Brook Bay.

- Watch the donkeys walk the treadwheel at Carisbrooke Castle.

- Cycle the Troll Trail.

- Explore Swiss Cottage Museum, Osborne House.

- Learn to sail, windsurf or kitesurf.

- Try Minghella ice cream.

- See Steve Hain's falconry display at Robin Hill Country Park.

Out & about Isle of Wight

Fun & free

Spot a squirrel

You can join a guided walk in search of the Isle of Wight's thriving population of red squirrels at Robin Hill Country Park (see page 55), but for something free and less formal there's a squirrel-viewing hide in Parkhurst Forest, located off the A3054 a short distance from Newport. Accessed by buggy-friendly trails, the hide is open year-round and provides excellent views of Britain's 'native Nutkins' – an endearing little critter measuring 35 cm from nose to tail and weighing just 350 g. Afterwards, take a walk in the forest, searching open rides for the pearl-bordered fritillary – a rare butterfly seen between late April and July. There are picnic tables near the carpark and two giant squirrel carvings by local artist Paul Sivell. Parkhurst's squirrel hide is part of the Isle of Wight's Gift to Nature initiative (gifttonature.org.uk) – a series of environmental projects aimed at getting people closer to the island's wildlife. You can also spot orchids and dragonflies at a wild meadow near Totland, while the Sandown Wetlands are home to kingfishers and water voles.

Catch a crab

Try Yarmouth Pier. You can buy crabbing lines from the RNLI shop opposite the ferry office and bait from the ironmongers in the town square. Crabbing off the seawall at Cowes is also popular, while other potentially good spots for dangling a line include the small harbours at Ryde and Ventnor.

Search for shrimps

You'll find pools teeming with anemones, shrimps and gobies at Bembridge Ledge, a series of rocky shelves exposed at low tide in Whitecliff Bay, south of Bembridge. It's also worth checking out the rock pools at Seaview, east of Ryde, and Bonchurch, near Ventnor.

Find a fossil

Keep off the cliffs! Not only are they dangerously unstable, but the best places to find fossils are the island's beaches. Dinosaur bones (see page 46) are top of every fossil hunter's wishlist, but you can also find turtle and crocodile remains on the foreshore at Yarmouth; fossilised fish and lobsters at Shepherds Chine; ammonites at Rocken End and brachiopods and other shells at Bembridge.

Visit Ventnor Botanic Garden

Why? The gardens are stunning – nine hectares of exotic flora from South Africa, Australia, New Zealand and the Americas. But even if you don't have any budding botanists in the family, kids love playing hide-and-seek and spotting green and brown wall lizards basking on the dry-stone wall in the northwest corner of the garden. You'll also find a play area and countless shady spots for spreading out a picnic rug. Paths are buggy-friendly, so it's ideal for littl'uns – particularly when you want a break from the beach.

Where? On the eastern outskirts of Ventnor just off the coastal A3055.

How? There's a large car park at the gardens which charges £0.90/hr. Admission to the Botanic Garden is free. You can also incorporate it into a circular walk combining Ventnor and Steephill Cove.

Contact Ventnor Botanic Garden, Undercliff Drive, Ventnor, T01983-855397, botanic.co.uk.

Walk this way

If the 67-mile Isle of Wight Coastal Path sounds a little daunting, try the 3.8-mile circuit of Yarmouth's Western Yar Estuary. It's flat, easy-going and shouldn't take longer than a few hours, although you may find yourself dawdling once you've glimpsed your first red squirrel. Don't forget to take binoculars – you'll need them for scanning the estuary's worm-riddled mudflats which entice a wide range of stilt-walking waders, from curlews to little egrets, as well as several varieties of duck. Prefer to pedal rather than walk? The trail on the right hand side of the estuary follows an old railway line and can be cycled in around 45 minutes. The 9-mile circuit of the Medina Estuary at Cowes also offers a mixture of footpaths and cycle ways.

Cycle with trolls

Although it stretches all the way from Cowes to Sandown, the most family-friendly section of the traffic-free Troll Trail is between Merstone's old railway platform and Shide. Conservationists have installed nestboxes for grey wagtails under several bridges along the route, so trolls are not the only things you might find living under the arches. There is also a meadow at Merstone Station, with hand carved picnic benches alongside a chalk and turf maze. See page 52 for cycle hire companies.

Fly a kite

Don't let the yachties and kite-surfers have all the fun! There's plenty of breeze to go round on the Isle of Wight, particularly on the southwest coast which feels the brunt of prevailing winds. Launch your kite off Tennyson Down for a shoulder-popping session or seek equally exhilarating conditions on the beaches at Bembridge, Sandown or Ryde.

Out & about Isle of Wight

Alum Bay

The famous coloured cliffs are the highlight of this pebbly beach, reached by steps or a chairlift (minimum height 1.4m if unaccompanied by an adult) from The Needles Park (see page 55). The multi-hued cliffs are off-limits, but there are good views of The Needles – and even better ones if you take the 20-minute boat trip from the beach (£4/adult, £3/child).

Bembridge

One of the quieter spots on the island's east coast, Bembridge has a mixture of pebble and sand beaches, with some good spots for shell-collecting and rock-pooling. Over on the north side of Bembridge Harbour, St Helens has sand, rock pools, and grass-covered dunes. Head south on the coastal path and you'll reach Whitecliff Bay – a sandy beach sheltered by spectacular cliffs. There's a café here, but limited parking.

Brook Bay

A mishmash of sand, rock and exposed bands of slippery mudstone, this is an explorer's beach. The main prizes are the dinosaur fossils that have been eroded from the friable and unsafe cliffs (see page 46), but don't overlook the strandline which often turns up other goodies, like cuttlefish bones and mermaids' purses.

Colwell Bay

Looking across to Hurst Castle in the Solent, Colwell Bay is mainly sandy – although it's quite compacted and gritty in places, so ambitious sandcastle builders might struggle without metal spades. Sheltered swimming makes this a popular spot for young families. Beachside cafés sell toasties and other snacks, while beach stalls offer everything from inflatable dolphins to ice creams.

Compton Bay

It's a bit of a scramble down steps that cling precariously to the low, crumbly cliffs at Compton Bay (the National Trust car park is steadily retreating as the sea nibbles away at the coast). But once on the beach this is a fine spot for swimming, surfing and fossil hunting. The gritty sand is roughly the consistency of cookie dough, so not bad for sandcastles. Don't expect much in the way of facilities. The car park has toilets, a tap to rinse your feet and – if you're lucky – an ice cream van.

Cowes & Gurnard

There's a shingle beach at

Above: Ventnor Bay.
Right: Boats bound for The Needles.

Princes Esplanade, while Gurnard Bay, further to the west, is a gently shelving swathe of sand and pebbles. Both are good for swimming, sailing and windsurfing.

Freshwater Bay

A small sand and shingle beach, Freshwater Bay has plenty of local diversions, including cliff walks, forays in Afton Marsh nature reserve and a golf course.

Ryde

A deservedly popular resort, Ryde has miles of sandy beach and a bustling Esplanade where you'll find an ice rink, bowling alley, swimming pool, boating lake and a playground. If you want lots to do, or some wet-weather bolt-holes, this is the beach for you.

Steephill Cove has seaside adventure written all over it

Garden (see page 48) or along the cliff path from Ventnor itself (a 20-minute stroll).

Totland Bay

A good choice for young families, Totland is quiet and sheltered with lots of facilities. Walk north along the prom to Colwell Bay, or south towards Alum Bay for rock pools.

Sandown

The Isle of Wight's golden-sand beauty, Sandown's 'full-spec' beach has everything from pedaloes and parascending to cafés and a pier. Consistently scooping UK sunshine records, the Victorian resort offers safe, sheltered swimming, but can get crowded in summer. Seek less trampled sands at Lake Beach to the south.

Seaview & Seagrove Bay

Park at Seaview and make for gently shelving Seagrove Bay. At low tide you can walk across miles of sand to equally unspoilt Priory Bay or to Puckpool Park where you'll find crazy golf and the Ryde 'hop-on' road train.

Shanklin

Linked to Sandown by a seafront walk, Shanklin boasts

as many activities and amenities as its neighbour. Expect all the trimmings of a traditional seaside resort, including excellent swimming. Shanklin town is up on the clifftop, but there's a lift if you don't fancy scaling the steps.

Steephill Cove

Secluded and peaceful, this little gem near Ventnor has seaside adventure written all over it. The beach is a mixture of sand and shingle, hemmed in by tumbled rocks and smugglers' cliffs, and backed by a ramshackle collection of old fishermen's cottages and beach shacks selling freshly caught crab. Brightly coloured buoys, lobster pots and fishing nets lie strewn across the slipway – there's not a burger bar or slot machine in sight. In fact, you won't even see cars here, since the only access is on foot from Ventnor Botanic

Ventnor Bay

Fine shingle with patches of gritty sand doesn't make Ventnor ideal for sandcastles, but this is still a lovely bay with an attractive promenade. Walk east to Bonchurch, a small shingle beach with rocks either side that are crying out for a low-tide prawning expedition.

Yarmouth

To the west of the town Fort Victoria Country Park (T01983-823893, fortvictoria.co.uk) has a maritime museum, aquarium and ranger-led walks along the shore and adjacent woodland.

Yaverland

A favourite spot for fossil hunters and watersports enthusiasts, Yaverland is linked to Sandown by an esplanade.

Out & about Isle of Wight

Action stations

Tree climbing
Goodleaf Tree Climbing
T01983-563573, goodleaf.co.uk.
£35/adult, £25/child 8-16, 5% off if
you travel by foot, bike or bus.
Get out on a limb for a unique
perspective of the Isle of Wight
with one of Goodleaf's all-
swinging, all-dangling arboreal
adventures. Each two-and-a-
half-hour session takes place in
a secluded field somewhere in
the island's Area of Outstanding
Natural Beauty – the exact
location is kept secret until you
book. A thorough safety briefing
by qualified instructors ensures
there's no monkey business and
then it's up to you how high
you go. Rates include locally
produced refreshments.

Fishing
Lisa Marie
Red Funnel Ferry Terminal, East
Cowes, T07971-282406.
£8.50/person, including rod hire.
Mackerel fishing and sightseeing.

Yarmouth River & Sea Cruises
Lifeboat Pontoon, Yarmouth,
T01983-759910. £3/person.
Birdwatching cruises on the Yar,
boat trips to The Needles and
mackerel fishing.

Horse riding
Allendale Equestrian Centre
Godshill, T01983-840258.
£24/adult, £23/child (minimum age
5) for 30-minute lesson, followed by
30 minutes riding on a bridleway.
Nestled in leafy countryside
around picturesque Godshill,
this BHS-registered stable offers
lessons for all abilities, plus some
excellent hacking.

Brickfields Riding Stables
Binstead, Ryde, T01983-566801,
brickfields.net. Daily 1000-1700, £6/
adult, £4.50, £17/family, £15/riding
lesson (minimum age 4).
A riding school and day-out
rolled into one. Meet donkeys,
Shetland ponies and shire
horses, visit the carriage
museum and gift shop, then
sign up for a riding lesson lasting
either 30 minutes or an hour.

Llama treks
Wight Llama Treks
T01983-551128, wightllamatreks.
co.uk. £60/family, minimum age 5.
Easy 90-minute walk with llamas
across the West Wight downs.

Safaris
**Shalfleet Manor Estuary
Safaris** T01983-531235.
£25/person, minimum age 12.
Discover the birdlife of Newtown
Estuary during a 90-minute
safari which includes an hour
aboard a six-passenger open
boat. Species often seen during
summer include sandwich tern,
osprey and shelduck.

Bikes to go

**1st Call Cycle Hire
Unit 15, College Close,
Sandown, T01983-400055.**
Bikes from £8/day, £30/wk;
family special (up to 4 bikes)
£30/day, £110/wk.

**Tav Cycles
High St, Ryde, T01983-812989,
tavcycles.co.uk.**
From £12/day to £69/fortnight.
Rates include helmet, lock, pump
and puncture repair kit. Bikes are
never more than two seasons old
and are regularly serviced.

**Wight Cycle Hire
The Old Works, Station Rd,
Yarmouth and Brading Station
Hire Centre, Station Rd,
T01983-761800,
wightcyclehire.co.uk.**
Adult bike £8/half day, £14/day;
child's bike £6/half day, £10/day;
child seat £5/half day, £8/day;
tag-along £6/half day, £10/day;
trailer £6/half day, £10/day.
Rates include helmet, lock,
backpack, maps and route
suggestions. Bikes can be
delivered to any island location.
Yarmouth hire centre is just 50 m
from the Yarmouth–Freshwater
cycle track.

Catch some air

UK Sailing Academy
Arctic Road, West Cowes
T01983-294941, uksa.org.
2-day weekend courses:
£205-235/adult, £175-205/child 8-16
5-day Mon-Fri courses:
£385-420/adult, £330-360/child 8-16
Courses include Windsurf Start,
Windsurf Improver, Kitesurf Taster
Weekend, Dinghy Start, Dinghy
Improver and Dinghy Advanced.

Whitewater Adventure
Watersports
Rew Close, Ventnor,
T01983 866269, wightwaters.com.
Sailing, windsurfing, kayaking and
other activities at Dunroamin Beach
between Shanklin and Sandown.
2-hr multi-activity Splash Sessions
for under 16s from £14/person.

X-Isle Sports
The Centre, Embankment Road,
Bembridge, T01983-873111,
x-is.co.uk.
Courses in kitesurfing, surfing,
windsurfing, sailing, wakeboarding
and waterskiing.

With its long-established yachting pedigree, reliable winds and excellent facilities, the Isle of Wight is one of the best places in Britain to learn how to sail, windsurf or kitesurf. For children who are just starting out, the UK Sailing Academy (UKSA) in Cowes provides introductory courses in dinghy sailing and windsurfing for mini-mariners aged eight and above. Their Dinghy Start course, for example, covers stages 1 and 2 of the RYA Dinghy Youth syllabus and covers everything from rigging and launching a boat to ropework, crewing, capsize recovery and understanding winds. An introduction to windsurfing, meanwhile, will get you standing, steering and performing 180-degree turns. Both courses take place over five days or two weekends.

In addition to tuition in sailing, windsurfing and surfing (all minimum age 8), X-Isle Sports offers kitesurfing lessons for adrenaline-addicts as young as 12 in which they will learn how to launch and fly kites safely before experiencing the thrill of body-dragging in the sea.

If that sounds too much like a white-knuckle ride, try a two-hour Splash Session with Whitewater Adventure Watersports where you can sail, windsurf, bodyboard and take part in beach games.

Out & about Isle of Wight

Carisbrooke Castle

Newport, T01983-522107, english-heritage.org.uk. Mar-Sep 1000-1700, Oct-Mar 1000-1600, £6.70/adult, £3.40/child (5-15), £16.80/family. Café and shop.

Donkeys steal the show at this fascinating fort where Charles I was imprisoned in 1648, prior to losing his head. Jigsaw, Jim Bob, Joseph, Jack and Jill take turns in demonstrating how a donkey-powered treadwheel was used for centuries to haul water from the castle's 50-m-deep well. The guardhouse, meanwhile, is home to a cartoon donkey called Jupiter who narrates a film about the castle's history in which the treadwheel becomes a time machine. You can relive moments yourself by donning chainmail in the armoury, firing a cannon and winding a crossbow. Allow 40 minutes to scale the keep and walk around the ramparts. Carisbrooke Castle hosts several events each summer, such as a medieval boot camp (in which children can hone their archery skills) and horrible history days where they can mix up their own plague cures.

Dinosaur Isle

Culver Parade, Sandown, T01983-404344, dinosaurisle.com. Apr-Sep 1000-1800, Oct 1000-1700, Nov-Mar 1000-1600, £4.95/adult, £2.95/child (3-15), £13.95/family. Guided fossil walks and shop. Food available at Browns Family Golf.

In case you were in any doubt as to the prehistoric significance of the Isle of Wight, a world map in this superb museum ranks the island alongside such famed dinosaur hotspots as Mongolia and Utah. Shaped like a giant pterosaur, Dinosaur Isle takes you on a journey back in time as you peruse cabinets crammed with Ice Age mammal bones and 100-million-year-old ammonites – all found on the island. The real wow factor comes, however, when you step into the huge dinosaur gallery to find yourself transported into a Cretaceous swamp complete with life-size models of an Iguanadon being stalked by a mean-

looking Neovenator. The hall echoes with dinosaur calls; an animatronic dilophosaur nods and bears its teeth and there's a touch table where you can grapple with the eight-inch tooth of a T-Rex. There's also plenty of geological info here, but much of it is presented in a fun and interactive way. Youngsters will enjoy making dinosaur skin rubbings and unearthing sauropod skeletons in the sandpits. Don't forget to bring along any fossils you've found on the island to have them identified by experts in the encounter zone.

Osborne House

East Cowes, T01983-200022, english-heritage.org.uk. Mar-Sep 1000-1800, Oct 1000-1600, Nov-Mar 1000-1600 Wed-Sun, £10.20/adult, £5.10/child (5-15), £25.50/family for entry to house and gardens. Restaurant, café and shop. There's a lot of ground to cover (both inside and out) at this seaside palace where Queen Victoria lived with her family. A picnic area (and excellent jungle gym) is located right next to the car park, so you can have an energy-boosting lunch or snack before getting stuck in. Allow 60-90 minutes for touring the house. That might sound like a drag, but most kids aged six and

Left: Lion statue at Osborne House.
Right: Kahn the steppe eagle, Robin Hill.

over will love finding out what life was like in a royal holiday home. Outside, it's a 15-minute walk to the Swiss Cottage – a playhouse fit for princes and princesses, complete with working kitchen appliances, vegetable plots and flower beds. Don't miss the nearby museum, crammed with a head-spinning array of artefacts collected by the royal children (and inspired by Prince Albert's travels). Look carefully and you'll find a giant centipede from Central America, a fragment of frieze from the Alhambra and a stuffed wolf shot by the King of Belgium.

Robin Hill Countryside Adventure Park

Downend, nr Arreton, T01983-730052, robin-hill.com. Mar-Nov 1000-1700, Jul-Aug 1000-1800, £8.50/person (under 4s free). Restaurant, café and shop.
Great value, even once you've factored in the extra £1.50 for the toboggan run, Robin Hill is a quirky but successful mix of woodland adventure centre, wildlife reserve and low-key theme park. Plan your day around Steve Hain's

falconry display (daily shows throughout summer at 1130 and 1445) when Harris hawks, saker falcons, buzzards and a steppe eagle take to the skies in a mesmerising display of natural hunting behaviour. You can also join a red squirrel safari (Fri, 1530), but these can be popular and noisy so you're probably better off waiting quietly on your own at the sculpture trail hide which overlooks a squirrel feeding station. Other peaceful spots include the nature pond and Driftwood Dome. Ultimately, though, Robin Hill is full-on, non-stop action with a treetop trail, assault course, lookout tower and adventure playground to name just a few of the rampaging highlights. Slightly out of kilter with its woody, wholesome theme, the park also has a stomach-churning swinging galleon and a motion simulator cinema – the graphics are OK, but you'll probably get more of a thrill from spotting a red squirrel.

Hit or miss?

Blackgang Chine
Nr Ventnor, T01983-730052, blackgangchine.com.
Mar-Nov 1000-1700 or 1900, £9.50/person (under 4s free), £35/4 people. Café and shop.
Originally opened in 1843, this eccentric theme park is often bemoaned as run-down and not worth the money. However, despite its eclectic, often old-fashioned range of attractions (from funny mirrors to a singing pet shop), most youngsters love the place. Kids aged nine and over might get bored once they've done the mildly wild Cliffhanger rollercoaster and the mildly wet Waterforce slide. Everything else is just quirky, innocent fun. Don't miss St Catherine's Quay with its model boats and whale skeleton, or the Wight Experience cinema film.

The Needles Park
Alum Bay, T0871-7200022, theneedles.co.uk.
Easter-end Oct 1000-1700, limited facilities during winter, free admission, £3 car parking
Brace yourself. This clifftop pleasure park can get horribly busy during peak periods as kids run amok from one pay-as-you-go attraction to another. When they've done Jurassic Golf, Junior Driver, the spinning tea cups and the carousel, they'll want to visit the Sweet Manufactory and the Sand Shop where they can use 21 shades of Alum Bay sand to create a unique souvenir. Don't miss the glass-blowers at Alum Bay Glass or the chairlift down to Alum Bay itself (see page 50).

Out & about Isle of Wight

Amazon World Zoo Park
Watery Lane, nr Arreton, T01983-867122, amazonworld.co.uk.
Year round, daily from 1000, £6.99/adult, £5.50/child (3-14), £24/family.
A taste of the tropics on the Isle of Wight, this superb zoo is firmly rooted in rainforest conservation with imaginative and informative exhibits featuring lemurs, ocelots, hummingbirds, crocodiles, poison dart frogs and lots more.

Arreton Barns Craft Village
Main Road, Arreton, T01983-539361, arretonbarns.co.uk. Year round, daily, free admission.
Watch local craftspeople get creative with wood, glass and ceramics. Children can make their own sculptures using air-dry clay at Ceramics Crafts during school holidays and weekends, 1100-1600.

Brading Marshes Reserve
Morton Old Rd, Brading, T01983-873681, rspb.org.uk. Year round, daily, free admission.
Collect a trail guide at Brading Station before exploring the beautiful valley of the lower River Yar – home to buzzards, little egrets, green woodpeckers, butterflies and dragonflies.

Brading Roman Villa
Morton Old Rd, Brading, T01983-406223, bradingromanvilla.org.uk.

Daily 0930-1700, £6.50/adult, £3/child, £18.50/family.
Protected under the roof of a snazzy, award-winning visitor centre, the remains of this 12-room villa (complete with mosaics, coins, pottery and tools) date from AD 50 and provide an intriguing glimpse of Roman life. Educational displays for Key Stage 1 and upwards.

Brighstone Village Museum
Brighstone, T01983-740689, nationaltrust.org.uk. Year round, times vary, free admission.
Small museum depicting Victorian village life.

Calbourne Water Mill
Calbourne, T01983-531227, calbournewatermill.co.uk.
Mar-Nov, daily 1000-1700, £7/adult, £4/child (5-16), £19/family.
Milling flour for its own delicious home-baked bread, the 17th century water mill at Calbourne grinds into action daily at 1500. You can also watch potters at the wheel and have a go yourself using air-dry clay (£2). Croquet (£1), pitch and put (£1) and pedalos (£5/30 minutes) are also available.

Donkey Sanctuary
Lower Winstone Farm, Wroxall, T01983-852693, iwdonkey-sanctuary.com. Easter-Oct, daily 1030-1630, free admission.
Relying entirely on charitable donations, this rescue centre is home to over 200 donkeys.

Black and white ruffed lemurs can be seen at both Amazon World and the Isle of Wight Zoo.

Isle of Wight Steam Railway
Havenstreet, T01983-884343, iwsteamrailway.co.uk. Mar-Oct, daily during school holidays, £9/adult, £4.50/child (5-15), £22.50/family.
Havenstreet station has a café, woodland walk and children's play area – then it's all aboard for the 10-mile round trip operated by locos dating from the 1870s.

Isle of Wight Zoo
Yaverland, T01983-403883, isleofwightzoo.com.
Feb-Mar 1000-1600, Apr-Sep 1000-1800, Oct 1000-1600, £5.95/adult, £4.95/child (5-16), £19.75/family.
Best known for its big cats, the Isle of Wight Zoo is home to ITV's *Tiger Island* fly-on-the-wall series. Meet the stars of the programme, but don't overlook the primate collections. Big Cat Tours take place at 1030 and 1530, lemur feeding at 1145.

Model Village
Godshill, T01983-840270, modelvillagegodshill.co.uk. Mar-Nov, daily from 1000, £3.30/adult, £1.95/

child (3-16), £10/family.
Miniature marvel of island life tucked away in a secret garden.

Mottistone Manor Garden

Mottistone, T01983-741302, nationaltrust.org.uk. Mar-Nov, Sun-Thu 1100-1730, £3.85/adult, £1.95/child, £9.65/family.
Grab an activity pack and follow the flowerpot man trail.

Needles Old & New Battery

Alum Bay, T01983-754772, nationaltrust.org.uk. Jul-Aug, daily 1030-1700, Mar-Jun and Sep-Nov, Tue-Sun 1030-1700, £4.85/adult, £2.45/child, £12.10/family.
Clifftop fort with a tunnel leading to a lookout high above The Needles. Discovery packs link to exhibits on ship wrecks.

Niton Maze

Niton Manor Farm, T07824-416197, nitonmaze.co.uk. Jul-Sep, daily 1000-1800, £4.50/adult, £3.50/child, £14/family.

Maize maze, plus extra activities, including a tyre assault course.

Owl & Falconry Centre

Wroxall, T01983-852484, appuldurcombe.co.uk. Mar-Sep, daily 1000-1600, £6.25/adult, £4.25/child (5-16), £20/family.
Held in the grounds of an 18th century mansion (or indoors if wet), 45-minute flying displays featuring vultures and owls take place at 1100, 1300 and 1500.

Seaview Wildlife Encounter

Springvale, T01983-612261, flamingoparkiw.com.
Mar-Sep, daily 1000-1700, Oct 1000-1600, £7.85/adult, £5.85/child (3-15), £26.50/family.
Penguins and meerkats are the stars at this popular little park where you can explore amazing free-flight tropical aviaries and feed ducks, geese and swans – and other, more exotic, species during the various daily demonstrations.

Wild zone

A National Trust programme designed to introduce children to the island's natural history, Wildzone activities last two hours and can include anything from birdwatching, bat detecting and bug hunting to rock-pooling and making nestboxes. Activities must be booked in advance (T01983-741020) and cost from £2/child (age 5 and over). Discovery Pack activities cost £5/pack (one pack is sufficient for each family).

Members' perks

Family membership (see page 5) entitles you to free entry to:

English Heritage
• Appuldurcombe House.
• Carisbrooke Castle.
• Osborne House.
• Yarmouth Castle.

National Trust
• Bembridge Windmill.
• The Needles Old & New Battery.
• Mottistone Manor Garden.

Rain check

Arts & Crafts
• Island Brass Rubbing Ctr, The Coach House, St George's Church, Arreton, T01983-527553.
• Quay Arts, Sea St, Newport, T01983-822490, quayarts.org.

Cinemas
• Cineworld, Newport, T0871-200 2000.
• Commodore, Ryde, T0845-1662387.

Ice skating
• Planet Ice, Quay Rd, Ryde, T01983-615155, planet-ice.co.uk.

Indoor play & amusements
• Jolly Roger's Plaice, Dodner Industrial Estate, Newport, T01983-559272, jrzone.co.uk. Mon-Fri 0930-1800, Sat-Sun 1000-1800, £3.95/person.
Giant multi-level maze of slides, ladders, swings and ball pits for 0-12 year-olds, plus laser gun wars (1600, £3) and disco (Fri 1600, £3.95) for 7-14 year-olds.
• Sandown Pier, Esplanade, Sandown, T01983-404122.
• Summer Arcade, Esplanade, Shanklin, T01983-867585, summerarcade.co.uk.

Indoor swimming pools
• Heights Leisure Ctr, Broadway, Sandown, T01983-405594.
• Medina Leisure Ctr, Fairlee Rd, Newport, T01983-523767.
• Waterside Pool, Esplanade, Ryde, T01983-563656.
• West Wight Sports Ctr, Freshwater, T01983-752168.

Ten-pin bowling
• LA Bowl, The Pavilion, Esplanade, Ryde, T01983-617070, Mon-Fri 1000-late, Sat-Sun 0930-late, family bowling £12.60/game.

Southland Caravan Club Site

Winford Rd, Newchurch,
T01342-316101, southland.co.uk or
caravanclub.co.uk. Apr-Sep, call for
ferry/camping package rates.

Showered with accolades,
including a David Bellamy
Gold Conservation Award, this
immaculate site is pervaded by
a strong sense of pride, from its
spotless toilet blocks to its neatly

clipped hedges and carefully
tended picnic area overlooking
the Arreton Valley. Kids can cycle
the park's network of gravel
tracks or tackle the adventure
playground, while the beaches
at Sandown and Shanklin are
just a three-mile drive away.

Heathfield Farm Camping

Freshwater, T01983-756756,
heathfieldcamping.co.uk.
May-Aug, from £9.25/2 adults,
£4.25/child (15+), £1.85/child (3-15).

Few campsites can claim to
have a resident population of
red squirrels, but this is just
one of the 'natural extras' at
Heathfield – a relaxed family site
a short walk from the beaches
at Colwell and Totland. You'll

also find a wildflower meadow,
native hedgerows and a playing
field for ball games.

Grange Farm Campsite

Brighstone Bay, T01983-740296,
brighstonebay.fsnet.co.uk.
Mar-Oct, £11-20/pitch, plus £3.50-
4/adult, £2-2.50/child (4-13).

Perched on a low cliff above
Brighstone Bay, this popular
site enjoys direct access to
an unspoilt sandy beach with
safe swimming. There's also a
wonderful playground and lots
of unusual animals to befriend,
from llamas to water buffaloes.
It can feel quite exposed and
blustery, though, so you might
want to opt for one of the farm's
caravans or barn conversions.

Island Yurts
Freshwater Bay, T07802-678591,
thereallygreenholiday
company.co.uk.
Apr-Sep, from £195-545/wk.

Rising from the verdant foliage of
an apple orchard like a cluster
of giant white mushrooms, these
fabulous yurts and bell tents sleep
up to five people. Forget inflatable
mattresses and damp flysheets
– inside the family yurts you'll find
a four-poster, wardrobe, dresser
and sofa bed, all on a wooden
floor strewn with rugs. A circular
skylight promises perfect stargazing,
while a wood-burning stove keeps

everything cosy. Breakfast is
available daily, but each yurt also
comes with a supply of Fairtrade
tea and coffee, as well as local
milk, butter, honey, bread, bacon
and eggs. Organic fruit, veg and
meat can be bought at nearby
Apple Tree Café (see page 61)
– then it's simply a case of firing up
the cooking brazier outside your
tent (using logs from sustainable
woodland). Other green touches
include recycling bins, picnic tables
made from
old doors,
composting
toilets (which
take a bit of
getting used
to) and solar
powered
showers.

Compton Farm Campsite

Brook, Newport, T01983-740215,
comptonfarm.co.uk. Apr-Oct, from
£6.50/adult, £3.50/child.

This is what child-friendly
camping is all about – acres of
downland on which to run wild,
hunt for minibeasts or fly kites;
a farmyard with rusty old
tractors and free-range chickens,
and an unspoilt beach that's just
a short walk away.

The Phillips family have
farmed this sheltered valley
on the southwest coast of the
island since 1926. You'll see
some of their 100-strong herd of
suckler cows as you drive up the
lane towards the farm. What you
won't see is a reception area or a
barrage of rules and regulations.
Just pop into the kitchen to let
the farmer's wife know you've

arrived, then choose a spot to
camp alongside the hedgerow.
Don't bother looking for pitch
numbers – they're aren't any.
The further up the field you go,
the better the westerly views of
the chalk cliffs looming above
Freshwater Bay. Keep your eyes
and ears open for barn owls,
yellowhammers and skylarks.

There's a small playground
onsite, plus easy walks on the
flower-speckled National Trust
downland above the campsite.
A modest toilet block with hot
showers and laundry room is
perfectly adequate. You can
also put cooler blocks in the
farmhouse kitchen's freezer. And
if it all sounds too basic check
out one of the static caravans
hidden in a small paddock
next to the farmer's impressive
vegetable garden.

Holiday parks

Appuldurcombe Gardens
Wroxall, T01983-852597,
appuldurcombegardens.co.uk.
Excellent facilities (from crazy
golf to scuba diving lessons), plus
wide range of accommodation.

Gurnard Pines Holiday Village
Gurnard, T01983-292395,
gurnardpines.co.uk.
Chalets nestled in woodland, with
nature walks, tennis academy and
heated pools.

Island View Holidays
T01923-721606,
islandviewholidays.co.uk.

Landguard Park Resort
T0871-200 6200,
landguardholidays.co.uk.

Ninham Country Holidays
T01983-864243,
ninham-holidays.co.uk.

Old Mill Holiday Park
St Helens, T01983-872507,
oldmill.co.uk.
Small family-run park overlooking
Bembridge Harbour.

Orchards Holiday Park
Newbridge, T01983-531331,
orchards-holiday-park.co.uk.
Five-star park with lots of green
space, lovely views and heated
indoor and outdoor pools.

Park Resorts Holiday Parks
T0871-200 2010, park-resorts.com.

Sandhills Holiday Park
T01983-872277,
sandhillsholidaypark.com.

Waverley Park
T01983-293452,
waverley-park.co.uk.

Whitecliff Bay Holiday Park
T01983-872671,
whitecliff-bay.com.

Best of the rest

Isle of Wight Camper Vans

Greatwood Lodge, Cowleaze
Hill, Shanklin, T01983-852089,
isleofwightcampers.co.uk. Breaks
from £325 Mon-Fri or Fri-Mon.
With room for two adults and
two children, these restored
1970s VW campers are perfect
for free-spirited roaming. Each
well-equipped van has a double
bed, pop-top bunks, cooker,
fridge and sink, plus a range of
nice little extras – fresh towels
and linen, CD player and iPod
converter and a hamper stuffed
with local island produce. Bike
racks are also available and,
if you need more space, an
awning can be attached to the
van to create an extra bedroom.

Niton Barns

Niton, T01983-731506, nitonbarns.
co.uk. St Catherine's Barn (sleeps
4-6), from around £470-1325/wk.
One of the latest additions
to the island's self-catering
scene, this handsome bevvy
of barn conversions combines
modern open-plan comfort with
traditional character. Each of
the five properties (which sleep
from 4-14 people) has luxurious
touches, including under-
floor heating and flatscreen
televisions in most bedrooms.
Outside there are patios and
barbeque areas with views of
the picturesque village of Niton.
St Catherine's Down and south
coast beaches are all close by.

Priory Bay Hotel

Seaview, T01983-613146,
priorybay.com. From £120-270/room
B&B based on two sharing, plus
£45/child (3-11), £20/infant (0-2).
Accommodation ranges from
suites to family cottages at this
elegant hotel set in a 70-acre
estate with outdoor pool, tennis
court and golf course. A path
leads through oak woodland
(home to red squirrels) before
emerging on Priory Bay, the
hotel's private sandy beach.

The Boathouse & Lighthouse

Cove Cottage, Steephill Cove,
T01983-852373, theboathouse-
steephillcove.co.uk. The Boathouse
from £450-1,150/wk, The Lighthouse
from £650-1,450/wk.
As if their location – right on the
beach at Steephill Cove – wasn't
sensational enough, these idyllic
three-bedroom properties have
lots of family-friendly touches.
The Lighthouse, for example, has
an octagonal kitchen/diner and
snug leading onto a deck where
you'll find an outdoor shower
for hosing off sandy children.
The Boathouse, meanwhile, has
everything from buckets and
spades to toddler stair gates.

Farm stays

Isle of Wight Farm & Country
Holidays (T01983-741422,
wightfarmholidays.co.uk) offers a
range of self-catering properties,
including converted stables and
dairies on working farms. See also
The Garlic Farm, opposite.

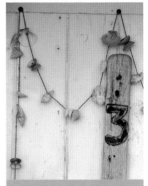

Cottage agents

**Appuldurcombe Holiday
Cottages** T01983-852484,
appuldurcombe.co.uk/cottages.
Select group of seven cottages in
the grounds of Appuldurcombe
House, with free access to the
Owl & Falconry Centre.

Home from Home Holidays
T01983-854340, hfromh.co.uk.
Choice of over 80 cottages on
the island sleeping up to 12.

Island Cottage Holidays
T01929-480080,
islandcottageholidays.com.
Over 75 properties island-wide,
including large farmhouses,
cottages with swimming pools
and houses beside the sea.

Island Holiday Homes
T01983-521113,
island-holiday-homes.net.

Wight Holiday Homes
T01983-874430,
wightholidayhomes.com.
Self-catering homes in
Bembridge and St Helens.

Wight Locations
T01983-811418,
wightlocations.co.uk.

Eating Isle of Wight

Apple Tree Café

Afton Park, Freshwater,
T01983-755774, rarebreeds.org/cafe.
Wed-Sun 1000-1600.
This peaceful café is just part
of an organic initiative that
includes a farm shop, plant
nursery, wildflower meadow
and apple orchard. Soups,
sandwiches, cream teas and
homemade cakes are available,
along with fresh apple juice and
a range of chutneys and jams.

Farmer Jack's Farm Shop

Arreton Barns, Arreton,
farmerjacks.co.uk. Daily from 1000.
A feast of island produce is sold
at Farmer Jack's, from sausages
to clotted cream. Try one of
the hampers – the £20 option
includes lemonade, stone-
ground organic flour, chilli-and-
sesame-seed rye biscuits, ginger
crunch cookies, homemade jam,
rosemary jelly, fruit chutney,
local garlic bulbs, blueberry juice
and Isle of Wight honey.

Isle of Wight Farmers' Markets

islandfarmersmarket.co.uk.
St Thomas' Sq, Newport, Fri 0900-1400
Ryde Town Sq, Ryde, Sat 0830-1230.
The island's ultimate showcase
for all things edible, Newport's
weekly farmers' market has over
20 stalls (10 in Ryde) featuring
specialists in poultry, bacon,
lamb, fish, cheese, honey and
garlic. It's a great spot to meet
locals and sample their produce.

Not to be sniffed at – a selection of seasonal fresh produce on display at The Garlic Farm.

Minghella Ice Cream

Minghella Centre, Wootton,
T01983-883545, minghella.co.uk.
La crème de la crème of ice cream
connoisseurs, Minghella was
founded on the Isle of Wight
in 1950 and now boasts over
140 flavours, from classic Old
English Toffee to radical Goo
Goo Cluster (chocolate, fudge
and marshmallow). Every scoop
is made with full-cream milk and
double cream from local farms,
with no artificial ingredients
or sweeteners. It's available
throughout the island.

The Garlic Farm

Mersley Lane, Newchurch,
T01983-865378, thegarlicfarm.co.uk.
Mon-Sat 0900-1700, Sun1000-1600.
Stock up on organic veggies
(including every vampire's worst
nightmare, the elephant garlic)
at this friendly shop on 300-acre
Mersley Farm – the UK's largest
garlic grower. Guaranteed to
titillate the tastebuds, one table
is laden with sample pickles and

chutneys (£3.50/jar) – be sure
to try Cheeky Monkey (banana
and garlic) and Vampire Extreme
(plum, garlic and chilli). You can
also stay at the farm in one of six
self-catering cottages. A week
in the Milking Parlour (sleeping
4-8) costs from around £400.

Three Gates Farm Shop

Shalfleet, T01983-531204,
calbourneclassics.co.uk. Daily.
The island's sole producer of
clotted cream, Three Gates is
also home to Country Cakes (try
a slab of Luxury Lemon Drizzle
Cake) and some seriously rich
ice cream. The warm cheese
scones and freshly made soups
are also delicious.

Fish & chips

Good quality fish & chips come
naturally to the Isle of Wight,
but three fryers that rise above
the rest are **Corries Cabin** (High
St, Cowes), **Fat Harry's** (High St,
Sandown) and **June's Fish Bar**
(High St, Shanklin).

Eating Isle of Wight

Quick & simple

Chequers Inn
Niton Rd, Rookley, T01983-840314.
Meals available 1200-2200.
Excellent family pub with an
adventure playground to keep
kids happy when they're not
munching through spaghetti
bolognaise (£3.95) or other
children's favourites. Good
range of adult dishes, from
ploughmans to pasta, plus a
carvery every lunchtime.

Crown Inn
Shorwell, T01983-740293.
Food 1200-1430, 1800-2100.
Village pub with trout stream
and play area. Menu includes
a good range of wholesome
children's options (£4.25-5.75).
For adult dishes expect to pay
around £6.25 for a half-pint of
prawns and £13.95 for a 10-oz
Shorwell beef sirloin steak.

Gossips Café
The Square, Yarmouth,
T01983-760646. Mon-Fri 0845-1730,
Sat-Sun 0845-1800.
Waterside café overlooking
the Solent. Huge range of
sandwiches and baguettes
(from £2.75), plus jacket
potatoes, fishermen's pie etc.

Windmill Inn
Steyne Rd, Bembridge, T01983-
872875. Food 1200-1430, 1730-2100.
One of the best children's
menus on the island, with not a
chicken nugget in sight. Instead,
choose from cheese omelette,
pasta carbonara, cod, chips and
peas, chicken with fresh veg and
potatoes, sausages and mash,
homemade curry and vegetable
lasagne (£3.95-4.50). Infant
meals also available. Varied adult
menu with main courses from
around £8. Carvery on Sundays.

Quay Arts
Sea St, Newport, T01983-822490.
Mon-Sat 0930-1630.
Vegetarian and fish dishes,
homemade soups and cakes,
ciabatta melts, salads and
baguettes. A good children's
option is the half jacket potato
platter with salad and fruit
(£2.75). Sit outside and watch
the ducks and swans.

Also recommended
Fisherman's Cottage
Shanklin Chine, T01983-863882.
Beachside pub dating from 1817.

Mr T's
Atherley Rd, Shanklin, T01983-863361.
Island's premier takeaway.

Puckpool Tea Gardens
Puckpool Hill, Seaview, T01983-615766.
Island's best stone-baked pizzas.

The Bugle Inn
High St, Brading, T01983-407359.
Family pub with indoor playzone.

Tilleys Café
Pier St, Ventnor, T01983-852284.
Fresh, good value food at a
friendly, family run café.

Crazy for crustaceans? Nip down to Ventnor.

Posh nosh

Baywatch on the Beach
The Duver, St Helens, T01983-
873259. Daily 0930-2130.
Great location, fresh local
seafood and gourmet burgers.

Salty's Restaurant
Quay St, Yarmouth, T01983-761550.
Fantastic seafood fresh from the
family fishing boat.

Spyglass Inn
The Esplanade, Ventnor, T01983-
855338. Food 1200-2130.
Overlooking Ventnor Bay, this
popular pub has a sun terrace
and an interior crammed with
nautical nicknacks. Local crab
and lobster are specialities, while
the kids' menu includes scampi
and cottage pie (£5.50).

Also recommended
Buddle Inn
St Catherine's Rd, Niton, T01983-730243.
Gastro pub with superb seafood.

Driftwood Beach Bar 'n' Grill
Sandown, T01983-404004.
Hot spot on Sandown's beach.

Essentials Isle of Wight

Getting there
By car Aim for car ferry ports at Lymington, Portsmouth and Southampton.
By train South West Trains (T0845-600 0650, southwesttrains.co.uk) offers combined rail and ferry tickets to the island, with regular services to Lymington, Portsmouth and Southampton.
By coach National Express (T0871-781 8181, nationalexpress.com) operates to Portsmouth and Southampton.
By ferry Red Funnel Ferries (T0844-844 9988, redfunnel.co.uk) runs a 55-minute vehicle service between Southampton and East Cowes and a 23-minute passenger service to West Cowes. Wightlink (T0871-376 1000, wightlink.co.uk) operates car ferries between Portsmouth and Fishbourne (40 minutes) and Lymington and Yarmouth (30 minutes), as well as an 18-minute FastCat service between Portsmouth and Ryde. Hovertravel (T01983-811000, hovertravel.co.uk) offers a fast, 10-minute service between Southsea and Ryde.

Getting around
By car If you're taking a passenger ferry to the island, two of the most convenient car hire companies are Esplanade, Ryde (T01983-562322) and Top Gear, Cowes (T01983-299056, top-gearhire.com). For beds-on-wheels, contact Isle of Wight Campers (see page 60). Money-saving All Island Council Parking Permits (valid 2-14 days)

are available from TICs (see below).
By train Island Line (T0845-600 0650, island-line.co.uk) links Ryde, Brading, Sandown, Lake and Shanklin along 8.5 miles of track. The Isle of Wight Steam Railway (T01983-882204, iwsteamrailway.co.uk) runs from Wootton to Smallbrook Junction, where you can connect with Island Line trains.
By bus Southern Vectis (T0871-200 2233, islandbuses.info) operates island-wide services. Rover Tickets provide unlimited travel for up to 30 days.

Maps
The Ordnance Survey OL29 Explorer is ideal for plotting walking and cycling routes. Choose the OS196 Landranger for more general touring.

Tourist Information Centres
Isle of Wight Tourism, Brading Rd, Ryde (T01983-813813, islandbreaks.co.uk). There are six TICs on the island, open Mon-Sat 0930-1700, Sun 1000-1530.
Cowes Fountain Quay.
Newport High St.
Ryde Western Esplanade.
Sandown High St.
Shanklin High St.
Yarmouth The Quay.

Hospital
St Mary's, Newport, T01983-524081.

Pharmacies
Cowes Lloyd's, Ferry Rd.
Newport Boots, High St.

Ryde Gibbs & Gurnell, Union St.
Sandown Moss, High St.
Shanklin Regent St Pharmacy.
Yarmouth Dorringtons, Quay St.
Ventnor Boots, High St.

Supermarkets
Cowes Co-op, Somerfield.
Newport Sainsbury's.
Ryde Co-op, Tesco.
Sandown Co-op, Somerfield.
Shanklin Co-op, Somerfield.
Freshwater Co-op, Somerfield.
Ventnor Somerfield.

Other shops
Baby supplies Mothercare, High St, Newport; Babyneeds, High St, Ryde; Tiddlywinks, High St, Shanklin.
Camping supplies Blacks, High St, Newport; Goodyears Outdoors, Regent St, Shanklin.
Toys & beach gear Toymaster, High St, Sandown; Paddingtons, High St, Ventnor.

Environmental groups
Gift to Nature, gifttonature.org.uk. Green Island Tourism, greenislandtourism.org. The Hampshire and Isle of Wight Wildlife Trust, hwt.org.uk.

Major Events
May Walking Festival.
Jun Music Festival.
Aug Skandia Cowes Week.
Sep Cycling Festival.

New Forest

A mosaic of woodland, heath and pasture, the New Forest was once jealously guarded as a royal deer hunting ground by William the Conqueror. Take a picnic into these wild woods 900 years ago and you'd have been lucky to escape with your head.

Nowadays, England's newest national park (created in 2005) looks more kindly on its visitors, with the death penalty long since replaced by a welcoming network of cycle tracks, footpaths and bridleways, several campsites and a range of child-friendly attractions. What makes this leafy corner of Hampshire so special, however, are its deep-rooted grazing traditions where some 400 Commoners put their ponies, pigs and cattle out to pasture,

with Keepers managing the forest's deer and other wildlife. A visit to the New Forest has more to do with simply mucking about in the woods – it's about experiencing a unique way of life.

Get your bearings
A lovely old town with half-timbered houses, thatched cottages and a high street crammed with everything from a teddy bear shop to a camping superstore, **Lyndhurst** lies at the hub of the forest where it can get snarled up with traffic during weekends and holidays. It's worth visiting, though, simply to peruse the **New Forest Centre** (T023-8028 3444, newforestcentre.org.uk, daily 1000-1700, £3/adult, under 16s free) where an excellent museum introduces the wildlife, habitats

Spot a deer

The New Forest is home to five species of deer: fallow, muntjac, red, roe and sika. For an almost guaranteed sighting, head for Bolderwood where an observation platform overlooks fields roamed by wild herds of fallow deer – the most common New Forest species, numbering around 1700. During summer, the animals are fed daily at 1330 and 1430. There's a car park, picnic area and toilets at Bolderwood, as well as several trails to take you deeper into the woods.

Main photo: Fallow deer, Bolderwood.
Right: Beaulieu village.

Ditch the car

Providing a squirrel's eye view from its open-top double decker buses, the New Forest Tour not only helps to reduce traffic, but it also offers a fun, stress-free way of reaching key attractions, as well as trailheads for walks and bike rides. Departing Lyndhurst's main car park hourly from 1015-1715, buses call at Hollands Wood campsite, Brockenhurst, Lymington High Street, Lymington Pier, Beaulieu Motor Museum, Beaulieu village, Exbury Gardens and Denny Wood campsite. Hop off at Hollands Wood for an easy 3-mile walk around Pignal Inclosure or a 6.5-mile cycle back to Lyndhurst using woodland tracks.
• **The New Forest Tour**, thenewforesttour.info. Daily throughout summer, £9/adult, £4.50/child (5-15), £22.50/group of five people, bikes carried free.

and traditions of the forest. Quiz sheets, interactive screens, a dressing-up area and plenty of 'touchy-feely' forest-themed displays make it accessible to all ages. Don't miss the impressive 25-ft-long embroidery upstairs, which depicts the wildlife and history of the forest. The New Forest Centre also has an information desk where staff can help you plan walks or book events run by the Forestry Commission or National Park Authority (see right).

Pitch your tent

Tucked away in the southwest corner of the New Forest, Holmsley is one of ten campsites run by **Forest Holidays** (T0845-1308224, forestholidays.co.uk, around £13.50-27.50/night for a family of four). With 700 pitches for tents, caravans and motorhomes, don't expect an intimate woodland experience. What you do get, however, is a wide range of facilities (showers, toilets, laundrette, shop and even pre-erected tents for hire), plus

Ramble with a ranger

The Forestry Commission (T023-8028 6840) organises a year-round programme of guided walks in the New Forest, ranging from gentle 4-mile strolls to strenuous 8-mile hikes (£4-6/person, minimum age 12). Other events suitable for families include Forest Fun Days (craft and nature activities), Family Stories on a Summer's Eve (storytelling at Blackwater Arboretum), Child of the Wild (forest challenges for 5- to 10-year-olds), plus various discovery sessions aimed at helping families find out about bats, fungi, deer and other wildlife. Prices from £6/adult, £3/child. For full details of these and other events run by The National Park Authority, pick up a free copy of the *New Forest Focus*.

Essential websites

Forestry Commission forestry.gov.uk/newforest.
New Forest National Park newforestnpa.gov.uk.
New Forest Tourism thenewforest.co.uk.

good access to the beaches at Bournemouth and Christchurch. To get more into the thick of the forest, set up camp beneath the oaks at Hollands Wood, a ten minute walk from Brockenhurst. Forest Holiday's Ashurst and Roundhill sites are also good family choices.

For camping on the wild side, unroll your sleeping bags in one of the secluded, lakeside tipis offered by **New Forest Safaris** (T07801-345264, newforestsafari.co.uk, £50/night for a family of four).

Stock up on local food
Farmers' markets are held each Sunday in Beaulieu, Fordingbridge, Lymington and Lyndhurst – an excellent opportunity to sample and buy bacon, cheeses, sausages and other local produce. Edible goodies fresh-from-the-forest are also available at Brockenhurst's **Setley Ridge Wine and Farm Shop** (T01590-622246, setleyridgevineyard.co.uk) and **Warborne Organic Farm** (T01590-688488, warbornefarm.co.uk). Look out for the New Forest Marque (newforestproduce.com), a sign that food has been grown, reared or created in the forest.

Pick a picnic spot
The New Forest is pretty much one giant picnic spot. Everywhere you go you'll find woodland glades and pony-cropped swathes of grass crying out for a picnic blanket. For a change of scene head to **Lepe Country Park** (T023-8089 9108, hants.gov.uk/lepe) where the forest meets the sea.

Plan a big day out
The two big family attractions in the region are **Beaulieu** (T01590-612123, beaulieu.co.uk, £43/family) and **Paultons** (T023-8081 4442, paultonspark.co.uk, from £48.50/family). Give them the choice and most children will go for Paultons' rollercoasters, water slides and animal park. Beaulieu is more sophisticated with its motor museum, Cistercian Abbey and Victorian gardens, but kids will still have fun here – particularly if you unleash them on Dipstick's Driving Circuit.

Don't overlook **Buckler's Hard** (T01590-616203, bucklershard.co.uk, £17.50/family) where Nelson's *Agamemnon* and other Royal Navy warships were forged from New Forest timber during the 18th century. The museum here has beautiful scale models of the vessels. Walk down the wide grassy avenue of the village and you can imagine the great man-o'-wars towering over the shipbuilders' cottages before they were launched and towed to Portsmouth for rigging. Swiftsure boats retrace the first part of that journey with 30-minute cruises on the Beaulieu River (£12/family), while a buggy-friendly walk follows the river two miles north to Beaulieu village.

Upping the action stakes, a day out at **Moors Valley Country Park** (T01425-470721, moors-valley.co.uk, £6-8/day car park) gets pulses racing with a treetop trail, adventure play area, cycle trails (bike hire from £4.50/90 minutes) and a **Go Ape** high wire forest adventure (T0845-643 9215, goape.co.uk, daily Mar-Nov, £25/adult, £20/child 10-17, minimum height 1.4 m).

Treat yourself to dinner

A thatched restaurant with shady outdoor eating area on the edge of Burley, the **Old Farmhouse** (T01425-402218, oldfarmhouseinburley.co.uk, daily 0900-1700, plus 1900-2100 Fri-Sat) serves excellent Sunday roasts (around £9/adult, £6/child), a good range of healthy children's meals, plus cooked breakfasts, cream teas, ploughmans and more. Made with New Forest Ice Cream the milk shakes are wicked – burn off the calories afterwards by hiring bikes at Forest Leisure Cycling (see right) and pedalling the 8.5-mile Woodland Trail through nearby forest inclosures.

A popular family pub on Bashley Common Rd, Wooton, **The Rising Sun** (T01425-610360) has a large outdoor play area and an excellent choice of dishes.

Don't miss

Exbury Gardens & Steam Railway
Nr Beaulieu, T023-8089 1203, exbury.co.uk.
Longdown Activity Farm
Ashurst, T023-8029 2837, longdownfarm.co.uk.
Otter, Owl & Wildlife Park
Ashurst, T023-8029 2408, ottersandowls.co.uk.
St Barbe Museum
Lymington, T01590-676969, stbarbe-museum.org.uk.

Ride a bike or a pony

Bike hire
AA Bike Hire, Gosport Rd, Lyndhurst, T023-8028 3349, aabikehirenewforest.co.uk.
Country Lanes Cycle Hire, The Railway Station, Brockenhurst, T01590-622627, countrylanes.co.uk.
Cyclexperience Brookley Rd, Brockenhurst, T01590-624204, cyclex.co.uk.
Forest Leisure Cycling, The Cross, Burley, T01425-403584, forestleisurecycling.co.uk.
From £13.50/day for adult bikes, £6-7/day for children's bikes, £7/day for tag-alongs and £3/day for child seats.

Horse riding
Burley Villa Riding School, New Milton, T01425-610278, burleyvilla.co.uk.
Offering both Western and traditional riding styles, Burley Villa is one of the forest's most family-friendly stables. A 30-minute lesson followed by a 90-minute ride in the forest costs £55 (minimum age 7), while a cowboy adventure day (beginner Western lesson, trail ride, lassooing and barbeque) costs £127. Traditional hacks cost £28/hr or £48/2 hrs (walk only for novices); 30-minute pony rides are £15.50 (minimum age 4).

Main photo: The village street at Buckler's Hard.
Top left: Cycling the Woodland Trail, near Burley.
Top right: Meeting the ponies at Burley Villa Riding School.

Can't camp won't camp

The best flysheet-free, family friendly accommodation in the New Forest is **Shorefield Country Park**, Milford-on-Sea (T0844-391 3354, shorefield.co.uk, from £265-1,045/wk for a 4-berth forest lodge). A full-blown holiday village with indoor pool, spa, crazy golf, supermarket, children's play areas and live evening entertainment, Shorefield's well-equipped self-catering chalets are scattered through 100 acres of parkland. An onsite nature centre organises family walks and wildlife detective activities for kids.
If, on the other hand, one of those chocolate-box thatched cottages beckons, contact **New Forest Cottages** (T01590-679655, newforestcottages.co.uk).

Body boarding at Whitesand Bay,
Sennen Cove, Cornwall.

Contents

70 Map

72 Isles of Scilly
73 Bath
73 Bristol
73 Somerset
73 Wiltshire

74 Jurassic Coast
76 Fun & free
78 Best beaches
80 Action stations
82 Big days out
84 Sleeping
86 Eating
87 Essentials

88 Devon
90 Fun & free
94 Best beaches
98 Action stations
102 Big days out
108 Sleeping
114 Eating
117 Essentials

118 Cornwall
120 Fun & free
124 Best beaches
130 Action stations
134 Big days out
140 Sleeping
146 Eating
149 Essentials

Southwest England

Big days out...

1 Abbotsbury Swannery & Children's Farm
2 Crealy: Devon's Great Adventure Park
3 Escot Gardens
4 Monkey World
5 Swanage Railway
6 Weymouth Sea Life
7 Wildlife Park at Cricket St Thomas
8 World of Country Life
9 Bicton Park Botanical Gardens
10 Pecorama
11 Seaton Tramway
12 The Big Sheep
13 National Marine Aquarium
14 Pennywell Farm
15 South Devon Railway
16 Lundy Island
17 Wildlife & Dinosaur Park
18 Woodlands Leisure Park
19 Arlington Court
20 Becky Falls
21 Buckland Abbey
22 Castle Drogo
23 Canonteign Falls
24 Clovelly
25 Dartington Crystal
26 Dartmouth Castle
27 Diggerland
28 Exmoor Zoo
29 Ilfracombe Aquarium
30 Living Coasts
31 The Milky Way
32 Miniature Pony Centre
33 Paignton Zoo
34 Powderham Castle
35 Prickly Ball Farm
36 RHS Garden Rosemoor
37 Cornwall's Crealy Great Adventure Park
38 Flambards
39 FutureWorld @ Goonhilly
40 Lanhydrock
41 The Lost Gardens of Heligan
42 National Maritime Museum
43 The Eden Project
44 St Michael's Mount
45 Tate St Ives
46 Tintagel Castle
47 Blue Reef Aquarium
48 Bodmin & Wenford Railway
49 Charlestown Shipwreck & Heritage Centre
50 Colliford Lake Adventure Park
51 Cornish Birds of Prey Centre
52 Cotehele & Cotehele Mill
53 Dairyland
54 Geevor Tin Mine
55 Hidden Valley Discovery Park
56 Lappa Valley Railway
57 Launceston Steam Railway
58 National Lobster Hatchery
59 National Seal Sanctuary
60 Newquay Zoo
61 Paradise Park
62 Pendennis Castle
63 Trebah Gardens

Isles of Scilly

Lying just 28 miles southwest of Land's End, the Isles of Scilly seem to have a toehold in the tropics. Nurtured by the Gulf Stream and one of Britain's sunniest climates, the archipelago's turquoise seas teem with corals, sponges and sea fans – don't forget to pack your mask and snorkel.

The hub of island life, Hugh Town on **St Mary's** has restaurants, shops, hotels and B&Bs. The **St Mary's Boatmen's Association** (scillyboating. co.uk) runs a fleet of 10 inter-island launches – sailing times are chalked up daily on quayside noticeboards and include cruises to the Bishop Rock Lighthouse and Western Rocks in search of shipwrecks, seals and seabirds. **Island Sea Safaris** (islandseasafaris.co.uk) can kit you out for snorkelling with seals, while **St Mary's Riding Centre** (horsesonscilly.co.uk) offers horse treks with children led on reins. St Mary's also has a bike hire centre (T01720-422289).

If you island-hop just once, make sure it's to **Tresco** (tresco.co.uk) where **Abbey Gardens** (built around the ruins of a 12th-century priory) runs riot with proteas, yuccas and other exotic plants. The best way to get around Tresco is by hiring a bike (T01720-422849). The island has some gorgeous sandy beaches to explore – not to mention some

Just the ticket

British International Helicopters (islesofscillyhelicopter. com) flies from Penzance to St Mary's and Tresco in around 20 minutes. **Isles of Scilly Travel** (ios-travel.co.uk) operates daily Skybus services to the islands from Bristol, Cardiff, Exeter, Land's End, Newquay and Southampton, using Twin Otter and Islander aircraft capable of carrying up to 19 people. The *Scillonian III* (islesofscilly-travel. co.uk) sails throughout the summer (Mon-Sat, plus occasional Sunday departures) leaving Penzance at 0915 and arriving at St Mary's around 1200.

of the Scilly's best accommodation, including the beachfront **Flying Boat Club**.

Smallest of the five inhabited islands, the coastline of **Bryher** (bryher-ios.co.uk) ranges from the white sands of Rushy Bay and the calm waters of Green Bay (ideal for kayaking) to rugged Shipman Head where Hell Bay receives the brunt of westerly gales. Accommodation includes the **Hell Bay Hotel** (part of the Tresco Estate), several self-catering cottages and a secluded campsite.

You can also pitch up at **St Agnes** (st-agnes-scilly.org) in the archipelago's 'wild west' where **Troytown Farm Campsite** (troytown.co.uk) hugs the foreshore and enjoys sensational sunsets. The island is joined to neighbouring Gugh by a sandy causeway – a favourite spot for families – while pubs, cafés and farms sell a mouthwatering range of local produce, from seafood to ice cream.

If you're going to be choosy, **St Martins** has the pick of the islands' beaches, with crystal-clear waters lapping sandy bays on the south coast. The food and accommodation isn't bad either – **St Martins on the Isle** (stmartinshotel.co.uk) has a Michelin-starred restaurant, while Poltreath Tea Rooms and Arthur Cafés are renowned for their home cooking. Work up an appetite with a fishing trip, farm tour or rock-pool ramble.
>> **simplyscilly.co.uk**

Bath

The pleasures of Bath range from boating on the **River Avon** (bathboating.co.uk) to exploring the magnificent **Roman Baths** (romanbaths.co.uk) where kids can 'meet the Romans' courtesy of a special audio tour.
>> **visitbath.co.uk**

Bristol

Head for the harbour where the vast propeller and rudder of Brunel's dry-docked *SS Great Britain* (ssgreatbritain.org) will astound kids. **Explore-at-Bristol** (at-bristol.org.uk) is a hands-on science museum, while highlights at **Bristol Zoo** (bristolzoo.org.uk) include the Monkey Jungle, Seal & Penguin Coasts and Explorers' Creek – a triple whammy of wet play area, tropical bird house and walk-through parrot feeding experience.
>> **visitbristol.co.uk**

Somerset

Traditional seaside fun is just a donkey ride away at Minehead, Burnham-on-Sea, Weston-super-Mare and Clevedon, while **Exmoor National Park** (exmoor-nationalpark.gov.uk) provides a rugged inland diversion. Top family attractions include **The Wildlife Park at Cricket St Thomas** (wild.org.uk), which has Britain's largest walk-through lemur exhibit, and **Wookey Hole Caves** (wookey.co.uk), where children can search for a petrified witch. **Cheddar Caves & Gorge** (cheddarcaves.co.uk) offers nature walks, caving and rock climbing (and isn't a bit cheesy), while **The Fleet Air Arm Museum** (fleetairarm.com) is packed with planes – including Concorde – and features a simulated journey to the flight deck of *HMS Ark Royal*. If you prefer supersoft animals to supersonic aircraft, get cuddling at **Animal Farm Adventure Park** (animal-fam.co.uk) or **Court Farm Country Park** (courtfarmcountrypark.co.uk).
>> **visitsomerset.co.uk**

Wiltshire

Ancient wonder or the ultimate ring of Mega Bloks? Whatever your take on **Stonehenge** (english-heritage.org.uk) you'll need some light relief after pondering its 45-ton sarsen stones. Try **Longleat** (longleat.co.uk) – the stately home won't hold kids rapt for long, but the drive-through safari park, hedge maze, adventure castle, petting zoo, railway and safari boats add up to a great family day out.
>> **visitwiltshire.co.uk**

Time travel by boat

A mere 65 million years old, the youngest rocks on the Jurassic Coast are found at Studland Bay. Head west from here and you effectively travel back in time, finally reaching Exmouth where the rocks were formed in a Triassic desert 250 million years ago. Boats are the best time-travel machines for the Jurassic Coast. As well as ogling the geology, you'll get to spy on seabirds and fish for mackerel.

• *Branscombe Pearl II*, Branscombe, T01297-680369.
• *Discoverer*, Weymouth, T07780-600233, underseaworld.co.uk. Glass-bottom boat trips.
• *The Fleet Observer*, Weymouth, T07778-286892, thefleetobserver. Glass-bottom boat trips.
• *Joint Venture*, Lyme Regis, T01297-442656.
• *Jozilee*, Lyme Regis, T07958-492953.
• *Loy Boy*, Seaton, T01297-23311. Mackerel fishing.
• *Lulworth Marine*, Lulworth Cove, T01929-400560.

• *Lyme Bay Boat Trips*, Lyme Regis, T07890-739625, lymebayboattrips.co.uk.
• *Lyme Bay Rib Charter*, West Bay, T07971-258515.
• *Marie F*, Lyme Regis, T07974-753287.
• *Marsh's Boats*, Swanage, T01929-427659, marshsboats.co.uk.
• *Sambe*, Beer, T01297-21955. Trips to Lyme Regis.
• *Stuart Line Cruises*, Exmouth, T07970-918418, stuartlinecruises.co.uk. Water taxi to Sidmouth.
• *Sunbeam*, Lyme Regis, T0777-5330973.
• *Susie B*, Lyme Regis, T01297-443674, susie-b.co.uk.
• *UK Sea Safari*, Weymouth, T01935-477585, ukseasafaris.co.uk.
• *Weymouth Whitewater*, Weymouth, T01305-781146, weymouth-whitewater.co.uk.
• *White Motor Boats*, Weymouth, T07749-732428, whitemotorboat.freeuk.com. Ferry to Portland.

West Bay harbour.

Jurassic Coast

England's first natural world heritage site, the 95-mile Jurassic Coast between Exmouth and Studland Bay adds prehistoric p'zazz to seaside holidays. You won't find the best of the South West's beaches here, but you will find beautiful scenery, traditional resorts and plenty of gentle family attractions.

Rubbing shoulders with the Grand Canyon, the Jurassic Coast was declared a world heritage site in 2002. A 185-million-year slice of earth history, this stretch of Dorset and East Devon shore is famed for its fossils. Spend a day on Charmouth beach, for example, and kids are just as likely to end up with ammonites in their buckets as blennies or crabs. There's a fossil forest near Lulworth Cove and dinosaur footprints on Portland, while 17-mile Chesil Beach is one of the world's finest shingle banks – a panoply of pebbles.

You don't have to be a rock fan, however, to enjoy the Jurassic Coast. **Swanage** is the starting point for steam train rides to Corfe Castle, while Studland Bay has superb sandcastle potential. Other Purbeck highlights include the rockpools at Kimmeridge Bay and Monkey World near Wool. Shrimps and chimps in a single day – child heaven.

Gateway to the Isle of Portland, **Weymouth** is the Jurassic Coast at its most urban, but kids will love the Sea Life Centre and running riot on the ramparts of Portland Castle. From Weymouth, the A3052 romps through rolling hills above Chesil Beach, dipping into Abbotsbury (with its wonderful swannery) before reaching **Bridport**. Nearby West Bay has a cutesy fishing harbour, but it's **Lyme Regis** that nets the most families – hardly surprising considering its fabulous seafront, sandy beach and Cobb-cosseted port.

Crossing into East Devon, **Seaton** doesn't quite have the charisma (or crowds) of Lyme Regis, but it comes up trumps with the bird-speckled Axe Estuary – best experienced from the top of one of the vintage trams that rattle back and forth to Colyton. Next door to Seaton, **Beer** has smugglers' cove written all over it, while **Branscombe** has one of the best beachside cafés on the entire coastline – not to mention some excellent walks to work up an appetite. Further west, **Sidmouth** is another family favourite with sand at low tide. **Budleigh Salterton** provides access to the glorious Otter Estuary, leaving just **Exmouth**, the westernmost outpost of the Jurassic Coast, with its long sandy beach and boat trips on the Exe Estuary.

You must

- Go mackerel fishing.
- Scour the beach at Charmouth for fossil ammonites.
- Ride the Seaton Tram.
- Follow the snorkel trail at Kimmeridge Bay.
- Meet your distant, hairy cousins at Monkey World.
- *Ooh* and *aah* at the fluffy cygnets at Abbotsbury Swannery.
- Explore the remains of Corfe Castle.
- Buy some souvenir dinosaur poo at the Fossil Shop in Lyme Regis.

Out & about Jurassic Coast

Goggle at gobies
A mesmerising window on the underwater world of the Jurassic Coast, the Fine Foundation Marine Centre at Kimmeridge Bay (dorsetwildlife.co.uk) has a camera focussed on the colourful seabed of Purbeck Marine Wildlife Reserve. You can also get nose-to-nose with tompot blennies, ballan wrasse and other local species in the centre's aquariums. The best way to see the fishes, however, is to don mask, snorkel and fins. A superb self-guided snorkelling trail has been laid out in a shallow, sheltered part of the bay where you can drift above swaying forests of rainbow wrack and coralline seaweed. Waterproof ID guides are available at the centre where you can also check tide information. Neap tides usually provide the best conditions for snorkelling, while low tide is the perfect opportunity for a rock-pool ramble, either on your own or as part of a warden-led event.

Watch the birdies
Seaton Marshes Nature Reserve (eastdevon.gov.uk) can be seen from one of the lovely old Seaton trams (see page 83), but for a free and more lingering birdwatching opportunity, park in Seaton's Harbour Road Car Park and walk along the cycle track to the nature reserve. Kingfishers often perch in front of the hide, while the grazing marsh and estuary attract curlews and little egrets.

Equally accessible, the Otter Estuary Nature Reserve near Budleigh Salterton has buggy-friendly paths and viewing platforms overlooking a saltmarsh teeming with birds.

Catch a crab
Try your luck at Stone Quay, Swanage, or in the sheltered harbour at West Bay, near Bridport. Axmouth Harbour, at Seaton, is also popular.

Walk on the wild side
The Axmouth to Lyme Regis Undercliffs National Nature Reserve (naturalengland.org.uk) is a riot of plant life with hart's tongue fern and wild iris jostling for space beneath a dense canopy of hawthorn. It's almost like stepping into a real-life Jurassic jungle. You won't encounter Veloceraptors, but

Visit The Donkey Sanctuary

Why? It goes without saying that the 400 or so rescued and retired donkeys here are irresistibly forlorn-looking and just crying out for some petting. But you'll also find an immaculate patchwork of paths and paddocks, an excellent visitor centre and a restaurant – all in beautiful countryside.

How? Open daily 0900-dusk, the sanctuary is just off the A3052 between Sidford and Seaton. Admission is free, although donations are welcome and there is a small charge for donkey walks and grooming sessions. The CoastlinX53 Jurassic Coast bus stops within easy walking distance.

Contact The Donkey Sanctuary, Sidmouth, T01395-578222, thedonkeysanctuary.org.uk.

Hunt for ammonites

This is what you're looking for: penny-sized, jewel-like ammonites (in shiny pyrite) plucked off the beach at Charmouth – by far the most family-friendly fossil-hunting patch on the Jurassic Coast. Start by visiting the excellent Charmouth Heritage Coast Centre (T01297-560772, charmouth.org, donations only) which has displays, touch tables and information on tides (a falling tide is the safest time to set out). You can sign up for a two-hour guided trip (£7/adult, £3/child) – an expert eye certainly helps, but most people go it alone.

Head east towards Golden Cap, remembering to stay clear of the cliffs. Not only are they very unstable and susceptible to landslides, but the best fossils are to be found on the beach. Keen fossil hunters should time their sorties to follow stormy weather when rain and heavy seas expose fresh fossils and wash them out. Look for shallow streams oozing from the base of the cliffs and spend some time sifting through the gritty sand where the water collects in pools further down the beach. Fossils can also get snagged between boulders.

Other nearby fossil hotspots include Monmouth Beach (west of the harbour at Lyme Regis) for giant ammonites, and Black Ven and Church Cliffs (between Lyme Regis and Charmouth) for ammonites and ichthyosaurs.

you should be prepared for a strenuous 7-mile hike.

Further west, between Beer and Branscombe, another series of huge landslips have created a similar 'undercliff forest'. It's quite a challenging walk, but much shorter than the one to Lyme Regis. Set out from the car park on the clifftop above Beer and keep your eyes peeled for peregrines. On a breezy day, you might want to stick to the clifftop path (rather than dropping into the undercliff) – there's no better place to fly a kite on the entire Jurassic Coast.

Stroll beside the sea

Worth Matravers and St Aldhelm's Head
Setting out from Worth Matravers (where the Square & Compass pub has displays of local fossils and shipwreck artefacts), this 5-mile circuit joins the South West Coast Path (southwestcoastpath.com) as it traces St Aldhelm's Head. Seabirds and dolphins can be sighted from the clifftops, while the Winspit Quarries were once used as a filming location for *Dr Who*.

Studland village to Old Harry
You can chalk up excellent views of the sea stacks at Old Harry on this easy 2-mile stroll. The Isle of Wight should also be visible, but don't overlook the detail at your feet, particularly during spring and summer when the area is ablaze with wild flowers and butterflies.

Lulworth Cove
Starting from the Heritage Centre (lulworth.com, free entry), this two-mile walk visits the famous Lulworth Crumple at Stair Hole before crossing Lulworth Cove to see the remains of a 135-million-year-old fossil forest.

Out & about Jurassic Coast

Best beaches

Beer

A natural suntrap sheltered by chalk cliffs, this pebble cove is strewn with fishing boats, and has an excellent café on the beach during summer.

Branscombe

Park at the beach or in the village (near the National Trust forge) from where there's an easy walk through farmland to Branscombe's two-mile-long swathe of pebbles.

Budleigh Salterton

Famed for its large flat cobbles, Budleigh's beach extends from Littleham Cove in the west to the Otter Estuary in the east.

Charmouth

Backed by austere grey cliffs that are prone to unleash mudslips across the shingle, Charmouth is not the prettiest beach on the Jurassic Coast, but it's the jewel in the crown for fossil hunters (see page 77). There are also rock pools at low tide, plus a grassy spot by the river where kids can fly kites and feed ducks.

Exmouth

A guaranteed hit with families, Exmouth has two miles of golden sand, rock pools at low tide, watersports galore, plus a seafront packed with amusements, from crazy golf to a miniature railway.

Kimmeridge Bay

A prime spot for rock-pooling, Kimmeridge Bay also has a snorkel trail (see page 76).

Lulworth Cove

A circular cove hemmed in by limestone cliffs, Lulworth Cove is a mixture of pebbles and rocks. Its iconic neighbour, Durdle Door, can be reached via the South West Coast Path, but it's a long walk with a steep descent to the beach. An easier option is to take the water taxi from Weymouth operated by the Bowleaze Boat Company (T01305-833315).

Lyme Regis

Following extensive coastal engineering, Lyme Regis has emerged with a newly-replenished sandy beach, plus an extended promenade between the Cobb and main town. Don't miss the Fossil Shop, an archaic Aladdin's Cave where shelves are festooned with prehistoric paraphernalia, or the Philpot Museum (lymeregismuseum.co.uk) which showcases Lyme's most famous fossil hunter, Mary Anning.

Seatown

A secluded beach with steeply shelving shingle rucked up against 630-ft Golden Cap, Seatown attracts fossil hunters rather than the bucket-and-spade brigade. The beachside Anchor Inn (page 86) is popular.

Sidmouth

Check the tides before visiting Sidmouth – sand and rock pools are exposed at low tide towards the Jacob's Ladder end of an

Sunset at Sidmouth – never too late for rock-pooling.

otherwise pebbly beach. The promenade at Sidmouth is a classic: pure Regency elegance.

Studland Bay

An arc of fine sand sweeping north of Old Harry Rocks, Studland Bay is divided into three child-friendly beaches. Knoll Beach, Middle Beach and South Beach each nuzzle shallow, sheltered waters, with Knoll Beach top of the podium thanks to its watersports hire shop (studlandwatersports.

co.uk) and excellent National Trust centre and café.

Swanage

With all the trimmings of a Victorian seaside resort, the sandy beach at Swanage is deservedly popular. Sailing, windsurfing and canoeing are available, while Swanage Pier is a renowned spot for angling.

West Bay

Split in two by a harbour

channel, the beach at West Bay varies from fine shingle to pebbles, with a dash of sand at low tide. The most sheltered spot is next to the Jurassic Pier.

Weymouth

Weymouth Beach is home to sand sculptor supremo, Mark Anderson (sculpturesinsand. com). But if that doesn't inspire you to dig for glory, there's a bucketload of other things to keep you busy, from Punch and Judy to Maggie's Donkeys.

Sea kayaking on the Jurassic Coast

Action stations

Bushcraft
Bushcraft Expeditions
Hereford, T01432-356700
bushcraftexpeditions.com.
3-day family courses from £95-120/
adult, £80/child (under 18).
Get back to nature in a 450-acre
woodland near Beaminster,
Dorset, where bushcraft experts
will hone your skills in shelter
building and wildlife tracking.

Cycle hire
Purbeck Cycle Hire
Wareham, T01929-550882,
purbeckcyclehire.com.
Adult bike £15/day, £10/half day;
child's bike £10/day, £8/half day.
Ideally located for exploring
Wareham Forest, Lulworth,
Swanage and Studland. Bikes
can be delivered.

Horse riding
**Budleigh Salterton Riding
School** Heatherways Stables,
Dalditch Lane, Budleigh Salterton,
T01305-823719, devonriding.co.uk.
Riding lessons, hacks, beach
rides and summer camps.

Windmill Stables
Weston, Portland, T01305-823719.
Horse treks lasting 1-2 hours,
plus tuition for all ages.

Llama treks
UK Llamas
New House Farm, Mosterton,
T01308-868674, ukllamas.co.uk.
Year round, full-day trek £85/adult,
£45/child (under 5s free).
Walk through beautiful Dorset
countryside with picnic-packing
llamas. Farm visits also available.

Watersports
Jurassic Kayak Tours
Secondwind Watersports, Bowleaze
Coveway, Weymouth, T01305-
835301, second-wind.co.uk.
£40/person (min age 12).
Using stable sit-on kayaks, this
is a unique way to explore the
coast between Weymouth and
Kimmeridge, with the added
bonus of spotting dinosaur
footprints in the coves around
Purbeck and the Isle of Portland.

**Weymouth & Portland
National Sailing Academy**
Osprey Quay, Portland,
T01305-866000, wpnsa.org.uk.
5-day Club Sunfish £185/child 5-7;
2-day Junior or Youth RYA Stage 1
course £155-165/child 8-16;
5-day Intensive RYA Stages 1 & 2
course £275-315/child 8-16.
Learn to sail at the 2012
Olympics sailing venue. The
SailLaser Centre offers numerous
courses, including Club Sunfish
– a fun-packed five days for five-
to seven-year-olds that features
rigging races, sailing for treasure
and a mini-Olympics. Older
children can sign up for two-day
RYA Stage 1 training or five-day
courses combining Stages 1 and
2 – a springboard to a whole raft
of intermediate sailing tuition.
Beginners' boats are usually
Bugs, Picos or Funboats.

Out & about Jurassic Coast

Abbotsbury Swannery & Children's Farm

Abbotsbury, T01305-871858, abbotsbury-tourism.co.uk. Mar-Nov, daily 1000-1700/1800 (Sep-Nov weekends and half term only at Farm), Passport Ticket to Swannery, Children's Farm and Subtropical Gardens £15/adult, £10/child (5-15), £40/family.

A cracking combo (or trio if you squeeze in the Subtropical Gardens), a day at Abbotsbury Swannery and Children's Farm has it all. Start by exploring the unique swan sanctuary – the only place in the world where you can stroll through a colony of nesting mute swans. Nest building begins around late March, while cygnets hatch from mid-May to late June. Don't miss the mass feeding of up to 600 swans (daily 1200 and 1600). There's a giant swan maze at the Swannery, but kids will probably be eager to get to the Children's Farm where there are toy tractors to race, rabbits to cuddle, ponies to ride and goats to feed and walk (when they're not taking part in the twice daily goat races). Good old-fashioned hay bales make a superb outdoor play area, while soft play in the Great Tithe Barn offers a wet-weather bolthole.

Crealy: Devon's Great Adventure Park

See page 102.

Escot Gardens

Ottery St Mary, T01404-822188, escot-devon.co.uk. Daily from 1000, £6.95/adult, £5.95/child (3-15), £24/family.

Kids hit the ground running here – there's so much to do, and it's all good, wholesome outdoor stuff. Top of their list will be the hedge maze with its cunning switch gates and wildlife quiz. Letterboxing (tracking down

Above: Not such ugly ducklings, Abbotsbury.
Opposite: Corfe Castle – Civil War survivor.

stamps hidden in the woodland) is also great fun. Then there are the falconry displays, walks and animals, such as otters.

Monkey World

Wool, T01929-462537, monkeyworld.org. Daily 1000-1700 (1800 Jul-Aug), £10.50/adult, £7.25/child (3-15), £31/family.

A strong sense of purpose pervades this 65-acre park that's home to over 160 primates rescued from laboratories and illegal smugglers. You'll find the largest group of chimps outside Africa, as well as capuchins, gibbons, orangutans, marmosets and a wonderful walk-through

Rain check

Cinemas
• Cineworld, Weymouth, T0871-200 2000.
• Radway, Sidmouth, T0871-230 3200.
• Regent, Lyme Regis, T01297-442053.

Indoor play
• Sharky's Soft Play and Laser Zone, Harbourside, Weymouth, T0871-222 5760, sharkysweymouth.co.uk.

Indoor swimming pools
• Bridport Leisure Ctr, Brewery Fields, T01308-427464.
• Flamingo Pool, Lyme Rd, Axminster, T01297-35800.
• Sidmouth Swimming Pool Ham Lane, T01395-577057.
• Splashdown, Tower Park, Poole T01202-716123, splashdownpoole.com.
• Weymouth & Portland Swimming Pool, Knightsdale Rd, Weymouth, T01305-774373.

Museums
• Dinosaurland Fossil Museum, Lyme Regis, T01297-443541, dinosaurland.co.uk.
• Discovery Interactive Science Centre, Weymouth, T01305-789007, discoverdiscovery.co.uk.
• Dorset County Museum, Dorchester, T01305-262735, dorsetcountymuseum.org.
• Teddy Bear Museum, Dorchester, T01305-266040, teddybearmuseum.co.uk.

All aboard the Swanage Railway

Leave your car at Norden Park & Ride (0800-2000, £1) before hopping on one of the Swanage Railway's steam locos. First stop is Corfe Castle to admire the 1,000-year-old ruins and explore the picture-postcard village with its Enid-Blyton-inspired Ginger Pop shop and Model Village. The next two stops (Harman's Cross and Herston Halt) provide access to good walking country, then it's full steam ahead to Swanage and a short walk from the station to the beach. Buses link to Studland or you could stay local and visit Durlston Country Park with its visitor centre and café.
• Swanage Railway, T01929-425800, swanagerailway.co.uk. Year round, times vary, £9/adult, £7/child (3-14), £26/family Norden-Swanage return.
• Corfe Castle, T01929-481294, nationaltrust.org.uk. Daily from 1000, £5.90/adult, £2.95/child, £14.75/family.

ring-tailed lemur enclosure. Don't miss the chimp nursery, the half-hour talks by keepers (1200-1530) or the huge jungle-style adventure play area.

Weymouth Sea Life

Lodmoor Country Park, T0871-423 2110, sealifeeurope.com. Daily from 1000, £17/adult, £13.50/child; check website for discounts.
With the added adrenaline buzz of Adventure Island (featuring rides like Giddy Galleon), this is the UK's best value Sea Life centre. Indoor displays include

Members' perks

Family membership (see page 5) entitles you to free entry to:

English Heritage
• Portland Castle.

National Trust
• Corfe Castle.
• Parking at Studland Bay.

RSPB
• Radipole Lake Nature Reserve, Weymouth.

a shark nursery, a walk-through turtle tunnel and a seahorse breeding centre. Seals, otters and penguins complete the marine menagerie. If it's hot, kids will want to round off the day frolicking in Splash Lagoon; if it's not they'll be dragging you next door to the Pirate Adventure Mini Golf.

The Wildlife Park at Cricket St Thomas

See page 73.

World of Country Life

Sandy Bay, Exmouth, T01395-274533, worldofcountrylife.co.uk. Mar-Nov, daily 1000-1700, £9.85/adult, £7.85/child (3-17), £32.50/family.
There's plenty of indoor fun here, with everything from soft play to a vintage car museum and Victorian street. But World of Country Life really comes into its own when the sun shines and kids can explore the animal paddocks, walk the pigmy goats, take a deer safari train ride, play crazy golf and run wild in the adventure playground.

More family favourites

Bicton Park Botanical Gardens

East Budleigh, T01395-568465, bictongardens.co.uk. Daily 1000-1800 (1700 in winter), £6.95/adult, £5.95/child, £22.95/family.
Bicton merges formal gardens and an arboretum with play areas, a nature trail and mini golf. Littl'uns love the 25-minute railway ride around the park.

Pecorama

Beer, T01297-21542, peco-uk.com. Mon-Fri 1000-1730, Sat 1000-1300, Sun 1000-1730, £6.60/adult, £4.50/child (4-14).
Pecorama has indoor and outdoor model railway layouts, including a mile-long, ride-on train through beautiful gardens.

Seaton Tramway

Seaton, T01297-20375, tram.co.uk. Feb-Dec, times vary, £8.35/adult, £5.85/child (3-14), £25.50/family Seaton-Colyton return.
Ride an open-top tram 3 miles, spotting birds before reaching Colyton station for a cream tea.

Sleeping Jurassic Coast

Burnbake Campsite

Rempstone, T01929-480570, burnbake.com. Apr-Oct, £7-9/pitch (1 person), £2-4/extra adult, £1-2/extra child.

A slide, swinging tyre and a stream – simple pleasures for children at this popular woodland site located between Corfe Castle and Studland Bay.

Eweleaze Farm

Osmington, T01305-833690, eweleaze.co.uk. Aug only, £6-12/adult, £3-6/child.

Solar-powered showers, earth toilets, an effective recycling scheme and a farm shop selling local organic food – Eweleaze certainly pays more than lip service to the environment. It's the private shingle beach, however, that guarantees happy days for families at this spacious site just east of Weymouth. Campfires add an extra spark of excitement for kids, and there's even a van selling wood-fired pizzas. Book early, though, as Eweleaze only opens in August.

Hook Farm

Uplyme, T01297-442801, hookfarm-uplyme.co.uk. Mar-Oct £10-22/pitch (2 people), £3/extra adult, £1.50/extra child.

Nuzzled in rolling countryside a mile from Lyme Regis, this peaceful site suits nature-loving families. Apart from a small climbing frame and swings, don't expect much in the way of special facilities. The local pub and general store are nearby.

Manor Farm

Seaton, T01297-21524, manorfarmcaravans.co.uk. Mar-Nov, £10-18/pitch (2 people), £3/extra adult, £2/extra child.

Kids can help feed the sheep, goats, chickens and Shetland ponies at this family-run site overlooking the Axe Valley. A farm shop sells local produce.

Oakdown

Weston, T01297-680387, oakdown.co.uk. Mar-Nov, £10.80-16.60 (2 people), £2.95/extra person.

A tidy site between Branscombe and Sidmouth, Oakdown has excellent facilities, including an impressive children's play area.

Sea Barn Farm

Fleet, Weymouth, T01305-782218, seabarnfarm.co.uk. Mar-Oct, £11-22/pitch (2 people), £4-5/extra adult, £1-2.50/extra child.

This place will blow away the cobwebs. It's perched high above the Fleet – a protected lagoon in the lee of Chesil Beach – with chest-swelling views east towards Portland and west towards Abbotsbury. Part of a 140-acre working farm, the campsite has spotless toilets, a children's play area and footpaths leading right down to the shores of the Fleet. A short stroll leads to the sister site of West Fleet Farm, another family favourite with an outdoor heated pool, licenced bar and entertainment – all available to Sea Barn Farm campers.

Wood Farm

Charmouth, T01297-560697, woodfarm.co.uk. Apr-Oct, £5.85-17.20/standard pitch, plus £4.40-6.35/adult, £1.95-2.95/child.

A mile from Charmouth, Wood Farm has a sheltered, terraced camping field. An indoor pool, tennis court, fishing lake and games room help to banish boredom come rain or shine.

Splashing out

Moonfleet Manor
Fleet, T01305-786948,
moonfleetmanorhotel.co.uk.
£170-205/double (2 adults,
1 child), £240-305/deluxe double
(2 adults, 2 children) dinner, bed
& breakfast; children sharing
parents' room pay only for meals.
A Georgian Manor crammed with
antiquities might seem like a
recipe for a family holiday disaster,
but not only are children positively
welcomed at this fabulous hotel,
but there are also all kinds of family-
friendly touches, from an indoor
pool and games room to children's
high tea and an OFSTED-registered
crèche. You're as likely to find *The
Beano* in one of the homely lounges
as a copy of *Vogue*. The food is
superb (often using local seafood),
while outside it's a two-minute
stroll to the edge of Fleet Lagoon.
Weymouth is just six miles away.

Best of the rest

Bookham Court Cottages
Alton Pancras, Dorchester, T01300-
345511, bookhamcourt.co.uk.
£225-1095/wk.
It might be a 30-minute drive
from the coast, but this stunning
farm development is paradise
for kids with its wildlife hide,
farm trail and fishing lakes.

Bulstone Hotel
Branscombe, T01297-680446,
childfriendlyhotels.com.
£90-110/room (2 adults, plus 2
children under 11) B&B.
Like Moonfleet (above), Bulstone
trumpets its family appeal – and
with good cause. Each family
suite has two bedrooms and
a bathroom, while the guest
kitchen is a nice extra for parents
who need to feed kids outside
meal times. Children's tea is
followed by a candlelit dinner for
adults only. The hotel has three
acres of grounds, surrounded by
East Devon countryside.

Knoll House Hotel
Studland Bay, T01929-450450,
knollhouse.co.uk. From around
£115/adult, FB. Discounts for children.
Walk five minutes through
the grounds of this upmarket
country hotel and you'll find
yourself on Studland's soft
sands. And as if location wasn't
enough, the family facilities
at Knoll House are top-notch,
with outdoor pool, adventure
playground, children's dining
room, golf course, tennis courts
and the nearby Studland Riding
Stables (minimum age five).

Holiday parks

Chesil Holiday Park
Weymouth, T01305-773233,
chesilholidays.co.uk.

Freshwater Beach Holiday Park
Bridport, T01308-897317,
freshwaterbeach.co.uk.

Ladram Bay Holiday Park
Otterton, T01395-568398,
ladrambay.co.uk.
With direct access to Ladram Bay,
this park is a good weatherproof
option with indoor pool, soft play
and crazy golf.

Littlesea Holiday Park
Weymouth, T0800-197 0058,
littlesea-park.co.uk.

Newlands Holiday Park
T01297-560259,
newlandsholidays.co.uk.

Swanage Bay View Holiday Park
T01929-422130, swanagebayview
holidaypark.com.

Waterside Holiday Park
Weymouth, T01305-833103,
watersideholidays.co.uk.
Five-star, all singing, all dancing
holiday park right on the beach at
Bowleaze Cove. Superb facilities
include pool, bowling and spa.

Farm stays

Rudge Farm Cottages
Chilcombe, T01308-482630,
rudgefarm.co.uk.
Ten cottages overlooking lake and
sleeping 2-6. Two miles from sea.

Westover Farm Cottages
Wootton Fitzpaine,
T01297-560451,
westoverfarmcottages.co.uk.
Four three-bedroom cottages
close to Charmouth.

Eating Jurassic Coast

Local goodies

Farmers' markets

Fresh local produce is sold at the market in Exmouth's Strand Gardens on the second Wednesday of every month (0900-1300), while Honiton Market takes place along the High Street, Tue-Sat, year round. Swanage Market is held Easter-Oct, Tue 0800-1500, and there's a market in Weymouth on the second Sunday of every month.

Locally-caught seafood can be bought in most harbour towns along the Jurassic Coast. There's a great little fish stall on the slipway at Beer, for example.

Crab House Café Ferryman's Way, Wyke Regis, T01305-788867. Simple shack, superb seafood.

Devon Juice Café The Strand, Exmouth, T01395-269222. Smoothies, salads and hot pots.

Hive Beach Café Beach Road, Burton Bradstock, T01308-897070. Lyme Bay hake, Portland turbot

Fish & chips

The harbourside stalls at West Bay are highly recommended, as is **The Beer Fish and Chip Shop** (Fore St), **Bloaters** of Sidford (Church St) and **Capels** of Exmouth (Imperial Rd). In Weymouth, pride of place goes to **Fish 'n' Fritz** (Market St) and **The Seagull** (Old Harbourside).

and other local seafood specials in a wonderful outdoor setting on Chesil Beach, near Bridport. The crab sarnies are excellent, as is the Lovington's ice cream.

Otterton Mill Otterton, Budleigh, T01395-567041. Watermill and bakery with scones and flapjacks to die for.

Quick & simple

Joe's Café South Beach, Studland Bay, T07931-325243. Daily during summer. This seriously cool beach café serves organic sandwiches and soup, homemade cakes and local Purbeck ice cream. The café's borrow-and-return policy with deckchairs, buckets, spades and other beach gear also goes down a treat.

The Sea Shanty Branscombe, T01297-680577. Easter-Nov, daily 1000-1700. Local crab is landed straight onto the beach in front of The Sea Shanty, so you'd expect the crab sandwiches here to be some of the best in Devon. But you'll also find delicious pasties fish and chips, homemade cakes, Devon cream teas and Sunday roasts (£7.50/adult, £3.50/child).

Also recommended
The Anchor Inn
Seatown, T01297-489215.
Cosy pub right on the beach.

Dukes The Esplanade, Sidmouth, T01395-513320. Good for snacks on the seafront.

The Elm Tree Inn Langton Herring, Weymouth, T01305-871257. Pub grub and cream teas.

Harbour Inn Marine Parade, Lyme Regis, T01297-442299. Pub classics served on a small terrace overlooking the beach.

The King's Arms Otterton, T01395-568416. Good selection of lunch specials; great value carvery.

Sunray Bar & Grill Chapel Lane, Osmington, Weymouth, T01305-832148. Grills, local seafood, daily carvery, children's play area.

Posh nosh

Ocean Bay Restaurant Ulwell Rd, Swanage, T01929-422222, oceanbayrestaurant.com. Daily 1230-1500, 1900-2045/2115. Funky decor, fresh seafood and a fantastic location on Swanage North Beach. Book a table for lunch on the terrace.

The Riverside Restaurant West Bay, Bridport, T01308-422011, thefishrestaurant-westbay.co.uk. Daily except Mondays. For seafood lovers it doesn't get much better than this. Lunch dishes from around £12.

Essentials Jurassic Coast

Getting there

By train Mainline rail from London connects Poole, Wareham, Wool, Dorchester and Weymouth. There's also a service from Salisbury and London to Axminster, Honiton and Exeter, from where you can change to Exmouth. Contact South West Trains (T0845-6000650, southwesttrains.co.uk) and First Great Western (T08457-000125 firstgreatwestern.co.uk).

By coach National Express (T0871-7818181, nationalexpress. com) serves Swanage, Weymouth, Bridport, Lyme Regis and Sidmouth.

Getting around

By bus CoastlinX53 (T0871-2002233) is a dedicated Jurassic Coast service, linking Poole and Exeter, with stops at Wareham, Wool, Weymouth, Abbotsbury, West Bay, Bridport, Charmouth, Lyme Regis, Seaton, Beer and Sidford. A Firstday Explorer ticket provides unlimited travel for a day and costs £6/adult, £4.50/child and £13/family. The 501 open-top bus runs hourly/daily from Weymouth to Portland Bill during the summer.

Maps

Choose sheets 115, 116 and OL15 from the Ordnance Survey Explorer series, or Landranger maps 192, 193 and 194.

Tourist Information Centres

There are several TICs along the Jurassic Coast, generally open Mon-Sat 1000-1700/1800 during summer months and 1000-1400/1500 in winter. A few, such as Lyme Regis and Weymouth TIC, also open on Sundays.

Bridport South St, T01308-424901, westdorset.com.

Budleigh Fore St, T01395-445275, visitbudleigh.com.

Exmouth Alexandra Terrace, T01395-222299, exmouth-guide.co.uk.

Lyme Regis Church St, T01297-442138, westdorset.com.

Seaton The Underfleet T01297-21660, seatontic.com.

Sidmouth Ham Lane, T01395-516441, visitsidmouth.co.uk.

Swanage Shore Rd, T0870-4420680, virtual-swanage.co.uk.

Weymouth Esplanade, T01305-785747, visitweymouth.co.uk.

Further Information

Jurassic Coast, jurassiccoast.com.

Hospital

Dorchester Dorset County Hospital, T01305-251150.

Sidmouth Victoria Cottage Hospital, T01395-512432.

Weymouth Community Hospital, T01305-760022.

Pharmacies

Bridport Co-op, East St.

Budleigh Lloyds, High St.

Exmouth Boots, Chapel St.

Lyme Regis Boots, Broad St .

Seaton Boots, Marine Place.

Sidmouth Boots, Fore St.

Swanage Co-op, Kings Rd.

Weymouth Boots, St Mary St; Asda, Newstead Rd.

Supermarkets

Bridport Co-op, Morrisons, Somerfield.

Budleigh Salterton Co-op.

Exmouth Somerfield, Tesco.

Lyme Regis Co-op.

Seaton Co-op.

Sidmouth Somerfield, Tesco, Waitrose.

Swanage Co-op, Somerfield.

Weymouth Aldi, Morrisons, Somerfield, Tesco.

Other shops

Baby supplies Mothercare, South St, Dorchester and St Marys St, Weymouth; Primary Colours, Broad St, Lyme Regis.

Camping supplies Jurassic Outdoor, High St, Swanage; Outdoor Sports & Leisure, North St, Wareham.

Toys & beach gear Frosts Toymaster, South St, Bridport; Rainbow, Bridge St, Lyme Regis; Rainbow, Harbour Rd, Seaton; Gliddons, Church St, Sidmouth; Early Learning Centre, St Mary St, Weymouth; Razzamataz Toymaster, St Alban St, Weymouth.

Environmental groups

Devon Wildlife Trust, T01392-279244, devonwildlifetrust.org. Dorset Wildlife Trust, T01305-264620, dorsetwildlife.co.uk.

Major Events

May International Kite Festival, Weymouth.

Aug Lyme Regis Carnival.

Aug Sidmouth Folk Week.

Aug Weymouth Carnival.

In a child's mind Devon is, first and foremost, about boat trips and sandcastles, surfing waves and rummaging in rock pools, building dams against the tide and dangling crab lines off the harbour wall.

Blackpool Sands.

Devon

A light, crumbly scone, strawberry jam so chocka with fruit it's almost impossible to spread and a big dollop of clotted cream. The best things in Devon come in threes, and that includes its tempting trio of family holiday highlights, from the surf-swept north coast to the rugged moors and idyllic South Hams.

No one is suggesting you try to cram in all three on a single holiday. One of the great things about Devon is that each coastline can easily be combined with either Exmoor or Dartmoor for a healthy dose of beach-relief – conquering a tor or two, horse riding or simply finding a secluded campsite or picnic spot next to a tumbling woodland stream.

Tucked into the leafy fringes of Dartmoor, attractive market towns like **Buckfastleigh** have more reasons to lure you away from the coast, whether it's a steam train ride on the South Devon Railway or farm fun at Pennywell. Exmoor, meanwhile, practically dabbles its toes in the sea, with **Lynton** and **Lynmouth** superbly placed for holidays that merge moor and shore.

But let's be honest. In a child's mind Devon is, first and foremost, about boat trips and sandcastles, surfing waves and rummaging in rock pools, building dams against the tide and dangling crab lines off the harbour wall. A family holiday in Devon which overlooks these obligatory rites of childhood is unthinkable. Like a scone without clotted cream.

North coast resorts, such as **Ilfracombe**, **Woolacombe** and **Croyde**, are magnets to surfers, but even here there are inland diversions. Hop on a bike at **Barnstaple** or **Bideford**, for example, and beautiful Devon countryside is just a short pedal away along the Tarka Trail.

Action on the south coast tends to revolve more around boats – learning to sail in trendy **Salcombe** or paddling a canoe on the River Dart or Tamar. There are some exciting boat trips available in **Dartmouth**, either hiring your own cabin cruiser or joining an organised 'seafari'. In the South Hams, just getting to the beach can involve a mini adventure – walking across wild and wonderful Bolberry Down to Soar Mill Cove, for example, or catching the ferry from Salcombe to South Sands. And, as you'd expect from one of Britain's flagship family holiday destinations, Devon is brimming with attractions, from the National Marine Aquarium at **Plymouth** and Living Coasts at **Torquay** to adventure parks like Crealy and Woodlands.

You must

- Surf at Woolacombe.
- Ride a horse on Exmoor.
- Cycle the Tarka Trail.
- Find a blenny in the rock pools at Wembury.
- Leap into the tidal pool at Tunnels Beaches.
- Sprint across Bantham.
- Paddle a canoe on the Dart Estuary.
- Learn to sail in Salcombe.
- Back the winning woolly at The Big Sheep races.
- Race sticks down a Dartmoor stream.
- Plan a Lundy adventure.

Out & about Devon

Spot an otter

Few mammal species are more charismatic than the otter, and Devon now supports one of the largest populations in England. But where to find them? Tarka Country, based around the ancient woods and flood meadows of the River Torridge in North Devon, is a good place to start – particularly Devon Wildlife Trust's Halsdon SSSI, near Great Torrington. Otters can also be found at the Upper & Lower Tamar Lakes (swlakestrust. org.uk) near Bradworthy. On Dartmoor, try Lydford Gorge, managed by the National Trust.

Fly a kite

Big beach, low tide, onshore breeze. Perfect! Top spots for kite flying in Devon include Woolacombe and Saunton on the north coast, and Bantham on the south coast.

Ramble through rock pools

Wembury, near Plymouth, clinches pole position in Devon's impressive line-up of rock-pooling hotspots. In fact, it's such a good place for intertidal critters that it forms part of the Wembury Voluntary Marine Conservation Area. Best of all, though, is that it's also home to the Wembury Marine Centre (T01752-862538, wemburymarinecentre.org, Easter-Oct, free admission), an ideal place to learn about the ecology and importance of rock pools. The centre organises guided rock-pool rambles (£1/person) where you'll search for rarities like the bloody-eyed velvet swimming crab and tompot blenny, as well as old favourites such as shore crabs

and beadlet anemones. If you set out on your own, remember that the best time for rock-pooling is about an hour either side of low tide. Always replace animals, rocks and seaweed where you found them and take care when using nets as they can easily rip seaweed off the rocks or damage fragile creatures like crabs. Remember, too, that rocks can be slippery and tides change quickly.

Seek shells

If you're really serious about shell collecting there's one beach in Devon you shouldn't miss. Known locally as Shell Beach, Barricane (located between Woolacombe and Mortehoe) turns up as many as 40 different varieties of shells, including blue-rayed limpets, cockles, necklace shells, netted dog whelks, painted topshells,

Visit Berry Head

Why? Because it's home to southern England's largest guillemot colony – part of a veritable seabird city of nesting fulmars, kittiwakes and shags, all crowded together on impressive 200-ft-high limestone cliffs. Eagle-eyed visitors might also spot stonechats and the nationally rare cirl bunting.

Where? Located on the South Devon coast, Berry Head National Nature Reserve is signposted from Brixham. Drive past Landscove Holiday Village up a single track road and you'll find the car park and visitor centre.

How? The RSPB operates a free watchpoint, Mar-Aug. Staff are at hand Sun-Thur, plus bank holidays, 1000-1600, to help visitors use telescopes and binoculars to identify the birds. For fair-weather twitchers there's also a CCTV link between the guillemot colony and visitor centre.

Contact The RSPB, T01392-432691, rspb.org.uk/datewithnature.

Dangle a crab line

No seaside family holiday in Devon is complete without a crabbing expedition. One of the best spots is the harbour wall and slipway at Lynmouth (pictured), but you stand equally good chances of hooking the nippers at hotspots like Stoke Gabriel in the Dart Estuary (see River Shack Café, page 115), Kingsbridge (see Crabshell Inn, page 115) and Dartmouth Quay.

periwinkles, razor shells, sand dollars, scallops, tellins and – the jackpot for most shell-seekers – tiny cowrie shells which are no bigger than your little fingernail and are said to have been carried from the Caribbean on the Gulf Stream.

Start Bay

Stride out on the South West Coast Path

In Devon there are several bite-size chunks of the 630-mile South West Coast Path (southwestcoastpath.com) that are suitable for families.

In North Devon, for example, the section of path between **Baggy Point** and Croyde Bay (starting at the National Trust car park) is an easy buggy-friendly stroll. You'll pass a memorial to Henry Williamson of *Tarka the Otter* fame before reaching the tip of the headland where a viewing area provides a vantage point for spotting seabirds.

For something slightly more challenging, head to **Hartland Point** where a two-mile circuit takes in the Coastguard Lookout and views of the lighthouse.

In South Devon, **Start Point** is the initial focus of what must surely rank as one of the most

spectacular short coastal walks in Britain. From the car park, the old lighthouse road (suitable for pushchairs) descends steadily to Start Point, offering sensational views across Start Bay towards the 'ghost village' of Hallsands (destroyed by storms in 1917) and beyond to the shingle-protected ley at Slapton – now a national nature reserve with a bird hide overlooking reedbeds.

You can visit Start Point Lighthouse (see page 105), but you will need to backtrack slightly in order to pick up the Coast Path heading west above a dramatic rocky coastline. Keep your eyes peeled for seals and basking sharks near the base of the cliffs, while further offshore, the submerged sandbank of The Skerries often attracts plunge-diving gannets. Be sure also to notice the wildlife at your feet – this section of coast is smothered in flowers during summer which, in turn, attract several species of butterflies.

Soon, you will reach Great Mattiscombe Sands, a quiet and secluded beach where wreckers once lured ships onto the rocks. From here, a footpath leads up the valley back to the car park, completing the two-mile circuit.

For an unusual twist on the South West Coast Path, dip into the 10-mile **Plymouth Waterfront Walkway** which meanders around Plymouth Sound and uses art, sculpture and poetry to showcase its

heritage and history. A free MP3 podcast, with commentary by Edward Woodward, can be downloaded from the Coast Path's website. The walk can also be combined with a visit to the excellent National Marine Aquarium (see page 102).

Salcombe

Get to know a Devon beauty

Covering 130 square miles of coastline and countryside and no fewer than five estuaries (the Avon, Erme, Dart, Salcombe-Kingsbridge and Yealm) the South Devon Area of Outstanding Natural Beauty (southdevonaonb.org.uk) is a magnet for holidaymakers. As well as the beaches of the South Hams (see page 97), free highlights include numerous family-friendly walks (you can download 30 circular routes from the website) and two easy-going cycle trails: the 2.5-mile Totnes to Dartington route and the 7-mile Plym Valley Trail on the south west edge of Dartmoor. The region also has some of Devon's most interesting towns, with Dartmouth, Kingsbridge, Salcombe and Totnes all worth a wander.

Discover Dartmoor

Covering some 368 square miles, Dartmoor National Park has plenty of pay-to-visit attractions (see page 106), but it's the simple and free pleasures, such as scrambling over a granite tor or boulder-hopping across a stream, that make the greatest impressions on children.

An excellent way to sample quintessential Dartmoor is to walk around Venford Reservoir (easily accessible from Ashburton) before continuing on to Combestone Tor.

One of the most popular family locations on Dartmoor is Dartmeet. There's a good café here, but if the weather is dry take a picnic and find a spot on the grassy bank next to the River Dart further upstream where it swirls between boulders and eddies through natural swimming pools. Children will happily while away an afternoon racing sticks through the mini-rapids or even taking a dip if it's warm enough.

The scenery is equally stunning at Avon Dam, the setting for a 2-mile surfaced and traffic-free trail from Shipley Bridge alongside the Avon River. It's one of many walks on Dartmoor that are particularly suitable for children. For details of others, call in at one of the information centres operated by the **Dartmoor National Park Authority** (dartmoor-npa.gov.uk). The most comprehensive is the High Moorland Visitor Centre at Princetown (T01822-890414, daily from 1000, free admission). Here you will find a range of displays on the history, culture and wildlife of Dartmoor, as well as information on walks and other activities.

To add extra incentives to your walks, letterboxing is not only a great way to introduce youngsters to the joys of exploring Dartmoor, but it will also improve their fitness and navigational skills! Basically,

Bleak and uninviting? If that's your impression of Dartmoor, then you haven't been to Dartmeet.

it involves a combination of orienteering and treasure hunting, using clues to locate boxes hidden on the moor. Each box contains a visitors' book and a rubber stamp. Find one and you can use the stamp to record the find in your own book before adding your personal stamp to the visitors' book. To get started, log on to Dartmoor Letterboxing (dartmoorletterboxing.org).

The Ranger Ralph Club

Organised by the National Park Authority, the Ranger Ralph Club is for children aged 5-12. Members receive a pack containing lots of goodies, a quarterly newsletter and a membership card that allows them to attend special events for free. All it costs to join is four second-class stamps. Visit dartmoor-npa.gov.uk/funzone for details.

Out & about North Devon Coast

Best beaches

Barricane Bay

Located half a mile from the main beach at Woolacombe, this shingle/sand bay offers excellent shell-collecting, as well as body-surfing and rock-pooling.

Combe Martin Bay

This sandy beach has only achieved minimum legal water quality standards in recent years, but it's still a popular spot for families with sheltered swimming and good facilities.

Croyde Bay

Much smaller than the neighbouring surf meccas of Woolacombe and Saunton, Croyde Bay can get crowded, but there's no denying the huge appeal of this beautiful sandy beach with its easy access.

Hele Bay

A sheltered cove between Ilfracombe and Coombe Martin, Hele Bay has sand and rockpools, and is close to Hillsborough Nature Reserve.

Instow

Sand without the surf, Instow's beach is snug in the Torridge Estuary where it's become something of a hotspot for the local fishing and sailing crowd.

Lee Bay & Woody Bay

West of Lynmouth, the Valley of the Rocks forms a rugged gateway to the most dramatic section of the North Devon coast. Crumbling rock spires inhabited by wild goats loom above cliffs draped with hanging forests of ancient oak. Lee Bay (rocky with sand at low tide) is tucked away here,

while further west, a toll road (£1 per car) twists and turns through the woodland, offering dizzying views of the sea below. Secluded Woody Bay can only be reached by a steep hike. For an easier sea-level perspective, join a tour boat from Lynmouth.

Lynmouth

You inevitably have to run the gauntlet of shops selling fudge, ice cream and sticks of rock to reach the seafront at picture-perfect Lynmouth. But the small, shingle beach has good skimming stones and rock pools. It's also a fine spot to eat fish and chips from Esplanade Fish Bar (page 116) or catch crabs from the harbour wall (page 91).

Saunton

Wrapping its tail end around the combined estuaries of the Taw and Torridge, Saunton Sands

stretches north in a long swathe of sand, sandwiched between impressive dunes and some of North Devon's most renowned surfing waters.

Tunnels Beaches
😎 🚻 🅿️ 🚫 🐕 🚻 🅿️

No matter how galling you may find the prospect of paying to visit a beach (£1.95/adult, £1.50/child, £6.50/family), this privately owned stretch of rocky shoreline on the western outskirts of Ilfracombe is not to be missed. The approach is supercharged with mystery and anticipation as you walk through tunnels, hand-carved in the 1820s, to emerge next to a sheltered cove dominated by a huge tidal pool that's visible for three hours either side of low tide. Kids love swimming, snorkelling or mucking about on inflatables in this stunning Victorian bathing lagoon, but don't overlook the natural rock

pools dotted around the beach – they're some of the best in the UK and are often the focus of rock-pool rambles run by the Devon Wildlife Trust. Kayaks are available for hire (£10/hr), while the Café Blue Bar is a top spot for family meals (see page 115).

Westward Ho!
😎 🚻 🚫 🐕 🚻 🅿️

This long sandy beach has a distinctive ridge of pebbles, behind which is the Northern Burrows Country Park. The surf isn't as good here as on beaches further up the coast, but being on the southern side of the Taw/Torridge Estuary does put you within easy reach of highlights like Clovelly (page 106) and Hartland Point (page 92).

Woolacombe Sands
😎 🚻 🚫 🐕 🚻 🅿️

This is the big one: nearly three miles of surf-strafed, squeaky clean sand, Woolacombe is

beach heaven whether you're a bucket-toting toddler or wave-riding teen. You'll pay around £5.50 to park in the field behind the beach, then it's a short walk down a slipway crammed with beach shops, cafés and surf school kiosks (see page 101). If it's summer, the northern part of the beach is likely to be staked out by a maze of windbreaks, but even when Woolacombe is heaving you can always find space for your picnic rug and a game of beach cricket. Wave-jumping, body boarding or surfing are also compulsory – as is building a sandy rampart to hold back the tide, the seawater warming as it slides in over those acres of sunbaked sand. Another family favourite, Putsborough is located at the southern end of the bay, near Croyde. With little more than a beach car park and a shop, it offers a more tranquil alternative to Woolacombe.

Tunnels Beaches, Ilfracombe

The approach is supercharged with mystery and anticipation as you walk through tunnels to emerge next to a sheltered cove.

Out & about South Devon Coast

Best beaches

Beesands

A mile-long, fine shingle beach, backed by the freshwater lake of Widdcombe Ley.

Bigbury-on-Sea

This large sandy beach is linked to Burgh Island by a low tide causeway or by sea tractor.

Challaborough

Just west of Bigbury, this sheltered, sandy cove has rockpools at low tide. Sailing, surfing and canoeing are popular and there is a good coastal walk to Ayrmer Cove.

Dawlish Warren

Backed by dunes, this sand and shingle beach lies close to the wildlife-rich Exe Estuary and offers safe swimming.

East Portlemouth

A string of sandy beaches facing Salcombe, including Fisherman's Cove, Smalls Cove and Mill Bay (see opposite). A foot ferry operates between Salcombe and East Portlemouth.

Lannacombe

Hidden down a long lane, just to the west of Start Point, Lannacombe is a peaceful beach, with sand and rock pools. There's not much left of it at high tide and parking is limited.

Salcombe

Lying just beyond the ruins of Salcombe Castle, North Sands is snug between wooded headlands and has limited parking, a shop and café. A little further towards the mouth of Kingsbridge Estuary and Bolt Head, South Sands has fine sand and can be reached by road, footpath or ferry from Salcombe

Slapton Sands

A three-mile ridge of shingle and gritty sand stretching across the southern edge of Start Bay, Slapton Sands is popular for watersports and there's a good fish and chip shop at Torcross. The beach was used by allied forces in 1943 to rehearse for the D-Day invasions – a Sherman tank from this period can be found in the car park, along with a birdwatching hide overlooking Slapton Ley Nature Reserve.

Thurlestone

There are two sand/shingle beaches here, the larger of which has Thurlestone Rock sea stack. Rock-pooling is excellent at low tide, while surfing, windsurfing and canoeing gear can be hired in summer.

Wonwell

Sandy beach on east side of Erme Estuary; Mothecombe, also sandy, lies opposite.

Plymouth

Wembury Beach (see page 90) is renowned for its rock-pooling and diving, while Bovisand has a wide expanse of sand at low tide – perfect for ball games.

Riviera at a glance

Torquay

Maidencombe, sand/shingle.
Watcombe, sand.
Oddicombe, sand/shingle with access by cliff railway.
Babbacombe, sand/shingle.
Anstey's Cove, shingle/rock.
Meadfoot, pebble/sand.
Torre Abbey Sands, sand, but covered at high tide.
Hollicombe Beach, sand.

Paignton

Preston Sands, sand.
Paignton, sandy beach with Paignton Pier at its centre.
Goodrington Sands, sandy beach with Seashore Centre and Quaywest Water park.
Broadsands, sand.

Brixham

Churston Cove, sand/shingle.
Fishcombe Cove, sand/shingle.
Breakwater Beach, shingle.
Shoalstone Beach, shingle/rock beach right next to outdoor seawater pool.
St Mary's Bay, sand/shingle.

Top 5 South Hams beaches

Bantham

It's impossible to hold your children back at Bantham. The moment you walk through the dunes to reach this beach beauty, west of Kingsbridge, they'll be off, sprinting across acres of soft, rippled sand, splashing in shallow tidal lagoons or skipping through waves clutching a surfboard. Apart from toilets in the car park, facilities are few and far between, but part of Bantham's free-spirited appeal lies in its wild, unspoilt nature.

Blackpool Sands

Driving south from Dartmouth, the A379 dips towards Start Bay where you'll find this immaculate turquoise cove nuzzled between headlands. The sand may be gritty at high tide (pretty useless for sandcastles) and the car park attendants don't always excel in the charm stakes, but you can't deny the almost Mediterranean beauty of Blackpool Sands. The swimming is sheltered and there's a lovely grassy area behind the beach for picnics – that is, if you can resist the excellent Venus Café (page 115).

Main pic: Mill Bay.
Left, from top: Hope Cove, Bantham, Soar Mill Cove and Blackpool Sands.

Hope Cove

This is the kind of place that lodges in childhood memories. A sleepy fishing village, fabulous rock pools, ample sand for beach cricket, gentle waters in which to swim and paddle a canoe, a harbour wall to fish from...

Mill Bay

You won't find a beach in Devon with softer sand or more sheltered swimming than Mill Bay, opposite Salcombe. A shallow stream on the left side of the bay is ideal for damming, while walkers can set off on a superb clifftop jaunt as far as Gara Rock, before looping back to the beach car park. You'll only find toilets here, but there's a café just up the lane above the jetty for the Salcombe-East Portlemouth ferry.

Soar Mill Cove

If you're after a secluded smugglers' cove with caves, cliffs and rock pools, look no further than this stunning cove. It's easily reached from Soar, but the longer walk across Bolberry Down is all part of the adventure of a day here. The sandy beach promises superb strandline treasure-hunting and has streams ripe for damming.

Out & about Devon

Action stations

Boat trips
African Queen
Dartmouth, T07885-246061,
theafricanqueen.co.uk.
Family rates negotiable.
Family cruises and fishing trips
up river or out to sea aboard a
15-m long ex-Royal Navy boat.

Dartmouth Boat Hire
Kiosk, North Embankment, T01803-
834600, dartmouth-boat-hire.co.uk.
Four-person boat £25/hr, including
fuel, life jackets and charts.
Self-drive cabin cruisers ideal for
exploring the River Dart, from
Dartmouth to Totnes. Skippered
RIB rides also available.

Exmoor Boat Trips
The Quay, Lynmouth, T01598-
753207. From £10/person.
Cruise past the spectacular coast
of the Valley of the Rocks, fish for
mackerel or visit Woody Bay.

Falcon Charters
Dartmouth, T01803-839245,
dartboat.com. Departures at 1100
and 1500 for 2-3 hr trips, from £10/
person, family rates available.
Seafaris on the Dart Estuary and
along the South Devon coastline
aboard the 9-m *Falcon*, with the
emphasis on wildlife watching.

Ilfracombe Princess
Pier Kiosk, Ilfracombe Harbour,
T01271-879727, ilfracombeprincess.
co.uk. Easter-Oct, £12/adult, £6/child
(5-15) for 90 minute cruise.

Carrying up to 100 passengers,
this is the largest and (being
twin-hulled) the most stable
cruise boat operating along
the North Devon coast. Two
cruises are available – head west
towards Morte Point in search
of seals and porpoises, or east
towards the soaring cliffs at
Hangman Point to spot nesting
seabirds and peregrine falcons.

Independent Charters
Bucks Mill, Bideford, T01237-431374,
independentcharters.co.uk.
Charter rates vary.
Sailing from Clovelly Harbour,
trips feature fishing, wildlife-
watching and drop-offs/pick-
ups at Lundy Island.

Salcombe Boat Hire
Salcombe, T01548-844475,
salcombeboathire.co.uk. Daily
estuary cruises, hourly from 1100.
Boat hire, Easter-Oct, daily.
Explore the sheltered estuary
waters of Salcombe and
Kingsbridge, either on an
organised cruise or on your
own. Each 12- to16-ft fibreglass
self-drive hire boat comes with
lifejackets and a detailed chart
to help you find the best spots
for seals, beaches and pubs.

Whitestrand Boat Hire
Whitestrand Quay,
Salcombe, T01548-843818,
whitestrandboathire.co.uk. Daily
from 0900-1800, 2-hr mackerel
fishing trips £15/adult, £10/child,
motor boat and Laser Pico dinghy

hire from £25/hr, £85/day; rowing
boat hire £20/hr, £75/day; double
canoe hire £13/hr, £55/day.
Great range of options for
getting you afloat, from
stable two-person kayaks to a
16-ft Fastliner with cabin and
outboard engine. Mackerel
fishing trips take place four
times daily (May-Sep) on the
skippered *Calypso*.

Canoeing
Canoe Adventures
Harberton, Totnes, T01803-865301,
canoeadventures.co.uk.
From £19/adult, £16/child (3-16).
Guided paddling trips exploring
the secret creeks of the Dart
Estuary in 12-seat Voyager
canoes, with lessons in bushcraft
thrown in. Each canoe comes
with a steersman, campfire
brazier, barbeque and shelter.
Family group paddles available.

Canoe Tamar
Kingsbridge, T0845-430 1208,
canoetamar.co.uk) £22/person,
free for children under 5.
Paddle the Tamar River
between the historic quays of
Morwellham and Cotehele using
stable Canadian canoes.

Singing Paddles
Kingsbridge, T0775-442 6633,
singingpaddles.co.uk. Day rates from
£40/person, £150/groups.
Tailor-made canoeing trips in
the South Hams suitable for all
ages and covering technique,
safety, navigation and bushcraft.

Bike the Tarka Trail

Biketrail
Fremington Quay,
T01271-372586, biketrail.co.uk.
Daily during holidays,1000-1800.
Adult bike £5.50/hr, £10/day;
child's bike £4/hr, £7.50/day;
family rate £32. Rates include
helmets, pannier bags, locks and
tool kits. Wide range of other bikes
also available, including tandems,
choppers and go-karts.

Tarka Trail Cycle Centre
Barnstaple Station
T01271-324202, tarkabikes.co.uk.
Daily Apr-Oct, 0915-1700.
Adult bike £8/half day, £10.50/day;
child's bike £5.50/half day, £7.50/day;
child seat £3/half day, £3/day;
tag-along £5/half day, £7.50/day.
Rail passengers receive £2 discount.

Torrington Cycle Hire
Old Town Station, Station Hill
T01805-622633.
Daily Feb-Nov, 0915-1700.
Adult bike £8/half day, £10.50/day;
child's bike £6/half day, £7.50/day;

Other hire centres:
Bideford Cycle Hire
East-the-Water, T01237-424123.
Otter Cycle Hire
Braunton, T01271-813339.

Tracing a 180-mile figure-of-eight across North Devon's worldclass biosphere reserve, the Tarka Trail offers traffic-free cycling and walking through countryside that inspired Henry Williamson's *Tarka the Otter*. The most family-friendly sections are between Braunton and Meeth.

Braunton to Barnstaple (6 miles) Flat, easy riding along the banks of the River Taw, linking Braunton Burrows (wildlife-rich dunes) with Barnstaple where you can find out about river life in the Museum of Barnstaple and North Devon (T01271-346747, devonmuseums.net). Three miles west of Barnstaple, the Ashford Bird Hide is a great spot to watch wading birds and wildfowl feeding on the mudflats – and there's a picnic spot nearby.

Barnstaple to Bideford (9 miles) There's more twitching to be had at RSPB Isley Marsh Reserve, but the highlight of this section of the Tarka Trail is the former china clay port of Fremington Quay with its glorious views of the Taw Estuary and superb café (see page 114). Further south, Instow has a sheltered beach as well as a ferry service to the fishing village of Appledore, while Bideford has a pannier market and 13th century bridge across the Torridge.

Bideford to Great Torrington (6 miles) Pedalling south, the trail straddles the River Torridge at the Landcross Viaduct – the setting for the Pool of Six Herons from *Tarka the Otter*. Then it's four miles of beautiful riverside scenery, including the stretch of the Torridge near Beam Aqueduct which Williamson describes as Tarka's birthplace.

Great Torrington to Meeth (10 miles) Dartmoor comes into view as you cycle this peaceful section of the trail with Dartington Crystal and RHS Garden Rosemoor as tempting diversions in Torrington.

Dotted along the Tarka Trail are 21 discovery posts containing information on history and wildlife. For further insights, download the Tarka Audio Trail (northdevonbiosphere.org.uk) to your MP3 player or mobile phone.

Out & about Devon

Cycling
See Tarka Trail, page 99.

Devon Cycle Hire
Sourton Down, T01837-861141, devoncyclehire.co.uk. Daily 0900-1700, adult bike £14/day, child's bike £10/day, tag-along £8/day. Ideally placed on Dartmoor's mainly level, traffic-free Granite Way Cycle Trail.

Falconry
Exmoor Forest Birds of Prey
T01643-831458, exmoorforestbirdsofprey.co.uk. Half-day basic falconry experiences £35. Learn how to handle harris hawks and other raptors with George Pile, one of Britain's youngest professional falconers.

Fishing
Blakewell Family Fishing & Trout Farm
Muddiford, Barnstaple, T01271-344533, blakewell.co.uk. Daily 0900-1700, £2.50/person to fish, £4.50/catch for 2 lb trout. A brilliant introduction to fishing, Blakewell provides all the fishing tackle and know-how to catch your own supper. Once you've hooked your trout, they'll even prepare and pack it ready for you to cook.

Horse riding
Dean Riding Stable
Lower Dean Farm, Parracombe, T01598-763565, deanridingstables. co.uk. £15/pony ride (minimum age 4), £26/1-hr lesson, £40/2-hr hack,

£48/half-day course including lesson, stable management and hack. Full-spec stables in Exmoor National Park offering everything from a half-hour 'taster' on a pony to a living-and-breathing-horses holiday, self-catering in the farmhouse.

Doone Valley Trekking
Cloud Farm, Oare, T01598-741234, doonevalleytrekking.co.uk. £20/1-hr starter ride, £37.50/2-hr trek, £97.50/day ride (minimum age 12). Located in one of Exmoor's most beautiful valleys, Doone Valley Trekking offers daily horse rides for complete novices, as well as longer treks for those who are competent at trot and canter. Even littl'uns can saddle up on the farm's miniature ponies. Accommodation is available in cottages or at Cloud Farm campsite (see page 108) and a cream tea at the café is a must.

Powerboating
RIBS 4 Kids
Salcombe Powerboat School, T01548-842727, salcombepowerboats.co.uk. Full-day RYA course in handling a RIB (minimum age eight).

Sailing
ICC Salcombe
Island Street, Salcombe, T01548-531176, icc-salcombe.co.uk. Two-day courses from £140/non-residents, £180/residents. Something of a legend and local landmark in Salcombe, the

Horse riding in the Doone Valley, Exmoor.

Island Cruising Club operates from the retired Mersey ferry *Egremont*, moored in the estuary. You can join live-aboard sailing courses or take a launch from Whitestrand Pontoon in the middle of Salcombe. ICC offers the full range of RYA sailing courses, lasting from two days to a week and suitable for children aged five and above. Boat hire and private tuition (for half or full days) is also available.

Salcombe Dinghy Sailing
East Prawle, T01548-511548, salcombedinghysailing.co.uk. 90-minute lessons from £45. Learn to sail in a Wayfarer or Laser Pico, or hire a six-person Drascombe Lugger (with sails *and* engine) for more leisurely exploration of the Salcombe Estuary. Family courses operate from Whitestrand Pontoon.

Surfing
Discovery Surf
Plymouth, T07813-639622, discoverysurf.com. Year-round, £38/2 hr lesson, minimum age 6.

Beach briefing – Nick Thorn surf school on Woolacombe Sands, North Devon.

Surf lessons at Bigbury on-Sea, plus a Fun Hour where kids can learn about sea safety and use surfboards to build a raft.

Nick Thorn Surf Coaching

Woolacombe, T01271-871337, nickthorn.com. Year-round, £30/2-hr lesson, £55/full day (two lessons), minimum age 8.
Boasting a superb beachfront location at Woolacombe, Nick Thorn lessons teach you how to paddle a surfboard, choose your waves and get to your feet.

North Devon Surf School

Bideford, T01598-710818, northdevonsurfschool.co.uk. Year-round, £28/2-hr lesson, £50/full day (two lessons), minimum age 8.
Learn to surf at Westward Ho! Private tuition available for children under eight.

Point Breaks

Croyde, T07776-148679, pointbreaks. com. £35/3hr lesson, minimum age 8. Croyde Bay's original surf school, also offering wakeboarding and waterskiing if the sea is flat.

Surfing Croyde Bay

Croyde, T01271-891200, surfingcroydebay.co.uk. Mar-Dec, £35/adult, £25/child (8-16).
Well established surf school with beach café, solar-powered showers and sandpit training area. Surfing lessons have a 5:1 student to instructor ratio.

Surf South West

Croyde Bay, T01271-890400, surfsouthwest.com. Mar-Oct, from £25-30/lesson, minimum age 8. Operates surf schools on Croyde and Saunton Beaches. Private tuition available for six- and seven-year-olds.

Wildlife watching
Devon Badger Watch

Nr Tiverton, T01398-351506, devonbadgerwatch.co.uk. Apr-Oct, Mon-Sat, from 1930, £10/adult, £7/child (7-15).
Not one for fidgets, Badger Watch promises spine-tingling encounters with Brock and his buddies. Up to 90 minutes are spent in a hide a few feet from where the badgers emerge.

Multi activities

H2Outdoor
Woolacombe, T07789-807424, h2outdoor.co.uk.
Coasteering, sea kayaking and mountain biking, plus 30-minute sessions for 6- to 8-year-olds.

Isca Outdoor
Exeter, T01392-494053, iscaoutdoor.co.uk.
Family programme of activities (half-day to full weekend) such as caving, climbing and bushcraft.

Mountain Water Experience
Kingsbridge, T01548-550675, mountainwaterexperience.co.uk.
Half- and full-day activities for families (minimum age 8), including coasteering around Start Point.

River Dart Country Park
Ashburton, T01364-652511, riverdart.co.uk. £6.50/person (5+), £3/infant (3-5).
Covering 90 acres, this Dartmoor park is an adventure paradise. Young children can run wild on the pirate ship, toddlers' beach and tree houses, while kids aged seven and over can sign up with Dare Devils – a range of extras (May-Sep, from £3/person) which includes canoeing and an 80-m zip wire. Rock climbing, abseiling, canoeing and caving on Dartmoor are also available. The River Dart Country Park also has an excellent campsite (see page 111).

Spirit of Adventure
Yelverton, T01822-880277, spirit-of-adventure.com.
Dartmoor family adventure weekends featuring rock scrambling, climbing, abseiling, kayaking and raft building.

Out & about Devon

Big days out

The Big Sheep

Bideford, T01237-472366,
thebigsheep.co.uk. Apr-Nov, daily
1000-1800, £9.95/person, £9.45/
person for groups of four or more,
children under 3-ft tall free, reduced
prices and facilities during winter.

Farm diversification gone mad,
The Big Sheep is utterly *baa*-rmy
– an indoor/outdoor mixture of
sheep-themed attractions that
is certainly Devon's most original
(and possibly most fun) day out
– and with modest admission
prices you won't feel fleeced
either. The highlight is definitely
the sheep racing where you can
place bets (using Ewe-ros, the
park's ubiquitous currency) and
cheer on Red Ram, Sheargar
and other favourites down
the 250-yard course. And if
you think that's bizarre, brace
yourself for the sheep duck
trials where border collies round
up gaggles of woolly-headed
runner ducks. There are also
traditional sheepdog trials, horse
whispering demonstrations,
pony rides, a farm safari, ride-
on tractors and a train ride
departing from – you guessed
it – Eweston Station. You'll find
all the cute-and-fluffies in the
Nursery Barn where puppies are
available for regular cuddling
sessions and newborn lambs
(Dec-Easter) can be bottle-fed.
Other barns house soft play
areas, a sheep-shearing arena,
restaurant and the all-important
Sheepy Shop. Somewhat at
odds with its innocent, organic
approach, The Big Sheep is
also the venue for Battlefield
Live – war games using
state-of-the-art 'eye-safe' laser
guns (minimum age 8). And if
teenagers simply find The Big
Sheep too silly, they can get
free entry to the South West
Mountain Boarding Centre.

Crealy: Devon's Great Adventure Park

Nr Exeter, T01395-233200, crealy.
co.uk. Daily from 1000, £7.78-
13.95/person, £6.80-13.45/person
for groups of four or more, children
under 92-cm tall free, reduced prices
available online and during winter.

This is what happens when you
cross Disneyland with a farm
park. Devon's Crealy (there's
another one in Cornwall – see
page 134) will have your kids
cuddling rabbits one minute,
then whooping it up on a log
flume the next. There are six
zones. Older children will make
straight for the Adventure
Realm where rides include the
El Pastil Coaster (runaway train
rollercoaster), Queen Bess Pirate
Ship (swing boat), Tidal Wave
Terror (12-m-drop water splash),
Battle of the Bears (interactive
ball-dodging adventure) and
Meteorite (stomach-lurching
vertical drop ride). Many of
these have a minimum height
restriction of 92 cm, but parents
with toddlers will find plenty
of tamed-down action in the
Magic Realm with its excellent
indoor play area. Action
Realm, meanwhile, keeps the
adrenaline pumping with its
go-karts, Dino-Blaster Bumper
Boats, Water Wars and Summer
Soak Zone (yes, you will get
wet). The three remaining realms
(Animal, Farming and Natural)
see Crealy going all soft and
soppy. You can feed lambs, ride
ponies, milk cows, tickle piglets,
cuddle hamsters and ride a train
to a quiet lakeside picnic spot.

National Marine Aquarium

Plymouth, T01752-600301,
national-aquarium.co.uk.
Daily from 1000, £11/adult, £6.50/
child (5-16), £30/family.

Once you've visited this water
wonderland, boasting over 4000
creatures from 400 species,
other aquariums might strike
you as damp squibs. Not only
will you find Britain's deepest
tank (holding 2.5 million litres of
water), but there are also 70-odd
sharks and a loggerhead turtle
that was rescued after being
washed up on a Cornish beach
in 1990. The aquarium is divided
into distinct zones – Atlantic
Reef, Mediterranean Sea, Weird
Creatures, Coral Seas and The
Shallows. As captivating as
these, often huge, displays are,
it's the Explorocean zone that
steals the show. Delving into
oceanography (with more than
a splash of fun), its interactive
exhibits include Mini SubMission
– an underwater assault course

using remotely operated vehicles. Equally high-tech is the 4D cinema where you get sprayed as a whale breaches and rocked in your seat when a shark nudges past.

Pennywell Farm

Buckfastleigh, T01364-642023, pennywellfarm.co.uk. Feb-Nov, daily 1000-1700, £9.95/adult and child, £6.95/infant (under 3).

This all-springing, all-prancing farm park should keep you busy for a whole day. Lambs, chicks, rabbits and miniature pigs are just some of the cute-and-cuddlies, with pony rides, falconry displays, pond-dipping and deer feeding also available. It's not all wild and woolly stuff though. Adventure activities include a quad bike circuit and a wonderful willow maze. If it rains, you can take cover in the animal barn or farmyard theatre.

South Devon Railway

Buckfastleigh, T0845-345 1420, southdevonrailway.org. Mar-Oct, limited timetable in other months, departure times vary, £9.90/adult, £5.90/child (5-14), £28.90/family Buckfastleigh–Totnes return.

Buckfastleigh Station oozes nostalgia – from the Great Western Railway steam locos hissing and puffing next to the platform to the cosy waiting room and old trolleys piled with trunks. But there's more to this beautiful 7-mile section of track alongside the River Dart than

Island of adventure

Lundy Island
Lundy Shore Office, Bideford, T01271-863636, lundyisland.co.uk.
Apr-Oct, sailing times vary, £32.50/adult, £17/child (4-16), £5/infant (under 4), £75/family day return from Bideford or Ilfracombe.
Sailing from North Devon, the 267-passenger *MS Oldenburg* takes under two hours to reach Lundy Island, a three-mile-long chunk of granite rising from the Bristol Channel, 11 miles north of Hartland Point as the gull flies.

Lundy has a chequered history. Vikings may well have used the island as a base for raiding Britain – 'Lund-ey' is Norse for puffin island. In the Middle Ages, Lundy was a popular lair for pirates, including a gang of Turks who threatened to burn Ilfracombe. This was followed by a pillaging band of Spaniards and, finally, by the French who hurled the islanders' livestock over the cliffs.

As you'd expect from such a turbulent past, a map of Lundy is littered with wicked place names, like Dead Cow Point, Devil's Kitchen and Brazen Ward. Making landfall at the island's jetty, it feels like you have been transported into the pages of a Famous Five novel.

It's a short walk to the Marisco Tavern, an atmospheric inn at the heart of Lundy's tiny settlement where you will also find a shop, church, the Old Lighthouse and a 13th century castle – one of a handful of historic buildings restored by the Landmark Trust to accommodate overnight visitors (see page 108). Don't miss the farm which has Soay sheep, ponies, chickens and ducks – you can wander at will as long as you remember to shut gates behind you.

One of the best places to spot wildlife is on the west side of the island. Follow the track from the settlement to South West Point, then head north along the clifftops towards Jenny's Cove, keeping an eye out for basking sharks, seals and seabirds. Your best chances of spotting puffins are during May and June, while guillemots and razorbills can be seen into July.

Lundy was designated Britain's first Marine Nature Reserve in 1986 on account of its clear water and rich cocktail of Atlantic and Mediterranean sea life. Warden-led events on the island include rock-pool rambles at Devil's Kitchen and snorkelling safaris (Jun-Sep) where you can glide through forests of kelp in search of Montagu's blennies and rare corals.

just another ride on a choo-choo. At Buckfastleigh you will find a museum, giftshop, café, picnic garden, play area and riverside walks – not quite enough to fill a whole day until you discover that the South Devon Railway cunningly links two additional attractions. At Buckfastleigh, Dartmoor Otters & Buckfast Butterflies features an underwater viewing area for European, Asian and North American otters, as well as a tropical house for butterflies, leaf-cutter ants and terrapins. At the other end of the line, meanwhile, the Rare Breeds Farm at Totnes has owls, red squirrels, goats, sheep and a hedgehog rescue centre. Discounted joint tickets are available for the railway and either attraction. A vintage bus service also links Buckfastleigh Station with Buckfast Abbey.

Wildlife and Dinosaur Park

Coombe Martin, T01271-882486, dinosaur-park.com. Mar-Nov, daily from 1000, £12/adult, £7.50/child (3-15), £34/family.

Life-size animatronic dinosaurs headline the attractions at this eclectic theme park where one moment you'll be cowering beneath a T-Rex or ducking to avoid a spitting Dilophosaurus and the next you'll be clinging to a Wild West runaway train as it lurches into a simulated earthquake. The park's snow leopards, lions, lemurs, gibbons, meerkats and other exotic creatures have no need for special effects, although the daily howling shows by Shaun Ellis certainly add an extra dimension to the wolf exhibit. You can also watch falconry displays, swim with sealions or take refuge from the wild things in the lovely gardens.

Woodlands Leisure Park

Blackawton, Totnes, T01803-712598, woodlandspark.com. Mar-Nov, daily from 0930, £11.45/person, £43.80/family, children under 92 cm free.

The entrance to Woodlands is deceptively tranquil with deer grazing in leafy paddocks. But step through the gates of this 10-zone theme park and life becomes a blur. Thrill rides include the 500-m Tornado Toboggan, White Knuckle Swing Ship and three water coasters. There are also pedal boats, zip wires, a commando assault course and plenty of less intense attractions for younger children, such as a Wild West play town. Calming moments can be sought at the fun farm (home to Terence the Champion Turkey), while wet weather will see everyone bolting for the excellent indoor play areas. Camping is also available.

Above: One of the day's more serene moments at Woodlands Leisure Park. Right: Chuffed to bits – getting fired up for a ride on the South Devon Railway.

See the light

Start Point Lighthouse Tours
T01803-770606, trinityhouse.co.uk.
Jul-Aug, daily 1100-1700,
times vary rest of year, £2.80/adult,
£1.50/child (5-16), £7/family.
Explore the cylindrical kitchen and listen
to tales of storms and wrecks in Start Bay.

Hit or miss?

The Gnome Reserve
Bradworthy, T01409-241435.
gnomereserve.co.uk. Mar-Oct, daily
1000-1800, £2.95/adult, £2.50/child.
Cynics may scoff, but where else
can you take a family of four for
under £12 *and* get free use of
gnome hats and fishing rods
into the bargain? So forget your
inhibitions, puff out your cheeks
and enjoy a day (OK, an hour
or two) at this 4-acre reserve,
populated by over 1000 gnomes.
You'll find the chirpy chappies
up to all sorts of fun and games,
including a motorbike scramble.

Members' perks

Family membership (see page 5)
entitles you to free entry to:

English Heritage
• Berry Pomeroy Castle, Totnes.
• Dartmouth Castle.
• Okehampton Castle.
• Totnes Castle.

National Trust
• Arlington Court, Barnstaple.
• Buckland Abbey, Yelverton.
• Castle Drogo, Drewsteignton.
• Killerton, Broadclyst.
• Lydford Gorge, Lydford.
• Overbeck's, Sharpitor.

Rain check

Arts & Crafts
• Krazy Krafts Workshops,
Lynmouth, T01598-753489.
• The Pottery, Cockington Crafts,
Torquay, T01803-606662.

Caves
• Kents Cavern, Torquay, T01803-
215136, kents-cavern.co.uk

Cinemas
• Embassy, Ilfracombe,
T01271-862323
• The Flavel, Dartmouth,
T01803-839530.
• The Reel Cinema, Kingsbridge,
T01548-856636.

Indoor play & amusements
• Atlantis Adventure Park,
Bideford, T01237-478888.
• Funder Zone, Barnstaple Trade
Ctr, T01271-328328.
• House of Marbles, The Old
Pottery, Bovey Tracey, T01626-
835285, houseofmarbles.com.

Indoor swimming pools
• Parklands Leisure Ctr,
Okehampton, T01837-659154.
• Quayside Leisure Ctr,
Kingsbridge T01548-857100.
• Totnes Pavilion & Swimming
Pool, T01803-862992.

Museums
• Dartmouth Museum, The
Butterwalk, T01803-832923.
• Ilfracombe Museum, Ilfracombe,
T01271-863541.
• Mortehoe Heritage Ctr,
Woolacombe, T01271-870028.
• Museum of Dartmoor Life,
Okehampton, T01837-52295.
• North Devon Maritime Museum,
Appledore, T01237-422064.
• Torquay Museum, Torquay,
T01803-293975.
• See also devonmuseums.net.

Pick of the pitches

Cloud Farm Campsite

Oare, T01598-741234,
doonevalleyholidays.co.uk.
Year-round, £5.50-7.50/adult,
£4-5.50/child (5-12).

Heather-blushed moorland, a stream tumbling over rocks into cool dark pools shaded by trees; grey wagtails fussing over moss-covered boulders and ponies grazing in riverside meadows. Doone Valley is quintessential Exmoor, and sitting pretty in the middle of it all is Cloud Farm. More than simply a farm with a camping field, this lovely old whitewashed property has three self-catering cottages, a tearoom and horse riding stable (see page 100). You can pitch your tent right next to the effervescent Badgworthy Water where kids will happily while away an afternoon netting water bugs, racing sticks through the rapids or taking a dip in one of the natural pools. Walk (or ride a horse) straight out of the campsite and you'll find yourself in the wilds of Exmoor National Park. And what better way to round off a day's hike than by sipping hot chocolate and toasting marshmallows around your very own campfire.

Doone Valley Campsite

Oare, T01598-741267, brendonvalley.
co.uk. Year-round, £5/adult, £3/child.

Almost opposite the track that leads to Cloud Farm (left), Doone Valley is a larger campsite with riverside fields (more space for frisbee and football) and excellent toilet facilities. It's not as pretty as Cloud Farm, but having the Buttery next door is a definite bonus. This riverside bar and café serves cream teas, light lunches and stone-baked pizzas.

Hidden Valley Park

West Down, nr Ilfracombe, T01271-813837, hiddenvalleypark.com.
Year-round, £15-22/pitch.

Creating a truly family-friendly campsite that inspires children to appreciate and respect nature requires careful planning and a healthy dose of imagination – and that's exactly what's gone into this exceptional park with its woodland nature trails, adventure play areas, organic

Cool & quirky

Lundy Island

c/o The Landmark Trust, Shottesbrooke, Berkshire SL6 3SW, T01628-825920, landmarktrust.org.uk. Year-round, £404-829/week for Castle Keep South (sleeps 4); £620-1426 for Government House (sleeps 5).
Thanks to the Landmark Trust, a charity which restores historic buildings and then rents them for self-catering holidays, Lundy Island offers a remarkable range of authentic accommodation. In all, there are 17 places to stay. By far the most ancient is the castle, originally built around 1250 and paid for by the sale of rabbits when Lundy was a royal warren. Castle

Keep South sleeps up to four, while other suitable family options (sleeping four or more) include Bramble Villa, Government House, Millcombe House, Old House South, Old Light, The Quarters and Stoneycroft. Limited camping is also available on the island.

Holiday parks

Hele Valley Holiday Park

Hele Bay, Ilfracombe T01271-862460, helevalley.co.uk.
Cottages, lodges, luxury caravans and camping on a peaceful site with nature trail and play area.

Ruda Holiday Park

Croyde Bay, T01271-890671, parkdeanholidays.co.uk.
Lively park with Blue Flag surf beach, tropical adventure pool and leisure programme.

Tarka Holiday Park

Ashford, Barnstaple, T01271-326355, tarkaholidaypark.co.uk.
Modest 10-acre site close to the Tarka Trail.

Relaxing by the river at Cloud Farm Campsite on Exmoor.

farm shop, eco store and fair trade coffee shop. Family camping pitches are a generous 14 m wide and feature both electric and TV hook-up points. There's a bath in the family washroom (a godsend if you have shower-resistant toddlers), while the separate wetsuit wash area stops the showers getting blocked with sand.

North Morte Farm
Mortehoe, T01271-870381, northmortefarm.co.uk. Easter-Sep, £5.90-8.30/adult, £2.50-3/child (2-15).

Location, location, location... this family-run site not only adjoins National Trust land, but it's also only 500 yards from Rockham Beach and five minutes' walk from Mortehoe which has shops, cafés and pubs.

Stowford Farm Meadows
Berry Down, Combe Martin, T01271-882476, stowford.co.uk. Year-round, £9.20-28/pitch (2 people), plus £1.50-4.50/extra person.

Located on the northern fringe of Exmoor, this 500-acre site offers an impressive range of facilities and activities, including an indoor heated swimming pool, horse riding centre, cycle hire, mini zoo, Kiddies' Cars and crazy golf. But far from being brash, Stowford manages to retain a tranquil atmosphere, particularly in the adjacent oak woodland which can be explored on a network of trails directly from the campsite.

Also recommended
Bay View Farm Camping Park
Croyde, T01271-890501, bayviewfarm.co.uk.

Channel View Camping Park
Lynton, T01598-753349, channel-view.co.uk.

Lobb Fields Camping Park
Braunton, T01271-812090, lobbfields.com.

Riverside Camping Park
South Molton, T01769-579269, exmoorriverside.co.uk.

Park life

Woolacombe Bay Parcs
Woolacombe, T01271-870343, woolacombe.co.uk. Year-round, check online for best deals.
If you want a good-value base on the North Devon coast that's as hassle-free (and rainproof) as possible, this group of four holiday villages at Woolacombe is ideal. **The Golden Coast** has the widest choice of accommodation, from villas to caravans. Not only is the place awash with rainy day retreats, from ten-pin bowling and softplay to a ceramics centre and cinema, but outside you'll find everything from waterslides and an adventure park to a rock-climbing wall and swing boat. The park even has its own pub, supermarket and beauty salon. What it doesn't have is walking access to a beach – you'll need to hop on a shuttle bus for that, or stay at one of the other parks. **Woolacombe Bay Holiday Park** has spectacular views of the coast and a wide range of facilities (staying at any park gives you access to the others). The evening entertainment is just as lively and it's a good spot to camp. With an Edwardian manor at its heart there's a slightly more refined air about **Twitchen House Holiday Park**. Not that it's stuffy in any way. Families will find lots to do here, but you really need to enjoy country walks to get the most from the location. Finally, **Easewell Farm Holiday Park** is billed as the most tranquil of the Woolacombe Bay Parc quartet – and its more modest facilities reflect this. It's the best option if you want to camp (there are also farm cottages and a luxury holiday caravan for hire), or play golf on the nine-hole course.

Sleeping Dartmoor

River Dart

Pick of the pitches

Barley Meadow
Crockernwell, T01647-281629, campingandcaravanningclub.co.uk. Mar-Nov, from £7.10/adult, £2.45/child, plus £6.46 non-member fee.

This small, immaculate park in the northeast of Dartmoor National Park is just five minutes' drive from Fingle Bridge, a mile's walk from the popular Drewe Arms and a short stroll to the Two Moors Way. Campsite comforts include firepits, a games room and a shop selling freshly baked croissants.

Churchill Farm Campsite
Buckfastleigh, T01364-642844. Easter-Sep, from £8-12/pitch.

A relaxed, clean and simple site on a working farm, Churchill has views towards Buckfast Abbey and is close to several attractions, including the South Devon Railway and Dartmoor Otters & Buckfast Butterflies.

Harford Bridge Holiday Park
Peter Tavy, Tavistock, T01822-810349, harfordbridge.co.uk. Year-round, from around £11/pitch.

Book early to stake out one of the wonderful riverside pitches next to the Tavy that runs along one side of this beautiful and well equipped park.

Langstone Manor Park
Moortown, T01822-613371, langstone-manor.co.uk. Mar-Oct, £12-15/pitch (2 people), plus £3-4/child.

Set in the grounds of a manor house in Dartmoor National Park, Langstone offers picture-perfect pitches in the shelter of grand trees or terraced sites with views across the moors. A cosy onsite bar serves evening meals.

Parkers Farm Holidays
Ashburton, T01364-654868, parkersfarm.co.uk. Easter-Nov, £7-24/pitch (2 people), plus £2/child.

Well placed for exploring the moors or making a break for the beaches in the South Hams, this terraced site is a guaranteed hit with kids. In addition to trampolines, a play room and a restaurant serving home-cooked family food, farm walks are available on which children can meet cows, pigs, goats, ponies, rabbits and other furry friends.

Also recommended
Beara Farm Camping Site
Buckfastleigh, T01364-642234.

Yeatheridge Farm
East Worlington, Crediton, T01884-860330, yeatheridge.co.uk.

View from Otter's Holt

Secret hideaways

Classic Cottages
T01326-555555, classic.co.uk. Otter's Holt, from £327-741/wk, Ludbrook, from £567-1503/wk.

There's something irresistibly exciting about a cottage on the moors – perhaps it has something to do with all those Famous Five adventures – and Classic Cottages has a couple of corkers. Ludbrook is tucked into a thickly wooded valley near Tavistock and has its own river frontage where you can fish for trout or swim in deep pools. It has a wild, away-from-it-all feel, with direct access onto Dartmoor through 80 acres of private land. The four-bedroom cottage has a spacious open-plan kitchen/dining area and games room. Otter's Holt near Tiverton, meanwhile, has views across riverside meadows (where you could actually spot an otter) and woodland in the Exe Valley. A converted cider barn (sleeping four), the cottage opens onto a farmyard where children can acquaint themselves with chickens, pigs and other animals.

Knowle Farm.

Brimpts Farm
Dartmeet, T01364-631450,
brimptsfarm.co.uk. From £75/
family room B&B.
In addition to cream teas and
farm walks, Brimpts Farm
offers climbing, abseiling,
orienteering and mountain
biking. Accommodation is in
self-catering barns with views of
Yar Tor.

Okehampton Youth Hostel
T01837-53916, adventure
okehampton.com. From £60/
adult, £51/child (under 14).
With ensuite family rooms in
a converted Victorian railway
building, this friendly hostel
makes a great base for an action-
packed break on Dartmoor.
Several family packages are
available, allowing you to have
a go at anything from gorge
scrambling, pony trekking and
raft building to archery, survival
skills and letterboxing.

River Dart Country Park
Holne Park, T01364-652511,
riverdart.co.uk. Apr-Sep,
£15-25/pitch (2 people), plus
£6-7/extra person.
The spacious campsite in this
woodland country park is just a
stroll away from numerous onsite
and free activities (see page 97).
Facilities include a shop, outdoor
heated swimming pool, tennis
courts, games room and a café.
Self-catering cottages (sleeping
6-9) and luxury B&B in Holne Park
House is also available.

• Looking for an activity centre
on the coast, but within range
of Dartmoor? Try **Skern Lodge**,
T01237-475992, skernlodge.com,
near Appledore in North Devon.

Farm favourite

Knowle Farm
Rattery, nr Totnes, T01364-73914,
knowle-farm.co.uk. Year-round, from
£285-1735/wk.
Arrive, unpack, stay put. That's
the beauty of Knowle Farm
– you won't feel the need to
go anywhere else. Not only
does this gorgeous 17th
century farmhouse have six
cosy cottages for rent, but
the grounds and facilities are
a rural paradise for children.
With 44 acres of South Devon
countryside to explore they'll be
able to spot a kingfisher at the
pond, roe deer in the fields, a
nuthatch in the woodland and,
with luck, an otter on the River
Harbourne. There's even a child-
friendly walking trail to follow.
Daily sightings are guaranteed
of the farm's resident kune kune
pigs, donkey, rabbits, alpacas,
sheep, chickens and ducks
– all of which demand regular
feeding and petting. Inside,
there's a 10-m heated swimming
pool opening onto a suntrap
patio, plus a well equipped play
barn with soft play, table tennis,
pool and other kids' games.
    Ideal for two families,
Woodbine Cottage sleeps up
to eight and features a galleried
living area with exposed beams.
With room for six, Moncks Green
has lovely views over the pond
and river, while Applecross
(sleeping four) is converted from
an old grain storage barn and
oozes character. Tucked into
the courtyard, Clematis sleeps
two adults and a child, while
Foxglove and Cow-mumble are
both two-bedroom cottages.

Sleeping South Devon

Slapton Ley

Pick of the pitches

Bolberry House Farm Caravan & Camping Park

Bolberry, nr Hope Cove, T01548-561251, bolberryparks.co.uk. Easter-Oct, £11-22/pitch (2 adults, 2 children).

This small, friendly park occupies a choice spot in the South Hams – and has the sea views to prove it. There are fine cliff walks across Bolberry Down which can be used to access beautiful beaches such as Soar Mill Cove. The campsite has lots of space for children to play and, as an added bonus, a fish 'n' chips van calls by once a week.

Leonards Cove

Stoke Fleming, Dartmouth, T01803-770206, leonardscove.co.uk. Easter-Oct, £7.50-15/pitch (2 people), plus £2/child.

With a choice of static holiday caravans, self-catering lodges and pitches for 40 tents and 14 touring caravans, Leonards Cove has a clifftop position just half a mile from much loved Blackpool Sands. Stoke Fleming (within easy walking distance) has shops, a pub and restaurant.

Slapton Sands Camping & Caravanning Club Site

Slapton, T01548-580538, campingandcaravanningclub.co.uk. Mar-Oct, from £5.53/adult, £2.45/child, plus £6.46 non-member fee.

A well run site overlooking Start Bay and close to the shingle beach of Slapton Sands and the nature reserve at Slapton Ley.

Also recommended
Karrageen Caravan & Camping Park

Bolberry, T01548-561230, karrageen.co.uk.

Widdicombe Farm Touring Park

Marldon, Torquay, T01803-558325, widdicombefarm.co.uk.

Cool & quirky

O'Connors Campers

Okehampton, T01837-659599, oconnorscampers.co.uk. Year-round, £375-850/wk.

Southwest Camperhire

Whitestone, T01392-811931, swcamperhire.com. £350-695/wk.

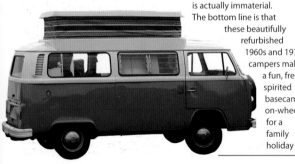

Everyone knows that VW campervan owners are ever-so-slightly obsessed with their vintage pop-up tourers, so it's hardly surprising to discover that O'Connors has personally christened its 13-strong fleet. Whether you opt for Bill, Mrs Orange or Shiny Norman, though, is actually immaterial. The bottom line is that these beautifully refurbished 1960s and 1970s campers make a fun, free-spirited basecamp-on-wheels for a family holiday – you could easily combine both Devon coasts in a week or venture further afield into Cornwall, Dorset or Somerset.

Each two- to six-berth van comes with a freestanding awning, inner tent and campbeds, mains hook-up, fridge, two-burner hob, sink with onboard water, cycle rack, roof rack, cooking equipment and CD player. O'Connors will also throw in a corkscrew and washing up liquid, arrange bike hire for you and even do your food shopping, so you can just get in and go.

Southwest Camperhire offers a mixture of classic VW campers and the modern VW Autosleeper Trooper which has newfangled extras like electric windows, power steering and a 180-degree rotating passenger seat.

A bright outlook – Sun Bay Hotel in Hope Cove is just a short stroll from the beach.

Best of the rest

Adventure Cottages
Halwell, T01548-821784, adventurecottages.co.uk. £340-1195/wk.
Superb farm complex with four self-catering cottages (sleeping 4-8), indoor pool, zip wire, games room and junior motorcycle academy (minimum age 7) in a soundproof arena.

The Cottage Hotel
Hope Cove, T01548-561555, hopecove.com. From around £50-80/adult B&B, £9.25/child (0-6), £19.50/child (7-12) sharing parents' room.
Relaxing hotel with 25 en suite rooms overlooking Hope Cove.

Mill Cottage
Wembury Beach, T0844-800 2070, nationaltrustcottages.co.uk. From around £320-1100/wk.
Four-bed Mill Cottage is so close to the beach that downstairs windows have shutters to keep the sea out during severe weather! There's a café and beach shop next door.

Sun Bay Hotel
Hope Cove, T 01548-561371, sunbayhotel-hopecove.co.uk. £40-50/adult B&B, £20/child sharing parents' room.
Friendly, old-fashioned seaside hotel with fabulous sun terrace and views across Hope Cove.

Thurlestone Hotel
Thurlestone, T01548-560382, thurlestone.co.uk. From £92-186/adult B&B, £28/child (3-7), £38/child (8-12) sharing parents' room.
This is not merely a luxury family hotel. It's a luxury family hotel with an Egon Ronay Henry the Duck award for excellence in catering and facilities for children. Not impressed? Then consider the simple fact that it occupies a priceless location just five minutes' walk from a prime stretch of rock-pooling, sand-digging heaven. The hotel also boasts a children's Dolphin Club, tropical gardens, two swimming pools, tennis courts and a nine-hole golf course.

Cottage agents

Big Houses Salcombe
T01548-843485, bighousessalcombe.com
Stunning homes sleeping up to 18 people.

Coast & Country Cottages
T01548-843773, coastandcountry.co.uk
Over 350 properties in and around the South Hams.

Dart Valley Cottages
T01803-771127, dartvalleycottages.co.uk
Cottages from Totnes and Dittisham to East Prawle.

Farm & Cottage Holidays
T01237-479698, holidaycottages.co.uk.
Southwest specialists.

Fulfords Holiday Cottages
T01548-856552, fulfords-holiday-cottages.co.uk
Waterside and country holiday homes in South Devon.

Toad Hall Cottages
T01548-853089, toadhallcottages.co.uk
High quality and unusual properties in South Devon.

Holiday parks

Golden Sands Holiday Park
Dawlish, T01626-863099, goldensands.co.uk.

Lady's Mile Holiday Park
Dawlish, T01626-863411, ladysmile.co.uk.

Whitehill Country Park
Paignton, T01803-782338, whitehill-park.co.uk.

Eating Devon

Cheristow Country Restaurant

Hartland, nr Bideford, T01237-441043, cheristow-restaurant.co.uk. Homemade soups and patés, locally sourced fish and meat dishes with fresh seasonal vegetables, and a selection of traditional puds.

Dartington Cider Press Centre

Shinners Bridge, Dartington, T01803-847500, dartingtonciderpress.co.uk. Mon-Sat 0930-1730, Sun 1030-1630. Everything from local organic food to crafts and toys. Lovely 'access-for-all' riverside walk and cycle path to Totnes.

Dartmouth Ice Cream

Lower St, Dartmouth, T01803-832157, dartmouthicecream.com. Forest fruits, ginger and other fancy flavours, plus homemade clotted cream fudge.

Occombe Farm

Paignton, T01803-520022, occombe.org.uk. Mon-Sat 0900-1730, Sun 0930-1630. Inspired organic farm with an award-winning farm shop, café, bakery, butchers, deli and nature trail. All profits go towards the conservation work of the Torbay Coast & Countryside Trust.

The Old Mill Café

Church Rd, Wembury, T01752-862314, oldmillwembury.co.uk. Closed during winter, but Beach Shop remains open for hot drinks, local pasties and ice cream. Stunning position on Wembury Beach. Home-made cakes, sandwiches and pasties, plus ice cream and cream teas.

The Quay Café

Fremington Quay, Fremington, T01271-378783, fremingtonquaycafe.co.uk. Daily 1030-1700 (closed Mon in school terms), lunches 1200-1500. A prime refuelling spot for cyclists on the Tarka Trail, this superb, family-run café overlooks the Taw Estuary and uses local, mostly organic, ingredients. The cream teas (£3.60) are legendary, using freshly baked scones, strawberry jam from Tiverton and clotted cream from Torrington. On the savoury front, there are home-made soups and baguettes (both £5), plus a small selection of light lunches (from £8.50), such as smoked salmon, paté and quiche. Kids' meals (£4.50) include veggie bites and plaice

Quay Café at Fremington, North Devon.

goujons served with sauté potatoes (chips would be far too unhealthy!). Wash it all down with a Luscombe organic soft drink (£2.25) and don't forget the Dunstaple Farm ice cream (£1.60 a scoop).

Quince Honey Farm

South Molton, T01769-572401, quincehoney.co.uk. Daily from 0900, shop only during winter. There's a real buzz about this place! Britain's largest honey farm not only offers a finger-licking opportunity to sample the sweet stuff (you must try the honey ice cream), but also contains a fascinating exhibition about the lives of honey bees.

Riverford Field Kitchen

Wash Barn, Buckfastleigh, T01803-762074, riverford.co.uk. Feb-Dec, daily during school holidays, plus weekends and selected weekdays. Lunch £15/adult, £7.50/child (3-12), dinner £16/adult, £8/child. Hearty, simple meals cooked

Market days

Barnstaple Pannier Market, daily.
Bideford Pannier Market, Tue, Sat.
Buckfastleigh Town Hall, Thu.
Dartmouth Old Market, 2nd Sat.
Exeter Fore St, Thu.
Honiton High St, Thu.
Ilfracombe Sun.
Ivybridge Glanvilles Mill, 3rd Sat.
Kingsbridge The Quay, 1st Sat.
Lynton Town Hall, 1st Sat.
Tiverton Pannier Market, 3rd Wed.
Torrington Pannier Market, daily.
Totnes The Civic Hall, last Sat.

from fresh, seasonal ingredients. Treat yourself to a decadent pud after all the healthy stuff. Farm tours also available.

River Shack Café
Stoke Gabriel, T07775-890959, therivershack.co.uk. Mar-Oct, from around 1030-1730, plus Friday evenings for summer barbeques.
Local suppliers are used as much as possible at the River Shack – apple juice and cakes from the village, seafood from Brixham and meat and dairy products from Devon farms. The views across the River Dart and Mill Pool are gorgeous – not that kids will notice; they'll be too busy catching crabs from the quay. It's such a hotspot for hauling in the crustaceans that the River Shack sells crablines, nets, buckets and bait.

Taverner's Farm
Lower Brenton, Kennford, T01392-833776, tavernersfarm.co.uk. Tue-Sat 1000-1700, Sun 1100-1600.
Ice cream using South Devon cows' milk – renowned for its richness – plus cream teas, cakes and milkshakes. Play area and farm shop.

The Venus Café
Blackpool Sands, T01803-770209; East Portlemouth, T01548-843558; Bigbury on Sea, T01548-810141, venuscompany.co.uk. Mar-June & Sep-Oct, Mon-Fri 1000-1700, Sat-Sun 0900-1700; Jul-Aug, daily 0900-1800; Nov-Mar, daily 1000-1600.

Something of a bright star in the South Hams, the Venus Company operates award-winning cafés at Bigbury-on-Sea, Blackpool Sands and East Portlemouth, as well as Tolcarne in Cornwall. You can eat al fresco at the outside tables (the East Portlemouth café has great views across the estuary to Salcombe) or take food with you to the beach. Children's box meals (from £3.95) come with a choice of cheese and ham bap, pasta, sausage roll or chicken drumstick, together with yoghurt, orange squash and crisps – all organic and locally sourced. There is also a good range of paninis (£4.50), salads, burgers, sandwiches, ice creams and a tasty crab bisque soup. But Venus is more than just good, wholesome nosh – the company carries out regular beach cleans and has teamed up with local wildlife trusts to support environmental education. You can also buy beach clothes, watersports gear, buckets and spades etc at their beach shops.

Café Blue Bar
Bath Place, Ilfracombe, T01271-879882, tunnelsbeaches.co.uk/cafebluebar. Mon-Thu 0900-2100, Fri-Sun 0900-2300.
Located at the entrance to Tunnels Beaches (see page 91), this courtyard café has an outdoor pirate play ship and indoor Play Hut (£2). Cream teas (£3.50) and snacks are served all day, while lunches (from £2.75) include ploughman's, tortilla wraps, jacket potatoes, salads, burgers and kids' sarnies (£1.75). For dinner, choose from old favourites like rump steak (£10.95) and wholetail scampi (£7.95) or go for one of the daily specials which often includes an excellent seafood platter. The puds (£3.95) are delicious – try the Eton Mess or fruit crumble with clotted cream. Kids' meals (pizza, spaghetti bolognaise etc) cost from £4.50.

Castle Tearooms
Dartmouth Castle, T01803-833897.
Nice spot for a snack right next to Dartmouth Castle. Sandwiches, jacket potatoes, pasties, cakes and desserts.

Crabshell Inn
Kingsbridge, T01548-852345.
Good pub nosh, but the real lure here is the quayside setting where kids can dangle crab lines and, with luck, catch sight of one of the local seals.

Eating Devon

Fingle Bridge Inn
Nr Drewsteignton, T01647-281287.
Riverside setting on northern edge of Dartmoor. Restaurant and bar meals, Sunday carvery and cream teas.

Jack Spratts
Island St, Salcombe, T01548-844747, jack-spratts.com.
Lively and fun family restaurant situated above The Oyster Shack (see right) and enjoying the same great views of Salcombe's estuary. Specialities include local beef burgers and fresh fruit smoothies. Eat in or take away.

Also recommended
Avon Mill Café
Loddiswell, T01548-550338, avonmill.com. Mon-Sun 1000-1700.
Devon cream teas and deli.

Badgers Holt
Dartmeet, T01364-631213. Mar-Jan, daily 1000-1800.
Tasty cream teas on Dartmoor.

Fish & chips
The Crowing Cock (formerly The Sea Shanty, Torcross, T01548-580747) serves some of the best fish and chips in the South Hams. Choose from cod, haddock, wholetail scampi and whitebait – eat in or take-away. In North Devon, **The Esplanade Fish Bar** (Lynmouth, T01598-753798) does a great haddock and chips (thin batter, chunky chips) for around £5. **Squires** (Braunton, T01271-815533) also dishes out decent fish.

Posh nosh

The Oyster Shack Salcombe
Island St, Salcombe T01548-843596, oystershack.co.uk. Wed-Sun, 1200-1500, 1800-2100.
One for grown-ups really, the Shack has oysters in numerous guises (from £1.95 each), plus a superb range of other seafood dishes. A Small Fry menu is available for lunch and there's a sister restaurant in Bigbury.

The Picnic Boat
Dartmouth, T01404-42449, thepicnicboat.co.uk. Mar-Dec.
It's hardly the high seas and it's definitely not the *Jolly Roger*. But there's no denying the fact that a pirate party aboard the delightful little Picnic Boat, pottering up the River Dart, is a perfect treat for mini mermaids and wannabee Blackbeards. Cruises last three hours and cost £250 for up to 12 passengers, including skippered boat hire, a hearty pirate feast, plus crabbing lines and bait. If that all sounds like a mutiny-in-the-making, opt for a more sophisticated alternative, such as a Devon cream tea cruise or luxury picnic.

The Pilchard Inn
Burgh Island, T01548-810514, burghisland.com/pilchard.
Haunted, 14th century smugglers' pub serving soup, baguettes and bar snacks at lunchtime and curries on a Friday night.

Dartmouth – all aboard the Picnic Boat for a pirate-themed cruise.

Resnova Floating Inn
Dartmouth, T07770-628967, resnova.co.uk. Tue-Sun.
Catch a water taxi to this Dutch barge moored in Dartmouth Harbour and tuck in to everything from bangers and mash to fresh lobster.

The Winking Prawn
North Sands, Salcombe, T01548-842326, winkingprawn.co.uk. Daily, Easter-Oct 0845-late, winter 1030-1700.
Located just across the road from North Sands, this popular brasserie has a serious selection of mainly seafood dishes. Daytime snacks range from tuna salad (£4.25) to whole cracked crab (£13.60), while the dinner menu pushes the boat out with a seafood platter costing around £20. Probably best for kids, the barbeque menu (from 1630) includes a choice of king prawns, rib-eye steak, salmon and chicken, served with salad and new potatoes.

Also recommended
Burton Farmhouse
Galmpton, nr Kingsbridge, T01548 56121, burtonfarmhouse.co.uk.
Local fare cooked with flair.

Essentials Devon

Getting there
By air The main hubs are Exeter International Airport (exeter-airport.co.uk) and Plymouth City Airport (plymouthairport.com).
By train First Great Western (firstgreatwestern.co.uk), South West (southwesttrains.co.uk) and Virgin (virgintrains.co.uk).
By coach National Express (nationalexpress.com).

Getting around
By train The Tarka Line operates between Exeter and Barnstaple, while The Riviera Line runs from Exeter to Newton Abbot and on to Torquay/Paignton. Contact First Great Western. Round Robin (T01803-834488, riverlink.co.uk) combines a steam train from Paignton to Kingswear, ferry to Dartmouth, river cruise to Totnes and bus to Paignton for £46/family.
By bus Stagecoach (T0871-200 2233, stagecoachbus.com) and First Group (T0845-600 1420, firstgroup.com).
By boat South Hams ferries include Kingsbridge–Salcombe (T01548-853607), Salcombe–East Portlemouth (T01548-853607) and Salcombe–South Sands (T01548-561035).

Maps
OS202 Landranger (South Hams and South Dartmoor), 191 (North Dartmoor), 180 (North Devon coast and Exmoor).

Tourist Information Centres
The Devon Tourist Board has a website at visitdevon.co.uk, with links to North Devon (northdevon.com), South Devon (visitsouthdevon.co.uk), Dartmoor (dartmoor.co.uk), Exmoor (visit-exmoor.co.uk), and the English Riviera (englishriviera.co.uk). Also try familyholidaysouthwest.co.uk, one of the official websites of South West Tourism. TICs can be found in most towns, including:
Barnstaple The Square, T01271-375000.
Bideford The Quay, T01237-477676.
Braunton Caen St, T01271-816400.
Dartmouth Mayors Avenue, T01803-834224.
Ilfracombe The Promenade, T01271-863001.
Kingsbridge The Quay, T01548-853195.
Lynton The Town Hall, T01598-752225.
Plymouth The Barbican, T01752-306330
Salcombe Market St, T01548-843927.
Totnes Coronation Rd, T01803-863168.
Woolacombe Beach Rd, T01271-870553.

Hospitals
North Devon District Hospital, Barnstaple, T01271-322577. Torbay Hospital, Torquay, T01803-614567.

Pharmacies
Barnstaple Boots, High St.
Dartmouth Boots, The Quay.
Kingsbridge Co-op, The Quay.
Plymouth Boots, Clairmont St.
Salcombe Alliance, Fore St.

Supermarkets
Barnstaple Somerfield, Sainsbury's.
Dartmouth Somerfield.
Kingsbridge Somerfield.
Plymouth Asda, Co-op, Morrisons, Sainsbury's.
Salcombe Somerfield.

Other shops
Baby supplies Mothercare, Wren Retail Park, Torquay; Green Lanes Shopping Ctr, Barnstaple and Charles St, Plymouth.
Camping supplies Ashburn Outdoor Experience, Chuley Rd, Ashburton; Devon Outdoor, Bear St, Barnstaple; Moor & Tor, Fore St, Bovey Tracey; OK Leisure, Fore St, Okehampton; Southface, Fore St, Kingsbridge.
Toys & beach gear Kaleidoscope Toys, Brook St, Tavistock; The Trading Post, Fore St, Kingsbridge; Venus Beach Shops, Bigbury-on-Sea, Blackpool Sands and East Portlemouth; Youings Toy Master, Boutport St, Barnstaple;

Environmental groups
Devon Wildlife Trust, T01392-279244, devonwildlifetrust.org.

Major Events
Jun National Sandcastle Competition, Woolacombe.
Jul Kingsbridge Fair Week.
Jul Mid Devon Show, Tiverton.
Aug Salcombe Regatta.

Kynance Cove.

Cornwall

It's not the surf. Or the beaches. It's not the estuary creeks, the fishing villages or the Eden Project. It's not even Stein's Fish & Chips. The reason families fall for Cornwall is that it epitomises the childhood-holiday idyll: tradition spiced with adventure; days on the beach that become days of discovery.

But be warned – Cornwall is addictive. With the A30 providing a fast-track through the Southwest, it's now a straightforward, if occasionally congested, matter to reach this far-flung corner of Britain. Whether you base yourself on the north or south coast depends on whether you prefer your sea rough or smooth. Popular north-coast resorts like **Bude** and **Newquay** are a sandy sprint from some of Cornwall's finest surf, while **Perranporth**, **Polzeath**, **Porthtowan** and the beaches fringing **Trevose Head** also offer that frothy cocktail of Atlantic breakers, surf schools and beach cafés.

However, not all towns and villages along the north coast have become shrines to neoprene. Pretty **Padstow** pays homage to local king of seafood, Rick Stein, while **Boscastle** and **Tintagel** are enshrouded with history – from Arthurian legends to the great flood of 2004. That's not to say the action stops outside the surf resorts. You can sea kayak from the rocky cove at **Port Quin**, hike to the clifftop lookout at Boscastle or cycle the Camel Trail from Padstow to **Wadebridge** and beyond towards **Bodmin** – gateway to a wonderfully wild and woody side of Cornwall that many overlook.

By contrast, the south coast of Cornwall is for messing about in boats. The sheltered estuaries of the **Fal**, **Fowey** and **Helford** are ideal for launching a canoe, while **Falmouth** has boat trips galore and the shipshape National Maritime Museum. A short ferry ride across the harbour leads to **St Mawes**, gateway to the **Roseland Peninsula** where narrow lanes fizzle out in sleepy fishing villages and peaceful coves. **St Austell**, of course, is synonymous with the iconic Eden Project, while other south Cornwall highlights include the fishing ports of **Charlestown**, **Looe** and **Mevagissey**.

Undecided? Then go for the tip of Cornwall where you'll find the best of both worlds – surf at **Whitesand Bay**, smugglers' coves on the **Lizard Peninsula**, fine art and fine food at **St Ives**, picture-book fishing villages like **Mousehole**, boat trips from **Penzance**, plus the big attractions of Land's End and St Michael's Mount.

You must

- Cycle the Camel Trail.
- Wade through the tide to St Michael's Mount.
- Visit the Eden Project.
- Learn to surf like a pro.
- Fall in love with Kynance Cove and Porthcurno.
- Camp near a beach.
- Explore the unspoilt Roseland Peninsula.
- Spot a basking shark.
- Get afloat on the Fowey or Helford River.
- Go ferry mad in Falmouth and St Mawes.
- Discover Heligan.

Get to the point

Distil everything that is magical about a family holiday in Cornwall – from surf, sand and rock pools to wild headlands and cutesy fishing villages – and you could well end up with this wonderful walk to Land's End. Following the South West Coast Path, the route starts at Gwenver, descending to a wave-pummelled beach at the northern end of Whitesand Bay. At low tide you can then stroll the best part of a mile along the entire scimitar curve of mainland Britain's most westerly beach, playing chicken with the waves, flying a kite, or simply enjoying the sensation of bare feet sinking into powder-soft sand. Approaching Sennen Cove you'll reach a lifeguard-patrolled zone where it's safe to swim or surf (wetsuits and boards can be hired from the surf shop), but be sure to leave enough time to explore the rock pools near the lifeboat ramp. Continue through the village, stopping at The Blue Lagoon for fish and chips, or Breakers Café for a pasty. Peruse the local crafts in the Round House Gallery, then rejoin the coast path for the steady climb to an old coastguard lookout. There's a superb view across Whitesand Bay from here, but it's to the west that your eyes are drawn – to heather-capped cliffs rearing from a filigree of waves and marching west towards Land's End. Follow the clifftop path, passing the remains of Maen Castle, an Iron Age fort, then celebrate your arrival at the edge of Britain with ice creams at the First and Last House. There's an RSPB Discovery Centre just below the Land's End signpost where, for free, you can use telescopes to scan for dolphins, seals and basking sharks. The walk from Gwenver to Land's End is around two miles. Buses run from Land's End to Sennen Cove and Penzance.

Opposite: Maen Cliffs near Land's End.
This page: shrimping at Sennen Cove; rusty chain
in the harbour; a fisherman returns to shore; distant Gwenver
Beach merges with Whitesand Bay; heather-clad clifftops;
Sennen Cove fishing boats; body boarding at Whitesand Bay.

Southwest England 121

Out & about Cornwall

Fun & free

Walk in the woods

You can have too much of a good thing in Cornwall, so when you feel 'surfed out' or just yearn for a beach-free day that doesn't resort to an expensive family attraction, head inland to Cardinham Woods, near Bodmin. Four waymarked trails weave through a mixed woodland of oak, rowan, alder, willow and beech, including the two-mile, 45-minute buggy-friendly Lady Vale Walk that follows a stream frequented by dippers and kingfishers. You might also spot buzzards spiralling above the treetops or glimpse a deer tiptoeing through the undergrowth. There's a picnic area (and playground) near the car park (£2/day) or you could treat yourself to homemade cakes or a cream tea at the Woods Café. Signposted from the A38 between Bodmin and Liskeard, Cardinham Woods is managed by the Forestry Commission (forestry.gov.uk).

Seek calmer waters

The South West Lakes Trust (T01566-771930, swlakestrust. org.uk) promotes recreation and conservation on several lakes and reservoirs in Cornwall. Some, like Stithians near Redruth, Siblyback on Bodmin Moor and Tamar Lakes near Bude, have fully-fledged watersports centres where you can hire boats or enrol on sailing, windsurfing and kayaking courses (see page 136 for further information on Siblyback). Apart from a modest car parking fee, however, you can easily enjoy a day out for free at these lakes – most have circular walks, nature trails, children's play areas and birdwatching hides. You'll find even more tranquil waters at the Trust's non-watersport lakes where the emphasis is on simply enjoying a peaceful day in the Cornish countryside. Argal, near Penryn, has a picnic site and play area, while Porth, near Newquay, is a bird sanctuary with nature trails and bird hides.

Spot a basking shark

Basking sharks are becoming an increasingly common sight around Cornwall during summer. Growing to a length of up to 11 m, these gentle, plankton-eating giants can be spotted from clifftops anywhere along the coast. Look for the broad, triangular dorsal fin breaking the surface. With binoculars, you might also be able to spot the white gape of the shark's mouth. If you join a boat trip in search of basking sharks and other wildlife (see page 130), be sure to choose an operator that's signed up to guidelines for minimal disturbance (wisescheme.org).

Walk into a good book

Antonia Barber's much-loved children's classic, *The Mousehole Cat* (Walker Books) describes the epic tale of an old fisherman called Tom and his cat, Mowzer, as they set sail into a terrible storm. The gripping yarn get's an extra splash of reality if, afterwards, you stroll around Mousehole (pronounced locally as 'Mowzel'), the fishing village near Penzance on which the book is based. A Cornish folktale by Charles Causley, *The Merrymaid of Zennor* (Orchard Books) has its roots in a small village near St Ives where a church chair bears the carving of a mermaid combing her hair.

Cruising in a bay near you – but don't worry, basking sharks are completely harmless.

Get all arty

Seek inspiration in Cornwall's myriad galleries, then equip your kids with a sketch pad, pencils and paints for an art session at a colourful fishing harbour. On the beach, make collages from strandline finds, fashion silly faces from shells and seaweed and build sandcastles modelled on St Michael's Mount. Don't forget that it costs nothing to visit the Falmouth Art Gallery, or that the Tate St Ives (page 136) is free for under 18s.

Fly a kite

North coast beaches like Gwithian and Watergate Bay are most likely to get you up, up and away. Alternatively, head inland to Bodmin Moor.

Watch the birdies

The Hayle Estuary RSPB reserve is a magnet for migrant waders during spring and autumn, while in summer you may be lucky enough to spot an osprey.

Bound over Bodmin

There are numerous walks on Bodmin Moor, but one of the most intriguing for children is the 2.5-mile Cheesewring trail which starts and finishes at the car park in Minions and offers plenty of opportunities for scrambling on rocks. It follows a clear track past standing stones and ancient graves to the higgledy-piggledy outcrop of Cheesewring Tor.

Boscastle Harbour.

Explore Boscastle

This fascinating north coast village made headlines during the devastating floods of 2004. It's sobering to stand in the newly renovated visitor centre (where a sign at ceiling level marks the extent of the floodwaters) and watch video footage of cars and campervans being swept downstream. There are also displays on geology and wildlife, as well as children's brass-rubbing activities and a giftshop. Nearby, you'll find a National Trust shop and the quirky Museum of Witchcraft (not for the easily spooked), while the village centre has craft shops, galleries, a bakery, cafés and restaurants. However, don't get too waylaid in browsing Boscastle's tourist traps. To fully appreciate the village's dramatic setting you need to hike the short, but fairly steep, footpath up to the coastguard lookout. Start by crossing the footbridge over to the left side of the famous dog-leg harbour, beyond which you are suddenly faced with dramatic vistas of sea cliffs, surging waves and wild Meachard Island. At low tide you can witness the Boscastle Blowhole at the base of the cliffs near the harbour entrance. Seals are often seen here too. Continue along the path, skirting a deep cleft where fulmars nest on narrow ledges, until you reach the lookout. Volunteers man this lonely outpost 365 days a year and you may well be invited inside the hut for a brief squint through powerful binoculars. On a clear day you can make out the buildings on distant Lundy Island. Another lovely walk follows the opposite side of Boscastle, past the little row of whitewashed cottages, to the vertiginous Pennally Point – a strictly hand-held adventure if you have young children!

Best beaches

>> For a round-up of some of the best surfing locations in Cornwall, see pages 126-127.

Bedruthan Steps

Cornwall's very own Twelve Apostles, Bedruthan Steps might not be quite on the scale of Australia's natural wonder, but it is still an impressive beach, dominated by gnarled sea stacks. Be warned, though, that not only is access via a very steep flight of steps, but swimming is dangerous due to strong currents. A fine beach to explore, but be alert to tides as it's easy to get cut off. There's a National Trust car park with shop and tea room at Carnewas.

Bossiney Haven

Like Bedruthan Steps, above, this is a beach for adventurous families. Park in Bossiney, near Tintagel, then follow the footpath to steep steps that lead down to the sandy cove, wedged in a narrow cleft in the cliffs. You'll be wasting your time at high tide when there is little or no beach. Locals claim Bossiney is a good spot for mussel collecting.

Crackington Haven

A mixture of shingle, rock and sand, this beautiful bay is sheltered by imposing headlands (which can be scaled using the coast path) and offers good swimming, surfing and rock-pooling.

Daymer Bay

A sheltered, sandy beach just north of Rock (which you can reach by ferry from Padstow – see opposite), Daymer Bay is gently sloping, making it a good choice for young families. For rock pools, check out the north side of the bay at low tide.

Hawker's Cove

Quite tricky to find, Hawker's Cove is tucked inside the mouth of the Camel Estuary on the Padstow side, just beyond the Old Lifeboat Station. Parking is available in a field at nearby Lellizzick Farm. Pack a picnic (and a map) and enjoy a day at this secluded, sandy haven.

Hayle Sands

Hayle Sands is the collective name for a series of beaches stretching three miles from the Hayle Estuary to Godrevy Point. There's good access to the middle section, Gwithian Towans, where you should find good surf as well as rock pools and caves to explore. As long as you take note of the tides this is a superb area for beach walks, particularly north towards the rockier beaches of Godrevy Towans, with its lighthouse and distant views of St Ives.

Holywell Bay

Just three miles down the coast from Newquay, this large, sandy beach is named after a holy well hidden in a sea cave at the northern end of the bay. Take great care when exploring the cave as it fills completely at high tide. Holywell Bay's family appeal is given a brash boost by the nearby fun park (holywellbay. co.uk) which features a range of pay-as-you-play attractions, such as F1 Carts and Adventure Golf.

Mawgan Porth

Located seven miles north of Newquay, Mawgan Porth has acres of golden sand at low tide and is a popular spot for swimmers and surfers. There is easy access to the beach, with toilets and parking nearby. The family-friendly Bedruthan Steps Hotel (see page 144) is perched on the cliffs above.

Mother Ivey's Bay

None

Overlooked by a caravan site (so seldom deserted) picturesque Mother Ivey's Bay is hidden away on the northern coast of Trevose Head, near Padstow. There are no facilities, so you will need to park at Harlyn Bay and walk 20 minutes along the coast path.

Porthcothan
🏄🚻🅿️♿🐕🚗

Located just north of Bedruthan Steps, sandy Porthcothan picks up some decent surf, but don't swim at low tide when dangerous currents often whip around the bay's headlands.

Porthgwidden
🏄🐕🚗🅿️

Just north of the harbour in St Ives, tiny Porthgwidden has big potential for sandcastle builders.

Port Isaac
🏄🐕🚗🅿️

There's not much of a beach at this historic port (dating from the Middle Ages), but Port Isaac is still worth a visit for those in search of quintessential Cornish fishing villages. You could try shrimping or crabbing at low tide, or head east to neighbouring Port Gaverne where there's a small, sheltered beach with an abundance of rock pools. A couple of miles to the west, Port Quin (rocky even at low tide) is a base for sea kayaking tours (see page 133).

Porthminster Beach
🦺🏄🐕🚻♿🚗🅿️

A beautiful beach with fine golden sand gently shelving into a sheltered corner of St Ives Bay, Porthminster is deservedly popular with families. The swimming is safe, there's a fabulous café (see page 148), and the St Ives Bay Line train from St Erth stops right behind the beach – so you don't have to endure the rigmarole of trying to park in St Ives. For a quieter alternative, hop off the train at Carbis Bay before you reach St Ives. Another Blue-Flag beauty, dune-backed Carbis covers acres of sand on the eastern side of St Ives Bay.

Rock Beach
🦺🏄🐕🚗🅿️

A long sandy beach stretching from Porthilly Cove to Daymer Bay on the East side of the Camel Estuary, Rock is linked to Padstow by a landing-craft-style passenger ferry (return tickets £3/adult, £1/child). Depending on the tide you land either on the slipway at Padstow Harbour or on Lower Beach just to the north of the town. Rock Beach is a popular spot for sailing and windsurfing and there's a lovely coastal walk north to Daymer Bay and Polzeath.

St George's Cove
None

A perfect excuse to combine Padstow, the coast path and one of Cornwall's quieter stretches of sand. To reach St George's Cove allow around 20 minutes to walk from the quay, past the war memorial to the ruined Napoleonic fortifications at Gun Point where, at low tide, St George's extends to Harbour Cove and Hawker's Cove.

Trevaunance Cove
🏄🐕🚗🚻🅿️

Located a mile or so from St Agnes, Trevaunance has a good stretch of sand at low tide when you can walk round to adjacent Trevellas Porth, exploring caves and rock pools along the way. The surfing is good too.

Treyarnon Bay
🏄🐕🚗🚻🅿️

A popular surf beach to the south of Constantine Bay, Treyarnon has a mixture of sand and rocky outcrops. Be wary of strong currents and waves.

Above: The Rock–Padstow ferry.
Below: Lifeguards patrol popular beaches.

Top 15 Cornish surf beaches

Bude

Providing shelter from prevailing southwesterly winds, the breakwater at **Summerleaze** (Bude's town beach) channels small, manageable waves into the harbour – ideal for novice surfers. At low tide Summerleaze merges with **Crooklets Beach**. Home to the Bude Surf Life Saving Club, Crooklets often has great surf – especially between mid- and high-tide with a light swell and easterly wind. Further up the coast, Northcott Mouth, Sandy Mouth and Duckpool are best left to experienced surfers – swimming can be dangerous at low tide, so focus instead on the rock pools. South of Bude, **Widemouth Bay** has over a mile of sand and promises excellent surfing for beginners to pros. There's a surf school and board hire here, plus lovely rock pools at low tide.

Newquay

If the surf's up, **Fistral** will be packed. Britain's best known, and original, surf spot, this iconic beach is located just to the west of Newquay. A large expanse of sand framed by headlands, Fistral often has 6- to 8-ft waves, while at the northern end of the beach, the Cribbar can generate 20-ft monsters – for experts only! A few miles out of town, **Watergate Bay** is Newquay's biggest and most spectacular beach with golden sands swept by reliable surf. If things get too serious on Fistral or Watergate, try Newquay's more sheltered town beaches. Not only are Great Western, Lusty Glaze, Porth and Towan ideal for novice board-riders, but they are also good, all-round family beaches. As well as surfing lessons, the Lusty Glaze Adventure Centre (see page 131) runs a Junior Baywatch programme

of basic surf rescue techniques and rock-pooling for children aged 8-14.

Perranporth & Porthtowan

Perranporth Beach has around three miles of sand at low tide, so it's a good choice if you want to escape the crowds (and are prepared to walk away from the busy town end of the bay). The waves are suitable for novice and intermediate surfers. Continue south past St Agnes and you'll find another top surfing beach at Porthtowan.

Polzeath

Cool Cornwall's surf central, Polzeath (Hayle Bay) squirms with neoprene during the height of summer when wetsuited bodies take to the sea in such numbers it can resemble a crowded seal colony. This superb family beach is so popular that part of it has long been commandeered as a car park. Everything crowds in on the beach: cars, surf shacks, snack bars – even ice cream vans drive out across the bay! There are good surf breaks along the beach, with waves for all abilities. If the sea gets too crowded, try New Polzeath on the north-east side of the bay. Alternatively, swap surf board for frisbee – there's usually plenty of unclaimed sand in the middle of the bay at low tide.

St Ives

Close to the town centre, **Porthmeor Beach** reaps some hefty Atlantic swells. There are rock pools either end of the bay and good facilities – including the Tate St Ives (page 136). On the eastern side of St Ives Bay, **Gwithian** is another gorgeous sandy beach with consistently fine surf. The fact that

Silver surfing – day's end at Trebarwith.

it's also popular with windsurfers and kitesurfers, however, reflects its quite exposed location.

Sennen Cove

Whitesand Bay, just to the east of Land's End, curves in a long scimitar of sand to Gwenver Beach. Although it bears the brunt of whatever the Atlantic hurls at Cornwall, this is a great family beach with fabulous

What is the best beach in Cornwall? Probably the one you've just spent the day on.

surfing, powder-fine sand and good facilities, including a surf school next to the beach car park at Sennen Cove. See page 120 for details of a walk from here to Land's End.

Trebarwith Strand

With no sand at high tide, beach-goers stake out the flat rocks at Trebarwith, near Tintagel, waiting for the tide to ebb. Families with young children might find getting across the rocks tricky, but once on the beach at low tide, Trebarwith is a gem with excellent surf, rock pools and natural paddling pools.

Trevose Head

Better known for its cutesy harbour, Padstow's nearest surf beaches are out to the west at Trevose Head. Fairly sheltered and with lovely sand and easy access, **Trevone** is probably the best option for young children;

Harlyn Bay is a wide crescent of sand popular with surfers and families alike, while **Constantine Bay** is the wildest of the trio. You're as likely to hear the piping of oystercatchers as the scream of excited children at this magnificent beach which is often scoured by treacherous waves and currents.

>> Most popular surf beaches have a lifeguard presence 1 May-30 Sep. Check rnli.org.uk for details.

Out & about South Cornwall Coast

Best beaches

Falmouth
😎 🏖 🏖 🏖 🏖 🚻 Ⓟ

There are several family beaches within easy reach of Falmouth. Closest to the town centre, Castle Beach is overlooked by Pendennis Castle (see page 139) and is a good spot for rock pools and a picnic; Gyllyngvase is Falmouth's sandy resort beach with watersports and a popular café; Swanpool is a sheltered, sand and pebble cove with crazy golf and a café, while a mile south of Falmouth, Maenporth is a sandy beach tucked out of the wind and offering a good range of watersports activities.

Fowey
🏖 🏖 🚻 Ⓟ

Closest to Fowey, Readymoney is a shingle and sand beach overlooked by the ruins of St Catherine's Castle. Two miles east of Fowey, Lantic Bay is a sheltered cove hemmed in by the 400-ft hulk of Pencarrow Head. It's a steep climb down to the beach, there are no facilities and swimming can be dangerous due to rip currents – but this is still a hidden gem for escaping the crowds.

Helford Passage
🏖 🏖 🏖 🚻 Ⓟ

Little more than a narrow strip of patchy sand and shingle, Helford Passage enjoys an idyllic location on the northern shore of the Helford River. A ferry runs to Helford village and Trebah Gardens (see page 139) or you can explore on your own with Helford River Boats (page 130).

Kennack Sands
🏖 🏖 🚻 Ⓟ

A sheltered beach of sand and fine shingle on the eastern side of the Lizard peninsula.

Kynance Cove
🏖 🏖 🚻 Ⓟ

The rough diamond in the Lizard's crown, Kynance is the stuff of childhood fantasy. The moment you first glimpse this wild cove on the half-mile walk down from the National Trust car park, countless beach adventures surge to mind – from delving in caves and rock pools to exploring the serpentine stacks and pinnacles that rear above this extraordinarily beautiful cove. Facilities are limited to a single beach café (see page 148), but it's the remoteness and solitude of Kynance that makes it so compelling. Aim to get there at least three hours before low tide when sugary sand envelops the bases of the rock formations. Take care when swimming as strong currents strafe the cove.

Looe
🏖 🏖 🚻 Ⓟ

Bounded on one side by Banjo Pier and on the other by rocks, East Looe Beach is always a safe bet for families. Boat trips operate from the harbour, while wilder stretches of sand can be found further east at Downderry and Tregantle.

Marazion
😎 🏖 🏖 🏖 🚻 Ⓟ

Better known as the stepping-off point for walking across to St Michael's Mount (see page 136), Marazion is also a fine beach in its own right, with gently sloping sand and fine shingle.

Mullion Cove
🏖 🏖 🚻 Ⓟ

Although the tiny beach only appears at low tide, this is a wonderful base for cliff walks or simply enjoying the atmosphere of a Cornish fishing village. The coves of Polurrian, Poldhu, Dollar and Gunwalloe Church lie a short distance to the north.

Porthcurno
🏖 🏖 ➕ 🚻 Ⓟ

The best family beaches hold secrets back, revealing them one by one as the tide ebbs and flows – and Porthcurno is a master of suspense. Stunning, even by Cornish standards, it nestles beneath the stone ramparts of the clifftop Minack Theatre, brilliant turquoise waters lapping its sweep of white sand. Then, as the tide drops, the beach slowly creeps along the rocky coast, stranding an enticing string of rock pools

and knee-deep lagoons. Tiny coves appear and, if you're lucky, a spit of sand emerges to form the perfect ephemeral wicket for beach cricket – best played as the tide turns again and fielders are sent splashing into the encroaching waves in pursuit of the ball. Porthcurno's most unusual secret is that it was once the site of the first transatlantic submarine cable telegraph station – a museum in the village reveals all. Keep your eyes peeled for glimpses of seals, dolphins and basking sharks near Porthcurno – particularly if you venture west towards Land's End, stopping perhaps for a snorkel in the craggy cove at Porthgwarra.

Praa Sands

🚻 🛟 🏊 ♿ ➕ 🐕 🅿️

One of Cornwall's most popular family beaches, Praa Sands (pronounced locally as 'Pray Sands') has a mile of golden sand, excellent swimming, great rock pools and even a dollop of surf when there's a south-coast swell. A spattering of beachfront

shops, a café and watersports centre makes Praa a doddle for a relaxed day-out.

Roseland Peninsula

🐕 🅿️

An easily overlooked cove, Towan beach is reached by a short walk across fields from the National Trust car park at Porth Farm. A mixture of coarse sand and pebbles, it is fringed by the sheltered, turquoise-dappled waters of Gerrans Bay and has rock pools at low tide. Further west, Pendower (or Carne) is a mile-long sandy beach overlooked by the Nare Hotel – recommended for its seafood.

St Austell

🚻 🛟 🐕 🅿️

A small crescent of sand, partly sheltered by a stone quay, Polkerris is about 7 miles east of St Austell and offers safe swimming. Closer to the town is the mile-long sandy beach of Carlyon Bay (also known as Crinnis Beach), while a few miles to the south lies Pentewan, another wide swathe of sand.

Top and middle: Kynance Cove, The Lizard.
Above: Towan Beach, Roseland Peninsula.

Out & about Cornwall

Action stations

Boat trips
Falmouth boat trips
Prince of Wales Pier, Falmouth, falriverlinks.co.uk. Check boards for details of departures and prices.
Wide choice of boat trips, plus ferries to St Mawes and Truro.

Fowey Marine Adventures
Fowey, T01726-832300, fowey-marine-adventures.co.uk. Forty-minute Family Special £16/adult, £8/child. One-hour Heritage Cruise £20/adult, £14/child.
Wildlife cruises with added 'oomph', the 12-seat, high-speed RIB *Kernow Explorer* whisks you out of Fowey in search of dolphins, seals, basking sharks, sunfish, seabirds and peregrine falcons. The Family Special nips over to Lantic Bay, stopping en route for rock-pooling and birdwatching, while the Heritage Cruise heads further out to sea where the best marine-life encounters are often to be had.

Fowey River & Sea Cruises
Fowey, T07891-516635, foweycruise.com. Apr-Oct, daily.
Choose from four 12- to 24-seat boats for trips to Charlestown, Polperro and around Fowey.

Fowey Town Quay Boat Hire
Fowey, T07989-991115, fowey-boat-hire.co.uk. Apr-Oct, daily.
Explore the tidal creeks of the River Fowey. Self-drive boats take up to five passengers.

Helford River Boats
Helford Passage, T01326-250770, helford-river-boats.co.uk. Apr-Oct. Six-person motor boats from £35/hr, £100/day, £600/wk; kayaks £10/hr, £50/day, £150/wk.
You can peek at it from the thickly wooded shoreline, but in order to really soak up the special atmosphere of the Helford River you need to get afloat and explore the myriad creeks. A ferry operates between Helford village and the boat rental base at Helford Passage.

Jubilee Queen
Padstow, T07836-798457, padstowboattrips.com.
Easter-Oct, check boards around harbour for rates and departures.
An old favourite for summer cruises out of Padstow, the 200-passenger *Jubilee Queen* is larger than most tour boats and even has a bar on board. Explore offshore islands or potter upriver to Wadebridge on a high evening tide.

Marine Discovery Penzance
Penzance, T01736-874907, marinediscovery.co.uk. One-hour Bay Discovery £18/adult, £14/child, £55/family. Two-hour Marine Discovery (minimum age 6) £32/adult, £24/child (6-15), £100/family. Ocean Discovery (minimum age 12) £38/person.
These adrenaline-charged cruises operate out of Penzance Harbour aboard the jet RIB *Shearwater*. The most popular trip is the Marine Discovery which, depending on weather conditions, surges west to Land's End via Porthcurno, or east towards Rinsey Cove. Both options return by an offshore route to maximise your chances of spotting common, bottlenose and Risso's dolphins, porpoises, basking sharks, sunfish and, if you're very lucky, a minke whale. The Ocean Discovery ventures out to Wolf Rock Lighthouse, while the Bay Discovery includes a stop at St Michael's Mount.

Mermaid Pleasure Trips
Penzance, T07901-731201, cornwallboattrips.com. Two-hour mackerel fishing trips, £12/adult, £8/child (6-8), £2/infant (under 6). Seal Cove trips (summer and school holidays) departing 1300 and 1500, £10/adult, £8/child (5-12), £5/infant (2-4). Longer fishing trips, snorkelling and Minack Theatre cruises available.
Having worked on local ferries and lifeboats, skipper Adrian Thomas knows the seas around Penzance like the back of his hand. He's also lived on St Michael's Mount, so a cruise aboard his boat, *Mermaid II*, is a great opportunity not only to catch mackerel, observe seals and haul in lobster and crab pots, but also to learn about the history and legends of this beautiful stretch of Cornish coast. The 33-ft boat is licensed to carry 35 passengers for summer cruising and up to 18 for fishing trips.

Left: Polzeath.

Surf schools

Animal Surf Academy
T01637-850808 (Newquay), T0870-242 2856 (Polzeath), animal.co.uk.

Atlantic Pursuits
Bude, T01288-321765
atlanticpursuits.co.uk.

BSX Surfing Centre
Bude, T0870-777 5111,
budesurfingexperience.co.uk.

Big Blue Surf School
Bude, T01288-331764,
bigbluesurfschool.co.uk.

Blue Wings Surf School
Newquay, T01637-874445,
bluewingssurfschool.co.uk.

Dolphin Surf School
Newquay, T01637-873707,
surfschool.co.uk.

Extreme Academy *
Watergate Bay, T01637-860543,
watergatebay.co.uk.

Falmouth Surf School
T01326-212144,
falmouthsurfschool.co.uk.

Global Boarders Surf School
Marazion, T0845-330 9303,
globalboarders.com.

Harlyn Surf School
Harlyn Bay, nr Padstow, T01841-533076, harlynsurfschool.co.uk.

Lusty Glaze Adventure Centre *
Newquay, T01637-872444,
adventure-centre.org.

National Surfing Centre
Newquay, T01637-850737,
nationalsurfingcentre.com.

Outdoor Adventure *
Widemouth Bay, Bude, T01288-362900, outdooradventure.co.uk.

Padstow Surf School
Trevone Bay, T01841-533382,
padstowsurfschool.co.uk.

Raven Surf School
Bude, T01288-353693,
ravensurf.co.uk.

Reef Surf School
Newquay, T01637-879058,
reefsurfschool.com.

Sennen Surfing Centre
Sennen Cove, T01736-871561,
sennensurfingcentre.com.

Shoreline Outdoor Pursuits *
Crooklets Beach, Bude, T01288-354039, shorelineactivities.co.uk.

Shore Surf School
Hayle, T01736-755556,
shoresurf.com.

St Ives Surfing Centre
Porthmeor Beach, T01736-793366,
st-ives.uk.com/surfing.

Surf's Up Surf School
Polzeath, T01208-862003,
surfsupsurfschool.com.

Waves Surf School
Padstow, T07792-574749,
wavessurfschool.co.uk.

The Winter Brothers Surf School
Newquay, T01637-879696,
winterbrothers.com.

Beginners' lessons cost from around £25-30 for a 2- to 3-hr session and cover beach safety, paddling technique, catching waves and how to stand and control your board. Minimum age from 6-8. * These operators offer multi-activities.

Out & about Cornwall

Mylor Boat Hire

Mylor Yacht Harbour, Falmouth, T01326-377745, mylorboathire. co.uk. Four-person motor boats from £17/hr, £70/day. Six-person motor boats from £25/hr, £90/day. Great range of craft, from family motorboats and traditional sailing yawls to zippy RIBs.

Newquay boat trips

Newquay, T01637-878886, newquay-harbour.com. May-Sep, £5/person. One- or two-hour cruises with a chance to spot seals and catch mackerel.

Padstow Speedboat Trips

Padstow, T0781-111 3380, padstowboattrips.com. Easter-Oct, daily, £5/person. Hold on tight for a 15-minute flit around the Camel Estuary on one of four speedboats.

St Ives boat trips

St Ives, T07821-774178, stivesboats. co.uk. From £9/adult, £6/child. Visit Seal Island (90 minutes) or join a two-hour fishing trip.

Camel riding
Cornish Camels

Rosuick Farm, St Martin, Helston, T01326-231119, cornishcamels.com. From £18-50/person. Take a ride on Frank, Myrtle or one of six other Bactrian camels that reside at this farm on the Lizard peninsula. Choose either a 15-minute farm walk or an hour-long trek, then enjoy a snack at the farm's organic café.

Canoeing
Fowey Kayak Hire

Fowey, T01726-833627, foweykayakhire.co.uk. May-Sep, double kayaks £12/hr, £36/day. Stable, easy-to-paddle sit-on kayaks – perfect for nosing about the creeks and sneaking up on herons and kingfishers. Guided canoeing expeditions also available from £24/person.

Encounter Cornwall

Lerryn, nr Lostwithiel, T01208-871066, encountercornwall.com. From £20/adult, £10/child. Guided canoe trips along Lerryn Creek and other idyllic spots on the River Fowey. Two-hour evening paddles or three-hour taster trips are ideal for novices or parents with young children. Stable, open-cockpit, single or double canoes are used. Children under 13 must share a double canoe with an adult. Canoe hire also available.

Coasteering
Cornish Coast Adventures

Port Quin, nr Polzeath, T01208-880280, cornishcoastadventures. com. £30/person (minimum age 8). Throw caution (and yourself) to the wind and sea on a two-and-a-half-hour coastal romp, leaping from ledges, swimming into sea caves, spinning in whirlpools and generally behaving like a crazed mermaid. Trips are led by qualified beach lifeguards, but under 18s must still be supervised by a parent.

Cycling: The Camel Trail

Allow 45-60 minutes each way for the popular five-mile pedal alongside the estuary between Padstow and Wadebridge. Cycle at low tide for a good chance of spotting little egret, curlew and oystercatcher. Encourage tired legs with the promise of Granny Wobbly's Fudge Pantry in Wadebridge or, if you're heading to Padstow, there's ice cream at Stein's Deli (see page 147). Intrepid cyclists can push on past Wadebridge to Bodmin, or try a circular route to Rock, taking the ferry back to Padstow.

Bike Smart

Wadebridge, T01208-814545.

Bridge Bike Hire

Wadebridge, T01208-813050, bridgebikehire.co.uk.

Padstow Cycle Hire

Padstow, T01841-533533, padstowcyclehire.com.

Trail Bike Hire

Padstow, T01841-532594, trailbikehire.co.uk.

All the above open daily from 0900. Adult bike £9-15/day, child's bike £4-8/day, tag-along or trailer £5-8/day.

Cycling: First & Last Trail

Part of this trail includes a level, mainly traffic free link between Penzance and Marazion, with lovely views across the bay to St Michael's Mount.

Mount's Bay Cycle Hire
Marazion, T01736-363044.

The Cycle Centre
Penzance, T01736-351671.

Pedals Bike Hire
Penzance, T01736-360600.

Cycling: Mineral Tramway Trail
Bike Chain Bissoe Bike Hire
Bissoe, T01872-870341, cornwallcyclehire.com. Daily from 0930. Adult bike £12-15/day, child's bike £8/day, tag-along £10/day. Direct access to the Portreath tram road. Café serving cream teas and other energizing treats.

Cycling: Pentewan Valley
Pentewan Valley Cycle Hire
Pentewan, T01726-844242, pentewanvalleycyclehire.co.uk. Daily 0900-1700. Adult bike £12/day, child's bike £8/day, tag-along £8/day. Pedal north on National Cycle Route 3 to St Austell and the historic port of Charlestown, or head south to Mevagissey.

Horse riding
Bosvathick Farm Riding Ctr
Constantine, Falmouth, T01326-340367, bosvathickridingstables.co.uk. Tue-Sun, lessons £16/hr (minimum age 6), lead rein rides £10/half hour (minimum age 4). Friendly, family-run yard.

Newton Riding Stables
Newton Farm, Mullion, T01326-240388, newton-equestrian.co.uk. Lessons £14/hr, hacks £15/hr.

Superb riding on the beaches and bridleways of the Lizard.

Kitesurfing
Mobius Kite School
Perranporth, T08456-430630, mobiusonline.co.uk. £65/2.5 hr intro session, £100/1 day BKSA/IKO beginner course (minimum age 12). Learn to kite surf at Perranporth, Hayle, Marazion or Pentewan.

Multi-activity
The following operators offer a range of activities, such as canoeing, sailing and cycling.

Active 8
Liskeard, T01579-320848, activecornwall.co.uk.

Adventure Cornwall
Lombard Farm, nr Fowey, T01726-870844, adventurecornwall.co.uk.

Tamar Lakes Watersports Ctr
Kilkhampton, nr Bude, T01288-321712, swlakestrust.org.uk.

Sailing
Dinghy courses are available at:

Fowey Maritime Centre
Fowey, T01726-833924, foweymaritimecentre.com.

Loe Beach Watersports
Feock, T01872-864295, loebeachwatersports.com.

Polkerris Beach Company
Polkerris, T01726-813306, polkerrisbeach.com.

Roseland Paddle and Sail
Portscatho, T01872-580964, paddleandsail.com.

Scuba diving
Cornish Diving
Falmouth, T01326-313178, cornishdiving.co.uk. Bubblemaker £29/child (8-11), Discover Scuba £49/person (minimum age 10). PADI courses, including the pool-based Bubblemaker for small fry and Discover Scuba which features a sea dive.

Sea kayaking
Cornish Coast Adventures
Port Quin, nr Polzeath, T01208-880280, cornishcoastadventures.com. £30/person (minimum age 8). Three-hour guided tours nosing about the inlets and sea caves of the north coast on sit-on kayaks.

Surfing
See pages 126-127 and 131.

Tree climbing
Mighty Oak Tree Company
Nanswhyden, nr Newquay, T07890-698651, mighty-oak.co.uk. Introductory climbs £120/group of 1-4 people (minimum age 4). Rekindle a childhood passion with a rope- and harness-assisted arboreal adventure.

Water skiing
Camel Ski School
Rock, T01208-862727, camelskischool.com. Waterskiing, wakeboarding and banana boat rides.

Out & about Cornwall

Cornwall's Crealy Great Adventure Park

Nr Wadebridge, T01841-540276, crealy.co.uk. Apr-Oct, daily from 1000, from £12.95/person, £12.45/person for groups of four or more, children under 92-cm tall free, reduced prices available online and during winter. Return free for a week. Divided rather grandly into six realms, Crealy is essentially a giant outdoor/indoor playground with lots of slides (wet and dry) and a handful of more high-tech rides, including a swing ship, log flume and 15-m-tall tower-drop called The Beast. There are also farm animals and a sunflower maze.

Flambards

Helston, T01326-573404, flambards.co.uk. Apr-Oct, daily from 1030 (1000 during school holidays), £16.50/adult, £11.50/child (3-15). With its Hornet Rollercoaster and cheek-pummelling Extreme Force and Thunderbolt rides, Flambards is an adrenaline blast for older kids, while littl'uns can get a buzz from gentle alternatives like the Cornish Mine Train. A good-value day out considering you also get the Really Wild Experience (animal show), Hands On Science Experience, live shows and a chance to meet Peppa the Pig.

FutureWorld @ Goonhilly

Helston, T0800-679593, goonhilly.

bt.com. Daily from 1000, £7.95/adult, £5.95/child (5-16), £26/family. If your child was plugged into a Nintendo DS or PSP for the entire journey to Cornwall, probably the last thing you want to do is take them somewhere where a room full of Xbox 360 play stations is one of the attractions. But don't zap FutureWorld from your plans too hastily because it's quite possibly Britain's most imaginative and stimulating science centre. As the name suggests, it's all about visions of the future. You can interact with a robot, send an email into space, design a city for the next century and experience an amazing 3D holographic television (everyone will want one in the future). And with live web-cam feeds from around the world, satellite dishes to twiddle and a fascinating film that takes you on a mission to find life in deep space, those Xboxes might – just might – be overlooked.

Lanhydrock

Nr Bodmin, T01208-265950, nationaltrust.org.uk. Garden year-round, daily from 1000, house Mar-Nov, Tue-Sun from 1100, £9.90/adult, £4.95/child (5-17), £24.75/family. A magnificent estate with vast grounds and an imposing gatehouse, the interior of Lanhydrock itself is surprisingly unpretentious and reflects the day-to-day – albeit very wealthy – lifestyle of a Victorian family.

Children can follow a quiz trail to explore the 50-odd rooms which include a nursery and the servants quarters 'below stairs'. Craft activities are held in the old stables across the courtyard from the café, while paths weave through park and woodland to the banks of the River Fowey (keep your eyes peeled for otters). Back near the car park there's a woodland play area.

The Lost Gardens of Heligan

Pentewan, T01726-845100, heligan.com. Daily from 1000, Adults £8.50/adult, £5/child (5-16), £23.50/family. Any child who's read *The Secret Garden* will be intrigued by Heligan which seems to sprout straight from the pages of Frances Hodgson Burnett's classic novel about a hidden, neglected garden nurtured back to life. Remember, though, that Heligan is now a large, working garden and conservation project – don't expect any fanciful forays into fairy-themed playgrounds or other children's attractions. Instead, let your imagination run wild as you follow boardwalks through tunnels of bamboo in the subtropical Jungle and discover natural sculptures on the Woodland Walk. Don't miss Horsemoor Hide which combines traditional wildlife I-spy (by overlooking a bird feeding area, wildlife pond, meadow and woodland) with live CCTV footage of bats, owls and badgers. Heligan's Northern

Gardens are festooned with fruit and veg and there's an excellent tearoom serving soups, roast lunches and snacks. At the entrance, Lobbs Farm Shop (see page 146) is the place to pick up local seasonal produce.

National Maritime Museum

Falmouth, T01326-313388, nmmc. co.uk. Daily 1000-1700, £8.75/adult, £6/child (6-15), £24/family.

The next best thing to messing about in boats on the sea, this outstanding museum (best reached by the excellent Park & Float from Posharden) is awash with nautical nuggets. The Set Sail gallery uses audio-visual displays to evoke epic voyages and daring maritime feats, while the main hall spins heads with its airborne flotilla suspended on wires from the ceiling. There are displays about incredible tales of survival at sea from the likes of Tony Bullimore and Ernest Shackleton, while The Cornish Galleries grab you with equally riveting yarns about smugglers and shipwrecks. Don't forget to climb to the Look Out with its panoramic views over Falmouth Harbour, or to immerse yourself in the Tidal Zone which provides a mesmerising window on the harbour's marine life – from mullet to barnacles. To prevent certain

Return to Eden

The Eden Project

Bodelva, nr St Austell, T01726-811911, edenproject.com. Year-round, daily from 1000 (car parks open 0900 during summer school holidays), £15/adult, £5/child (5-15), £36/family, reduced prices (children free) if you arrive by walking or cycling.

Bulging from an old china clay pit like a giant string of silvery frog spawn, Eden's vast biomes have become an icon, not just of British tourism, but of sustainability. Visiting this hallowed shrine to vegetation has almost become a rite of family holidays in Cornwall – a peat-free pilgrimage that's right up there with surfing and Stein's fish 'n' chips. And it's hardly surprising. Not only is the Eden Project immensely fun and educational for kids, but it also reconnects them with the environment, plunging them into an earthy succession of habitats, from jungle to global veggie patch.

Zig-zagging along paths below the visitor centre, most people make straight for the Rainforest and Mediterranean Biomes, but don't overlook the outdoor space – it's riddled with shortcuts, hideaways, stepping stones, spy-holes and sandpits. You might also bump into a Pollinator, one of Eden's resident interpreters who act as guides and impromptu storytellers. Everything you need for building a den can be found in the play area, while the Mechanical Theatre uses robots, puppets and film to bring plant stories to life. And, of course, everywhere you look you'll see real plants, growing, flowering, fruiting and generally giving your senses a thorough workout.

Brace yourself for the Rainforest Biome. Littl'uns might wilt in the hot and humid atmosphere, so take your time and make use of the water fountains scattered throughout this record-breaking greenhouse. As well as identifying tropical fruits and spices, you'll find out, through imaginative displays, how rubber, chewing gum and cola drinks are derived from rainforest plants. There's also a waterfall and jungle settlement to discover, while sharp-eyed explorers might spot a tree frog or praying mantis.

The Mediterranean Biome is just as mesmerising with its cork and citrus plantations, grape vines and perfume garden. There's a lot to see at the Eden Project, but try to leave a good hour or two for tinkering about with the interactive exhibits in The Core educational centre. The elaborate nut-cracking machine is addictive!

Out & about Cornwall

mutiny be sure to take plenty of 50p coins – you'll need them for the radio-controlled yachts which can be steered across an indoor pool that's ingeniously strafed by an artificial breeze. The museum is part of a snazzy waterfront development with everything from boat trips to Pizza Express.

St Michael's Mount

Marazion, T01736-710507, stmichaelsmount.co.uk. Mar-Oct, Sun-Fri from 1030, £6.60/adult, £3.30/child (5-17), £16.50/family.
It's a cliché, but getting here really is part of the adventure. Few Cornish landmarks are more evocative, or enticing, than St Michael's Mount, especially at low tide when a cobbled causeway emerges from the sea, extending an irresistible invitation to walk across to the rocky islet crowned with its medieval castle and church. Better still, wait for an ebbing tide, roll up your trousers and wade across. Boats shuttle back and forth at high tide. Once on the island, you may be surprised to find a thriving little community, complete with harbour, gardens, shops, café and restaurant. Collect children's quiz sheets before walking up the steep, but short, path to the castle. The views are spectacular, while the castle itself is a small, but fascinating time capsule with coats of arms, battlements and an exquisite chapel.

Tate St Ives

Porthmeor Beach, St Ives, T01736-796226, tate.org.uk. Mar-Oct, daily 1000-1720, Nov-Feb, Tue-Sun 1000-1620, £5.65/adult, free for under 18s.
How do you sell a day out at a modern art gallery to children? You could mention that the Tate St Ives is renowned for its child-friendliness and has a busy programme of family activities that sometimes spills onto Porthmeor Beach. You could add that St Ives is the epicentre of Cornwall's thriving art scene and that a visit to the Tate embodies the region's creativity. Or you could simply slip in the gallery as part of a fun-filled day trip that starts with a scenic 12-minute train ride on the St Ives Bay Line from St Erth (far better than trying to park in St Ives), an hour or two on Porthminster Beach (plus a snack at the superb beach café – see page 148) followed by a spot of browsing and crabbing along the harbourfront as you amble towards the Tate. Treat them to an ice cream after visiting the gallery – but only if they agree to a quick look around the nearby Barbara Hepworth Sculpture Garden.

Tintagel Castle

Tintagel, T01840-770328, english-heritage.org.uk. Year-round, daily from1000, £4.90/adult, £2.50/child 5-15), £12.30/family.
Like St Michael's Mount, a large part of Tintagel's appeal lies

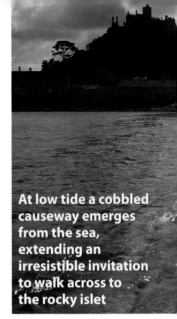

At low tide a cobbled causeway emerges from the sea, extending an irresistible invitation to walk across to the rocky islet

Wade to go – barefoot to St Michael's Mount.

in its location – perched on surf-scoured cliffs where the only access is by a long flight of uneven steps and a dramatic footbridge. In fact, at Tintagel you won't find much of a castle at all. Crumbling walls are all that remain of the 13th-century fort. It's what Tintagel could have been, however, that puts a spring in the step of all who venture here. The discovery of the inscribed 6th-century Artognou Stone fuelled tantalizing speculation that Tintagel was the birthplace of King Arthur – a great excuse for the riveting myths and legends recounted during summer by a local storyteller. There's also a beach café and a giftshop selling Arthurian nicknacks.

Hit or miss?

Land's End Experience
T0871-720 0044, landsend-landmark.co.uk. Easter-Oct, from 1000, Nov-Easter from 1030, £10.95/adult, £6.95/child, £24.75/family all-inclusive. Or pay for individual attractions. Dr Who gets everywhere (as you'd expect with a Time Lord), but do you really need to see him, along with the Daleks and Cybermen at Land's End? It's just one of the exhibits at Land's End Experience which also includes a multimedia show on Cornish legends, a film about air-sea rescue, a restored 200-year-old farm (with craft workshops) and The Land's End Trading Co. It all adds up to a fun day out, but don't forget to pop outside and check out the view. See page 116 for a taste of Land's End for free.

Members' perks

Family membership (see page 5) entitles you to free entry to:

English Heritage
• Pendennis Castle, Falmouth.
• St Mawes Castle.
• Restormel Castle, nr Lostwithiel.
• Tintagel Castle.

National Trust
• Antony, nr Torpoint.
• Cornish Mines & Engines, Pool.
• Cotehele & Cotehele Mill.
• Glendurgan, Mawnan Smith.
• Godolphin, nr Helston.
• Lanhydrock, nr Bodmin.
• Levant Mine, Trewellard.
• St Michael's Mount, Marazion.
• Trelissick, Feock.
• Trengwainton, Madron.
• Trerice, Kestle Mill.
• Car parking at various beaches, such as Kynance Cove.

Rain check

Arts & Crafts
• Becky Biddle's, Market Place, Falmouth, T01326-212333.
• Dillydollies, Fore St, Mevagissey, T01726-844870.
• Dish-n-Doodles, St Dominic St, Truro, T01872-273095.

Cinemas
• Cinedrome, Padstow, T01841-532344.
• Falmouth Arts Centre, T01326-314566.
• Filmcentre, St Austell, T01726-73750.
• Plaza, Truro, T01872-320003.
• Rebel, Bude, T01288-361442.
• Regal, Wadebridge, T01208-812791.
• Royal, St Ives, T01736-796843.
• Savoy, Penzance, T01736-363330.

Indoor play & amusements
• Ben's Playworld, St Austell, T01726-815553.
• Kids' Kingdom, Colliford Lake, T01208-821469.
• Trethorne Leisure Park, nr Launceston, T01566-86324.

Indoor swimming pools
• The Dragon Leisure Ctr, Bodmin, T01208-75715.
• Ships and Castles Leisure Ctr, Falmouth, T01326-212129.
• Oasis, Hendra Holiday Park, Newquay, T01637-875778.
• Waterworld, Newquay, T01637-853829.
• St Ives Leisure Ctr, T01736-797006.
• Penzance Leisure Ctr, T01736-874744.

Museums
• Royal Cornwall Museum, Truro, T01872-272205, royalcornwallmuseum.org.uk.

Out & about Cornwall

Blue Reef Aquarium
Newquay, T01637-878134, bluereefaquarium.co.uk. Daily from 1000, Adult £8.95/adult, £6.95/child (3-14), £30/family.
Sharks lurk just metres away from the bucket-and-spade brigade at Newquay's Towan Beach, but don't worry – they're all behind glass at this excellent aquarium which features a Tropical Shark Lagoon and huge reef display with walk-through tunnel. Other highlights include seahorses, cuttlefish and a giant Pacific octopus – try to see them at feeding time.

Bodmin & Wenford Railway
Bodmin General Station, Bodmin, T0845-125 9678, bodminandwenfordrailway.co.uk. Mar-Dec (daily May-Sep), from £7.50/adult, £4/child (3-16), £21.50/family return Bodmin General-Boscarne Junction or Bodmin Parkway.
This six-mile steam train ride can be used to link with the Camel Trail (page 132) at Boscarne Junction or Lanhydrock (page 134) at Bodmin Parkway.

Charlestown Shipwreck & Heritage Centre
Charlestown, T01726-69897, shipwreckcharlestown.com. Mar-Nov, daily 1000-1700, £5.80/adult, £2.90/child (under 10s free).
As close to a real-life treasure chest as you'll ever get, this wonderfully cluttered museum showcases artefacts from over 150 shipwrecks. You can also board the lifeboat *RNLB Amelia* and walk through a tunnel (once used for transporting china clay) to Charlestown's docks where square riggers and other historic ships are moored.

Colliford Lake Adventure Park
Bodmin Moor, nr Jamaica Inn, T01208-821469, collifordlakepark. com. Daily from 1030, £6/adult, £5/child (3-12), £19.80/family.
This is Bodmin on the wild side, whichever way you look at it. At one extreme you've got the 50-acre Moorland Kingdom with walking trails and wildlife hides and, at the other, there's Kids' Kingdom, an indoor adventure zone with ball pit, net mazes and drop slide. Woodland Kingdom has more energy-sapping stuff and there's also a Beast of Bodmin display.

Cornish Birds of Prey Centre
St Columb Major, T01637-880544, cornishbirdsofprey.co.uk. Easter-Oct, daily 1000-1700, £6.50/adult, £5/child (3-13), £20/family.
Eyeball hawks, owls, falcons, vultures and eagles and watch them fly at 1200, 1400 and 1600.

Cotehele & Cotehele Mill
St Dominick, T01579-351346, nationaltrust.org.uk. Garden daily from 1000, house & mill Mar-Nov, Sat-Thu (mill daily) from 1100, £9.20/adult, £4.60/child (5-17), £23/family. Calstock ferry, T01822-833331.

Seal of approval – the sanctuary at Gweek is enjoyed by both kids and orphaned pups.

This delightfully dingy Tudor manor has grounds running down to an old quay on the River Tamar that can be reached by ferry from Calstock. A short walk downriver, the watermill has workshops featuring a blacksmith, carpenter, saddler and wheelwright.

Dairyland
Nr Newquay, T01872-510349, dairylandfarmworld.com. Daily 1000-1700, £7.95/person (3-59), £33/family (up to 5 people).
Milk Clarabelle with her realistic udders, pat a pet and ride in a Lamborghini (that's a type of tractor by the way). Dairyland is a gold-top, full-fat farm park with vast indoor and outdoor adventure play areas. A half-pint by comparison, the nearby Springfields Fun Park (T01637-882132, springfieldsponycentre. co.uk) features pony rides and duck racing.

Geevor Tin Mine
Pendeen, T01736-788662, geevor. com. Year-round, Sun-Fri, from 0900 (mine tours hourly 1000-1600), £8.50/

adult, £4.50/child (5-16), £25/family.
A working mine until 1990,
Geevor's tunnels are now open
to visitors for guided walks.

Hidden Valley Discovery Park
Nr Launceston, T01566-86463,
hiddenvalleydiscoverypark.co.uk.
Apr-Oct 1000-1700, £6.25/adult,
£5.25/child (5-15), £21/family.
Allow at least two hours to solve
clues leading to crystals hidden
in this attractive woodland park.
Each crystal is worth a certain
amount of time in the Vault
where you tackle challenges to
win a prize. Treasure hunts are
available in three difficulty levels.

Lappa Valley Railway
St Newlyn East, T01872-510317,
lappavalley.co.uk. Apr-Oct, from
1030, £9.50/adult. £7.50/child (3-15),
£30/family.
Steam train rides to the old tin-
mining site at East Wheel Rose
where you will find the mine's
renovated engine house, a café,
crazy golf and a canoeing lake.

Launceston Steam Railway
Launceston, T01566-775665,
launcestonsr.co.uk. Easter, plus May-
Sep, Sun-Fri, from 1100, £8.25/adult,
£5.50/child, £25/family Launceston-
Newmills return.
Five-mile round trip on narrow
gauge steam locos chuffing
through the Kensey Valley to
New Mills Farm Park.

National Lobster Hatchery
Padstow, T01841-533877,

nationallobsterhatchery.co.uk. Daily
from 1000, £3/adult, £1.50/child.
Quirky quayside attraction at the
head of the Camel Trail – good
for all kinds of nippers.

National Seal Sanctuary
Gweek, T01326-221361,
sealsanctuary.co.uk. Daily from
1000. £13/adult, £10/child (3-14),
£36/family.
Home to sea lions, fur seals
and otters, this is primarily a
rescue and rehabilitation centre
for local common and grey
seals. Seal Rescue provides a
fascinating glimpse into the
whole process, from rescue to
release, and enables children
to see pups at various stages of
recuperation and even take part
in mock medical examinations
using a lifelike model.

Newquay Zoo
Newquay, T01637-873342,
newquayzoo.org.uk. Apr-Sep
0930-1800, Oct-Mar 1000-1700,
£10.95/adult, £8.20/child (3-15),
£32.90/family.
A 3-acre African Savannah,
which sees wildebeest and
warthog rubbing shoulders with
ostrich and zebra, is the latest
addition to Newquay Zoo. Junior
Keeper days are available for
8- to 14-year-olds.

Paradise Park
Hayle, T01736-751020, paradisepark.
org.uk. Daily from 1000, £10.99/adult,
£8.99/child (3-14), £38.50/family.
Home to the World Parrot Trust,

Paradise Park boasts a 150-ft
freeflight aviary. Buy a pot of
nectar to feed the lorikeets.

Pendennis Castle
Falmouth, T01326-316594, english-
heritage.org.uk, year-round, daily
from 1000, £5.70/adult, £2.90/child
(5-15), £14.30/family.
Largest and most intact of
Cornwall's castles. Don't miss
the gun deck simulation in the
Tudor Keep. For a fort-filled day,
take the ferry across Falmouth
Harbour to the smaller St Mawes
Castle – a fine spot for a picnic.

Trebah Gardens
Mawnan Smith, T01326-252200,
trebah-garden.co.uk. Daily from
1030, £7.50/adult, £2.50/child (5-15).
Beautiful Cornish ravine garden
leading to a secluded beach
on the Helford River. Children's
activities, trails and adventure
play areas, including a zip wire.

Also recommended
Screech Owl Sanctuary
Indian Queens, T01726-860182,
screechowlsanctuary.co.uk.

Tamar Otter & Wildlife Centre
Nr Launceston, T01566-785646,
tamarotters.co.uk.

Trelissick Gardens
Feock, Truro, T01872-862090,
nationaltrust.org.uk.

Trevarno Gardens
Crowntown, T01326-574274,
trevarno.co.uk.

Sleeping Cornwall

Ayr Holiday Park

St Ives, T01736-795855,
ayrholidaypark.co.uk. Apr-Sep,
£3.75-6/adult, £2-3/child (5-16),
£5.50-18.50/tent

The beaches, galleries and other
highlights of St Ives are just a
short stroll from this popular
clifftop site. Rates are a bit steep,
but they're worth it for the
excellent facilities and chest-
swelling views across the bay.

Boscrege Caravan & Camping Park

Ashton, nr Helston, T01736-762231,
caravanparkcornwall.com. Mar-Nov,
£8.50-17.50/pitch.

A short drive from Praa Sands,
this quiet, well-run site has a
nature trail and games room.

Carlyon Bay Camping Park

Carlyon Bay, T01726-812735,
carlyonbay.net. Apr-Sep, £11-27/
pitch (2 people), plus £4/child (3-15).
The icons here
Just 2 miles from the Eden
Project and a short walk to the
beach, this tidy site has a pool,
playground and crazy golf.

Dennis Cove Camping

Padstow, T01841-532349,
denniscove.co.uk. Apr-Sep, from
around £13/pitch.
The icons here
Close to the start of the Camel
Trail and overlooking the

estuary, this small campsite is
within easy walking or cycling
distance of Padstow.

East Crinnis Camping & Caravan Park

Lantyan, East Crinnis, T01726-
813023, crinniscamping.co.uk.
Easter-Oct, £10-18/pitch.
The icons here
A leafy, well-landscaped park
with its own fishing pond, East
Crinnis makes a good base for
exploring south coast beaches
(Carlyon Bay is only a mile away),
as well as the Eden Project
and the fishing villages of
Mevagissey and Fowey.

Gwithian Farm Campsite

Gwithian, T01736-753127,
gwithianfarm.co.uk. Apr-Sep, £12-
22/pitch (2 people), plus £2/child.
The icons here
You can almost smell the surf
at this friendly campsite 10
minutes walk from Gwithian's
golden sands. After a day on the
beach, the family shower room
is a welcome change from the
limb-crunching cubicles you
find at many sites – and there's a
good pub opposite.

Siblyback Lake

Nr Liskeard, T01579-346522,
swlakestrust.org.uk. Apr-Oct, £6/
adult, £3/child (5-14), £14/family.
The icons here
A popular watersports centre on
Bodmin Moor, Siblyback Lake
has a meadow campsite that's
an ideal base for the wide range

of activities on offer. You can hire
kayaks, windsurfers and rowing
boats from £10-16/hr, enrol on
a two-day sailing course (£145)
or try three different sports on
a Wet 'n' Active Day (£45). Tamar
Lake (another site managed
by the SW Lakes Trust) also has
a good family campsite with
excellent watersports facilities.

South Penquite Farm

Blisland, nr Bodmin, T01208-850491,
southpenquite.co.uk. May-Oct,
camping £6/adult, £3/child (5-16),
yurts £220-360/wk.
The icons here
Set on a 200-acre organic farm
on Bodmin Moor this sheltered
campsite has solar-powered
showers, family bathrooms
and a children's play area. For
a Mongolian twist try one of
the four yurts (sleeping up to
six). Each has a wood-burning
stove, rugs, futons and a roof
light for star-gazing. Farm-made
lamb burgers and sausages
are available for your campfire
barbecues, while a lovely farm
walk takes you to a Bronze Age
settlement and wildlife-rich
ancient woodland.

Southwinds

Polzeath, T01208-862215,
polzeathcamping.co.uk. Apr-Oct,
from around £20-35/pitch.
The icons here
Half a mile from the sea,
Southwinds offers a peaceful
(families and couples only)
alternative to its sister site,

Tristram, which is perched right above Polzeath's beach.

Tollgate Farm Caravan & Camping Park

Perranporth, T01872-572130, tollgatefarm.co.uk. £4-6/adult, £2-3/child (6-14), £5-7/tent

A well thought out family site, Tollgate Farm has a large play area, as well as a paddock where kids can pet and feed miniature pigs, pygmy goats, chickens, rabbits and guinea pigs. The nearest beach is a 20-minute walk through sand dunes to Perran Bay.

Treveague Farm

Gorran, T01726-842295, treveaguefarm.co.uk. Apr-Oct, £6-18/pitch. Tipi £345-495/wk.

The perfect spot for wildlife lovers, Treveague Farm has a state-of-the-art hide with night vision cameras allowing you to watch the nocturnal antics of badgers and foxes. Everything from peregrine falcons to hummingbird hawk moths have been recorded at the farm and there's a resident expert on hand to take you on nature walks. Located on the Roseland Peninsula, Treveague has wonderful coastal views. Footpaths lead to the fishing village of Gorran Haven, as well as the secluded Vault and Hemmick beaches. The farm's restaurant serves organic

produce, while a storyteller visits during peak season to recount traditional folk tales.

Trevedra Farm

Nr Sennen Cove, T01736-871818, cornwallfarwest.co.uk/trevedra. Apr-Oct, £4.50/adult, £2/child (5-15).

Occasionally windy, but with a superb location above Whitesand Bay, Trevedra has direct access to the coastal path leading to Gwenver Beach (see page 120). Book early to secure a pitch in the field with sea views.

Also recommended
Little Trevothan
Trevothan, T01326-280260, littletrevothan.co.uk.

Lower Pennycrocker Farm
Nr Boscastle, T01840-250257, pennycrocker.com.

Porth Joke Campsite
Treago Mill, Crantock, T01637-830213, treagomill.co.uk.

Treen Farm Campsite
St Levan, nr Penzance, T01736-810273, treenfarmcampsite.co.uk

Tregedna Farm Holidays
Maenporth, nr Falmouth, T01326-250529, tregednafarmholidays.co.uk.

Holiday parks

Hendra Holiday Park
Newquay, T01637-875778, hendra-holidays.com.

Hentervene Holiday Park
Bude, T01840-230365, hentervene.co.uk.

Juliot's Well Holiday Park
Nr Camelford, T01840-213302, juliotswell.com.

Mullion Holiday Park
Nr Helston, T0871-641 0191 parkdeanholidays.co.uk.

Perran Sands Holiday Park
Perranporth, T01872-573742, havenholidays.com.

Porth Beach Tourist Park
Newquay, T01637-876531, porthbeach.co.uk.

St Ives Bay Holiday Park
Upton Towans, T01736-752274, stivesbay.co.uk.

Sandymouth Bay Holiday Park
Sandymouth Bay, T01288-352563, sandymouthbay.co.uk.

Seaview International
Mevagissey, T01726-843425, seaviewinternational.com.

Sun Valley Holiday Park
Pentewan, T01726-843266, sunvalleyholidays.co.uk.

Tencreek Holiday Park
Looe, T01503-262447, dolphinholidays.co.uk.

Trevornick Holiday Park
Holywell Bay, T01637-830531, trevornick.co.uk.

Wooda Farm Park See page 138.

Sleeping Cornwall

Adventure Cornwall

Lombard Farm, nr Fowey, T01726-870844, adventurecornwall.co.uk. Houses, Feb-Oct, £420-1620/wk; yurt, May-Oct, £320-780/wk.

Proof that the action isn't always confined to Cornwall's north coast, Adventure Cornwall runs canoeing trips on the River Fowey and rock climbing on Bodmin Moor from its base at Lombard Farm. As well as two contemporary cottages (both sleeping six), there's a five-berth yurt with wood burner and hot tub, plus a large tipi for overnight camps. Fowey is within easy walking distance, while a more adventurous 50-minute hike will take you to rarely crowded Lantic Bay.

Bosinver Holiday Cottages

Trelowth, nr St Austell, T01726-72128, bosinver.co.uk. Year-round, £460-2420/wk.

Bosinver combines the rural idyll of a farmstay (30 acres of wildflower meadow, farm animals wandering past your doorstep etc) with the pick-and-mix appeal of a self-catering cottage agency and the facilities of a holiday park. There is a choice of no less than 19 highly individual and stylishly furnished cottages (sleeping 3-12) scattered through this hidden valley between St Austell and Mevagissey. Local characters include Lovejoy and Tinker

the Shire horses, and Chalky, a tree-climbing Pygmy goat that's fond of digestive biscuits. As well as feeding the animals, kids will love the play barn, games room, adventure playground, tennis court and outdoor pool. Bikes are available for hire (the Pentewan Valley Trail is nearby), while groceries can be pre-ordered from the local store.

Pollaughan Farm Cottages

Portscatho, T01872-580150, pollaughan.co.uk. From around £450-1600/wk. Weekend and midweek breaks Nov-Mar from £340.

A haven for wildlife and a paradise for children, Pollaughan is a 22-acre farm on the tranquil Roseland Peninsula. Dragonflies, and moorhens make a beeline for the wildlife pond, while kids make a fuss of the pony, two donkeys, five pygmy goats and assorted chickens and ducks. There's also a soppy black labrador called Bryher, a trampoline, tennis court and a pick-you-own veggie patch. Porthcurnick beach, meanwhile, is just a 20-minute stroll away. Choose one of three well-equipped, open plan cottages (sleeping 4-6) or opt for the three-bedroom wing of the Victorian farmhouse.

Wooda Farm Park

Poughill, nr Bude, T01288-352069, wooda.co.uk. Apr-Oct, 5-6 berth holiday homes £200-770/wk.

A holiday park with a rural twist,

Kid friendly – the farmstay at Pollaughan.

Wooda Farm has tractor rides, woodland walks, fishing, archery and a mini-menagerie of chickens, goats and lambs.

Also recommended
Beacon Cottage Farm

St Agnes, T01872-552347, beaconcottagefarmholidays.co.uk.

Coombe Mill

St Breward, nr Bodmin, T01208-850344, coombemill.com.

Fentrigan Manor Farm

Warbstow, nr Launceston, T01566-781264, fentriganmanor.co.uk.

Mount Pleasant Farm

Bodmin, T01208-821342, mountpleasantcottages.co.uk.

Tredethick Farm Cottages

Lostwithiel, T01208-873618, tredethick.co.uk.

Penally Cottage (left) and Atlantic House.

Atlantic House

Sennen Cove, T01326-555555, classic.co.uk. £540-1422/wk.
This gorgeous, open-plan New England-style property sleeps seven and is crisp, fresh and uncluttered – exactly how you wished your own home could be. The path to surf-sensation, Whitesand Bay, is steep, but the views more than compensate.

Bamham Farm Cottages

Launceston, T01566-772141, bamhamfarm.co.uk. £295-1395/wk.
Attractive farm complex with eight cottages (sleeping 4-8), indoor pool and games room.

Bassets Acre

Portreath, nr St Ives, T01209-842367, bassetsacre.co.uk. £325-1100/wk.
Six apartments (sleeping up to seven) in a Georgian house with heated indoor pool and an acre of sub-tropical gardens.

Penally Cottage

Boscastle, T01326-555555, classic. co.uk. £438-1092/wk.
Another characterful gem from Classic Cottages (see Atlantic House, above), Penally is the first in a row of fishermen's cottages perched above Boscastle Harbour. Traditional features like wooden shutters, tongue-and-groove panelling and window seats haven't been compromised by a slick makeover which includes a modern kitchen and a useful utility/shower room for postbeach wash-downs. The patio in front of the cottage is ideal for barbecues – but beware the steep drop beyond.

Trevone Beach House

Trevone Bay, nr Padstow, T01841-520469, trevonebeach.co.uk. £35-40/adult B&B, £25-30/child (2-12).
Comfortable, nine-room guest house in an enviable location.

Also recommended
Crylla Valley Cottages

Notter Bridge, nr Saltash, T01752-851133, cryllacottages.co.uk.

Mayrose Farm

Helstone, nr Camelford, T01840-213509, mayrosefarmcottages.co.uk

Wooldown Farm Cottages

Marhamchurch, nr Bude, T01288-361216, wooldown.co.uk.

Cottage agents

Blue Chip Vacations
T01803-855282, bcv.itrk.co.uk.
Newquay, Bude, St Ives and Looe.

Classic Cottages
T01326-555555, classic.co.uk.
West Country specialists.

Cornish Horizons
T01841-533331, cornishhorizons.co.uk.
Cottages in North Cornwall.

Cornwall Coast Holidays
T0208-4407518, cornwallcoastholidays.com.
Cottages near Fistral Beach.

Duchy of Cornwall
T01579-346473, duchyof cornwallholidaycottages.co.uk.
Luxury cottages in Cornwall.

Farm & Holiday Cottages
T01237-459888, holidaycottages. co.uk. Cornwall-wide properties.

Harbour Holidays
T01841-533402, padstow-self-catering.co.uk.
North Cornwall properties.

Mullion Cottages
T01326-240333, mullioncottages. com. Properties on the Lizard.

Padstow Cottage Company
T01841-532633, padstowcottagecompany.co.uk.
Cottages in and around Padstow.

West Cornwall Cottage Holidays
T01736-368575, westcornwallcottageholidays.com.
Cottages at the tip of Cornwall.

West Country Cottages
T01803-814000, westcountrycottages.co.uk.

Sleeping Cornwall

Best of the rest

Bedruthan Steps Hotel

Mawgan Porth, T01637-860555, bedruthan.com. £77-142/adult DB&B, £19-35/infant (1-2), £38-71/child (3-6), £52-95/child (7-12). Don't feel intimidated by the smart, contemporary style of this clifftop hotel – it's as child-friendly as they come. In fact, with its indoor and outdoor play areas, daily entertainment, heated pools, OFSTED-registered clubs and special mealtimes, children could be forgiven for thinking that it was made exclusively for them. In a way it was. But grown-ups get a fair share of goodies too. There's the sumptuous Ocean Spa and the award-winning Indigo Bay Restaurant (for adults only), as well as exemplary childcare for those moments when you crave some 'me-time'. The simple but tastefully decorated bedrooms often have spectacular sea views and they come in all shapes and sizes – from spacious family rooms to villas and apartments.

Falmouth Beach Resort Hotel

Gyllyngvase Beach, T01326-310500, bw-falmouthbeachhotel.co.uk. £67-75/adult B&B, £17-19/child (5-10), £33-38/child (11-15); cottage and apartments £465-975/wk. Enjoying prime position on one of Falmouth's best beaches, this popular hotel offers versatile accommodation, including family suites, two self-catering apartments and a three-bed cottage. Facilities range from baby sitting and early mealtimes to a children's swimming pool.

The Hotel & Extreme Academy

Watergate Bay, Newquay, T01637-860543, watergatebay.co.uk. Family suites from £210-372/night B&B. Cornwall's ultimate base for surf and chic, Watergate Bay's The Hotel is right on the beach, with its own watersports centre and no less than four places to eat, including the Beach Hut and Living Space (both of which have children's menus) and Jamie Oliver's Fifteen Cornwall (see page 148). The hotel has playrooms, swimming pools, a parents' kitchen and baby-listening service, while family suites feature a king-size bedroom and bunk room for children. Plasma televisions and DVD players come as standard – for those rare moments when you can tear yourself away from the ocean views. Interconnecting rooms, some with balconies overlooking the bay, are also available.

Porthminster Hotel

St Ives, T01736-795221, porthminster-hotel.co.uk. £60-150/adult B&B, £30-75/child (6-11), £45-112/child (12-16). With private access through sub-tropical gardens to the Blue-Flag Porthminster Beach (see page 125), you might expect

Cuisine and decor at Bedruthan Steps Hotel.

this hotel to be pretty special – and it is. Location may be everything, but the Porthminster Hotel backs up its position with a range of family-friendly touches, including indoor and outdoor heated pools, family suites, children's dinners and a room listening service.

The Rosevine

Nr Portscatho, Truro, T01872-580206, rosevine.co.uk. £930-2400/wk. Designed with families in mind, this classy coastal retreat consists of a Georgian house divided into 12 apartments and suites – each with one or two bedrooms, a sitting and dining area and small kitchen. You can eat 'downstairs', self-cater or do a bit of both. There's even a deli service providing breakfast boxes, packed lunches and freshly prepared supper dishes that you can heat up for a quiet meal in. Rosevine also hits the spot with its excellent facilities – a children's den, indoor pool and wooden play area to name a few. The hotel overlooks Gerrans Bay and has a sandy beach just 140 m from its garden gate.

Sands Resort Hotel
Porth, T01637-872864, sandsresort.co.uk. £50-77/adult B&B, £11/baby, £15-23/infant (1-2), £25-38/child (3-6), £35-54/child (7-14).
A genuinely family friendly hotel, Sands does more than most to make parents and children feel welcome and well catered for. Most of the rooms are suites with separate children's sleeping areas. There are sports facilities, play areas and children's clubs for all ages; the Surf Shack has wetsuits and boards, while two beach adventure centres are just minutes away. Little ones get pre-dinner entertainment, grown-ups get a health spa.

Also recommended
Crantock Bay Hotel
Newquay, T01637-830229, crantockbayhotel.co.uk.

Fowey Hall Hotel
Fowey, T01726-833866, foweyhallhotel.co.uk.

Hengar Manor Country Park
Bodmin, T01208-850382, hengarmanor.co.uk.

Polurrian Hotel
Mullion, T01326-240421, polurrianhotel.com.

Cool & Quirky

Cornish Tipi Holidays
Pendoggett, nr St Kew, T01208-880781, cornishtipiholidays.co.uk. Apr-Oct, from £375-745/wk, plus £50/person (age 4+) to cover fuel etc.
Tipis have popped up all over Britain, but not only was this the first site to add a touch of 'pow-wow' to camping holidays, it is arguably still the best. That probably has something to do with the setting – a 16-acre woodland crowded around a spring-fed quarry lake where parents and kids can play real-life *Swallows and Amazons*, swimming, fishing, boating or simply watching the dragonflies whizz past. Then there's the tipi experience itself – ducking inside to flop on cosy rugs and rolling on to your back to gaze up at the 18-ft high cone of canvas and locally sourced poles, lashed together with twine and hessian and daubed with authentic Native American designs. There are 40 tipis here, sleeping up to 10 and arranged either in village fields (complete with totem poles) or tucked away in private clearings. Each one comes with its own cooking fire and woodpile. There's a gas stove for back-up (plus flush toilets and hot showers at either end of the site), but essentially this is no-frills, back-to-nature camping where, in the absence of electricity, tipis take on a warm, magical lantern glow at night. A friendly warden that lives on site will be able to point you in the direction of Port Isaac (10 minutes drive away) and other north-coast highlights.

Eating Cornwall

Local goodies

Callestick Farm
Nr Truro, T01872-573126,
callestickfarm.co.uk.
You've probably slurped it at
countless places across Cornwall
– now visit the farm to find
out how Callestick ice cream is
made. As well as sampling the
sticky stuff at the dairy parlour,
you can indulge in other local
foods at the farm's café and deli.

Carruan Farm
Polzeath, T01208-869584,
carruan.co.uk. Daily, 0730-2030.
Around 1,000 Poll Dorset ewes
and 25 beef suckler cows
– that's the mainstay of Mike
and Clare Parnell's farm, but like
so many farmers they've also
diversified into tourism with
tractor tours and play areas etc.
The Parnells stand out from the
herd, however, with their superb
Farmhouse Kitchen which serves
breakfasts, light lunches, cream
teas and dinners, including
Sunday roasts. Best of all are
the family barbecues and hog
roasts (Jul-Sep, from 1730) when
special events like sheep racing,
storytelling, farm olympics,
sheepdog trials and bird of prey
handling are run alongside a
feast of lamb chops, burgers,
sausages, steaks, veggie kebabs
and homemade puddings.

The Chough Bakery
The Strand, Padstow, T01841-
532835, thechoughbakery.co.uk.
The ultimate Padstow snack-
attack – a hot, flaky (and
award-winning) Cornish pasty
fresh from the harbour bakery
and nibbled while dangling your
legs over the quayside.

Cornish Cyder Farm
Penhallow, Truro, T01872-573356,
thecornishcyderfarm.co.uk.
No one's suggesting you initiate
the kids to Cornish Scrumpy or
Rattler (that's your holiday treat).
Instead, they'll get a kick out of
the tractor rides, meeting farm
animals and completing the
quiz on a tour through the Cyder
Farm's press house, bottlery, jam
kitchen and museum.

Lobbs Farm Shop
Heligan, T01726-844411,
lobbsfarmshop.com. Year-round,
Mon-Fri 0930-1730 (1700 in winter),
Sat-Sun 1030-1630.
Fabulous farm shop at Heligan
Gardens (see page 134) with
meat and cheese counters,
fruit, vegetables, dairy products,
bread, jams, biscuits, ice cream,
smoked fish and other local
produce – much of it sourced
from the owner's Kestle Farm
(30-minute tours available
during spring and summer).

Oggy Oggy Pasty Shop
Arwenack St, Falmouth,
T01326-318662.
Pasties to eat in or take away.

Padstow Farm Shop
Trethellick Farm, Padstow, T01841-
533060, padstowfarmshop.co.uk.
Tue-Sat, 1000-1600.
Locally reared meat, fresh eggs,
Cornish cheeses, seasonal
vegetables and salads, honey,
jams, chutneys and ice cream.

Porteath Bee Centre
Nr Polzeath, T01208-863718,
porteathbeecentre.co.uk, Easter-Oct.
Try hive-fresh honey in fudge,
jams, ice cream or dripping
from the end of a spoon. And
as if that wasn't a sweet enough
temptation, this busy little
centre has a Living Honey Bee
Exhibition, a Winnie the Pooh
shop and a chance for children
to make their own beeswax
rolled honeycomb candles.

Purely Cornish Farm Shop
St Martin by Looe, T01503-262680,
purelycornish.co.uk.
Cheese, clotted cream, pasties
and other local produce is
available from Purely Cornish
which also runs the Chillout
Bar serving light meals, organic
coffee and smoothies. The
Purely Cornish Deli in East Looe,
meanwhile, is the place to go
for hand-picked hampers.

Ralph's
Portscatho, T01872-580702.
Daily 0700-1900.
Hidden away in an old pilchard
fishing village on the Roseland
Peninsula, this general store sells
tasty pasties (£1.80), plus a good
range of locally caught seafood
and other Cornish produce.

Fresh fish at Stein's Deli, Padstow.

Roskilly's

Tregellast Barton Farm, St Keverne, T01326-280479, roskillys.co.uk. Farm open daily; restaurant 1000-1800 (summer), 1100-1600 (winter), closed Jan. Free entry.

The Creamery is the one part of Roskilly's farm that isn't open to visitors, but you can still watch the legendary ice cream being made at the Ice Cream Kitchen – and even have a go at making your own flavour. The cows are milked between 1630 and 1700, a hundred-odd Jerseys filing into the barn which has a viewing gallery. A restaurant serves homemade pizzas, pasties, salads, pies and cakes along with the farm's very own apple juice. Evening barbecues are held weekly during summer.

Stein's Deli

South Quay, Padstow, T01841-532700, rickstein.com. Daily, 1000-1600.

A gastronomic Aladdin's Cave, Stein's Deli is a feast for the eyes

Market days

Bodmin Public Rooms, 4th Sat.
Bude Parkhouse Ctr, alternate Fri.
Callington Town Hall, 2nd, 4th Fri.
Falmouth The Moor, Tue.
Helston Guildhall, Mon.
Launceston Town Square, 1st Sat.
Penzance Wharfside, Sat.
Redruth Market Way, 2nd, 4th Fri.
Truro Lemon Quay, Sat and Wed.

with fresh seafood and seasonal fruit and vegetable arranged on counters like natural works of art. There is also a good range of local meat (try the lamb and mint sausages on your barbecue), lots of preserves, a cookshop and a selection of luxury Treleaven's ice cream for £1.60 a scoop. Of course, anyone with a genuine sweet tooth should make for Stein's Patisserie on Lanadwell St where the shelves are packed with cakes and pastries. For a sit-down treat, visit Stein's Café or The Seafood Restaurant. See page 148 for Stein's Fish & Chips.

See page 148 for Stein's Fish & Chips.

Beach

Sennen Cove, T01736-871191, thebeachrestaurant.com. Mon-Sat 1000-1630, 1845-2045, Sun1000-1730.

Located right above Whitesand Bay, the Beach restaurant practically dabbles its toes in the Atlantic. There's a surf shop underneath it, so no excuses for not working up an appetite for lunchtime bites such as mezze (£7.45), crab soup (£7.25) and Cornish brie frittata (£6.25) – best enjoyed on the large terrace with views of the beach and distant Cape Cornwall. The children's menu features fish goujons and chips (£5.95) and meatballs with pasta (£6.45), while dinner is a more refined affair with dishes like Cornish duck, lemon sole and linguine with mussels costing from £10-18. Try the fish of the day – it's often fresh off the restaurant's boat *Rosebud*.

Blue

Porthtowan, T01209-890777, blue-bar.co.uk. Daily from 1200.

This bar-brasserie has a fantastic beach location, perfect for sunset gazing. The chips 'n' dips (£5.50) makes a great snack, but for something more substantial try one of the burgers (from £8.75), stonebaked pizzas (from £5.50) or a special like pan-fried seabass on wilted spinach (£13.50). The kids' menu has posh fish and chips (battered pollock with handcut chips and minted pea puree) for £5, as well as pasta and bangers and mash.

Custard

The Strand, Padstow, T0870-170 0740, custarddiner.com. Mon-Fri, 0900-1500, 1900-2100; Sat-Sun 0900-1600, 1900-2130. English diner serving simple, tasty food for breakfast, lunch and supper. Dishes include Cornish crab sandwiches (£8.95), Padstow mackerel fillets (£11.95) and local rib-eye steak (£17.50).

Kynance Cove Beach Café

Kynance Cove, T01326-290436, kynancecovecafe.co.uk. Dating from the 1920s, this whitewashed café presides over the quintessential Cornish cove

Fish & chips

Harbour Lights (Falmouth) offers a good choice of fish, from haddock to seabass – eat in with views of the harbour or grab a takeaway and stroll to the quay. Stein's Fish & Chips (Padstow) serves ever-so-posh battered fish cooked in beef dripping and served with a lemon wedge, parsley and chips or a salad. Oysters, scallops and tiger prawns are also available. You can eat in or take away, but be prepared to queue. Also try the The Port and Starboard Café Fish & Chip Shop (Indian Queens), Barny's Fish & Chip Restaurant (Wadebridge), Sam's Fish & Chips (Fowey) and Porthminster Beach Café Takeaway (St Ives).

(see page 128). Sandwiches, baguettes, jacket potatoes, ploughmans, pasties and a tasty range of salads are all on the menu – just make sure you leave room for the home-made caramel and apple cake; it's one of a mouthwatering selection of sweets that all come with a dollop of Rodda's Clotted Cream or Kellys Ice Cream. The café has a small shop selling beach gear.

The Pea Pod

Port Isaac. T01208-880223. Small deli offering pies, cakes, sandwiches and baguettes – ideal for provisioning a picnic.

The Strand Café

Trebarwith, T01840-779109, thestrandcafe.co.uk. Easter-Sep, 1000-1800. Bacon rolls, crab sandwiches, salads, ciabattas, soups, burgers, chips and cream teas – to eat in or take away. Across the road is the more basic Shop in the Strand Café where surfers queue up for pasties followed by fresh doughnuts (£1.50 for 4) dunked in creamy hot chocolate.

Also recommended
Lifeboat Café
Polkerris, T01726-812223. Pizza and pasta on the beach.

The Three Mackerel

Falmouth, T01326-311886, thethreemackerel.com. A taste of the Mediterranean overlooking Swanpool Beach.

Posh nosh

Fifteen Cornwall

Watergate Bay, T01637-861000, fifteencornwall.co.uk. Daily, 0830-1030, 1200-1700, 1815-2400. Children are welcome for breakfast and lunch at Jamie Oliver's pukka beach restaurant, but 7- to 12-year-olds are only allowed for dinner from 1815-1900. A Mini Brekkie fry-up for kids costs £4.40, while lunchtime dishes start at around £6. In the evening tuck into the Tasting Menu (£48.95) which uses lamb, seafood and other local produce in irresistible Italian recipes.

Porthminster Beach Café

St Ives, T01736-795352, porthminstercafe.co.uk, 1200-2200. A sunny café with a zesty menu, fusing local seafood with imaginative Asian and Italian recipes. For lunch, try steamed Fowey mussels with chorizo, saffron, coriander and basil butter (£9), and for dinner, push the boat out with crab linguini, monkfish curry or scallop risotto.

Also recommended
New Harbour Restaurant
South Quay Hill, Newquay, T01637-874062, finns2go.com. Seafood for lunch or dinner.

Seven Bays Bistro

St Merryn, nr Padstow, T01841-521560, sevenbaysbistro.co.uk. Fresh Cornish ingredients with a Mediterranean zing.

Essentials Cornwall

Getting there
By air Air South West
(airsouthwest.com) to Newquay.
By train First Great Western
(firstgreatwestern.co.uk).
By coach National Express
(nationalexpress.com).

Getting around
By train Scenic lines (carfreedays
out.com), include the Looe Valley
Line (Looe-Liskeard), Atlantic Coast
Line (Par-Newquay), Maritime Line
(Falmouth-Truro) and St Ives Bay
Line (St Ives-St Erth).
By bus First Group (T0845-600
1420, firstgroup.com) and Western
Greyhound (T01637-871871,
westerngreyhound.com).
Ride Cornwall One-day travel
pass valid on all train and most
bus services available from First
Great Western for £24/family.
By boat The Mevagissey-Fowey
Ferry (T07977-203394) runs
daily, Apr-Oct, with returns
for £10/adult, £5/child. King
Harry's Ferry (T01872-862312,
kingharryscornwall.co.uk, daily,
£4.50/car) saves 27 miles on the
road trip between St Mawes and
Falmouth. King Harry's also runs
the St Mawes Ferry (£19/family
return) between the two towns,
as well as Falmouth's Park & Float
ferry between Ponsharden and
Custom House Quay (£15/car,
including parking and ferry). A
network of ferries, boats, buses
and trains, Fal River Links (T01872-
861914, falriverlinks.co.uk) is a
one-stop shop for car-free travel in
the Falmouth area.

Maps
OS Explorer 102-109 and 111.

Tourist Information Centres
Cornwall Tourist Board's website
is visitcornwall.com. Also try
visitnorthcornwall.com, visit-
southeastcornwall.co.uk and visit-
westcornwall.com. TICs include:
Bodmin Shire Hall, T01208-76616.
Boscastle T01840-250010,
visitboscastleandtintagel.com.
Bude Crescent Car Park, T01288-
354240, visitbude.info.
Camelford North Cornwall
Museum, T01840-212954.
Falmouth Prince of Wales Pier,
T01326-312300, acornishriver.co.uk.
Fowey South St, T01726-833616,
fowey.co.uk.
Launceston Market St, T01566-
772321, visitlaunceston.co.uk.
Looe Fore St, T01503-262072.
Mevagissey St Georges Square,
T01726-844857.
Newquay Marcus Hill, T01637-
854020, visitnewquay.org.
Padstow North Quay T01841-
533449, padstowlive.com.
Penzance Station Approach,
T01736-362207.
St Austell Southbourne Rd,
T01726-879500.
St Ives Guildhall,
T01736-796297.
St Mawes The Square, T01326-
270440, roselandinfo.com.
Tintagel Bossiney Rd,
T01840-779084.
Truro Boscawen St,
T01872-274555.
Wadebridge Town Hall,
T01208-813725.

Hospital
Royal Cornwall, Truro,
T01872-250000.

Pharmacies
Falmouth Boots, Market St.
Newquay Drury's, St Thomas Rd.
Padstow Alliance, Market St.
Penzance Boots, Market Jew St.
St Austell Boots, Fore St.
St Ives Boots, High St.
Truro Alliance, Lemon St.

Supermarkets
Falmouth Sainsbury's, Tesco.
Newquay Morrisons, Somerfield.
Padstow Sainsbury's, Tesco.
Penzance Morrisons, Tesco.
St Austell Asda, Tesco.
St Ives Sainsbury's, Tesco.
Truro Sainsbury's, Somerfield.

Other shops
Baby supplies Mothercare, Pydar
St, Truro.
Camping supplies Aztec Leisure,
Trevellas, St Agnes; Millets, Market
Jew St, Penzance.
Surf supplies Cornwall Surf Ctr,
Kingsley Village, Fraddon.
Toys & beach gear Toymaster,
Arwenack St, Falmouth; Venus,
Tolcarne; Wonder Years, Bude.

Environmental groups
Cornwall Wildlife Trust, T01872-
273939, cornwallwildlifetrust.org.uk.

Major Events
May 'Obby Oss Festival, Padstow.
Jul RAF Culdrose Air Day.
Jul Sea & Sail Festival, Penzance.
Aug Fowey Regatta.

Contents

152 Map

154 Oxford
154 Warwickshire
154 Shropshire
154 Nottinghamshire
154 Cotswolds

156 Forest of Dean
158 Fun & free
160 Action stations
162 Big days out
164 Sleeping
166 Eating
167 Essentials

168 The National Forest

174 North Norfolk
176 Fun & free
178 Best beaches
180 Action stations
182 Big days out
186 Sleeping
188 Eating
189 Essentials

Central & East England

Big days out...

1 Oxford
2 Cotswolds
3 Clearwell Caves
4 Dean Forest Railway
5 Dean Heritage Centre
6 Dick Whittington Farm Park
7 Perrygrove Railway
8 Puzzlewood
9 AMazing Hedge Puzzle
10 Caldicot Castle
11 Goodrich Castle
12 Tintern Abbey
13 Westbury Court Gardens
14 Wye Valley Butterfly Zoo
15 BeWILDerwood
16 Dinosaur Adventure
17 Hunstanton Sea Life Sanctuary
18 Pensthorpe
19 Snettisham Park
20 Animal Ark
21 Bure Valley Steam Railway
22 Elizabethan House Museum
23 Gressenhall Farm
24 North Norfolk Railway
25 Sea Life Great Yarmouth
26 Sheringham Park
27 Time & Tide Museum
28 Wells & Walsingham Railway
29 Welney Wetland Centre

Great escapes
Oxford

Let slip to your kids that the Great Hall of Christ Church College doubles as Hogwarts School in the Harry Potter movies and they'll be dragging you to Oxford quicker than a golden snitch in a game of Quidditch. Add fact to fiction at the anthropological **Pitt Rivers Museum** (prm.ox.ac.uk) and the **Oxford University Museum of Natural History** (oum.ox.ac.uk).
>> visitoxford.org

Warwickshire

The Shakespeare Birthplace Trust (shakespeare.org. uk) manages five properties in Stratford-upon-Avon, all linked to the life of the great bard. One of the most interesting for children is Mary Arden's where you can experience what life was like on a 16th-century farm, complete with long-horn cattle and Gloucester old spot pigs. For a history lesson with more oomph, **Warwick Castle** (warwick-castle.co.uk) delivers with a passion. Kids can lay siege to haunted towers, torture chambers and medieval banqueting halls, but it's the legendary activities they'll remember most. Jousting, archery and falconry displays are held daily throughout summer, while winter sees a skating rink installed at the fort.
>> visittheartofengland.com

Shropshire

With 10 museums and the world's first iron bridge as its star attraction, there's nothing rusty about **Ironbridge Gorge Museums** (ironbridge.org.uk), a World Heritage Site commemorating the Industrial Revolution. At Blists Hill Victorian Town costumed actors evoke a bygone era when steam engines and horses powered industry, while at the Enginuity centre children can scheme away at their own technological innovations
>> shropshiretourism.co.uk

Nottinghamshire

With its family nature trails, cycling and horse riding opportunities, the historic royal hunting patch of **Sherwood Forest** (sherwoodforest.org.uk) is a great place to set free your 'inner Robin Hood'. Designed for under-10s, **Sundown Adventure Park** (sundownadventureland.co.uk) has gentle rides and story-book-themed attractions.
>> visitnottingham.com

Don't miss

Birdland Parks & Gardens
Bourton-on-the-Water, birdland.co.uk.
Corinium Museum
Cirencester, cotswold.gov.uk/go/museum
Cotswold Farm Park
Nr Guiting Power, cotswoldfarmpark.co.uk.
Cotswold Motoring Museum
Bourton-on-the-Water cotswold-motor-museum.co.uk.
Gloucestershire Warwickshire Railway
Toddington, gwsr.com

Cotswolds

With its honeystone market towns and rolling hills peppered with sheep, nowhere does traditional England better than the Cotswolds – the region that inspired a million jigsaw puzzles. You don't have to look far, however, to discover some unexpected surprises – zebras grazing in front of a Victorian manor house, for example.

Located near Burford, the **Cotswold Wildlife Park** (cotswoldwildlifepark.co.uk) provides a grand setting for wolves, rhinos, lions and other rare species. The 160-acre park even features a walled garden where enclosures for meerkats, otters and penguins nestle between glorious flower borders. Another highlight is the walk-through Madagascar exhibit which is home to ten species of lemur.

Cotswold surprises don't come much greater than the **Cotswold Water Park** (waterpark.org) which has the sandiest beach in Britain furthest from the coast. Activities here include sailing, canoeing, raft-building, angling and water skiing.

Kids can also burn off energy on the **Cotswold Way** (nationaltrail.co.uk), a 100-mile trail between Chipping Campden and Bath (sample it at Dover's Hill near Chipping Campden). The 2000-acre park at **Blenheim Palace** (blenheimpalace.com) is ideal for an active day out with its maze and adventure playground, while **Hidcote Manor Gardens** (nationaltrust.org.uk) and **Westonbirt Arboretum** (forestry.gov.uk) are crying out to be explored.

Don't miss **Snowshill Manor** (nationaltrust. org.uk) with its mesmerising collection of artefacts (from old bicycles to Samurai armour). The trout will also need feeding at **Bibury** (biburytroutfarm. co.uk), pocket money must be spent at the toy shop in Bourton-on-the-Water and scones need scoffing at **Badgers Hall Tearoom** (badgershall. com) in Chipping Campden.

>> cotswolds.com

Cotswold Wildlife Park.

River Wye from Symonds Yat Rock.

Forest of Dean

What could be better than mucking about in the very woods that inspired weird and wonderful ideas to take root in the minds of Tolkien and Rowling? The Forest of Dean is a leafy fantasy world rife with ents and whomping willows. But it's a river, not a tree, that elevates this forest to 'gold leaf' status.

Uncoiling like a lazy green python, the River Wye kinks and curls along the western fringes of the 27,000-acre Royal Forest of Dean. Over 40 miles of the Wye lie in an Area of Outstanding Natural Beauty and nowhere is that better admired than at **Symonds Yat Rock** where dense woodland spills over towering limestone cliffs rising sheer from a bend in the river.

Tintern Abbey and Goodrich Castle also make fine vantage points over the Wye, but it's only from a canoe that you get to truly appreciate the wildlife, scenery and moods of this unspoilt river. You can plan paddling odysseys from several locations, including **Symonds Yat West**, **Monmouth** and **Ross-on-Wye**, loading four-seater Canadian canoes with picnics and letting the river's steady current do most of the work.

Snagging traffic from the tail-end of the M50, Ross-on-Wye clings to a rocky bluff above a horseshoe bend in the river and forms the northern gateway to the Forest of Dean. To the south, at the Wye's confluence with the Severn, **Chepstow** diverts visitors from the M4/M48, while other regional centres include **Newent** in the Vale of Leadon, the old Severnside port of **Lydney** and the market towns of **Coleford** and **Cinderford** – both of which have the forest practically growing in through their windows.

Several attractions are dotted around the Forest of Dean, including the Clearwell Caves, Dean Forest Railway, Dean Heritage Museum, Perrygrove Railway and Puzzlewood. Don't overlook the simple (and free) pleasures, though, of a walk in the woods. There are numerous waymarked trails, ranging from half-mile easy-access saunters at Forestry Commission visitor sites like Mallards Pike to more epic jaunts on the long-distance Gloucestershire Way. Cycling, too, is available for all abilities. The Family Cycle Trail follows 11 miles of the forest's disused railway network, while the Sallow Vallets area is reserved for more experienced mountain bikers. And if you were wondering what the tree-climbing potential of the Forest of Dean was like, look no further than the Go Ape high wire forest adventure course.

You must

- Paddle a canoe down the River Wye.

- Spot the peregrines at Symonds Yat Rock.

- Cycle the Family Trail deep into the forest.

- Swing out at Go Ape.

- Let your imagination run wild at Puzzlewood.

- Camp in the woods.

- Find the treasure at the end of the Perrygrove Railway line.

- Explore Clearwell Caves.

- Cook Gloucester Old Spot bangers on a forest barbeque.

Out & about Forest of Dean

Walk the Sculpture Trail

Each of the visitor sites described in the box opposite provides access to walking trails in the Forest of Dean. A good option for families with buggy-bound children is the half-mile walk around the lake at Mallards Pike. There are also easy-access trails at Soudley Ponds and Cyril Hart Arboretum. The most popular walk in the forest, however, follows the Sculpture Trail which is marked by blue-ringed posts starting – and finishing – near the picnic site at Beechenhurst Lodge. Although the whole trail is 4.5 miles long, there are two shortcuts back to the lodge – shortcut A reduces the walk to just over 2 miles and includes the first six sculptures, while shortcut B is 3 miles long and features 14 sculptures. A leaflet (available from the lodge for £1) describes the inspiration behind each work of art. For example, Black Dome (a pile of 900 tapered and charred larch logs) symbolises the forest's history of charcoal production, while Iron Road uses carved railway sleepers to evoke its industrial heritage. The concepts can be quite high-brow (particularly for kids), but part of the appeal of doing this walk with children is to see how *they* interpret the sculptures – and it doesn't really matter if they're right or wrong.

Natural cycle

An excellent way to explore the forest, the Family Cycle Trail traces an easy 11-mile circuit on specially surfaced tracks that are suitable for all ages. You can join the bike path by following links from Coleford, Lydbrook or Cinderford, but most people set off from the Pedalabikeaway Cycle Centre (see page 160) which is located right on the trail. The circuit can be pedalled in two hours, but allow a whole day to include a picnic at Mallards Pike or Beechenhurst Lodge, a stroll at Cannop Ponds and some birdwatching at New Fancy (where you can sometimes see goshawks from the viewpoint). Another trail, known as The Peregrine Path, provides a level ride alongside the River Wye between Hadnock Road, Monmouth, and Symonds Yat East.

Forest centres

With access to both the Sculpture Trail and Family Cycle Trail (see left), **Beechenhurst Lodge** makes an ideal base from which to explore the forest. Facilities include a café, toilets, picnic site, barbecues and a play area featuring wooden sculptures of animals, a horse pulling a timber cart, lumberjacks at work and a ship under construction. As well as being home to the Go Ape high-wire forest adventure course (see page 160), **Mallards Pike** also has toilets, picnic and barbecue sites, and a cabin serving hot and cold snacks during summer. You can also join the Family Cycle Trail here, or walk the 1.6-mile Pluckpenny Trail. **Cannop Ponds** and **Wenchford** are also popular picnic spots with seasonal refreshments available. You can often see Mandarin ducks at Cannop; the top pond is a nature reserve with good numbers of dragonflies, including the broad-bodied chaser, pictured above.

Forest events

The Forestry Commission ranger service (T01594-833057, forestry. gov.uk) organises a programme of events throughout the year in the Forest of Dean. These can include ranger-led walks in search of anything from bats to bluebells, as well as more hands-on activities such as den building, wild camping and Junior Ranger days. During summer holidays there are often drop-in ranger activities at Beechenhurst Lodge and Symonds Yat Rock.

Visit Symonds Yat Rock

Why? It's one of the best places in Britain to see peregrine falcons. They've nested on the 400-ft-high cliffs of Symonds Yat Rock every year since 1982. It's not only a safe place to rear young, but also the perfect spot to ambush pigeons and other prey – a task that peregrines accomplish with deadly accuracy during high-speed stoops which can reach 200 miles per hour.

How? You can zoom in on the world's fastest animal using the telescopes at the Symonds Yat Rock Peregrine Viewpoint operated by the RSPB. Scopes are mounted at child and adult height and there are volunteers on hand (Mar-Sep, weekdays 1100-1800, weekends 1000-1800) to help you focus on the birds and answer any questions. Goshawks, ravens and barn owls also nest in the area, while bird feeders at the viewpoint regularly attract nuthatches, finches and tits. The viewpoint is free (donations welcome), but you'll need to pay for parking (£3/day, valid at all Forestry Commission car parks). A nearby cabin serves drinks and snacks.

Where? Symonds Yat Rock is signposted off the B4432 from Coleford.

Contact The RSPB, T07736-792511, rspb.org.uk/datewithnature.

Bird bonanza

If the peregrines at Symonds Yat Rock have got you all twitchy, the RSPB manages a couple of reserves nearby where, with luck, you can glimpse two more rather special birds. Spring is the best season to visit Nagshead when pied flycatchers are investigating the nest boxes, while Highnam Woods resound with birdsong at this time of year – including the unforgettable medley of breeding nightingales. Both reserves are open year-round, while Nagshead has an information centre (Easter-Aug, weekends 1000-1600).

Out & about Forest of Dean

Boat trips
Kingfisher Cruises
Symonds Yat East, T01600-891063, wyenot.com. Mar-Oct, 1100-1700, £5.50/adult, £3/child.
If canoeing on the River Wye sounds too much of an ordeal, try one of these hour-long cruises instead. Each boat carries up to 50 passengers.

Cycle hire
Pedalabikeaway Cycle Centre
Cannop Valley, nr Coleford, T01594-860065, pedalabikeaway.co.uk. Apr-Oct, weekends and school holidays, 1000-1700; Nov-Mar bookings only. Adult bike £8/2 hr, £10/3 hr, £14/day; child's bike £6/2 hr, £7/3 hr, £10/day; trailer from £4, child seat from £2. Tool kits and helmets included.
For Pedalabikeaway Cycle Centre Monmouth: T01600-772821.
Pedalabikeaway operates two cycle hire centres – one in the Cannop Valley with access to the circular Family Cycle Trail in the middle of the Forest of Dean; the other in Monmouth where you can follow the Peregrine Way to Symonds Yat. See page 158 for details of both routes.

Horse riding
Severnvale Equestrian Centre
Tidenham, nr Chepstow, T01291-623412, severnvale-equestrian.com. Children's Saturday Club £20.50. Highly regarded riding school offering children's clubs, fun days and camps during holidays.

Llama treks
Severnwye Llama Trekking
Smallbrook Farm, Alvington, nr Lydney, T01594-528482, severnwyellamatrekking.co.uk. From £120/trek using 2 llamas for up to 3 people (half price for children 10-16, free for children under 10), £50/camel accompanying llamas, £25/donkey and trap.
If you go down to the woods today you might be surprised to meet a procession of llamas, accompanied by a camel, a donkey and a mule – the four-footed contingent of these novel treks. Children can hitch a ride on the camel or in the donkey trap, but everyone else walks. The llamas are for carrying your day gear and gourmet picnics. Formal introductions are held at Mallards Pike Lake where you meet your llamas and learn how to handle them. Then it's off into the forest, walking with a heightened awareness as the llama's superb eyesight and hearing help to fine tune your senses to the forest.

Quad biking
Chepstow Outdoor Activity Centre
Sedbury, T01291-629901, chepstowoutdooractivities.co.uk. £27/hr, minimum age 12.
Tackle farm trails in the Severn Vale on fully automatic bikes.

Tipi adventures
Forest Adventure Activity Ctr
Doberhill Lodge, Joyford, nr Coleford, T01594-861666, tipiadventure.co.uk. Apr-Oct, from £130/nt, plus canoe hire at £40/day. Combine a Canadian canoe expedition on the River Wye with one or more nights in a luxury riverside tipi. Each one sleeps up to seven and provides pampered camping with futons and sheepskin rugs snug around a central fire pit. Luggage and food is transported for you.

Woodland adventures
Go Ape
Mallards Pike, Parkend, T0845-643 9215, goape.co.uk. Mar-Oct, daily 0900-1700, Feb half-term, plus weekends in Nov. From £25/gorilla (18+), £20/baboon (10-17). Minimum age 10, minimum height 1.4 m, under 18-yr-olds must be accompanied by participating adult. One of 21 Go Ape arboreal adventure courses in Britain, the Forest of Dean site is a heady mix of high wires, rope bridges, zip slides and Tarzan swings draped through the treetops like the web of some deranged spider. The highest point is 50 ft above ground, while the longest zip wire is 590 ft. Attached to safety lines by a harness, you climb, scramble, pigeon-step and slide your way around the 3-hr course, completing one section at a time (when you have an opportunity to rest or call it a day). Mallards Pike has other, more down to earth, activities available, including walking and cycling trails.

Paddle the Wye

Monmouth Canoe & Activity Ctr
Old Dixton Rd, Monmouth, T01600-713461, monmouthcanoe.co.uk.
Canadian canoes £33/day,
£26/half-day (for 2 people),
plus £5/extra adult, £3/extra child.
Double kayaks £36/day, £30/day.

Ross-on-Wye Canoe Hire
Symonds Yat West, T01600-890883,
thecanoehire.co.uk.
4-person canoes from £30.

Symonds Yat Canoe Hire
Symonds Yat West,
T01600-891069, canoehire.co.uk.
4-person canoes £40/full day,
£30/half-day.

Wyedean Canoe & Adventure Ctr
Symonds Yat East,
T01594-833238, wyedean.co.uk.
4-person canoes £39/full day,
£30/half-day.

Wye Pursuits
Kerne Bridge, T01600-891199,
wye-pursuits.co.uk.
4-person canoes £40/full day,
£30/half-day.

Rates include buoyancy aids,
helmets and drysack. Transport costs
to launch sites are usually extra.

River Wye canoeing operators might give the impression of being gung-ho – they're bound to tell you not to worry about hippos because the crocodiles ate them all – but the fact is that safety is taken very seriously on these self-guided paddling adventures. Buoyancy aids are compulsory for all, while anyone under 18 must also wear a helmet. Families can either add extra seats to a canoe or lash two canoes together to form a twin-hulled (and stable) raft.

The Wye can be paddled from Glasbury to Chepstow, a 100-mile, week-long epic, but there are several half- or full-day options that suit most families, such as Symonds Yat–Redbrook and Kerne Bridge–Monmouth.

A steady current carries you downstream, the Wye a smooth green slick, streaked with tendrils of weed. As well as perfecting paddling technique there are plenty of opportunities to simply go with the flow, watch the balsam-blushed riverbanks pass by and keep a tally of the kingfishers you spot.

Canoeing beneath Symonds Yat Rock provides a dramatic perspective of the towering cliffs, but the real excitement begins around the next bend where a V-shaped shute of water swoops you into mildly wild Grade 2 rapids. A string of beaches (littered with nuggets of iron ore) is just below the rapids on the right-hand bank – the perfect spot to pull ashore for a well-earned picnic. Then it's all aboard for the final push towards Monmouth. The river loses some of its tranquillity as you come within earshot of the A40, but this is still a fantastic family adventure, spiced with a real sense of achievement.

Out & about Forest of Dean

Clearwell Caves

Clearwell, nr Coleford, T01594-832535, clearwellcaves.com. Mar-Oct, daily 1000-1700, £5.80/adult, £3.80/child (5-16), £17.30/family.
Iron ore has been mined here for over 4000 years – and ochre pigments are still extracted for artists' paints. You can explore nine caverns and visit blacksmith and ochre workshops. If you're feeling adventurous and don't mind getting dirty, join a caving expedition (from £10/person), crawling through passages 200 ft underground where, many years ago, children would have worked.

Dean Forest Railway

Lydney, T01594-845840, deanforestrailway.co.uk. Mar-Oct, All-day rover fares £9/adult, £5/child (5-16), £26/family.
Steam trains and diesel locos ply the 9-mile route between Lydney Junction and Parkend. Start at Norchard where there is a railway museum, café and shop, as well as riverside and forest walks. Northbound trains head for Parkend station in the heart of the forest. Renowned for its pied flycatchers (see page 159), RSPB Nagshead Reserve is within walking distance. Head south to Lydney for shops and the playground at Bathurst Park.

Dean Heritage Centre

Camp Mill, Soudley, T01594-822170, deanheritagemuseum.com. Daily from 1000, £4.90/adult, £2.50/child (5-16), £14/family.
A traditional forester's cottage, with Gloucestershire Old Spot pigs snuffling around in the yard, is just one of the 'living history' exhibits at this excellent museum where kids can take part in craft activities, learn how charcoal is made and then burn off energy in the adventure playground. The mill pond garden is a lovely spot for a picnic or barbeque.

Dick Whittington Farm Park

Longhope, T01452-831000, dickwhittington.info. Daily 1000-1700, £4.50/person (over 10), £5.00/child (3-10), £4/infant (under 3).
A good option for younger children, this 100-acre farm park has everything from ponies to a pedal cart track, while the play barn features a café, aquarium, and reptile room, as well as all the usual soft play shenanigans.

Perrygrove Railway

Coleford, T01594-834991, perrygrove.co.uk. Easter-Nov, weekends and school holidays, £4.95/adult, £3.95/child.
In a young child's mind there's only one thing more thrilling than a steam train ride, and that's a steam train ride in search of treasure. The narrow gauge Perrygrove Railway climbs and winds through woods and farmland on a 1.5-mile return trip, during which children hunt for clues that will unlock a treasure chest back at the station. Once they've bagged the booty, there's a treetop adventure and play area in which to let off steam.

Puzzlewood

Coleford, T01594-833187, puzzlewood.net. Mar-Sep, daily 1000-1730, Oct 1100-1630, £4.80/adult, £3.40/child (4-16), £15/family.
The fact that Puzzlewood was used as a filming location for the BBC drama series, Merlin, gives you an inkling of the enchanted, eerie feel of this pre-Roman opencast iron ore mine – long since smudged over by moss and reclaimed by ancient woodland. Tolkien, a frequent visitor to the Forest of Dean, is said to have found inspiration for Middle Earth here, and it's certainly a magical place for children to explore, with a mile of pathways weaving through ravines and over bridges, grappling with bizarre rock formations and confounding you with dead ends. To solve the puzzle, you must find seven items hidden in the forest. To be honest, though, most children become obsessed with personal quests for fairies, dragons or Bilbo Baggins. Allow at least two hours for your visit – longer if you want to meet the miniature goats, Shetland ponies and other farm animals that reside at Puzzlewood. There's also a café and indoor Wood Puzzle.

aMazing Hedge Puzzle

Jubilee Park, Symonds Yat West, T01600-890360, mazes.co.uk. Daily from 1100, £3.75/adult, £2.50/child. Joint tickets for maze and Wye Valley Butterfly Zoo (see right) £7/adult, £4.50/child, £20/family. Solve one of 12 routes to the centre of the Jubilee Maze (the shortest is only 180 m, but there are 13 dead ends), then lose yourself in the absorbing museum and Puzzle Shop. If you prefer cereal maizes, get stuck into Elton Farm Giant Maize Mazes (T01452-760795, eltonfarm-leisure.co.uk).

Caldicot Castle

Caldicot, T01291-420241, caldicotcastle.co.uk. Apr-Oct, daily 1100-1700, £3.75/adult, £2.50/child (5-17), £12/family.
A medieval castle set in 55 acres of parkland, Caldicot has lots to keep children occupied, from pond dipping to designing their own shields and armour.

Goodrich Castle

Goodrich, T01600-890538, english-heritage.org.uk. £5.20/adult, £2.60/child, £13/family. Mar-Oct, daily from 1000; closed Mon-Tue, Nov-Feb.
With a commanding position over the River Wye, Goodrich boasts some of the most intact medieval domestic buildings of any English castle. A visitor centre explores life at the fort from the 11th century until

its fall in 1646 when Royalists surrendered to 'Roaring Meg', an infamous Civil War mortar wielded by the Parliamentarians.

Tintern Abbey

Tintern, nr Chepstow, T01291-689251, cadw.wales.gov.uk. Year-round, 0900-1700, £3.60/adult, £3.20/child, £10.40/family.
Sorry kids, the name might be similar, but this Cistercian abbey, founded in 1131, has nothing to do with Hergé's famous cartoon character. Instead, you'll find the remarkably intact ruins of a splendid Gothic monastery with soaring pillars reminiscent of a Greek temple. According to folklore, the abbey is haunted by a mail-clad knight known as Strongbow. Sounds like a mystery for Tintin and Snowy...

Westbury Court Garden

Westbury-on-Severn, T01452-760461, nationaltrust.org.uk. Mar-Oct, Wed-Sun 1000-1700, daily Jul-Aug, £4.70/adult, £2.35/child (5-17), £12.15/family.
The only restored Dutch water garden in Britain, Westbury Court is an elegant blend of canals and clipped hedges. Kids can explore using a quiz trail.

Wye Valley Butterfly Zoo

Symonds Yat West, T01600-890360, butterflyzoo.co.uk. Daily from 1000, £4.25/adult, £2.75/child.
Walk with free-flying exotic butterflies and watch them sipping nectar and laying eggs.

Also recommended

Cinderbury Iron Age Experience

Clearwell, nr Coleford, T0870-6093219.

International Centre for Birds of Prey

Newent, T01531-820286, icbp.org.

Rain check

Arts & crafts
• Reckless Designs Pottery, Gloucester Rd, Coleford, T01594-810504.
• Taurus Crafts, Lydney Park Estate, T01594-844841, tauruscrafts.co.uk.

Cinemas
• Palace, Cinderford, T01594-822555.
• Savoy Theatre, Monmouth, T01600-772467.

Indoor play & amusements
• Symonds Yat West Amusement Park, T01600-890770.

Indoor swimming pools
• Forest Leisure Cinderford, Causeway Rd, T01594-824008.
• Forest Leisure Coleford, Berry Hill, T01594-835388.
• Forest Leisure Lydney, Church Rd, T01594-842383.
• Forest Leisure Newent, Watery Lane, Newent, T01531-821519.
• Forest Leisure Sedbury, Beachley Rd, T01291-625347.

Museums
• Chepstow Museum, Chepstow, T01291-625981.
• Nelson Museum, Monmouth, T01600-710630.

Sleeping Forest of Dean

Pick of the pitches

Bracelands, Christchurch & Woodland Camping Sites

Christchurch, nr Coleford, T0845-130 8224, forestholidays.co.uk. Mar-Oct, £8-14/pitch, (2 people), £4.25-6.25/extra adult, £1.75-3.25/extra child, £1 discount for families.

This terrific trio has family camping in the Forest of Dean well and truly zipped up. Operated by Forest Holidays (see pages 18-19), each site has a unique feel – from the spacious, 520-pitch Bracelands, with its far-reaching views, to the more intimate 280-pitch Christchurch, a gently sloping site with a children's play area. Woodland, meanwhile, is nestled in a forest glade with room for 90 caravans and motorhomes – wild pigs like it here too, so no tents are allowed. All three sites are immaculately maintained and provide easy access to walking and cycling trails, as well as the peregrine viewpoint at Symond's Yat Rock (see page 159). A well stocked shop next to reception at the Christchurch site sells camping supplies and groceries, plus a few treats, such as paninis and ice cream.

Doward Park Campsite

Great Doward, T01600-890438. Mar-Oct, £12.50-16.50/pitch, (2 people), £2.50/extra adult, £2/extra child.

South-facing, terraced site with a private woodland where children can make dens.

River Wye Camping

Symonds Yat West, T01600-890672, riverwyecamping.com. Mar-Oct, £7/adult, £3/child.

With a riverside setting and canoe hire, this friendly site rings all the right bells – until you discover that it also has a fairground! Great fun for some...

Woodlands View Camping

Clearwell, nr Coleford, T01594-835127. Mar-Oct, £13-16/pitch.

Small, welcoming site, within walking distance of Puzzlewood.

Pitch-perfect – Bracelands Campsite has views over Highmeadow Woods.

Cottage agents

Edenwall Holiday Cottages, T01594-832583, edenwallholidaycottages.co.uk. Small selection of farmhouse cottages near Coleford.

Forest of Dean Holiday Cottages, T01594-562219, forestofdeanholidays.co.uk. Thirteen converted farm buildings in a courtyard setting.

Hideaways, T01747-828170, forest-of-dean-cottages.co.uk. Cottages in the Forest of Dean, Wye Valley and Welsh Borders.

Steppes Farm Cottages, T01600-775424, steppesfarmcottages.co.uk. Six cottages near Monmouth.

Yearning for a yurt? You're spoilt for choice in the Wye Valley/Forest of Dean area with no less than two Mongolian ger campsites, including the one at Woodlands Farm, above.

Hidden Valley Yurts
Lower Glyn Farm, Llanishen
nr Chepstow, T01600-861856,
hiddenvalleyyurts.co.uk. Apr-Sep,
3- or 4-night breaks £260-330/yurt.
At Lower Glyn Farm, the five yurts
(or gers to use their proper term)
are the genuine thing – imported
from Mongolia with elaborately
painted interiors, thick felt linings
and a removable rain cap for
star-gazing. Walk inside one and
you'll experience one of life's 'Tardis
moments' as you take in the kingsize
bed, day beds and futons that
can sleep up to six people – with
room to spare for a wood burning
stove and perhaps a Welsh dresser,
Mongolian chest and an extra child
or two. There are also lots of nice
little touches, such as spare wellies,
wet-weather clothing, books, games
and candles.

Each ger squats on a large
deck with table, chairs, barbeque
and chiminea, while a communual
kitchen is well equipped with
everything from dishwasher to
ice-making machine. The kitchen
building is constructed from larch,
felled and milled on the farm as
part of the owners' drive to be
as environmentally friendly as
possible. The green theme is also
evident in the composting toilets
and the small waterfall where hardy
Mongolian warrior types can take an
invigorating dunk. Softies not only
have the luxury of solar-heated
showers, but can also take pleasure
in toilets flushed by pure Welsh
spring water – all drained and
cleansed through a natural reedbed
filtration system.

Between the kitchen and
showers is a south-facing deck
overlooking the campfire circle and
boules pitch. There's also a games
shed – but chances are it won't get
much of a look-in. Not when there's
a stream to dam, over 40 acres of
wood to explore, kingfishers and
herons to spot on the lake and a
herd of Peruvian alpacas to become
acquainted with.

St Briavels Castle Youth Hostel
St Briavels, nr Lydney, T0845-371
9042, yha.org.uk. From £12/adult,
£9/child (under 18) B&B.
Built as a hunting lodge for King
John in 1205, this moated Norman
castle was fortified in 1293 to form
part of the Ring of Stone around
Wales. Accommodation is fairly basic
and families will want to make sure
they book one of the two rooms
with just four or six beds. Don't
miss the medieval banquets which
take place on most Saturdays and
Wednesdays during August.

Woodland Tipis and Yurts
Woodlands Farm, Little Dewchurch,
T01432-840488, woodlandtipis.
co.uk. Apr-Sep, 3-night weekends
from £220-280/tipi, £250-340/yurt;
4-night mid-week breaks £200/tipi,
£230-260/yurt; 7 nights during
summer holidays £500/tipi,
£550-590/yurt.
There's a serene, almost spiritual,
feel to this idyllic Herefordshire
farm where a cluster of six yurts
and tipis nuzzle in woods less than
a mile from the River Wye. Just
because it's a farm, however, don't
expect tractor tours or animal
feeding sessions. This is more like
a woodland retreat where children
run wild with the fairies – and build
them miniature wigwams of sticks
and leaves decorated with petals
and feathers. A fenced, six-acre
tangle of ancient woodland is
perfect for den-building, playing
hide and seek, scaling rope ladders
or collecting firewood for the
traditional clay pizza oven. Hop over
a stile and you find yourself on a
grassy slope that's ideal for picnics
or simply sitting quietly, waiting
for a glimpse of one of the local
buzzards or badgers.

Sleeping four or five people
comfortably, each tipi and yurt
has an outdoor firepit, picnic table
and hammock. Inside, there's a
cosy jumble of blankets, cushions,
rugs and mattresses with a wood-
burning stove or chiminea. A
separate wooden shelter has flush
toilets, hot showers, a lovely old
roll-top bath and a kitchen area with
ovens, washing up sinks and fridges.
Bread, milk, eggs and organic
vegetables are all available locally.

Eating Forest of Dean

Abbey Mill

Wye Valley Centre, Tintern,
T01291-689228, abbeymill.com.
Daily 1030-1730.
This friendly little craft centre
on the banks of the River
Wye occupies the original
mill site of Tintern Abbey
(see page 163). After you've
watch the trout and browsed
the handicrafts, pop into the
Coffee Shop and Restaurant for
local specialities like mill wheel
teacake and fiery dragon pie
(made only from locally grown
Welsh dragons).

Hunter & Todd Delicatessen

High St, Newnham-on-Severn,
T01594-516211, hunterandtodd.
co.uk. Mon-Fri 0845-1900,
Sat 0800-1700.
Operating from a lovely old
beamed building dating from
1647, this well established
deli stocks a vast range of
local food, from Gloucester
Old Spot sausages to Wye
Valley ice cream. Kit out your
picnic with local cheeses and
chutneys, fresh-baked bread
and Ragman's Lane organic
fruit juices. If you're after food
for the barbecue, don't forget

Market days

Coleford Market Square, 2nd Fri.
Lydney The Co-op, last Wed.
Chepstow Senior Citizens Centre,
2nd and 4th Sat.
Ross-on-Wye Market Hall, 1st Fri.

to pick up a bottle of Severn
Sauce (produced by Claire's
Kitchen in The Forest of Dean)
to add a bit of zing to your
burgers and steaks.

Shepherd's Farm Shop

Three Shires Garden Centre,
Newent, T01531-828590,
shepherdsfarmshop.co.uk. Mon-Sat
0900-1730, Sun 1030-1630.
Susie Keenan has created
a mouthwatering shrine to
local produce at this award-
winning farm store. A one-stop
shop, it sells everything from
Hereford beef and Malvern
lamb to Chedworth yoghurt
and good old Stinking Bishop
cheese from Gloucester. Picnic
goodies include pies, pasties,
homemade cakes and organic
fruit juices. Alternatively, sit
down to delicious soups and
other wholesome dishes at
Shepherd's Deli Café (Church St,
Newent, Mon-Sat 0900-1700).

Also recommended
Crumbs

Gloucester Rd, Coleford, T01594-
811177, crumbscraftsngifts.com.
Traditional teas, cakes and crafts.

Field Fayre

Broad St, Ross-on-Wye,
T01989-566683.
Local, organic produce.

Pengethley Farm Shop

Pengethley Garden Ctr, Peterstow,
Ross-on-Wye, T01989-730430.
Seasonal, farm-fresh food.

The Old Dairy Tearoom

Harts Barn Craft Centre,
Longhope, T01452-830954,
hartsbarncraftcentre.co.uk.
Tue-Sun from 1000.
Daily specials, plus homemade
soups, sandwiches, jacket
potatoes and cream teas.

The Ostrich Inn

Newland, Coleford, T01594-833260,
theostrichinn.com.
Daily 1200-1430, 1830-2130.
Cosy, old-fashioned pub
without the slightest whiff
of 'gastro' about it. Try the
Forester's Feast – three local
cheeses, a hunk of bread, salad
and a dollop of chutney for £8.

Also recommended
The Greyhound Inn

The Slad, Popes Hill, Newnham,
T01452-760344. Tue-Sun from 1200.
Friendly pub with large garden,
stream and children's play area.

Saracens Head Inn

Symonds Yat East, T01600-890435.
Daily 1200-1430, 1830-2100.
Treat yourself to lunch or
dinner at this 17th-century pub
on the banks of the River Wye.
Children's meals include local
sausages and mash (£5.25),
while a 10-oz Herefordshire
steak with handcut chips, field
mushrooms and a red wine jus
will set you back around £18.

Essentials Forest of Dean

Getting there

By train CrossCountry Trains (T0844-811 0124, crosscountrytrains.co.uk), First Great Western (T08457-000125 firstgreatwestern.co.uk) and London Midland (T0870-609 6060, londonmidland.com) serve Cheltenham Spa and Gloucester, from where Arriva Trains Wales (T08709-000773, arrivatrainswales. co.uk) runs to Lydney just south of the forest.

By coach National Express (T0871-781 8181, nationalexpress. com) has services to Chepstow, Gloucester, Monmouth, Newent and Ross-on-Wye.

Getting around

By bus Stagecoach (T0871-200 2233, stagecoachbus. com) operates several routes in the region, including 30/31 (Gloucester–Cinderford–Coleford), 32/132 (Gloucester–Newent– Ross-on-Wye), 34 (Ross-on-Wye–Monmouth), 35 (Ross-on-Wye–Coleford–Monmouth), 38 (Ross-on-Wye–Hereford) and 73 (Gloucester–Lydney–Chepstow). A local family business, James Bevan Coaches (T01594-842859, jamesbevancoaches.com) runs services linking Coleford, Cinderford and Lydney. George Youngs Coaches (T01531-821584) runs a Mon-Fri service between Monmouth and Symonds Yat, while Chepstow Classic Buses (T01291-625449) operates between Coleford and Symonds Yat, Tue, Thu and Fri.

Maps

The Ordnance Survey Explorer map OL14 covers the Wye Valley and Forest of Dean, while the Landranger 162 map takes a wider view of Gloucester and the Forest of Dean.

Tourist Information Centres

Coleford High St, T01594-812388, visitforestofdean.co.uk. Apr-Sep, Mon-Sat 1000-1700, plus Sun 1000-1400 Jul-Aug; Oct-Mar, Mon-Sat 1000-1600.
Monmouth Priory St, T01600-713899, visitwyevalley.com. Apr-Sep, daily 0930-1700, Oct-Mar, Mon-Sat 1000-1600.
Newent Church St, T01531-822468.
Ross-on-Wye Edde Cross Street, T01989-562768, visitherefordshire. co.uk. Apr-Sep, Mon-Sat 0930-1730, Sun and bank holidays 1000-1600, Oct-Mar, Mon-Sat 1000-1630.

Further Information

The Forestry Commission, T01594-833057, forestry.gov. uk/forestofdean.

Hospitals

Lydney Lydney and District Hospital, T01594-598220.
Gloucester Gloucestershire Royal Hospital, T08454-222222.

Pharmacies

Chepstow Boots, High St.
Cinderford Alliance, Market St.
Coleford Lloyds, Railway Drive.
Lydney Co-op, Newerne St.

Newent Day Lewis, Broad St.
Monmouth Boots, Monnow St.
Ross-on-Wye Boots, Market Pl.

Supermarkets

Chepstow Tesco.
Cinderford Co-op.
Coleford Co-op, Somerfield.
Lydney Co-op, Somerfield, Tesco.
Newent Costcutter, Budgens.
Monmouth Marks & Spencer, Somerfield, Waitrose.
Ross-on-Wye Morrisons, Somerfield.

Other shops

Baby supplies Mothercare, St Oswalds Rd, Gloucester.
Camping supplies Escape, Croft Court, Ross-On-Wye; Millets, Monnow St, Monmouth.
Toy shops Toyzone, Gloucester Rd, Ross-On-Wye.

Environmental groups

Gloucestershire Wildlife Trust, T01452-383333, gloucestershirewildlifetrust.co.uk. Herefordshire Nature Trust, T01432-356872, wildlifetrust.org.uk/hereford.

Major Events

Apr/May Dean Outdoors Festival (various venues).

Other Events

The Dean Heritage Centre (see page 162) has a programme of walks, craft activities etc, while Forestry Commission rangers run events at Beechenhurst Lodge and Symonds Yat (see pages 158-159).

Willow Swamp

Sculpture

Lakeside Trail

Great escapes

National Forest

A family holiday in the Midlands?
Surely not. It's all motorways and
cities, and you'll be about as far
from a beach as it's possible to
get in Britain. What could possibly
possess you to stop here for a holiday?

Trees. Lots of trees. In fact, a whole new
forest of them taking root across a 200-square-
mile swathe of former coal-mining land. One
of Britain's boldest environmental projects, the
National Forest is turning parts of Leicestershire,
Staffordshire and Derbyshire from black to green.
Since the project was initiated in the 1990s, over
seven million saplings have been planted, shading
in the gaps between two existing fragments of
ancient woodland – Charnwood in the east and

Needwood in the west.
It doesn't pretend to
be like the New Forest
or Sherwood. This is a
forest-in-the-making
and will never be
wall-to-wall trees.
Instead you will find
a multi-purpose
woodland, spreading
like a green tide
between the towns
of Coalville, Ashby-
de-la-Zouch and
Burton upon Trent.
The National Forest

Walk in the park

Sence Valley Forest Park (nr Ibstock, T01889-586593, forestry.gov.uk, daily from 0830, free) is one of several community woodlands in the National Forest where you can walk, cycle and picnic. A haven for wildlife, it has a hide overlooking a lake with an artifical nesting wall for sand martins. Otters, ospreys and water voles have also been spotted here.

Kids will be like squirrels on steroids the moment they scurry inside the Discovery Centre at Conkers.

Wildlife Trail

Post haste – time to make up your mind at Conkers (see below).

Don't miss

Conkers, Moira, T01283-216633, visitconkers.com, daily from 1000, £7.95/adult, £5.95/child, £24.95/family. A nature reserve, adventure playground and science museum rolled into one, this 120-acre park is an outdoor/indoor forest-themed free-for-all. Kids will be like squirrels on steroids the moment they scurry inside the Discovery Centre to find the Enchanted Forest play area and an education zone packed with exhibits designed to stimulate young minds on everything from caterpillars to climate change. Outside, there are endless paths to explore – encircling lakes, probing swamps, delving in woods – plus an assault course for teenagers, a willow labyrinth for younger children and a lookout tower. And just when you think they'll run out of puff, along comes the miniature railway and you find yourselves steaming towards the neighbouring Waterside Centre. More paths, more wildlife and, to top it all, an amphitheatre where regular live-animal shows are held during summer (good for resting your feet for an hour if nothing else). Time to go home? Not if you haven't done a ranger activity or visited the shop...

is as much for people as wildlife, with farmers, local communities and conservation groups sharing a vision for a dynamic, reinvigorated landscape. And with this positive mood (and frenzy of tree-planting) has come a natural growth spurt in tourism where the emphasis lies very much on outdoor discovery, local heritage and rural traditions.

Time then, to remove the blinkers as you speed north or south on the M1 or M6. There's a leafy gem in the heart of the Midlands ripe for exploration – if only for a few days.

Great escapes National Forest

Get your bearings
Reaching the National Forest isn't difficult. In fact, you've probably driven through it several times without even realising. The M1 clips the eastern reaches of the forest, just above Leicester. Leave the motorway at junction 22 and the A511 whisks you past Coalville to Ashby-de-la-Zouch, a small market town at the heart of the National Forest. The M42/A42 provides a fast track to Ashby where you'll find the tourist information centre on North Street (T01530-411767, Mon-Fri 0930-1700, Sat 0930-1600). The A511 continues west, crossing the A38 at Burton upon Trent, the forest's largest town, which has the excellent Coors Visitor Centre on Horninglow Street (T01283-508111, Mon-Fri 0900-1700, Sat 1100-1600).

Check out the hostel
Just like the National Forest as a whole, the youth hostel near Moira has an enlightened, eco-friendly feel to it. Forget musty old buildings with dingy dorms and a shared bathroom at one end of the corridor. The Youth Hostel Association is an altogether different beast to the one of twenty or thirty years ago. Opened in 2007, **YHA National Forest** (T0845-371 9672, yha.org.uk, year round, from £15.95/adult, £11.95/child under 18) has ensuite family bedrooms with a restaurant/bar, lounge and self-catering kitchen opening onto a terrace surrounded by lawns and newly-planted trees. It recycles rainwater for flushing toilets, has a bio-fuel boiler using wood chips sourced sustainably from the forest and supplements this with solar power. There's even a touch-screen monitor in reception where you can find out about local attractions. The bedrooms are small and basic, but clean and light, and you get a hermetically sealed bedding pack for each bunk. The food served in the restaurant isn't at all bad: Derbyshire oatcakes stuffed with wild mushrooms and stilton cheese (around £6.50)

and for the kids, salmon fillet with potato wedges and salad (from £3.50). Still think youth hostels are a bit dreary and backward?

Pitch your tent
There are numerous options for camping in the National Forest. One of the best sites is right next to the youth hostel at the 90-pitch **Conkers Camping & Caravanning Club Site** (T01283-224925), while another good option is near Swadlincote, where **Beehive Farm Woodland Lakes** (T01283-763981) has 25 pitches spread across a 66-acre mosaic of woodland, meadow and wetland habitats.

Treat yourself to a forest lodge
It only seems natural that the National Forest should be leading the way in luxury timber lodges (from sustainable sources, of course) and you'll find some of the most thoughtfully designed at Rosliston Forestry Centre (see page 172). Not only are **Forest Lodges** (T01283-595795, roslistonforestrycentre.co.uk, year round, from £341-880/wk) well equipped with mod cons and high-quality furnishings, but they also offer excellent access for wheelchair users. Each of the six cabins (sleeping up to 10) is discreetly tucked away in its own grassy forest clearing.

Stock up on local food
Marmite comes from Burton on Trent, so it would seem churlish not to buy a jar (even if you're of the Vegemite persuasion). But local food in the National Forest goes way beyond yeast extract. There are farmers' markets at Ashby-de-la-Zouch and Swadlincote on the third Saturday of every month, while **Scaddows Farm Shop** (Ticknall, T01332-865709, Mon-Sat from 0830, Sun from 1000) has pick-your-own fruit in summer. At the wonderful waterfront development of Barton Marina, near Barton-under-Needwood, the **Appletree** (T01283-712332, Mon-Sat 1000-1700, Sun 1100-1700) has a fine deli counter

encouraging wildlife

Model cars at Toys of Yesteryear, Barton Marina; Wild Man of the Woods sculpture at the Ferrers Centre; earthy decor at Forest Lodges; archery at Rosliston Forestry Centre; old colliery buildings at Snibston.

Great escapes National Forest

serving homebaked cakes, local cheeses and fresh sandwiches. Next door, the **Butcher, Baker & Ice Cream Maker** (T01283-711002, Mon-Sat 0900-1700, Sun 1100-1600) has award-winning pork pies, bangers and bacon, plus bread, cakes and pastries. Its delicious Jersey Ice Cream comes straight from a farm in Staffordshire.

Get wise in the woods
Peter Wood is a busy man, running traditional craft workshops at his rustic camp in Spring Wood, near the Ferrers Centre for Arts & Crafts (see below). With any luck, though, he'll be able to fit you into a family session where children can make willow weavings of butterflies and fish and learn how to master a foot-powered pole lathe to fashion anything from a spinning top to a chair leg. It's an immensely satisfying way to spend a few hours, made all the more rewarding by Wood's gentle and patient manner with kids. For details, contact **Greenwood Days** (T01332-864529, greenwood-days.co.uk).

If bushcraft is more your thing, **Woodland Ways** (T07843-064114, woodland-ways.co.uk) offers overnight survival courses for £300/family, during which you'll learn essential skills, such as shelter building, collecting and purifying water, lighting a fire and making damper bread.

Plan a big day out
You'd be bonkers not to visit **Conkers** (see page 169), but you can have almost as much fun at **Rosliston Forestry Centre** (Rosliston, T01283-563483, roslistonforestrycentre.co.uk, year round, daily 0730-dusk, parking £0.80/hr or £2/day). Having parted with your very reasonable car-parking fee, you could quite happily enjoy a free day-out here, exploring the woodland trails and sensory gardens, picnicing by the lake and setting the kids loose on the adventure playgrounds. Most families, however, dip into their pockets for a few extras. Drop-in activities (from £2.50/person for a 20-minute session) include archery, laser combat, laser clay shooting and a climbing wall. You can also go fishing (£5/adult, £4.50/child), rent bikes (from £3) or take part in an orienteering course or one-hour falconry session (prices vary with group size). The centre's Hub Café, meanwhile, serves hot and cold snacks from 1000-1600.

Action stations
Moira Furnace Cycle Centre, Moira, T01283-224667, justbikesashby.com.
National Forest Llama Treks, Barton-under-Needwood, T01283-711702, nationalforestllamatreks.co.uk.

Set on the site of a former colliery, **Snibston Discovery Museum** (Coalville, T01530-278444, snibston.com, year round, daily from 1000, £6.75/adult, £4.50/child, £20/family) is the National Forest's best ticket for a rainy day. The interactive exhibits in the Extra Ordinary Gallery are inspired. Kids can use energy and oxygen to make fire, operate electromagnets to lift a Mini off the ground, create a tornado out of a spiralling column of smoke and vote for their favourite invention since humans discovered fire (a popular one for teenage boys if the all-time winner – the brassiere – is anything to go by).

Other galleries explore coal mining, transport and engineering. There's a mighty beam engine on display, plus a collection of old buses, fire engines and aircraft. Rather incongruously, you'll also find a fashion gallery with the largest display of historic and contemporary costume outside London. Essentially, though, Snibston is about coal and machines. The outdoor play area has some terrific mining-themed challenges, while nearby you can join ex-miners on a colliery tour (£1.75/adult, £1/child) of the old mine buildings and railway. And it wouldn't be the National Forest without some greenery, so Snibston also has a 100-acre country park (free admission) with fishing lakes, nature ponds, walking trails and picnic areas.

Just south of the National Forest, **Twycross Zoo** (T01827-880250, twycrosszoo.org, year round, daily from 1000, £11/adult, £7/child, £33/family) is the place to go for visiting your distant hairy cousins. A breeding centre for all kinds of endangered primates, from bonobos and gorillas to orang-utans and lemurs, the zoo blends monkey business with serious conservation. By far the most imaginative enclosure is the Borneo Longhouse Aviary – a contrast to the rather austere brick-wall quarters belonging to the gorillas and chimpanzees. Other species include giraffes, lions, leopards, penguins, tapirs, prairie dogs and Asian elephants. None are more charismatic, though, than the gibbons which, if you're lucky, will whoop themselves into a singing frenzy, the black siamangs using their balloon-like throat pouches to amplify their extraordinary calls.

Treat yourself to dinner

Combine lunch with shopping at the **Ferrers Centre for Arts & Crafts** (Staunton Harold, ferrerscentre.co.uk, Tue-Sun 1100-1700) where **Staunton Stables Tea & Luncheon Rooms** (T01332-864617) serves delicious light bites, including summer salads (from £7.25) and soup (from £4). Occupying a Georgian stable block, the centre also has a gallery and craft studios. Other good places to eat out in the National Forest include the **Honey Pot Tea Rooms** (Rosliston, T01283-763980), **The Shoulder of Mutton** (Oakthorpe, T01283-522811) and **Zamani's Italian Restaurant** (Ashby-de-la-Zouch, T01530-560719).

Essential websites

The National Forest nationalforest.org.
Forestry Commission forestry.gov.uk.
Tourist information nwleics.gov.uk, enjoystaffs.co.uk.

Amaze yourself

The National Forest Maize Maze is so fiendishly difficult that you carry flags to wave should you get really lost and want to be rescued. Sometimes people stagger out after five hours, having finally solved the riddles hidden in the convoluted crop. An adjacent field has a village fête atmosphere. Parents can relax with a cup of tea while children leap about on space hoppers or the giant bouncy pillow, race go-karts, squirt each other with hoses or pet the llamas, calves and lambs.
• **The National Forest Maize Maze**, Tatenhill, T07812-333315, nationalforestmaze.co.uk, Jul-Sep, daily 1030-1800, £5.95/adult, £5.25/child, £19.95/family.

Morston Quay.

North Norfolk

Norfolk might lag behind Devon and Cornwall in the seaside glamour stakes, but this is no turkey when it comes to family holidays. Not only does it boast some of Britain's wildest beaches topped by the biggest skies this side of Arizona, but it's also bursting with wildlife and adventure opportunities.

A large swathe of North Norfolk's coast is designated an Area of Outstanding Natural Beauty. Follow the coastal A149 west from **Hunstanton** (famed for its striped cliffs and Sea Life centre) and you soon begin to see why. Flinty hamlets, fishing villages and the occasional windmill fringe a pristine shoreline of long sandy beaches, salt marsh and tidal creeks.

The RSPB reserve at **Titchwell** is one of several havens for North Norfolk's extraordinary birdlife. Avian A-listers include the reed-skulking bittern and elegant, stilt-legged avocet. Nearby **Brancaster** and **Holkham**, meanwhile, are two of the coast's undisputed beach beauties – perfect for sandcastles, beachcombing, flying kites or reinacting Gwyneth Paltrow's carefree stroll across endless sands in the closing scenes of *Shakespeare in Love*.

Throwing all pretensions to the wind (and it can be a tad brisk on this North Sea coast), **Wells-next-the-Sea** is an old-fashioned blend of fishing boats, fudge shops and the odd flash of neon from an amusement arcade. Most children, however, seem more interested in casting crab lines from the quay or riding a steam train to the ancient pilgrimage centre of **Walsingham**. Further west, Poppy Line locos chuff between the Georgian market town of **Holt** and the Victorian seaside resort of **Sheringham**.

Don't overlook the stretch of coast between Wells and Sheringham. Not only do the villages of **Morston**, **Blakeney**, **Cley** and **Salthouse** ooze charm (and mud at low tide), but they also offer North Norfolk's freshest seafood. Tour boats set out daily from Morston Quay to sidle up to the seals at Blakeney Point, while the visitor centre at Cley Marshes is the starting point for birdwatching rambles among the reedbeds.

With its pier and traditional seaside fun, **Cromer** forms part of a chain of Blue Flag beaches stretching from Sheringham to **Mundesley** and **Sea Palling**. Further south lies **Great Yarmouth**, but its boisterous seafront shenanigans are no match for a few days exploring **The Broads**: paddling canoes, treading secret boardwalks and searching for the ever-elusive bittern.

You must

- Ride a steam train.
- Canoe on the Broads.
- Get a tick for avocet, bittern and marsh harrier.
- Cruise out to Blakeney Point to see the seals.
- Run wild on the acres of sand at Holkham Bay.
- Catch a crab or three at Wells-next-the-Sea.
- Cycle in the woods at Kelling Heath.
- Feel the magic at BeWILDerwood.
- Explore a windmill.
- Learn to sail.

Out and about North Norfolk

Fun & free

Comb the beaches
Norfolk's long sandy beaches are gold dust for strand-stalkers, turning up anything from mermaid's purses to fossil shark teeth. Holkham is your best bet for strandline treasures, while Hunstanton is rich in Cretaceous fossils of fish, sea urchins and shells. Remember to keep off the crumbly and unstable cliffs.

Smell the lavender
Pretty in purple from Jun-Aug, Norfolk Lavender (T01485-570384, norfolk-lavender. co.uk) packs a perfumed punch with 100 acres of the aromatic herb cultivated around Caley Mill, Heacham. It's not only a bloomin' marvellous spectacle, but an education in the culinary and medicinal uses of herbs too. There are gardens to explore, as well as tours of the lavender oil distillery (£3/adult, £1.50/child). Daily from 0900.

Catch a crab
You'll be hauling them in by the bucketload at the quays in Wells, Blakeney and Burnham Overy.

Bike the byways
No excuses now. It's mostly flat, the back roads are quiet and there are plenty of cycle hire shops if you need them (see pages 180-181). Norfolk is ideal country for a two-wheel family adventure. You can explore country lanes around Bircham Windmill or go off-road at Kelling Heath Holiday Park. The Broads by Bike (thebroadsbybike.org.uk) features nine circuits, including several that are suitable for families. One links Hickling Broad (see opposite), following 5.5 miles of lanes, while a 14.5-mile route heads east from Potter Heigham to How Hill nature reserve. See page 181 for other route suggestions.

Fly a kite
Miles of empty space and a steady breeze – take your pick of just about any Norfolk beach at low tide. You could also try the clifftops at Cromer.

Plan a shrimping expedition
Some of the best rock pools can be found at Old Hunstanton and Sheringham. Even on sandy beaches, it's worth checking the groynes at low tide where pools can be seething with shrimps. Just keep an eye on the tide – the sea can sweep in rapidly across those acres of sand.

Visit a horse sanctuary
Caldecott (T0870-040 0033, redwings.co.uk) pampers ponies, horses and other needy nags in 70 acres of paddocks. Entry is free, but you can support the centre's work by buying horsey gifts, taking out an adoption or getting stuck into the Nosebag Café. Mar-Oct, daily 1000-1700.

Focus on birds

Haven't got a telescope? Worried that your binoculars aren't up to scratch, or that you might confuse ruffs with redshanks? Professional twitchers flock to Norfolk in such numbers that it's easy to feel a bit intimidated, but don't let this stop you from experiencing one of the county's great natural wonders. Not only are there numerous superb birdwatching locations in Norfolk, but many have excellent visitor centres, trails and hides managed by charities like the Norfolk Wildlife Trust (norfolkwildlifetrust.org.uk) and the RSPB (rspb.org.uk). Most cost nothing to visit, but by becoming members you not only get free entry to all nature reserves but also help to fund vital conservation work and take part in special events, walks and activities.

Easy ticks – oystercatcher, greylag goose and cormorant. Inset: Ranworth Broad boardwalk.

Berney Marshes and Breydon Water RSPB reserves

Grassland attracts redshanks and lapwings in spring, while the estuary throngs with ducks and geese during winter. Open year round.

Cley Marshes NWT reserve

One of the UK's best birdwatching sites, Cley Marshes' ticklist exceeds 300 species, with star sightings including avocet, bearded tit, bittern and marsh harrier. The snazzy new visitor centre has audio-visual presentations, a remote-controlled wildlife camera, café and giftshop – not to mention green kudos, thanks to its wind turbine, 'living' sedum roof and rainwater-harvesting system. Open year round 1000-1700, £4/adult, children and members free.

Foxley Wood NWT reserve

Norfolk's prime patch of ancient woodland is a haven for tawny owls, sparrowhawks and woodpeckers.

Hickling Broad NWT reserve

A large swathe of reedbeds and open water, Hickling Broad is best explored on the Water Trail – a boat tour (May-Sep) weaving through quiet backwaters to the Tree Tower. Summer highlights include bittern, Cetti's warbler, water rail and swallowtail butterfly, while a winter raptor roost (Oct-Mar) promises sightings of marsh harriers, merlins and hen harriers, plus cranes and pink-footed geese. Kids' wildlife packs are available free from the visitor centre, open Apr-Sep 1000-1700; reserve open daily, £3.25/adult, children and members free.

Mid-Yare Valley RSPB reserves

Strumpshaw Fen is the most popular of this trio of reserves located east of Norwich and open year round. A mosaic of reedbeds, woods and meadows, gold-star species include marsh harrier and swallowtail butterfly. Family explorer backpacks and trail booklets are available. Nearby Buckenham Marshes attract large numbers of breeding waders, as well as flocks of overwintering bean geese, while Surlingham Church Marsh has an intimate mile-long circular walk around reedbeds, fens and pools where you may well glimpse kingfishers, marsh harriers and reed warblers.

North Denes

The UK's largest colony of little terns nests on this beach adjacent to Great Yarmouth racecourse. RSPB wardens protect the site which can be visited from mid-May-end July.

Ranworth Broad NWT reserve

A magical spot for children, Ranworth has a floating visitor centre packed to the rafters with hands-on learning activities. You reach it by a boardwalk nature trail that probes a tangle of flooded 'carr' woodland (Norfolk's very own Everglades) before delving through thick reedbeds. A water taxi shuttles back and forth between the visitor centre and Malthouse Broad where there's a café. Nature reserve open daily, visitor centre Apr-Oct 1000-1700.

Snettisham RSPB reserve

A birding icon, Snettisham hosts two of Britain's great avian spectacles – vast flocks of wading birds pulsing over The Wash as high tide forces them to leave the mudflats, plus the winter roosting (at dawn and dusk) of thousands of pink-footed geese. The hides at Snettisham (reached by a 30-minute walk) are ideally placed to witness the 'touchdown' of both events. During summer, avocets, ringed plovers and oystercatchers nest on the shingle beach in front of the hides. Open year round.

Titchwell Marsh RSPB reserve

If you're new to birding, Titchwell provides a rewarding introduction. A five-minute stroll from the visitor centre and café (open daily from 0930) and you're deep in reedbeds, peering from a hide into prime habitat for warblers, bearded tits and marsh harriers. Another path passes a series of lagoons that become progressively brackish until you crest a line of dunes overlooking the sea. The result is a microcosm of Norfolk at its natural best. Summer highlights include nesting avocets and terns diving for fish. Open year round. Pond-dipping available for children during summer.

Out and about North Norfolk

Best beaches

Brancaster

🐕 🚗 🚽 🅿️

There's more to this gorgeous stretch of soft sand than first meets the eye. Managed by the National Trust (T01485-210719, nationaltrust.org.uk), Brancaster encompasses a huge area of bird-rich saltmarsh and sandflats, so you can be building sandcastles one minute and watching sandpipers the next. It's also the site of Branodunum Roman fort and Scolt Head Island National Nature Reserve (to which there is a ferry service). The Brancaster Millennium Activity Centre offers family fun days and courses in weaving, birdwatching and painting.

Cley

🅿️

A minor road runs through marshes north of Cley to reach a lonely shingle beach – the starting point for a 3-mile walk to Blakeney National Nature Reserve. Most people join boat trips from Morston Quay to see the seal colonies at Blakeney Point (see page 185). You won't be allowed to get as close on foot, but a walk along the shingle spit towards Blakeney Point is still a rewarding and invigorating experience. Check tide times before setting off and see if you can spot rare shingle-dwelling plants like the yellow horned poppy and sea beet.

Cromer

🐕 🚗 🚽 🏄 🍴 🚗 ➕ 🚗 🚗 🅿️

Dominated by its pier – built in 1901 and housing a lifeboat station, RNLI museum and theatre – Cromer's beach is a mixture of sand and shingle running along the base of low cliffs. Crab boats still operate from the beach and, if you're lucky, you can see fishermen unloading their catch. Try your luck shrimping in rock pools at low tide or catch a wave with Glide Surf School (glidesurfschool.co.uk) which offers surfing lessons, May-Oct, on the east side of the pier.

Great Yarmouth

🐕 🚗 🚽 🏄 🍴 🚗 ➕ 🚗 🚗 🅿️

One of Britain's most popular seaside resorts, boredom is banished at Great Yarmouth thanks largely to Pleasure Beach (pleasure-beach.co.uk) with its rollercoaster, log flume and swing ship, plus less stomach-churning carousel and snail rides. You can also go bowling at Wellington Pier or catch a show at the Hippodrome Circus. Other crowd-pullers include the Sea Life Centre, Amazonia and Time and Tide Museum (see pages 183-184), while boat trips to see the seals at Scroby Sands are advertised along the seafront. Don't forget the beach though! Great Yarmouth's sands have been scientifically proven to make some of Britian's finest and sturdiest sandcastles.

Top: Sandflats at Wells. Above: Hunstanton. Right: The pier and lifeboat ramp at Cromer.

Hemsby

🚗 🚽 🏄 ➕ 🚗 🚗 🅿️

Sandy beach with dunes, safe swimming and surf board hire.

Holkham

🚗 🅿️

A 24-carat-gold nugget in North Norfolk's long necklace of sandy beaches, Holkham sits pretty in one of Britain's largest nature reserves and also lies within the magnificent estate of Holkham Hall (holkham.co.uk). From wind-rippled dunes and whispering pine woods to sheltered lagoons, teeming saltmarsh and four miles of pristine sand, Holkham is easily reached by following footpaths from car parks at Burnham Overy (free), Lady Ann's Drive or Wells Beach Road. It's also accessible by bike (see page 181). Take a picnic, some binoculars and a sense of adventure and go exploring.

saltmarsh. A causeway links town and beach, so you can drive directly to a beach car park (where you'll find a café, ice cream van and a caravan park with crazy golf, trampolines and a fish and chip shop). During summer, a miniature railway chugs back and forth to the beach (£1.20/adult, £1/child), but you'll get far better views of the estuary by walking along the top of the embankment. Backed by dunes and pine trees, the beach at Wells is part of the Holkham Estate (see left) and stretches for miles. Be wary of venturing too far to the east as it's easy to get trapped on the wrong side of the channel when the tide comes in. A siren usually sounds to warn of an incoming tide. It's also worth checking the tide tables so you can be at the quay in Wells at high water – prime time for crabbing. Several shops in the town sell crab lines and if you need bait, try Arthur Howell butchers on Staithe Street for bacon off-cuts. Moored against the quay, the 1899 twin-masted *Albatros* serves delicious pancakes.

Hunstanton

A rarity in Norfolk, Hunstanton (or 'Sunny Hunny' as it's known locally) faces due west – just the job for watching the sunset as you munch fish and chips on the seafront. Famed for its red-and-white-striped cliffs (best seen from cruises aboard the Wash Monster – page 180), Hunstanton is a buzzing resort with donkey rides on the beach, pitch and putt, amusement arcades, funfair and a Sea Life Sanctuary (see page 182). Low tide can expose a mile of sandy beach, creating rockpools around the groynes. During summer, a land train runs the length of the promenade.

Mundesley

Clifftop gardens and beach huts form a traditional backdrop to this sandy beach that's good for swimming and surfing.

Sea Palling

A series of shallow, sheltered bays protected by artificial offshore reefs, the large sandy beach at Sea Palling offers safe paddling and swimming.

Sheringham

Better known as the home of the Poppy Line steam railway (see page 184), Sheringham is a traditional seaside town with a handful of crabbing boats dragged high-and-dry on a beach of sand and pebbles, a slipway festooned with nets and buoys, and rows of seaweed-clad groynes jutting into the sea.

Wells-next-the-Sea

Wells has a split personality – a pristine sandy beach on the coast and, about a mile inland, a bustling fishing town perched on an estuary of sandflats and

West Runton

A quiet, sand and shingle beach located between Cromer and Sheringham, West Runton often has decent surf.

Out and about North Norfolk

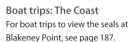

Action stations

Boating: The Broads
Broadly speaking there are four ways to get afloat in Norfolk's great wetland. You can embark on a river cruise, hire a self-drive launch, paddle a canoe or sail a yacht. Rental boats come in various guises. Day boats (right) usually seat up to eight people, are simple to drive and have fold-down covers to protect you from the elements. Picnic boats have extra creature comforts – a proper cabin with hob, sink and toilet – while day cruisers really push the boat out with a sliding canopy and fridge. See also broads-authority.gov.uk.

Canoe hire
Around £30/day, £20/half-day for two- or three-seater canoes.

Bank Dayboats, Wayford Bridge, T01692-582457, bankboats.co.uk.

Barnes Brinkcraft, Wroxham, see right.

Martham Boats, T01493-740249, marthamboats.com.

Outney Meadow Caravan Park, Bungay, T01986-892338, outneymeadow.co.uk.

Salhouse Broad, T07795-145475.

Sutton Staithe Boatyard, T01692-581653.

Waveney River Centre, Burgh St Peter, T01502-677343, waveneyrivercentre.co.uk.

Whispering Reeds, Hickling, T01692-598314.

Barnes Brinkcraft
Wroxham, T01603-782625, barnesbrinkcraft.co.uk. Mar-Nov, daily from 0900. Day boats £14-16/hr, £79-102/day; picnic boats £85-120/day.

Broads Tours
Wroxham, T01603-782207 and Potter Heigham, T01692-670711, broads.co.uk. Mar-Oct, daily from 0900. Day boats £14-16/hr, £79-102/day; cruisers £125-145/day; river trips from £6.50/adult, £5/child (5-16).

The Canoe Man
See page 187.

Day Cruisers
Horning, T01692-631111 and Burgh St Peter, T01502-677343, daycruisers.co.uk. Year round, daily from 0900. Luxury day cruisers £95-131/day, day boats £74-84/day.

Fineway Leisure
Wroxham, T01603-782309, finewayleisure.co.uk. Year round, daily from 0900. Day boats £11-13/hr, £63-80/day.

Moonfleet Marine
Stalham, T01692-580288, moonfleetmarine.co.uk. Mar-Oct, daily from 0900. Day boats £12-20/hr.

Wroxham Launch Hire
Hoveton, T01603-783043, russellmarine.co.uk. Mar-Oct, daily from 0900. Day boats £12-14/hr, £67-90/day; picnic boats £46-66/half-day, £90-110/day.

Boat trips: The Coast
For boat trips to view the seals at Blakeney Point, see page 187.

Searles Sea Tours
Hunstanton, T0783-132 1799, seatours.co.uk. Year round, times vary. Seal tours £12/adult, £6/child. Searles operates a quirky fleet of tour boats out of Hunstanton, including the LARC XV – an amphibious landing craft used by American Forces in Vietnam that still sports its original shark's head livery. Not surprisingly it's become known as the Wash Monster, the preferred form of transport for the five cruises offered by Searles. Most last 20-30 minutes and potter along the coast viewing the striped cliffs of Hunstanton that resemble a giant slab of coconut ice. You'll also see the lighthouse and even a wreck or two. More exciting for kids, though, is the Seal Island Tour (where you're ferried in the Monster to a 60-seater tour boat moored offshore before setting out to see some of the 3000 common seals that live in The Wash) and the Sandbank Special where the Wash Monster lowers its ramp and disgorges passengers onto tidal banks.

Cycling: North Norfolk
Bircham Windmill
Great Bircham, T01485-578393, birchamwindmill.co.uk. Mar-Sep,

daily 1000-1700. Adult bike £5/hr, £11/day; child's bike £3.50/hr, £9/day; trailer from £6. See also page 190. With its museum, bakery, tea room, gift shop, farm animals and children's play area, Bircham Windmill makes a fine base for a cycling adventure, with circuits lasting from an hour to a full day.

Huff & Puff Cycles
Kelling Heath Holiday Park, Weybourne, T07788-132909, cyclenorfolk.co.uk. School holidays, daily 1000-1700, phone for other times. Adult bike £9/day, child's bike £6/day, tag-along £5/day.
The 250-acre Kelling Heath Holiday Park (see page 187) is riddled with traffic-free trails. Alternatively, strike out on quiet lanes to Sheringham Park. Families with older children can saddle up for a more epic 9-mile cycle to Salthouse, while steam train fans can combine a 5.5-mile circuit with a ride on the North Norfolk Railway between Sheringham and Holt. Special fares are available to cycle hirers.

On Yer Bike Cycle Hire
Wighton, nr Wells-next-the-Sea, T01328-820719, norfolkcyclehire.co.uk. School holidays, daily 1000-1700, phone for other times. Adult bike £13/day, child's bike £7-9/day, tag-along £7/day.
Pack a picnic and set out for the day, pedalling through Holkham Estate towards the sandy beach at Holkham and Wells-next-the-Sea (see pages 178-179).

Cycling: The Broads
Broadland Cycle Hire
Bewilderwood, nr Hoveton, T07887-480331, norfolkbroadscycling.co.uk. School holidays, daily 1000-1700, phone for other times. Adult bike from £10/day, £7/half-day; child's bike £6/day, £4/half-day; tag-along and trailer from £4.
Broadland Cycle Hire provides access to several circular routes in the Broads. A 7-mile jaunt leads to Coltishall, returning via Wroxham Barns Craft Centre. You can also cycle to Ranworth Broad (page 177) or follow a traffic-free trail alongside the Bure Valley Railway (page 184). Other cycle hire centres in the Broads include Clippesby Hall (T01493-367800), Ludham Bridge Services (T01692-630489) and Stokesby Riverside Stores (T01493-750470).

Sailing
Norfolk Etc
Blakeney, T01263-740704, norfolketc.co.uk. Two-day course £195/person; 3-day course £255-265/person; private tuition £155/day. RYA dinghy courses, from beginner to advanced, for children and adults, sailing from Morston Quay. Powerboating courses also available.

Sailcraft Sea School
Brancaster Staithe, nr King's Lynn, T01485-210236, sailcraft.co.uk. Short Sailing Session £105/2 hrs, Young Mariner Course from £165/2 days. Short Sailing Sessions provide an ideal introduction for parents with children aged 5-7, while Young Mariner Courses follow the RYA Junior Scheme Stages 1-2 and teach a basic grasp of handling a dinghy.

Try Sailing
Barton Broad, nr Wroxham, T01603-782897, trysailing.com. One-day taster course from £59/person. Learn to sail a 24-ft Pegasus yacht, covering boat handling, rigging, rules, knots and safety.

Woodland adventures
BeWILDerwood
See page 184.

Extreeme Adventure
Weasenham, T07775-593477, extreemeadventure.co.uk. Mar-Nov, daily 0900-1600, ropes course £25/adult, £23/child (minimum age 10). High ropes course with 1000-ft zip wire and fan descender jump as optional extras. Junior course for children under 10 (£2), plus woodland walk and treasure hunt (free).

Hilltop Outdoor Centre
Sheringham, T01263-824514, hilltopoutdoorcentre.co.uk. School holiday adventure sessions £16/half-day, £32/day (minimum age 6). Superb woodland adventure centre offering adrenaline-charged days where assault courses, zip wires, climbing walls, ropes courses and super swing are just some of the daredevil pursuits.

Out & about North Norfolk

BeWILDerwood

Hoveton, T01603-783900,
bewilderwood.co.uk. Feb half-
term, Mar-Nov, daily from 1000,
£10/person (over 105 cm), £6/child
(under 105 cm), free for children
under 92 cm.

A brilliantly conceived arboreal
fantasyland, BeWILDerwood is
like Tarzan, The Hobbit and The
Faraway Tree rolled into one. A
breath of fresh forest air, it not
only rekindles every child's tree-
climbing ambitions, but also
sparks their imagination as they
discover an enchanted world
inhabited by Boggles, Twiggles,
Thornyclods and Crocklebogs.

Based on the book, *A Boggle
at BeWILDerwood* by Tom
Blofeld, children follow the
daring exploits of the elf-like
Swampy, reliving his adventures
through a beautifully
crafted succession of rope
bridges, tree houses, zip
wires, slippery slides, mazes,
obstacle courses, nature
trails and den-building. Apart
from a Crocklebog lurking in
Sccaaaaary Lake, you don't
see the characters
themselves. There
are glimpses of Boggle
and Twiggle villages
as you navigate the
Broadland swamp
by boat or boardwalk just
beyond the entrance to
BeWILDerwood – but other
than that it's mostly left to

children's
imagination.
If anything,
it's almost too
subtle, with
kids becoming
blinkered by
an 'adrenaline
high' as they
rampage
through the
woods. Be sure
to rein them in occasionally to
help them make the connection
between the action and the
story. Ultimately, though, a
day at BeWILDerwood can be
summed up by a sign near the
exit daubed with the words
'Home boring home.'

Barking up the right tree – BeWILDerwood has turned woodland
adventure into a fantasy experience. Just watch out for the Crocklebog.

Dinosaur Adventure

Lenwade, T01603-876310,
dinosauradventure.co.uk.
Year round, daily from 1000,
from £7.55/person, under 3s free.

A pack of T-Rexes is loose
in the woods and it's your
mission to find them
using radios, lookout
towers and fieldstations.
Dinosaur Adventure could
so easily have become yet
another park full of
plastic prehistoric
paraphernalia. Instead,
kids get taken
on an interactive
foray through a
lost world. After tracking the
Tyrannosaurs and collecting
passport stamps in their free
Adventurer's Guides, there's

a fossil dig and scavenger hunt
to get stuck into. And, of course,
it just wouldn't be the Jurassic
without dino-themed crazy golf,
raptor racer karts or a climb-a-
saurus. There's even a mini-zoo
with real-life dinosaur lookalikes
such as iguanas and bearded
dragons. After that little lot,
the deer safari and bunny barn
somehow seem altogether too
cute and cuddly.

Hunstanton
Sea Life Sanctuary

Hunstanton, T0871-423 2110,
sealsanctuary.co.uk. Year round, daily
from 1000, £12/adult, £9/child (3-14),
check online for offers.

Despite being smaller than Sea
Life Great Yarmouth (page 184),
Hunstanton's aquarium has the
added appeal of a seal rescue
centre and marine hospital, as
well as sanctuaries for otters
and Humboldt penguins. You
can practice rescue and feeding
techniques on dummy seals
and find out about the true-life
dramas of pups rescued along
Norfolk's coast. New arrivals

will be under intensive care in the rescue centre, while outpatients will be building up their strength in the pool ready for release back to the wild.

Pensthorpe

Nr Fakenham, T01328-851465, pensthorpe.com. Year round, daily from 1000. Park admission £8.50/adult, £5/child (4-15), £23/family; park admission plus Wensum Discovery Tour £12.75/adult, £8.25/child (4-15), £38/family.

A 500-acre mosaic of lakes, meres, ponds, meadows, heath and woodland, Pensthorpe is a haven for an extraordinary range of wildlife. Over 170 bird species have been recorded, including Norfolk's terrific trio – the avocet, bittern and marsh harrier. But that's not why you're forking out over £20 to take your family here (you can see these birds at several Norfolk nature reserves for free – see page 177). What makes Pensthorpe special is its unique crane conservation project. No less than eight varieties of these long-legged beauties breed here. The Wensum Discovery Tour delves into the reserve in search of the cranes and other wildlife; Norfolk's very own Land Rover safari where children are armed with spotter sheets and binoculars. You can also tackle nature quizzes, follow a bug trail, go pond dipping, join bird-feeding walks and explore huge free-flight aviaries. Surrounded

by beautiful gardens, the centre has a café and gift shop.

Snettisham Park

Snettisham, T01485-542425, snettishampark.co.uk. Feb-Nov, daily 1000-1700. Park admission £5.50/adult, £4.50/child (3-16), £18/family; park admission plus deer safari £8.95/adult, £6.95/child, £30/family.

A 45-minute tour of the deer park (Easter-Oct) is the highlight of a visit to this farm park where you can also follow a wildlife discovery trail, run wild on a huge adventure playground, bottle feed lambs, piglets and goats and enjoy tea and cakes in the orchard. Horse riding lessons and hacks are available at Park Farm Riding Stables (T01485-543815), while a shop sells local farm produce and farm-related toys and books.

Members' perks

Family membership (see page 5) entitles you to free entry to:

English Heritage
• Castle Acre Priory, nr Swaffham.
• Castle Rising, nr Kings Lynn.
• Great Yarmouth Row Houses.

National Trust
• Blickling Hall, nr Aylsham.
• Felbrigg Hall, nr Cromer.
• Horsey Windpump, nr Martham.
• Oxburgh Hall.
• Sheringham Park.

RSPB
• Strumpshaw Fen reserve.
• Titchwell Marsh reserve.

Rain check

Arts & Crafts
• Sticky Earth Café, Cromer, T01263-519642.

Cinemas
• Hollywood, Dereham, T01362-691133.
• Hollywood, Fakenham, T01328-856765.
• Hollywood, Great Yarmouth, T01493-852600.
• Majestic, King's Lynn, T01553-772603.
• Odeon, Norwich, T0871-224 4007.

Circus
• Hippodrome Circus, Great Yarmouth, T01493-844172.

Indoor play & amusements
• Aylsham Fun Barns, Aylsham, T01263-734108.
• Captain Willie's Soft Play, Hunstanton, T01485-536019.
• Elephant Playbarn, Knapton, nr Mundesley, T01263-721080.
• Funstop, Cromer, T01263-51497.
• Playland, Wells-next-the-Sea, T01328-711656.
• Run Wild, North Walsham, T01692-500666.

Indoor swimming pools
• Oasis, Hunstanton, T01485-534227.
• Pinewood Park, Sheringham, T01263-821208.

Museums
• Cromer Museum, T01263-513543.
• Elizabethan House, see page 184.
• Shell Museum, Glandford, nr Holt, T01263-740081.
• Time and Tide, see page 184.

Ten-pin bowling
• Wellington Pier, Great Yarmouth, T01493-843635.

Out & about North Norfolk

Animal Ark

Great Witchingham, T01603-872274, theanimalark.org. Easter-Nov, daily from 1000, £6.50/adult, £5.50/child. Always a winning combination, the well-run Animal Ark has a good mix of adventure play and farm animals, with a few 'exotics' like wallabies and parakeets.

Bure Valley Steam Railway

Aylsham, T01263-733858, bvrw. co.uk. Year round, return fares £11/ adult, £6/child (5-16), £29/family. A fun way to arrive in the Broads, this 15-inch-gauge line runs 9 miles between Aylsham and Wroxham. Train- and boat-ride combo tickets are available.

Elizabethan House Museum

Great Yarmouth, T01493-855746, nationaltrust.org.uk. Apr-Oct, daily 1315-1700, call for admission prices. A lesson in history that kids will love, this hands-on museum explores life in a 19th-century scullery and investigates the skulduggery surrounding the trial and execution of Charles I.

Gressenhall Farm

Nr Dereham, T01362-869263, museums.norfolk.gov.uk. Year round, daily from 1000. £8.10/adult, £5.80/child (4-16). Through good times and hard times, Norfolk is alive and kicking at this superb museum where you can dress up in the Victorian Workhouse (and get goosebumps in its punishment cell), take a cart ride around a traditional farm and then hurtle back to the future at the woodland playground.

North Norfolk Railway

Sheringham, T01263-820800 (T01263-820808 for talking timetable), nnr.co.uk. £10.50/adult, £7/child (5-15), £35/family. Stepping on to the platform at Sheringham is like being transported into an old movie. The restored 1950's station is a gem with piles of old trunks and other memorabilia. Add a magnificent steam train and you're set for nostalgic nirvana as you ride the scenic Poppy Line 5.5 miles to Holt, stopping at Weybourne and Kelling Heath.

Sea Life Great Yarmouth

T0871-4232110, sealifeeurope. com. Year round, daily from 1000, £12.55/adult, £9.50/child (3-14), check online for offers. Jellyfish, sharks, turtles, rays, seahorses – they're all here at this water-wonderland where touchpools, a sea-life nursery and SOS (Save our Seas) display help to get across marine conservation issues.

Sheringham Park

Upper Sheringham, T01263-820550, nationaltrust.org.uk. Garden year-round, daily, dawn-dusk; visitor centre Mar-Oct, daily 1000-1700, plus weekends in winter. £4/car. A riot of rhododendron blossom in May and June, Sheringham Park has trails (including a link to the North Norfolk Railway station at Weybourne), viewing towers and interactive displays in the visitor centre.

Time and Tide Museum

Great Yarmouth, T01493-743930, museums.norfolk.gov.uk. Year round, daily from 1000, £5.20/adult, £3.80/ child (4-16). Great Yarmouth's maritime heritage brought to life through hands-on displays and activities.

Wells & Walsingham Railway

Wells-next the-Sea, T01328-711630, wellswalsinghamrailway.co.uk. Mar-Nov, daily, times vary, return fares £7.50/adult, £6/child (4-14). Narrow gauge steam railway running 30 minutes between Wells and Walsingham.

Welney Wetland Centre

Welney, nr Wisbech, T01353-860711, wwt.org.uk. Daily for 0930 (summer) and 1000 (winter), £6.30/adult, £3.10/child (4-16), £16.90/family. Huge wetland renowned for its overwintering whooper and Bewick's swans. Floodlit swan feeds take place Nov-Feb, while other activities include pond-dipping (Apr-Oct), family trails and a Fenland Discovery Area in the innovative visitor centre.

Pick up a free copy of the *Broadcaster* for details of family events run by the Broads Authority.

See the seals

Beans Boat Trips
Blakeney, T01263-740505
or Morston, T01263-740038,
beansboattrips.co.uk.

Bishop's Boats
Blakeney, T08000-740754,
norfolksealtrips.co.uk.

Roy Moreton Seal Trips
Blakeney, T01263-740792,
roymoretonsealtrips.co.uk.

Temples
Morston, T01263-740791,
sealtrips.co.uk.

Trips operate daily, Feb–early Nov,
£8/adult, £4/child (under 14).
Advance booking recommended
during summer holidays. Tickets
usually need to be collected from
Blakeney Quay, a 30-minute walk
or 5-minute drive to Morston
Quay from where boats depart.
For Temples boat trips, collect
tickets from The Anchor Pub in
Morston village. Most trips operate
in traditional clinker-build boats
with little or no protection from
the elements, so remember to take
warm, weatherproof clothing.

Grey seals frolicking in the shallows at Blakeney Point.

Managed by the National Trust (nationaltrust.org.uk), Blakeney National Nature Reserve provides one of Britain's best wildlife-watching spectacles for families. Not only is the 3.5-mile spit of sand and shingle a favourite haul-out for both common and grey seals, but it's also an internationally important nesting site for no less than four species of tern – arctic, common, little and sandwich. What makes this mass gathering of flab and feathers all the more riveting is that to see it up-close you don't have to gag the kids and creep into a hide. Boat trips operating from Morston Quay take you to within a whisker of the seals. Those that aren't flopping on the beach will often approach to within a few metres, while the terns – also unfazed by the boats – are busy fussing over their eggs and chicks or dive-bombing fish.

There's a colony of around 500 seals at Blakeney Point, but numbers fluctuate throughout the year. Common seals give birth on remote sandbanks during summer, the fluffy white torpedoes most abundant during June or July. Four weeks later, after being weaned, the seals return to Blakeney Point ready for mating in September. Grey seals (which, confusingly, are more common) give birth in November and December. You can tell the two species apart by peering at their noses – common seals have V-shaped nostrils, while grey seals have W-shaped nostrils. Common seals are also slightly smaller than grey seals and have cuter, more rounded faces.

The terns' breeding season is from April to July when you should also be able to spot other nesting birds, such as oystercatchers and ringed plovers. In autumn and winter, look out for brent geese, wigeon, dunlin and curlew.

Boat trips usually last about an hour – longer if the tides allow a landing on the reserve where you can tiptoe amongst the rare shingle vegetation and visit the old lifeboat house which has displays inside. There's an information centre, café and toilets at Morston Quay.

Sleeping North Norfolk

Pick of the pitches

Clippesby Hall

Nr Great Yarmouth, T01493-367800, clippesby.com. Apr-Oct, £10.50-25/pitch (2 people), plus £5/extra adult, £2.50/extra child.

With its family pub, crazy golf, café and swimming pool, Clippesby Hall has shades of a holiday park, but manages to retain the feel of a relaxed, rural campsite. That's largely due to the secluded pitches scattered around the manor's 30-acre patchwork of woods and parkland. Cedar Lawn, for example, has open glades for children to play in, while The Rabbits Grove, hidden amongst mature trees, is ideal for wildlife lovers. A bike-hire centre makes exploring the Broads a piece of cake, while Great Yarmouth, if you want it, is just 10 miles away.

Deepdale Farm

Burnham Deepdale, T01485-210256, deepdalefarm.co.uk. Year round, camping £4.50-9/adult, £2.50-5/child; tipis £40-80/nt (1-2 people), £72-114/nt (3-6 people).

An eco-friendly budget bolthole on the North Norfolk coastline, Deepdale Farm has five camping paddocks (for tents and small campervans), a backpackers' hostel (with family rooms) and a smattering of tipis (with faux fur sleeping mats and chimineas). A strict noise policy maintains an air of tranquillity at this lovely village site. Local beaches, Brancaster and Holkham (see page 178) are two of Norfolk's finest, while next door the Deepdale Café (T01485-211055, deepdalecafe.co.uk, daily 0730-1600) will set you up with a cooked breakfast, snack, coffee and croissant or a picnic lunch.

Deer's Glade

Hanworth, T01263-768633, deersglade.co.uk. Year round, nightly rates £5.25-7.75/adult, £2-3/child, £14.50-19.50/family.

A level, sheltered site with immaculate facilities, Deer's Glade scooped a David Bellamy Gold Conservation Award in 2008. You can spot deer on woodland walks (or even see them wandering past your tent). A fishing lake and cycle hire are nice extras, while Muntjac Meadow (Aug only) offers basic pitches for tents with a communal campfire each night.

Also recommended

Forest Park

Cromer, T01263-513290, forest-park.co.uk.

Searles Leisure Resort

Hunstanton, T01485-534211, searles.co.uk.

West Runton Camping & Caravanning Club Site

West Runton, T01263-837544, campingandcaravanningclub.co.uk.

Cottage agents

County & Coast
Cromer, T01263-513139, countyandcoast.co.uk.
Cottages in and around Cromer.

Countryside Cottages
Holt, T01263-713133, holiday-cottage-norfolk.co.uk.
High quality, character cottages.

Farm Stay East Anglia
T01359-231013, farmstayanglia.co.uk.
Eighty farms offering B&B and self-catering accommodation.

Kett Country Cottages
Fakenham, T01328-856853, kettcountrycottages.co.uk.

Keys Holidays
Sheringham, T01263-823010, keys-holidays.co.uk.

Norfolk Country Cottages
Holt, T01263-715779, norfolkcottages.co.uk.

Boating holidays

Hoseasons Boating in Britain
T0844-499 0088, hoseasons.co.uk.

Le Boat T0844-463 3593, leboat.co.uk.

Maffett Cruisers T01508-520344, maffett-cruisers.com.

Moore & Co T01603-783311, boatingholidays.co.uk.

Pacific Cruisers T01508-520321, pacificcruisers.co.uk

Richardson's T01692-582277, richardsonsgroup.net.

Waterways Holidays
T0845-127 0050, waterwaysholidays.co.uk.

Cley Windmill
Cley-next-the-Sea, T01263-740209, cleywindmill.co.uk. Self-catering £385-530/wk, B&B £78-155/room, plus £20/child (under 12) sharing with parents. Wheel, Stone and Wheat rooms not suitable for young families.
Teetering over reedbeds and just a few minutes from the sea as the bittern flies, Cley Windmill is the original master of spin – a magnificent 18th-century windmill offering Norfolk's most unique (and sought after) B&B and self-catering accommodation, along with fine dining. Sleeping four, the snug, flint-walled Dovecote cottage is adjacent to the Mill's garden and has two doubles, a bathroom and open-plan kitchen and living area. For B&B you can choose cosy circular rooms in the mill itself or go for the square Barley Bin, Miller's Room, River Room or converted boathouse.

Best of the rest

Kelling Heath
Weybourne, T01263-588181, kellingheath.co.uk. Mar-Dec, two-bedroom lodge £484-1220/wk, three-bedroom lodge £558-1362/wk, holiday homes £237-753/wk. Short breaks and camping also available.
The timber lodges and holiday homes are pretty snazzy, but it's the great outdoors that makes Kelling Heath special – 250 acres of woodland and heathland to explore on foot, by bike or as part of the excellent Acorn programme which includes activities such as pond-dipping, bat walks, bushcraft and kite-flying. There's also a children's adventure playground, assault course, cycle-hire centre, indoor and outdoor pools, health centre and a smart Village Square with restaurants, shops and evening entertainment.

Also recommended
Ivy Farm Holiday Park
Cromer, T01263-579239, ivy-farm.co.uk.

Pinewoods
Wells-next-the-Sea, T01328-710439, pinewoods.co.uk.

Weybourne Forest Lodges
Weybourne, T01263-588440, weybourneforestlodges.co.uk.

Canoe Trails

The Canoe Man
T07810-838052, thecanoeman. com. Weekend packages from £80/person.
Explore the peaceful backwaters of the Broads, paddling a canoe on an overnight expedition, gliding silently past wildlife and delving into the parts that motorboats can't reach. A weekend package includes canoe hire, transport to and from your start and finish points, camping or B&B accommodation, tuition and a route map. The Canadian canoes can easily accommodate two adults and two children, plus all your camping gear and luggage. Guided and unguided trips are available and you can also hire canoes from £40/day.

Eating North Norfolk

Local goodies

Bircham Windmill
See page 180 for contact details, opening times and bicycle hire. Although the mill finally ground to a halt in the 1920s, Bircham Windmill's original bakery still gets fired up for a tasty range of breads and cakes. Children can have a go at baking rolls and mini-loaves, daily 1000-1300.

Cley's Smokehouse
Cley, T01263-740282, cleysmokehouse.com. Herring, slit in two, gutted and cleaned, brined, then smoked over oak – you've got to try traditional North Norfolk kippers and this is the place to get 'em.

Cookies Crab Shop
Salthouse, T01263-740352, cookies. shopkeepers.co.uk. Daily, 0900-1900 (summer), 1000-1600 (winter). Crabs, prawns and fish, straight off the boats and into salads and sarnies to take away or eat in.

Docwras Rock Factory
Great Yarmouth, T01493-844676. Heaven for kids, hell for dentists, the world's largest rock shop churns out 80,000 sticks of the molar-cracking stuff every week.

Picnic Fayre
Cley, T01263-740587, picnic-fayre.co.uk. Mon-Sat 0900-1700, Sun 1100-1600. The ultimate picnic pick 'n' mix, this irresistble deli has speciality bread, cheese, chutney and jam.

Also recommended
The Fish Shed
Brancaster Staithe, T01485-210352. Fresh fish and sushi to go.

The Humble Pie
Burnham Market, T01328-738581. Goodies galore in gold-star deli.

Walsingham Farms Shop
Little Walsingham, T01328-821877. The best of local seasonal fare.

Wells Deli
Wells-next-the-Sea, T01328-711171. Quayside deli selling paninis, sandwiches, drinks and snacks.

Look out for local ice cream, such as **Norfolk Farmhouse**, **Parravani's** and **Ronaldo's**.

Quick & simple

The Old Barn Restaurant Café
Wroxham Barns, Hoveton, T01603-783762, wroxhambarns.co.uk. Daily 1000-1700. Worth a visit for its local crafts and children's farm as much as for its food, Wroxham Barns has a fudge shop and country food store as well as a friendly restaurant serving cream teas (£6.95), snacks and main meals. The kids' menu has traditional favourites like bangers and mash for £5.25, while local dishes like smoked haddock chowder cost around £9.

Also recommended
Deepdale Café See page 186.

Posh nosh

The White Horse
Brancaster, T01485-210262, whitehorsebrancaster.co.uk. Daily, 1200-1430, 1900-2130. With mesmerising views across tidal marshes and beyond to Scolt Head Island, there's no better place to enjoy fine, local cuisine than the conservatory restaurant and sun terrace at The White Horse. Local mussels poached in white wine, cream and parsley costs from £7.50, while kids can tuck into salmon fishcake, chips and peas (£4.25).

Bolton's Bistro
Cromer, T01263-512543. Daily, 1200-1400, 1800-2200. Seafood, steaks and salads on the seafront.

Market days
Cromer Fri.
Fakenham Thu and 4th Sat.
North Walsham Thu.
Sheringham Wed (Easter-Oct) and Sat.
Stalham Tue and Sat (twice monthly).

Fish & chips
Battered to perfection, top fryers in North Norfolk include **Daves** (High St, Sheringham), **Downham Fryer** (Bridge St, Downham Market), **Mary Jane's** (Garden St, Cromer) and **The Three Cottages** (Bacton Rd, North Walsham).

Essentials North Norfolk

Getting there
By train National Express East Anglia (T0845-600 7245, nationalexpresseastanglia.com) operates trains from London to Norwich, Great Yarmouth and Sheringham, while First Capital Connect (T0845-026 4700, firstcapitalconnect.co.uk) runs from London to King's Lynn.
By coach Daily services with National Express (T0871-781 8181, nationalexpress.com) link London with several Norfolk destinations, including Cromer, Sheringham, Holt and Fakenham.

Getting around
By train The Bittern Line (T08700-409090, bitternline.com) runs daily from Norwich to Salhouse, Hoveton & Wroxham, Worstead, North Walsham, Gunton, Roughton Road, Cromer, West Runton and Sheringham. Ideas for walks and cycles are available for each station. Offering unlimited travel on Bittern Line trains, plus travel on CoastHopper buses (see below), the Bittern Rover costs £7/adult and £3.50/child, available any time at weekends and after 0845 weekdays.
By bus Norfolk Green (T01553-776980, norfolkgreen.co.uk) operates CoastHopper buses year round (hourly during summer and on a two-hour basis at other times) between Cromer and Hunstanton (£5.40/adult, £3.60/child), providing a useful link to north coast highlights as well as sections of the Norfolk Coast Path

(nationaltrail.co.uk/peddarsway). Family tickets are available for twice the adult fare plus £1. Norfolk Green also runs buses from Norwich and King's Lynn.

Maps
Ordnance Survey Explorer maps 250 (King's Lynn & Hunstanton), 251 (Wells-next-the-Sea & Fakenham), 252 (Cromer & North Walsham), OL40 (Broads) and Landranger maps 132 and 133.

Tourist Information Centres
Cromer The North Norfolk Information Centre (Louden Rd, T0871-200 3071, visitnorthnorfolk.com, daily, from 1000) is the region's flagship TIC.
Aylsham Bure Valley Railway Station, T01263-733903.
Great Yarmouth Maritime House, T01493-846345.
Holt Market Place. T0871-200 3071.
Hoveton Station Road, T01603-782281, broads-authority.gov.uk.
Hunstanton Town Hall, T01485-532610.
King's Lynn The Custom House, T01553-763044.
Norwich The Forum, T01603-213999, visitnorwich.co.uk.
Sheringham Station Approach, T0871-200 3071.
Wells-next-the-Sea Staithe St, T0871-200 3071.

Hospital
Norfolk & Norwich University Hospital, T01603-286286.
Cromer Hospital, T01263-513571.

Pharmacies
Aylsham Lloyds, Market Place.
Cromer Lloyds, Church St.
Hunstanton Boots, High St.
Sheringham Alliance, High St.
Hoveton Roys, Station Rd.

Supermarkets
Aylsham Budgens, Somerfield.
Cromer Rainbow, Morrison.
Fakenham Budgens, Morrison, Rainbow, Tesco.
Great Yarmouth Asda, Budgens, Sainsbury's, Tesco.
Hunstanton Rainbow, Tesco.
Norwich Budgens, Morrison, Sainsbury's, Tesco, Waitrose.
Wells-next-the-Sea Leftley's.

Other shops
Baby supplies Babyland, Wendover Rd, Rackheath; Youngster's World, Norfolk St, King's Lynn.
Camping supplies Cotswold Outdoor, Theatre St, Norwich.
Toys & beach gear Toys R Us, Norwich; Roys Toys, Stalham Rd, Wroxham; Starlings Toymaster, Wrights Walk, Dereham.

Environmental groups
Norfolk Wildlife Trust, norfolkwildlifetrust.org.uk.

Major Events
Jun-Sep Cromer Seaside Special.
Jul Lobster Potty Festival, Sheringham.
Jul Worstead Festival.
Aug Carnivals in Cromer, Wells and Sheringham.
Aug Wells Regatta.

Whitby.

Contents

192 Map

194 Peak District
195 Blackpool
195 Manchester
195 Liverpool
195 Durham
195 Newcastle

196 Yorkshire
198 Fun & free
200 Best beaches
202 Action stations
204 Big days out
208 Sleeping
211 Eating
213 Essentials

214 Lake District
216 Fun & free
220 Action stations
222 Big days out
224 Sleeping
227 Eating
229 Essentials

230 Northumberland

North England

Big days out...

1 Castle Howard
2 The Deep
3 Eureka!
4 Flamingo Land
5 Jorvik Viking Centre
6 The Forbidden Corner
7 Fountains Abbey
8 North Yorkshire Moors Railway
9 Scarborough Sea Life
10 Bempton Cliffs RSPB Reserve
11 Eden Camp
12 Harewood House
13 Murton Park
14 Scarborough Castle
15 York Maze
16 Aquarium of the Lakes
17 Lakeside & Haverthwaite Railway
18 Honister Slate Mine
19 Mirehouse
20 Muncaster
21 Ravenglass & Eskdale Railway
22 Cars of the Stars
23 Trotters World of Animals
24 The World of Beatrix Potter

North Sea

Morpeth

Newcastle
Gateshead

Sunderland

Easington

Hartlepool

ockton-
n-Tees
Middlesbrough

arlington

Whitby

North York Moors

Osmotherley

Pickering

Helmsley

Thornton-
le-Dale

Thirsk

Malton

Filey

Bridlington

York

EAST RIDING
OF YORKSHIRE

Beverley

Kingston
upon Hull

Barton-upon-Humber

Scunthorpe

NORTH LINCOLNSHIRE

Grimsby

Doncaster

Nettleton

Waddingham

Gainsborough

Market
Rasen

Louth

heffield

hesterfield

Lincoln

Horncastle

Ashby
by Partney

Skegness

NOTTINGHAMSHIRE

LINCOLNSHIRE

Mansfield

Newark-on-
Trent

Sleaford

Boston

Wells-next-
the-Sea

Cromer

Ambergate

erby

Nottingham

Donnington

Sandringham

Fakenham

Erpingham

Happisburgh

Castle
Donnington

Melton
Mowbray

Grantham

Spalding

Holbeach

King's Lynn

NORFOLK

EICESTERSHIRE

Empingham

Stamford

Swaffham

Norwich

Great
Yarmouth

eds

York

Harrogate

rewood

Thirsk

Ripon

Newcastle

Gateshead

Morpeth

Motorway
Primary route
A Road
Airports
Ferries

Leeds

Wakefield

Selby

Harewood

Numberland
AONB

Great escapes

Peak District

Designated Britain's first national park in 1951, the heather-clad moors and wooded valleys of the Peak District are ideal stomping grounds for active families. The **Peak District National Park Authority** (peakdistrict.org) operates visitor centres in the Upper Derwent Valley and Edale (the flagship Moorland Centre) where you can find out about the landscapes and wildlife of the national park and plan walks and picnics.

A good spot to break in the boots of mini-trekkers, **Ilam Park** (nationaltrust.org.uk) is within easy walking distance of Dovedale, where kids can have fun crossing the famous stepping stones.

The national park also has several family-friendly cycle rides. The Monsal Trail runs from Bakewell to Blackwell Mill, while the Tissington Trail follows an old railway line from Ashbourne where you can hire bikes from **Peak Cycle Hire** (peakcyclehire.com) for the easy 3-mile ride to the village of Tissington. Just to the west, the Manifold Track covers 9 miles between Waterhouses (hire bikes at Brown End Farm) and Hulme End, passing Thror's Cave – a bolt-hole for Stone Age man.

The limestone of the Peak District is riddled with show caves, including **Treak Cliff Cavern** (bluejohnstone.com) near Castleton, where guided tours reveal the source of Blue John Stone (a rare form of fluorspar) and chambers studded with fossils and spiked with stalactites and stalagmites. Nearby **Peak Cavern** (peakcavern.co.uk) boasts the largest natural cave entrance in Britain, while **Speedwell Cavern** (speedwellcavern.co.uk) can be explored on an exciting underground boat ride.

There are more subterranean shenanigans at the **Heights of Abraham** (heightsofabraham.com) where a return ticket on the gondola ride gets you free entry to a hilltop park with show caves, woodland trails, café and fossil shop.

Back down to earth (and not delving into it) the vintage trams at **Crich Tramway Village** (tramway.co.uk) trundle along cobbled streets and out into the open countryside for spectacular views. There's also a woodland walk and sculpture trail here.

Other family favourites in the Peak District include the farmyard and adventure playground at **Chatsworth** (chatsworth.org), the **Museum of Childhood at Sudbury Hall** (nationaltrust.org.uk) and **Gulliver's Kingdom** (gulliversfun.co.uk), a theme park at Matlock Bath for children aged 2-13.
>> visitpeakdistrict.com/trailtribe

Ilam Park.

Blackpool

The Great British family holiday was practically invented in the Lancashire seaside resort of Blackpool. Thrill-city-central, **Blackpool Pleasure Beach** (blackpoolpleasurebeach.com) has over 125 rides and attractions, including the 87-mph Pepsi Max Big One rollercoaster (see page 27). There's also Britain's largest indoor water park (sandcastle-waterworld. co.uk), an aquarium (sealifeeurope.com) and waxworks (louistussaudswaxworks.co.uk). For nostalgia mixed with fun, don't miss the iconic, 518-ft tall **Blackpool Tower** (blackpooltower.co.uk) where you'll be relieved to discover that the 2-inch glass floor at the Tower Top's Walk of Faith can withstand the weight of five baby elephants. Views, ballroom dancing, circus shows and one of Europe's largest indoor adventure playgrounds will further conspire to keep you off the beach.
>> blackpooltourism.com

Manchester

Footie fans will want to make straight for Old Trafford where the **Manchester United Museum and Stadium Tour** (manutd.com) takes you into the hallowed heart of the world's most popular football team. You can strut down the player's tunnel, drool over the trophy cabinet and sit at the dressing-room peg of your favourite player. For fancy footwork on the high street, Manchester's shops will satisfy all fashion fans, while the city's mighty industrial heritage is celebrated at the **Museum of Science and Industry** (mosi.org.uk). For family-friendly culture in Manchester, you can't beat the galleries and theatres of **The Lowry** (thelowry.com).
>> visitmanchester.com

Liverpool

Not to be outdone by the likes of Rooney et al, the **Liverpool FC Museum and Stadium Tour** (liverpoolfc. tv) pays homage to The Reds. But there's another attraction in Merseyside's great city that overshadows even football. Your kids may never have heard of The Beatles, but that's no reason why you shouldn't at least attempt to improve their music tastes. Of the many 'Fab Four' tours and attractions, your best bet with kids is **The Beatles Story** (beatlesstory.com) which now has an interactive Discovery Zone where kids can create their own newspaper and play a Beatles tune on a giant piano. From rocking the world to exploring new ones, **Spaceport** (spaceport.org.uk) at Seacombe on the Wirral (ride the Mersey ferry to get there) takes you

Durham

Dominated by its fine Norman cathedral and castle, Durham (durhamtourism.co.uk) has gentle woodland paths and rowing boats to hire on the River Wear. The open-air museum at **Beamish** (beamish.org. uk) recreates life in the northeast prior to the First World War, complete with a farm, railway, high street and coal mine.

on a virtual journey through the cosmos. The nearby **Blue Planet Aquarium** (blueplanetaquarium.com) has a moving walkway through a 230-ft underwater tunnel, a nifty new nautilus exhibit and Bubblemaker diving courses for children aged 8-15. Further south, **Chester Zoo** (chesterzoo.org) has imaginative and educational enclosures, such as Realm of the Red Ape – a little piece of Indonesian rainforest that's home to a family of endangered orang-utans. Highlights north of Liverpool include the beaches, dunes and red squirrel reserve at **Formby Point** (nationaltrust.org.uk) and **Splash World** (splashworldsouthport.com), a water park at Southport with slides, fountains and a lazy river ride.
>> visitliverpool.com

Newcastle

The Centre for Children's Books, **Seven Stories** (sevenstories.org.uk) uses workshops, crafts, dressing-up and story-telling to spark the imagination of even the most reluctant young readers, while the high-tech **Centre for Life** (life.org.uk) has a planetarium and 3D Motion Ride cinema. One of the best days out from Newcastle, **Hadrian's Wall** (hadrians-wall.org, see also page 235) snakes 73 miles across northern England. Easily reached by metro from the city, **Segedunum Roman Fort** (twmuseums.org.uk) once guarded the eastern end of the Wall. Reconstructions and an interactive museum reveal what life was like for the garrison of 600 soldiers. Touring Hadrian's Wall west of Newcastle is straightforward – just follow the B6318 which signposts all the major sites, such as **Vindolanda** (vindolanda.com) and **Housesteads Fort and Museum** (english-heritage.org.uk).
>> visitnewcastlegateshead.com

Main photo: Robin
Hood's Bay. Abo
right: York Minster.

Yorkshire

The Moors and Dales, Scarborough, Whitby and York. Not bad for starters, but delve deeper into this right-grand county and you'll also discover a dinosaur coast, cliffs swarming with seabirds, vast forests, a lost Viking city, iconic steam trains and one of the world's most breathtaking aquariums.

Yorkshire is big, beautiful and bewildering. Huge swathes are designated as national parks, areas of outstanding natural beauty or heritage coast. For family holidays, though, the county's heather-honeypot has to be the North York Moors – a sweet concoction of coast, forest and moorland. A single day in this national park could easily be divided between rock-pooling at **Robin Hood's Bay** and a picnic at **Danby** in the Esk Valley; you could hike or cycle in **Dalby Forest**, stroll through honey-stone villages like **Thornton-le-Dale** or ride the North Yorkshire Moors Railway between the market town of **Pickering** and the fish-and-chip mecca of picturesque **Whitby**.

Stretching from **Boulby** to **Cloughton**, Yorkshire's heritage coast forms a series of towering cliffs (rich in Jurassic fossils), rocky coves and sweeping bays – a suitably rugged finale to the North York Moors National Park where it plunges into the North Sea. Further south lie the popular family resorts of **Scarborough** and **Filey**, their sandy beaches giving way to chalky, gannet-festooned cliffs at **Bempton**. Nearby **Bridlington** marks the start of a great scoop of coastline reaching down to the mouth of the Humber where The Deep aquarium in **Hull** takes you on an unforgettable undersea journey.

Underground is the best way for kids to explore **York**. Delve into the Jorvik Viking Centre and DIG, and they'll get a hands-on insight into the city's remarkable 2000-year-old history. The National Railway Museum, meanwhile, has to rank as Yorkshire's best free attraction.

West of York, **Harrogate**, **Ripon** and **Skipton** are southern gateways to the Yorkshire Dales National Park where gentle river valleys nuzzle stark limestone hills. They might lack the coastal appeal of the North York Moors, but the Dales more than compensate with superb walking and must-see attractions, like Fountains Abbey and The Forbidden Corner.

South of the Dales, the Yorkshire Pennines offer woodland walks at Hardcastle Crags near **Hebden Bridge**, while **Halifax** is home to the innovative children's museum, Eureka!

You must

- Go viking at Jorvik Viking Centre in York.

- Spy on the gannets at Bempton Cliffs.

- Hike or bike in the Dales.

- Go fossil-hunting on the heritage coast.

- Eat fish and chips with mushy peas in Whitby.

- Join a ranger activity in Dalby or Cropton Forest.

- Visit The Deep in Hull.

- Explore Robin Hood's Bay.

- Picnic in the Esk Valley.

- Ride a steam train across the North York Moors.

Out & about Yorkshire

Fun & free

Find a shore thing

Robin Hood's Bay (see page 200) is the place to go for hermit crabs, starfish, gobies and other rock-pool critters. While you're there, don't forget to visit the Old Coastguard Station (daily during school holidays, free entry) which has an aquarium full of all the things you'd like to net. Binoculars and telescopes are also available for scanning the rocky shore for wading birds and, if you're lucky, a seal or two.

Follow the fish trail

A pavement sculpture trail of life-size fish, Hull's Seven Seas Fish Trail starts at the tourist information centre (trail leaflets cost £0.40) and sends you casting for clues through the old town and down to the riverfront. Find all 41 sculptures (from diminutive anchovies to a 10-ft ray) and you'll receive a certificate. The shark, naturally, is to be found outside a bank.

Bound over barmy boulders

There's nowt so strange as Brimham Rocks in Nidderdale, near Harrogate. These weird and wonderful formations sprout from the moor like giant stone mushrooms – perfect for picnics, hide-and-seek and boulder-hopping. Equally curious are the Bridestones in the North York Moors National Park.

Track down a dinosaur

Yorkshire's Dinosaur Coast is a hotbed of Jurassic and Cretaceous fossils. The chalk that forms the 400-ft-high cliffs at Flamborough, for example, was deposited 100 million years ago in a subtropical sea inhabited by sharks and marine reptiles – scour the beach at South Landing for fossil teeth, as well as sea urchins and ammonites.

The old limestone quarries at Forge Valley Woods National Nature Reserve (just inland from Scarborough) are ideal hunting grounds for Upper Jurassic ammonites and plesiosaurs.

Further north, between Scalby and Ravenscar, sandstone from the Middle Jurassic reveals fossils of ferns and cycads, as well as reptilian footprints – evidence that Yorkshire, 150-180 million years ago, was a lush floodplain roamed by dinosaurs.

The Lower Jurassic, exposed at Whitby and Robin Hood's Bay, is rich in shales and limestones containing fossils of ammonites, belemnites, crinoids and some of the coast's best preserved icthyosaurs and plesiosaurs.

Scarborough and Whitby Museums have fossil displays, while the Dinosaur Coast partnership (T01723-384503, dinocoast.org.uk) organises family fun days and fossil hunts.

Walk this way

Everyone loves to stride out on the Moors and Dales, but don't overlook Ogden Water (ogdenwater.org.uk) and Hardcastle Crags (nationaltrust. org.uk) – two excellent family walking locations near Halifax.

Visit The National Railway Museum

Why? Because it's the one of the few places in Britain where train-spotting is really cool. The Great Hall is a shrine to iconic locos like the Mallard (world's fastest steam train), the Japanese Bullet and a replica of Stevenson's Rocket. Other highlights include the giant Chinese locomotive and Queen Victoria's royal carriage. There's also a Flying Scotsman workshop and a simulator (£3/ride) that whisks you from London to Brighton in just four minutes.

How? Open daily 1000-1800. Stoke hungry tummies at the Brief Encounter restaurant or Signal Box café and don't miss the Thomas gift shop. Children can also let off steam in the outdoor playground.

Contact The National Railway Museum, York, T08448-153139, nrm.org.uk.

Terrific trio – Mallard, Bullet and Thomas.

Explore moor

North York Moors National Park
visitthemoors.co.uk.

The Moors National Park Centre
Nr Danby, Esk Valley,
T01439-772737.

Sutton Bank National Park Centre
Nr Thirsk, T01845-597426.

Both centres:
Apr-Oct, daily 1000-1700;
Nov, Dec & Mar, daily 1030-1530;
Jan-Feb, weekends 1030-1530.

Information can also be found at
the Old Coastguard Station in Robin
Hood's Bay, the Dalby Forest Visitor
Centre (see page 203) and the
Pinchinthorpe Visitor Centre.

The North York Moors is one of Britain's most diverse national parks. You'd
expect to find plenty of heather moorland (and you won't be disappointed),
but the 554-square-mile national park also includes picnic-perfect dales, the
best slice of Yorkshire's coast and healthy dollops of forest.

With so much to see and do, start by getting your bearings at one of
the park's visitor centres (see left). The Moors Centre is particularly good for
families and makes a great day out in its own right. Inside, there's an engaging
exhibition with lots for children to get their hands on. They can stroke models
of the North York Moors 'Big Five' (merlin, red grouse, curlew, golden plover
and lapwing) to hear their distinctive calls, make brass rubbings of an otter
and hone their skills on a climbing wall. The centre's beautiful grounds,
meanwhile, have a sculpture trail (look out for the giant willow otters), a
riverside walk and adventure playground. Daily events and activities (usually
involving a small charge) are chalked up on a board and can include anything
from a teddy bears' picnic to lessons in bushcraft. The National Park Authority
also publishes an annual events guide, while walking leaflets are available at
any of the information centres.

Five family-friendly walks

1 hr	**Thornton le Dale–Ellerburn**	Gentle 2-mile circuit from one of the Moors' prettiest villages.
2 hr	**Castleton–Commondale**	Easy 2.5-mile walk; return the same way or use the Esk Valley Railway.
2 hr	**Farndale**	Follow the banks of the River Dove 2.5 miles from Low Mill to Church Houses.
3 hr	**Bilsdale–Urra Moor**	Five-mile yomp across the national park's highest moors.
4 hr	**Helmsley–Rievaulx Abbey**	Six-mile jaunt through woods and fields. Catch the Moorsbus back.

The Moors Centre – wildlife inside and out.

Out & about Yorkshire

Bridlington North Beach

British seaside at its most traditional, Bridlington's sand and pebble beach comes with a full supporting cast of amusement arcades, fairground rides, crazy golf, indoor leisure pool and the nostalgic Beside the Seaside Museum for those who like to roll up their trouser legs for a paddle in the past. Across the bay loom the chalk cliffs of Flamborough Head, best viewed on boat trips from Bridlington Harbour (see page 202). Popular watersports at Bridlington include canoeing, sailing and windsurfing. About 2 miles south of Bridlington, the sandy beach at Fraisthorpe is popular with naturists.

Filey

One of the best stretches of sand on the Yorkshire coast, Filey's 5-mile golden strand is the perfect beach for sandcastles, beach cricket, kite flying and even surfing when conditions are right. There are deckchairs on the prom, donkeys on the beach and rock pools towards the northern end of the bay at Filey Brigg. To the south, meanwhile, Reighton Sands is overlooked by several holiday parks perched on the cliffs above.

Hornsea

The coastline south of Bridlington is less visited than more scenic bays like Filey and Scarborough to the north, but Hornsea (and Withernsea, even further south) still come up trumps for those in search of fine sand, good swimming and a lively promenade.

Robin Hood's Bay

If Filey and Whitby are Yorkshire's quintessential seaside resorts, then Robin Hood's Bay is its cutesy smugglers' cove. Clinging to a steep hillside like a random stack of Mega Bloks, the delightful, red-roofed fishing village spills onto a slipway where visitors are funnelled into the vast expanse of the bay. Don't expect much in the way of sand. Robin Hood's Bay is largely composed of rocky reefs which, at low tide, become studded with pools. There simply isn't a better place in the entire North East to wield a shrimping net – and you can find out what to look for by perusing the aquarium in the Old Coastguard Station. First, however, you need to reach the beach. Car parks are located at the top of the village, from where it's a steep walk down a cobblestone street winding between irresistible shops like Browns with its chocolate fountain and shelves laden with sweets. Finally, you come to the slipway where The Bay Hotel once famously had its windows smashed by a ship that got too close. Bear right for the best of what sand there is. Donkey rides are available, but at £2 for a stingy couple of minutes you're better off saving your money for a strawberry and marshmallow kebab drenched in chocolate from Browns. You can always compensate by cycling to Robin Hood's Bay along the disused railway track between Whitby and Scarborough – see page 202.

Runswick Bay

Like Robin Hood's Bay, left, Runswick is one of Yorkshire's favourite coastal pin-ups with honey-coloured stone cottages cascading down a hillside onto a mile-wide arc of sand. And that's about it – there's no promenade, no donkeys, no deckchairs; just a lovely unspoilt beach where days are wiled away with simple pleasures like picnics, rock-pooling and beachcombing. Keep your eyes peeled for ammonites, belemnites and fragments of fossil wood (Yorkshire's famous jet) that are often exhumed from the cliffs after a downpour or heavy seas.

Sandsend

A small, picturesque fishing village, 2 miles north of Whitby, Sandsend is a good place for rock-pooling and fossil-hunting. Surfers rank it as one of the best spots on the Yorkshire coast, while families with young children stick to the shallow, placid waters of the estuary.

Scarborough North Bay

There's everything here for a relaxed, if often crowded, family day at the beach. Sandcastle-builders can find inspiration in the ruins of the Norman fort that preside over the beach, while sporty types can go body-boarding or crazy-golfing. The historic miniature railway and water chute (nbr.org.uk) are as popular as ever, while the Sea Life centre (page 206) could occupy you for most of a day.

Staithes

Crab-pot boats still set out from this once vibrant fishing port, but surfers now claim the waves are the biggest catch. A small sandy beach emerges at low tide, along with a large expanse of rock or scar – definitely worth a shrimping expedition. You can also join a boat trip to spot seals or go fishing.

Tunstall

A quiet, sandy beach midway between the resorts of Hornsea and Withernsea, Tunstall is good for paddling, swimming and building sandcastles.

Whitby West Cliff

Don't be put off by the long, zigzag path down to Whitby's two-mile sandy beach – you can always take the cliff lift back up. This is a deservedly popular family beach with plenty of facilities and lots going on. Other Whitby beaches include Tate Hill, a sheltered, sandy patch within the harbour. If you want rockpools, try East Cliff Flats (beyond the pier) where a large expanse of mussel-encrusted rock is exposed at low tide. The sea sweeps in quickly here, so don't wander too far.

Withernsea

Sand and shingle stretch for miles either side of this traditional seaside resort, famous for its lighthouse, but also sporting an attractively redeveloped promenade.

Robin Hood's Bay.

Clinging to a steep hillside like a random stack of Mega Bloks, the delightful red-roofed fishing village spills onto a slipway where visitors are funnelled into the vast expanse of the bay.

Out & about Yorkshire

Action stations

Boat trips
Bark Endeavour
Nr West Pier, Whitby, T07813-781034, endeavourwhitby.com. Year-round, sailing times depend on tide and weather, phone for details.

Captain James Cook began his seafaring career in Whitby where he enrolled on a Baltic Sea collier at the age of 18. Find out about the master mariner, as well as the geology and wildlife of the North Yorkshire coast as you sail on a replica of Cook's *Endeavour* – built by Whitby craftsmen at 40% of the ship's original size.

Whitby Coastal Cruises
Brewery Steps, Whitby, T07941-450381, whitbycoastalcruises.co.uk. Year-round, sailing times vary.

The 100-passenger *Esk Belle II* runs daily 25-minute boat trips along the coast towards Sandsend. Whale-watching trips operate Sep-Nov when cetaceans arrive off the coast of Whitby in pursuit of vast shoals of herring that migrate here to spawn. The most common species seen is the minke whale, but sightings of humpback and pilot whales are not unheard of.

Sea-fishing boats operate out of several harbours along the Yorkshire coast. You could also try angling from Whitby's piers. Shoals of mackerel usually arrive in June and stay throughout the summer months.

Yorkshire Belle
Bridlington, T07774-193404, yorkshire-belle.co.uk. Apr-Oct, daily. Prices vary, phone for details.

Cruises to Flamborough Head and the seabird colonies at Bempton Cliffs.

Cycling
See also Dalby Forest, opposite.

Bob Trotter Cycles
Lord Mayor's Walk, York, T01904-622868, bobtrottercycles.com. Daily from 0900. Adult bike £15/day, child's bike £13/day.

Set off along traffic-free paths beside the River Ouse or explore further afield on country roads. To the south of York, a scale model of the solar system has been created on the York–Selby cycle track, where the Sun is 2.4 m in diameter and Pluto (6 miles away) a mere 5.9 mm.

Dales Bike Centre
Fremington, T01748-884908, dalesmountainbiking.co.uk. Daily, 0900-1700, Adult bike from £18/day, trailers and tag-alongs £10/day.

A café, bike shop and hire centre rolled into one, this is the perfect base to plan a two-wheeled adventure in the Yorkshire Dales, following moorland tracks or quiet lanes.

Trailways
The Old Railway Station, Hawsker, nr Whitby, T01947-820207, trailways. info. Mar-Nov, daily from 1000. Adult bike £17/day, £14/4 hrs; child's bike £8.50/day, £7/4 hrs; tag-along £12/day, £10/4 hrs.

Cycle all or part of the 20-mile Scarborough–Whitby Rail Trail. It's just a couple of miles from Trailways to Robin Hood's Bay and 8 miles to Ravenscar. The hire centre also links into the challenging Moors to Sea route.

Watersports
Allerthorpe Lakeland Park
Nr Pocklington, T01759-301444, allerthorpelakelandpark.co.uk. RYA training centre. Kayaks and dinghies available for hire.

Woodland adventures
See also Go Ape, opposite.

Aerial Extreme
Camp Hill, nr Bedale, T0845-652 1736, aerialextreme.co.uk. Feb-Nov, from 1000, £22/adult, £17/child. Minimum age 10, minimum height 1.4 m.

Explore a beautiful oak forest, your heart in your mouth as you negotiate 25 tree-top challenges, including the knee-knocking Sky Walk and a simulated parachute jump.

Saddle up

Snainton Riding Centre
Snainton, T01723-859218, snaintonridingcentre.co.uk.

Staintondale Trekking Centre
Staintondale, nr Scarborough, T01723-871846.

Yorkshire Dales Trekking Ctr
Malham, T01729-830352, ydtc.net.

Discover Dalby

Dalby Forest Visitor Centre
Forestry Commission,
nr Pickering, T01751-460295,
forestry.gov.uk/dalbyforest.
Daily, 0930-1630, £7/vehicle, free
admission for passengers on the
Moorsbus (see page 211).

Go Ape
Dalby Forest Visitor Centre,
T0845-643 9215, goape.co.uk.
Mar-Oct, daily 0900-1700,
Feb half-term, plus weekends in Nov.
From £25/gorilla (18+), £20/baboon
(10-17). Minimum age 10, minimum
height 1.4 m, under 18-yr-olds
must be accompanied by
participating adult.

Purple Mountain Bike Centre
Dalby Courtyard (next to the
visitor centre), T01751-460011,
purplemountain.co.uk.
Adult bike from £20/3hrs, £45/day;
child's bike £10/3hrs, £15/day;
tag-along, trailer or child's seat
£10/3hrs, £12/day. Rates include
helmet, pump and repair kit.

Dalby Forest can be accessed via
Pickering on the A169 or from
Thornton-le-Dale on the A170.

A dense cloak of pine, spruce, oak and beech spread over the southern flanks
of the North York Moors, Dalby Forest is the perfect setting for an action-
packed day out. Make the Forestry Commission visitor centre your first stop.
Inside you'll find information on Dalby's history and wildlife, a restaurant,
shop and a ranger desk with details of events, walks and cycle trails.

Particularly suitable for families, the 2.5-mile Dalby Beck Walk
follows mostly level tracks to Ellerburn Pond, passing a bird hide and bat
hibernaculum (an artificial cave where bats can spend the winter). Family
events, meanwhile, can include anything from fungi forays and woodland
art to badger watching, stargazing and bushcraft. There are some 55 miles
of cycle trails in the forest, including child-friendly circuits like the 2.5-mile
Allerburn route and the 8-mile Adderstone trail. Bicycles can be hired from
Purple Mountain which also operates a café.

Picnic sites and barbeque stands are dotted throughout the forest, but
Sneverdale and Adderstone Field have the added attraction of adventure
playgrounds. To get pulses really thumping, sign up for a treetop adventure
with Go Ape which features a 50-ft Indian Bridge and 820-ft zip wire.

Stay at one of Forest Holidays' cabin sites in nearby Cropton Forest (see
page 210) and you'll get woodland adventures right on your doorstep.

Out & about Yorkshire

Castle Howard

Nr York, T01653-648333,
castlehoward.co.uk. Mar-Nov 1100-
1600; gardens, playground, shops
and café year round, 1000-1700, £11/
adult, £7/child (4-16), £29/family.
There's nothing stuffy or aloof
about this magnificent estate,
designed by Sir John Vanbrugh
in 1699. The Howard family
have flung open the doors to
the public with gusto, sparking
children's imagination with
quiz sheets, activity workshops
and adventure trails themed
on Dragons & Unicorns, The
Lazy Giant and The Fairy Twins.
A land train trundles across
1000 acres of gardens to the
Great Lake where a fabulous
adventure playground (for big
kids and little kids) includes a
9-m-high pyramid slide. You
can also take boat trips on the
lake, play games on the vast
lawns and treat yourself to
homemade chocolate in one of
the courtyard shops.

The Deep

Hull, T01482-381000,
thedeep.co.uk. Year round, daily
1000-1800, £8.95/adult, £6.95/child
(3-15), £28.50/family.
A world-class marine marvel,
The Deep goes way beyond
the walk-through tunnels that
other public aquariums rely
on as crowd-pullers. Instead,
you'll witness incredible sea life
during an interactive journey

that not only takes you
from polar waters to
teeming coral reefs,
but also from the past
to the future. Along
the way, children
are challenged to
design a prehistoric
sea monster, investigate
the impacts of rising sea
levels and devise an ocean
research station for the year
2050 – just some of the hands-
on exhibits that are skilfully
blended with jaw-dropping live
displays like the 2.5-million-litre
Endless Oceans tank with its
dozen species of sharks. Other
highlights include the abyssal
depths of the Twilight Zone and
a glass lift ride through a 10-m-
deep aquarium. There's also a
Monsters of the Deep 4D movie,
a soft-play area themed on the
Humber Estuary and a chance
to discover how slime keeps the
animal world moving.

Eureka!

Halifax, T01422-330069,
eureka.org.uk. Year round, daily
1000-1700, £7.25/person, £2.25/
infant (1-3), £31/family.
The hands-on science museum
to displace all others, Eureka!
provides total immersion for kids
through an absorbing range of
challenges, experiments and
role play. Hundreds of must-
touch exhibits are arranged in
six galleries. SoundGarden and
Desert Discovery are specially
designed for under fives and

Left: Get on
down to The
Deep where this
yellow tang is just
one of 3500 fancy fish.

take soft play into the realms
of an enchanted garden and
desert den. The four remaining
galleries are aimed at three-
to 11-year-olds and include
SoundSpace (where you can
experiment with special effects
on a musical spaceship), Our
Global Garden (where Gordon
the Gnome helps you get stuck
into various habitats) and Me

Members' perks

Family membership (see page 5)
entitles you to free entry to:

English Heritage
• Brodsworth Hall and Gardens.
• Middleham Castle, nr Leyburn.
• Richmond Castle.
• Rievaulx Abbey, nr Helmsley.
• Scarborough Castle.
• Whitby Abbey.

National Trust
• Beningbrough Hall and Gardens.
• East Riddlesden Hall.
• Fountains Abbey, Ripon.
• Nostell Priory and Parkland.
• Nunnington Hall, nr Helmsley.
• Treasurer's House, York.

RSPB
• Bempton Cliffs Reserve.
• Blacktoft Sands Reserve, nr Goole.

& My Body (where anatomy comes under the spotlight). There's also a new Outdoor Playscape built from eco-friendly materials, but the most popular gallery at Eureka! remains Living & Working Together – a pint-size town square complete with bank, garage, post office, supermarket and house where children can learn what it's like to be grown-up.

Flamingo Land

Kirby Misperton, nr Malton, T0871-911 8000, flamingoland.co.uk. Mar-Oct, daily 1000-1700, £23/person (children under 3 free), £82/family. It's one of Britain's big family attractions, with prices and queues to match. Throw in four Q-Buster fast-passes and the basic cost for a family of four tops £100. Is Flamingo Land worth it? Well, it certainly gives Chessington World of Adventures (Surrey's version of the zoo-cum-theme-park) a run for its money. Flamingo boasts six extreme rides, including the 56-mph, quadruple inversion Kumali coaster, plus other less stomach-churning options like the Lost River Ride. There's also a water park, 4D cinema and indoor soft play. To keep thrill-seekers on a high, the zoo is full of A-listers from the animal kingdom, including lions, tigers, rhinos, chimps and lemurs, as well as a few surprises such as condors and baboons.

The Forbidden Corner

Tupgill Park Estate, Middleham, T01969-640638, theforbiddencorner.co.uk. Apr-Oct, Mon-Sat 1200-1800, Sun 1000-1800, Nov-Christmas Sun only, £9/adult, £7/child (4-15), £30/family. Pre-booked tickets only. It sounds straightforward: use clues on your ticket to find your way around a 4-acre garden in the Yorkshire Dales. But this is no ordinary garden. Spooky follies, curious grottoes, bizarre statues, secret underground chambers, a network of tunnels, a huge glass pyramid and a revolving room conspire to thwart your efforts. At every turn there are decisions to make and tricks to beware of – and no map to help you if you get stuck. Originally

Meet the Vikings

Jorvik Viking Centre, Coppergate, T01904-615505, jorvik-viking-centre. co.uk. Year round, daily from 1000, £8.50/adult, £6/child, £26/family. Prebook to guarantee a timed entry slot. DIG, Saviourgate, T01904-615505, digyork.co.uk. Year round, daily from 1000, £5.50/adult, £5/child, £18.50/ family. Visits last two hours. Joint tickets for Jorvik, DIG and the restored medieval townhouse of Barley Hall £13.50/adult, £10/child, £42/family.
York makes a fantastic day out with kids. You can climb the 275 steps to the top of York Minster's Central Tower, admire the steam trains at the National Railway Museum (see page 198), cruise the River Ouse and delve into the city's horrible history at the York Dungeon. But if you really want to get under the city's skin, there are two attractions you shouldn't miss.

Standing on the actual site of a Viking city (excavated by archaeologists 30 years ago), one half of the Jorvik Viking Centre consists of a ride which weaves through a diorama of houses, backyards and market stalls – complete with authentic aromas of manure, fish and roasting boar. The rest of the centre features galleries where you'll meet 'real-life' Vikings, a few holographic Viking ghosts and a fascinating array of artefacts and interactive exhibits.

For real hands-on stuff, though, combine Jorvik with a visit to DIG where kids are given trowels and challenged to unearth Roman, Viking, Medieval and Victorian remains from special excavation pits. Archaeologists are on hand to help them work out what artefacts would have been used for and how people lived in the York of ages past.

Jorvik Viking Centre.

Sleeping Yorkshire

Crow's Nest Caravan Park

Gristhorpe, nr Filey, T01723-582206, crowsnestcaravanpark.com. Mar-Oct, £15-22/pitch (up to 4 people), 6-berth caravan from £220/wk.

Crow's Nest has luxury caravans for hire, plus a clifftop camping field with far-reaching views across Gristhorpe Bay towards Scarborough Castle. There's lots to do on-site, with an indoor pool, adventure playground and evening entertainment. And with its own bus stop on the Scarborough–Bridlington route, Crow's Nest could be the ideal base for a car-free holiday.

Hook's House Farm Campsite

Robin Hood's Bay, T01947-880283, hookshousefarm.co.uk. Year round, £5/adult, £2/child, £3/electric hook-up.

As the B1447 winds up the hillside out of Robin Hood's Bay, the sea views get wider and grander until you reach Hook's House Farm Campsite, a modest, family-run affair with a Royal-Box view of prime Yorkshire coast. The facilities are simple – just a basic washroom and kitchen. And those views don't come without the occasional feisty North Sea breeze. If you want more comfort, though, the farm has a self-catering cottage (sleeping up to seven) and a four-berth caravan for hire. You can also bring your horse on

holiday, with DIY livery available at £20/wk.

Knight Stainforth Hall

Little Stainforth, nr Settle, T01729-822200, knightstainforth.co.uk. Mar-Oct, £11-22/pitch (2 people), plus £2.50/extra adult, £1.50/extra child (5-16).

Nestled in the green-velvet folds of the Yorkshire Dales National Park, this fine campsite is part of the 45-acre estate of Knight Stainforth Hall, just 2 miles north of the market town of Settle. It's the perfect base for a walking holiday, with several routes leading from the site (a handy information kiosk will set you on the right track). Nearby attractions include Malham Cove and Skipton Castle, while the River Ribble, tumbling along one side of the campsite, is the perfect spot for a lazy picnic and a game of Pooh sticks from the stone bridge.

Middlewood Farm

Fylingthorpe, T01947-880414, middlewoodfarm.com. Year round, £11-22/pitch (2 people), plus £3/extra person, 2-bedroom holiday homes from £165/wk.

Closer to the sea than Hook's House Farm Campsite (see left), Middlewood Farm is just a 10-minute walk from Robin Hood's Bay across fields and a nature reserve. Located on the outskirts of Fylingthorpe (which has a

pub, general store and a baker/pizzeria), this is a small, friendly site with gleaming washrooms, and a children's adventure play area. A mobile takeaway calls by most mornings and evenings.

South Cliff Caravan Park

Bridlington, T01262-671051, southcliff.co.uk. Mar-Nov, £18-23/pitch, 2/3-bedroom holiday homes £240-580/wk.

With everything from football coaching to Don the Duck's party games, there's never a dull moment at South Cliffs. Catering mainly to caravans, the park has 160 hard standings and 20 tent pitches. Facilities include a mini market, fish and chip shop and amusement arcade, while the beach is just a short stroll away.

Spiers House Campsite

Cropton Forest, nr Pickering, T0845-130 8224, forestholidays.co.uk. Apr-Jan, £11-16/pitch, (2 people), £4.75-6.25/extra adult, £2.75-3.75/extra child, £1 discount for families.

A thick stubble of conifer woodland on the southern edge of the North York Moors, Cropton Forest has three Forest Holidays sites, including the excellent Keldy and Cropton Cabins (see page 210). Located alongside the latter, Spiers House Campsite has recently refurbished washrooms and offers ranger-led walks and activities, as well as bike hire.

Bay-watch beauty – Hooks House Farm campsite is perched above Robin Hood's Bay.

Wold Farm Campsite
Flamborough, T01262-850536,
woldfarmcampsite.tk. Mar-Oct,
£5/pitch.

A short walk from the seabird
colonies at Bempton Cliffs (page
206), Wold Farm Campsite
enjoys a lofty position on the
edge of Flamborough, with
views across to the lighthouse
and Danes Dyke Nature Reserve.

Also recommended
Golden Square Caravan Park
Nr Helmsley, T01439-788269,
goldensquarecaravanpark.com.

Goosewood Caravan Park
Sutton-on-the-Forest, nr York,
T01347-810829, goosewood.co.uk.

Howgill Lodge Bolton Abbey,
T01756-720655, howgill-lodge.co.uk.

Riverside Caravan Park
High Bentham, T015242-61272,
riversidecaravanpark.co.uk.

Rosedale Rosedale Abbey,
T01751-417272, flowerofmay.com.

Vale of Pickering Caravan Park
Allerston, T01723-859280,
valeofpickering.co.uk.

Holiday parks

The Bay
Filey, T0844-847 1356,
hoseasons.co.uk.
Prestigious development of
holiday cottages with 600-m
beach frontage and superb pub.

Blue Dolphin Holiday Park
Gristhorpe Bay, Filey,
T0871-231 0893, haven.com.
One of a trio of Haven parks along
the Yorkshire coast, Blue Dolphin
has a fabulous clifftop location,
plus tons to do inside and out –
from go-karts and a TumbleWave
Slide pool to bowling, kids' clubs
and a soft-play area.

Cayton Bay Holiday Park
Nr Scarborough, T0844-847
1356, hoseasons.co.uk.
Lively park with indoor
waterworld and kids' activities.

Flower of May Holiday Park
Lebberston Cliff, Scarborough,
T01723-584311, flowerofmay.com.
Award-winning, five-star holiday
park with luxury caravans and
leisure centre.

Skirlington Leisure Park
Skipsea, T01262-468213,
skirlington.com.
Family-run park on 70 acres,
with fishing lake, pitch-and-putt,
indoor pool and bowling.

Primrose Valley Holiday Park
Filey, T0871-231 0892,
haven.com.
Direct beach access, boating lake,
fun fair, state-of-the-art pool
complex and kids' clubs.

Reighton Sands Holiday Park
Reighton Gap, T0871-231 0892,
haven.com.
Clifftop park with tractor ride
down to a long, sandy beach.

Sleeping Yorkshire

Best of the rest

Beech Farm Cottages

Wrelton, nr Pickering, T01751-476612, beechfarm.com. Year round, £255-1850/wk.

Idyllic farmstay with eight cosy stone cottages (sleeping 2-10), a heated indoor pool, children's playground and a paddock with horses, ponies and llamas.

Cropton and Keldy Cabins

Cropton Forest, nr Pickering, T0845-130 8223, forestholidays.co.uk. Year round, £272-965/wk for a 4-bed Copper Beech cabin. See pages 14-15.

Offering style and comfort in the heart of Cropton Forest, both of these cabin sites feature Forest Retreats where you can buy local food and book ranger activities, pony trekking, bike hire, archery and laser combat. Keldy also has a games room and educational Forest Experience Room, while Cropton, opened in May 2009, boasts new-style, single-storey cabins with underfloor heating and floor-to-ceiling windows.

Farsyde Farm Cottages

Robin Hood's Bay, T01947-880249, farsydefarmcottages.co.uk. Year round, £195-630/wk.

A 10-minute walk from Robin Hood's Bay, these five superbly located cottages (sleeping 3-5) also have footpath access to Boggle Hole beach – a favourite spot for a swim. The larger Mistal Cottage has a small indoor pool.

York Lakeside Lodges

Moor Lane, York, T01904-702346, yorklakesidelodges.co.uk. Year round, £220-785/wk.

Located in parkland just 2 miles from York, these 16 lakeside lodges make an ideal rural base for visiting the city.

Also recommended

Abbey House Youth Hostel

East Cliff, Whitby, T0845-371 9049, yha.org.uk.

Wrea Head Country Cottages

Scalby, nr Scarborough, T01723-375844, wreahead.co.uk.

Splashing out

Swinton Park

Nr Masham, T01765-680900, swintonpark.com. From £160/room B&B, plus £35/child sharing.

This luxurious castle-hotel has 30 designer bedrooms and a reputation for fine cuisine. How do kids fit in? Very nicely, thanks to a playroom-cum-cinema, cookery classes and a birds of prey centre where children can handle hawks and owls.

For a York city break, try the **Novotel** (Fishergate, T01904-611660, novotel.com). Five minute's walk from the city centre, it not only has an indoor pool, playground, kids' menus and family rooms, but accommodation and breakfast are free for two children (under 16) sharing with their parents.

Cottage agents

Dales Holiday Cottages
T0844-576 2545, dales-holiday-cottages.com. Over 600 cottages throughout northern England and Scotland.

North Yorkshire Cottages
T01751-476653, northyorkshirecottages.co.uk. Cottages in and around Pickering.

Robin Hood's Bay Cottages
T01947-821803, robinhoodsbaycottages.co.uk.

Yorkshire Cottages
T01228-406701, yorkshire-cottages.info.

The Lodge Holidays collection from **Hoseasons** (T0844-847 1356, hoseasons.co.uk) features quality properties throughout Yorkshire, including Westholme Lodges, a peaceful retreat on the banks of Bishopdale Beck in the heart of the Yorkshire Dales. Lodges feature open-plan living areas and private terraces, while the site has a playground, brasserie and direct access to fine walking country. Captain Cook's Haven, meanwhile, is a cluster of cottages beside the River Esk, near Whitby – a great spot for exploring the Moors and Heritage Coast. The cottages sleep up to six and have shared use of an indoor heated pool. Weekly rates are £274-995 for Westholme Lodges and £225-782 for Captain Cook's Haven.

Eating Yorkshire

Local goodies

The Balloon Tree

Gate Helmsley, nr York, T01759-373023, theballoontree.co.uk. Farmshop: Mon-Sat 0900-1800, Sun 1000-1700. Café: Mon-Sat 0930-1630, Sun 1030-1630.

You could happily spend a half-day at The Balloon Tree. A pick-your-own trail weaves through fields growing 50 types of fruit and veg, while the farm shop is brimming with fresh produce – from rare-breed meats to local honey and ice cream. There's also a café where you can sample Phyllis Thompson's legendary lemon drizzle cake and fresh cream roulade while watching the kids play on the vintage tractor in the adjacent play area.

For traditional ice cream from Yorkshire dairy farms, look out for **Mr Moo's Real Dairy Ice Cream** (mrmoos.co.uk), **Ripley Ice Cream** (ripleystore.com), **Ryeburn of Helmsley** (ryeburn.com), **Swales Yorkshire Dales Ice Cream** (yorkshiredalesicecream.co.uk), **Yorvale** (yorvale.co.uk) and the **Yummy Yorkshire Ice Cream Company** (yorkshiremilk.co.uk). At the village of Sneaton, near Whitby, **Beacon Farm** (beacon-farm.co.uk) not only makes its own ice cream (try the eight-flavour Beacon Belly Buster), but also has a café, farmshop and family-friendly campsite.

Castle Howard Farm Shop

Castle Howard, T01653-648529, castlehoward.co.uk. Daily 1000-1700.

You don't have to pay to visit Castle Howard's Courtyard where the farm shop boasts one of Yorkshire's best butchers', as well as a deli counter selling cheeses, pork pies and other regional specialities. Fresh fish from Scarborough is available every Thursday.

The Farmer's Cart

Towthorpe Grange, nr York, T01904-499183, thefarmerscart.co.uk. Mon-Sat 0930-1730.

Like The Balloon Tree (left), The Farmer's Cart teeters towards a great day out with its award-winning farm shop, bakery and café complemented by child-friendly activities, such as ride-on tractors, animal feeding and pig racing (Jul-Aug).

The Forge Farm Shop & Sandwich Bar

The Old Smithy, Bondgate Green, Ripon, T01765-698249.

Freshly-made sandwiches, cakes, soups and salads.

The Ginger Pig Shop

Market Place, Pickering, T01751-477211. Mon-Sat 0900-1700.

This traditional grocers' sells everything from local cheeses to freshly baked cakes and quiches, but if you buy one thing make sure it's the dry-cured bacon, pork sausages or picnic-perfect sausage rolls.

John Bull World of Rock

Bridlington, T01262-678525, john-bull.com. Mar-Oct. Factory tours: Mon-Thu 1100-1730, £2/adult, £1.50/child. Shop & café: Mon-Fri 0930-1700, Sat-Sun 1000-1600.

Have a go at making your own rock and lollipops, sample chocolates, biscuits and fudge, then round off the ultimate sweet-tooth fantasy with cake and ice cream in the café.

The Stonehouse Bakery

Danby, T01287-660006. Year round, Mon-Sat.

Stock up on freshly-baked bread, pasties, pies and buns, then find a quiet spot for lunch next to the river Esk or spread a picnic rug in the grounds of the nearby Moors Centre (page 199).

Fish & chips

Whitby's most celebrated chippie, the **Magpie Café** (Whitby) serves fish and chips with mushy peas from £5.35. Expect long queues for both the restaurant and take away – and remember to avoid eye contact with the loitering herring gulls if you decide to eat out by the harbour. Other good fish bars include **Audreys** (Bridlington), **Inghams** (Filey), **Mother Hubbards** (Scarborough), **Mariondale** (Robin Hood's Bay), **Quayside** (Whitby, see page 212) and the **Wetherby Whaler** (York).

Eating Yorkshire

The Wensleydale Creamery

Hawes, T01969-667638, wensleydale.co.uk. Year round, Mon-Sat 0930-1700, Sun 1000-1630.
"Cheese, Gromit, cheese!" There's nothing like a nice bit of Wensleydale, and everyone's favourite play-dough-duo have done wonders for sales of the light, crumbly Yorkshire cheese with the slightly sweet aftertaste. The Wensleydale Creamery offers 30- to 90-minute tours where you can witness the entire cheese-making process, while a museum takes you back in time to the original farmhouse dairy.

Market days

Driffield Showground, 1st Sat.
Grassington 3rd Sunday.
Harrogate Cambridge St, 2nd Tue.
Pickering Mon.
Ripon Market Square, Thu; farmers' market 3rd Sun.
Settle, 2nd Sun.
Skipton 1st Sun.
Thirsk 2nd Mon.

This should keep the kids going during a busy day sightseeing in York: the **Gourmet Burger Kitchen** (Lendal, off Museum St, T01904-639537, Mon-Fri from 1200, Sat-Sun from 1100) offers no fewer than 28 burgers, from the no-frills Classic (£5.95) to the signature Kiwiburger (£7.95) – a jaw-dislocating feast of beef, cheese, beetroot, egg, pineapple, salad and relish.

Quick & simple

Blacksmith's Arms

Lastingham, T01751-417247.
A 17th-century village inn on the edge of the moors serving home-cooked meals using local ingredients. Main dishes from £8.95.

Glass House Bistro

Scarborough, T01723-368791, glasshousebistro.co.uk. Sun-Wed 1000-1600; Thu-Sat from 1800. Stylish café/bistro in Northstead Manor Gardens. Lunchtime snacks include jacket potatoes and sandwiches from £3.95.

The Harbour Bar

Sandside, Scarborough, T01723-373662.
Almost frozen in time since Giulian Alonzi opened it in 1945, this classic milk bar on Scarborough's seafront is a shrine to formica, neon and knickerbocker glories.

Quayside

Whitby, T01947-602059, fuscowhitby.com. Mar-Oct, daily from 1100. One of Whitby's plethora of fish and chip shops (see also page 211), Quayside has an 80-seater restaurant with great views over the harbour. Whitby haddock, coated in batter and fried in beef dripping, costs from £8.45. Alternatively, try the delicious home-made fishcakes with parsley sauce (£6.75) or the fish pie, thick with cod, salmon and prawns (£7.25).

Also recommended
Tricolos Italian Restaurant

Scarborough, T01723-367842. Scarborough's original, and still its most authentic, pizzeria.

Wit's End

Whitby, T01947-893658, witsendcafe.co.uk. Fri-Wed 0900-1700. Seaside café with a walled garden and lovely views across Sandsend Bay.

Posh nosh

The Star Inn

Harome, nr Helmsley, T01439-770397, thestaratharome.co.uk. Mon from 1830; Tue-Sat 1130-1400, 1830-2130; Sun 1200-1800. Andrew Pern is one of Britain's most talented young chefs, and his Michelin-starred pub is a glowing testament to his skills. The menu is sophisticated and pricey (Pern's speciality is black pudding and foies gras), but you will also find wholesome dishes like North Sea fish pie (£16) and local rump steak with chunky chips (£23). Lunchtime salads and sandwiches start at £8.

Also recommended
Kapadokya

York, T01904-622500, kapadokya-restaurant.co.uk. Daily from 1200. Delicious Turkish cuisine with marinated kebabs and seafood sizzling straight off the grill.

Essentials Yorkshire

Getting there
By train Grand Central (grandcentralrail.co.uk) has a non-stop service from London to York; National Express East Coast (nationalexpresseastcoast.com) operates between London and Edinburgh, via York; Cross Country Trains (crosscountrytrains.co.uk) links the Midlands with Leeds and York, while the TransPennine Express (tpexpress.co.uk) has direct services from Liverpool and Manchester airports.
By coach Destinations in Yorkshire served by National Express (nationalexpress.com) include Bridlington, Filey, Harrogate, Hull, Pickering, Ripon, Scarborough, Skipton, Thirsk and Whitby.

Getting around
By train Transpennine Express runs to Hull and Scarborough. Northern Rail (northernrail.org) links the Dales with the North York Moors and coast, and also operates the Esk Valley Railway between Middlesborough and Witney. See page 206 for the North Yorkshire Moors Railway.
By bus Moorsbus (moors.uk.net) operates across the North York Moors, with fares from £8/family. Services include M3 (Danby–Sutton Bank), M6 (Thornton-le-Dale–Dalby Forest–Ayton), M15 (York–Helmsley) 128 (Sutton Bank–Pickering–Scarborough), and 840 (Pickering–Goathland–Whitby). In the Yorkshire Dales, Dalesbus (dalesbus.org) runs a Sunday service during summer.

Maps
Ordnance Survey Explorer 301 (Scarborough, Bridlington & Flamborough Head), OL26 & 27 (North York Moors), OL2 & 30 (Yorkshire Dales).

Tourist Information Centres
Yorkshire Tourist Board (yorkshire.com), Yorkshire Moors & Coast (yorkshiremoorsandcoast.com), Hull & East Yorkshire (realyorkshire.co.uk), Scarborough, Whitby and Filey (discoveryorkshirecoast.com). There are two TICs in York, located in Exhibition Square and at York Railway Station, T01904-550099, visityork.org, Mon-Sat 0900-1700 (1800 in summer), Sun 1000-1600 (1700 in summer). TICs can also be found in most towns, including:
Bridlington Prince St, T01262-673474.
Filey John St, T01723-383636.
Grassington National Park Centre, T01756-751690.
Helmsley Helmsley Castle, T01439-770173.
Hull Paragon St, T01482-223559.
Pickering The Ropery, T01751-473791.
Ripon Minster Rd, T0845-389 0178.
Scarborough Sandside & Brunswick Shopping Centre, T01723-383636.
Skipton Coach St, T01756-792809.
Whitby Langborne Rd, T01723-383636.

Further information
North York Moors National Park, T01439-770657, visitnorthyorkshiremoors.co.uk.

Yorkshire Dales National Park, T0300-456 0030, yorkshiredales.org.uk.

Hospital
York Hospital, Wigginton Rd, York, T01904-631313.

Pharmacies
Bridlington Late Night, Promenade.
Hull Asda, Mount Retail Park.
Pickering Wrothwell, Market Place.
Ripon Boots, Market Place.
Scarborough Heaps, Ramshill Rd.
Skipton Boots, High St.

Supermarkets
Bridlington Morrison, Somerfield.
Hull Asda, Morrison, Tesco.
Pickering United Co-op.
Scarborough Sainsbury's, Tesco.
Skipton Morrison.
York Asda, Budgens, Morrison, Sainsbury's, Somerfield, Tesco.

Other shops
Baby supplies Mothercare, Clifton Moor Retail Park, York.
Camping supplies Cave & Crag, Market Place, Settle; Crag & Moor, Victoria Rd, Scarborough; Millets, Market St, York.
Toys & beach gear Bubbles Toys, Gillygate, York.

Environmental groups
Yorkshire Wildlife Trust, T01904-659570, ywt.org.uk.

Major Events
May Moor and Coast Festival.
Jun/Jul Filey Festival.
Jul SeaFest, Scarborough.
Aug Whitby Regatta.

Ullswater

Lake District

Driving towards Cumbria on the M6 you can almost smell the Nikwax and hear the swish of trekking poles against Goretex. Boasting England's five tallest peaks, the Lake District is a stomping ground for the high-and-mighty, but family holidays in this gem of a national park are far more down-to-earth.

Pitch a tent with a lake view, skim stones, collect fir cones, second-glance a red squirrel, sail a stick down a gurgling beck. No trekking poles required. And if you want to raise the adventure stakes a little, rent a canoe and paddle out to a deserted island with a picnic and a copy of *Swallows and Amazons* (toddlers might prefer Beatrix Potter and a chance to feed the Jemima Puddle-ducks on the shores of Windermere).

England's largest national park is remarkably accommodating, whether it's teens hell-bent on conquering Helvellyn or tots who dare to dabble their toes in Rydal Water. The real challenge for families is deciding where to go.

Many tend to gravitate towards Lake Windermere where **Ambleside** and the linked towns of **Windermere** and **Bowness-on-Windermere** form the region's southern hub of tourism, awash with attractions and places to eat, sleep and shop. Likewise, **Keswick** is a popular centre in the Northern Lakes, with Derwent Water and Borrowdale right on its doorstep, while **Penrith** is just minutes from **Pooley Bridge** at the tip of Ullswater.

It's all too tempting, though, to let fingers wander over a map of the Lakes. Before you know it, you're lost in a tangle of lanes around the sleepy old market town of **Hawkshead** (gateway to Tarn Hows and Grizedale Forest), or drifting west towards **Coniston** where the Old Man looms above Coniston Water. Then there's the stunning drive from **Skelwith Bridge**, past **Elterwater** and into the Langdale Valley. Or the great Lake District 'thoroughfare' north from Ambleside to **Rydal** and **Grasmere**, hemmed in by Helvellyn and Thirlmere, with Skiddaw looming ahead.

You'll also find it hard to resist the passes of Honister, Kirkstone, Wrynose and Hardknott – each one a window to 'hidden' Lakeland gems, like Buttermere and Brothers Water. Be warned though. It's only once you've ventured west beyond Hardknott (the road unravelling through exquisite Eskdale) that you realise just how close the Cumbrian coast is. Mountains, lakes and now beaches. Deciding where to go just got a whole lot harder.

You must

- Find the perfect skimmer at Buttermere.
- Meet Peter Rabbit.
- Watch ducks dive at the Aquarium of the Lakes.
- Learn to sail or abseil.
- See red squirrels at Whinlatter Forest Park.
- Take a ride on a steam train or lake cruiser.
- Explore a slate mine.
- Take a hike around a lake, on a fell, through a forest or to a summit.
- Ride a pony on a beach.
- Eat Grasmere Gingerbread.

Get yer boots on

Lung-bursting assaults on Helvellyn are all very well if you have older children game for a challenge, but most families set their sights lower. That's the beauty of the Lake District. You don't have to be a fell-bagging fitness fiend with thighs of iron to enjoy a good walk. There are plenty of options suitable for kids of all ages.

An occasionally bumpy, but buggy-friendly, path casts a 2-mile loop around exquisite **Tarn Hows**, nestled in forest near Hawkshead. There are great views of the Langdale Pikes – although kids are likely to be too busy exploring streams and spotting red squirrels to notice.

At **Buttermere**, a short stroll from the car park leads you to the northern end of the lake where the shore is littered with some of the best skimming stones you'll find anywhere. Nearby, the mere overflows into a small river (perfect for stick-racing), while Sour Milk Gill, tumbling from Red Pike, is another essential diversion. Sooner or later, though, the 4-mile circuit around Buttermere beckons. It's an easy walk, with peaks looming all around.

Ideal for a gentle amble or cycle, the farm track at the head of the **Great Langdale Valley** (near the Old Dungeon Ghyll Hotel) meanders across flat pastures. For a riverside ramble surrounded by high fells, try **Cockley Beck** between Wrynose and Hardknott Passes.

An easy summit for kids, a well-trodden path leads to **Gummers How**, near the southern end of Lake Windermere. Slightly more ambitious, but with equally stunning views, a trail from Ambleside climbs past Stock Ghyll Force and on up towards **Wansfell Pike**. In the Northern Lakes, combine a boat trip from Keswick to Hawes End with a hike on **Cat Bells** above the western shore of Derwent Water.

Opposite: Sour Milk Gill at Buttermere.
This page: Bridge over Cockley Beck near Hardknott Pass; farm track from Middlefell Place towards Bow Fell in the Langdale Valley; reflections at Tarn Hows; Lake Windermere from Wansfell Pike.

Out & about Lake District

Fun & free

Plan a Lake District safari

Your top ticks have to be red squirrel and osprey – and, surprisingly, neither should be too elusive. Red squirrels are found in forests throughout Cumbria (it's one of their major strongholds), but your best chance of spotting one is in Whinlatter Forest Park (see right). From Oct-Apr, the visitor centre has a CCTV link to a red squirrel feeder, but if you think that's cheating, try stalking the Squirrel Scurry Trail (maps are available at the visitor centre), keeping your eyes turned skyward for that tell-tale flash of ochre-red fur.

For further information on the Lake District's red squirrels, contact Save our Squirrels, saveoursquirrels.org.uk.

During the summer months, ospreys gain TV celebrity status at Whinlatter, courtesy of live camera footage beamed from a nest at nearby Bassenthwaite Lake. Ospreys hadn't bred in England for over 150 years when they began using this site in 2001. RSPB volunteers at the Dodd Wood Viewpoint (rspb.org. uk/datewithnature, Apr-Aug, daily 1000-1700) will help you train telescopes on the raptors as they catch fish on the lake and carry food to their chicks. The best way to reach both the viewpoint and Whinlatter Visitor Centre is on the Osprey Bus (74) which operates a summer service around Bassenthwaite Lake from Keswick.

Make a break for the coast

A day at the seaside might not be something that naturally springs to mind when visiting the Lake District. It's hard to see beyond all those mountains and lakes. But the Cumbrian coast is not only close-by, but also boasts some wonderfully unspoilt beaches. Better known as the starting point of Wainwright's Coast to Coast walk, St Bees (4 miles south of Whitehaven) has a long sandy beach with rock pools near the base of St Bees Head. You can get good views of the seabirds that nest on this red sandstone bluff either by joining a boat trip from Whitehaven (see page 220) or following the clifftop path towards Fleswick

Visit The Lake District Visitor Centre

Why? It's the perfect spot to lull yourself into the Lakes and dabble your toes – literally if you like – in what the national park has to offer. As well as exhibitions and displays, the centre has an information desk where you can plan walks and days out, while the terrace café commands stunning views across Lake Windermere and the fells beyond. The grounds at the centre are brilliant for kids. They'll want to make a bee-line for the adventure playground or putting green, but try to coax them around the lakeshore and woodland walk first. During school holidays, children can also get a taste of adventure during special activity days – some of which involve a small fee.

Where? Brockhole, between Troutbeck Bridge and Ambleside.

How? Gardens and adventure playground open year round, dawn-dusk; centre, café and shop, daily 1000-1700. Park in the pay-and-display car park, catch the 555 or 599 bus or take the launch from Ambleside.

Contact The Lake District Visitor Centre, T015394-46601, lake-district.gov.uk.

Count the stones

Legend has it that if you count the standing stones at Castlerigg, near Keswick, you'll never reach the same total twice. The 5000-year-old stone circle is officially made up of 38 megaliths, plus an additional 10 that form a curious rectangle at one side of the ring. A larger, though less well-known, stone circle at Little Salkeld near Penrith, Long Meg and her Daughters are believed to be witches turned to stone for dancing on the Sabbath. Think twice about counting these stones – if you get the same number twice, the curse will be undone.

Stone Circle.

at low tide that's ideal for kite-flying and beach games.

Go down to the woods
Grizedale and Whinlatter Forest Parks (forestry.gov.uk/northwestengland) offer action-packed days of walking, cycling and wildlife-watching. The mile-long Ridding Wood Trail at Grizedale has around 20 interactive sculptures (including a forest xylophone) and is suitable for pushchairs, while the much more demanding Carron Crag walk rewards hikers

of the
is equally
both
work of
hire bikes
ic areas,
-wire
ge 221).

liscover
ionaltrust.
e quarter of
the Lake District National Park, including 24 lakes and tarns, 90 tenanted farms, England's highest mountain (Scafell Pike) hundreds of paths and miles of dry-stone walls. Members can park for free at over 20 car parks, including popular family walking spots like Aira Force, Buttermere, Elterwater and Tarn Hows. You can learn more about the Trust's work in Cumbria by popping into the quirky little information centre at Bridge House, Ambleside, or visiting Fell Foot Country

Park at Newby Bridge – a peaceful retreat on the shores of Windermere with picnic-perfect gardens sweeping down to the lakeshore and a Victorian boathouse where you can hire rowing boats and buy ice cream.

Escape the rain
Beat those rainy-day blues at The Rheged Centre (Penrith, T01768-868000, rheged.com, daily 1000-1700), which has exhibitions on Cumbria, shops and cafés specialising in local produce, a soft play area and giant cinema screen.

The Lake District National Park Authority (lake-district.gov.uk) organises an annual programme of events, including family activities such as farm walks, an introduction to map reading, *Swallows and Amazons* cruises and summer activity days at Brockhole Lake District Visitor Centre (see left).

Sleeping Lake District

Low Wray.

Castlerigg Hall Caravan and Camping Park

Keswick, T017687-74499, castlerigg.co.uk. Mar-Nov, £5.50-6.75/adult, £2.50-3.30/child (5-15). Caravan pitches from £15.50; 4-berth holiday caravans from £220/wk.

🅐 😊 🄾 🅑 🄲 🄾 🆆🄲 🄸 😊

Caravans and tents share lovely views over Derwentwater at this terraced site which has a well-stocked shop, gleaming washrooms, games room and play field. With an onsite café (great breakfasts) and a pub just outside the entrance, this is an ideal site for lazy campers – although you'll probably feel you've earned a meal out after hiking the 25-minute (steepish) walk down to Keswick and back a few times.

Fisherground Campsite

Eskdale, T01946-723349, fishergroundcampsite.co.uk. Mar-Oct, £5.50/adult, £2.50/child, £2.50/vehicle.

🅐 🄾 🄾 🄾 🅑

A campsite with a play area is always a bonus for kids. And one that allows campfires is a guaranteed hit. But just imagine a campsite that not only has marshmallow-toasting potential, but also boasts a rafting pond, tree house, zip wire, adventure course *and* a steam railway station. Welcome to Fisherground, a children's paradise with its own halt on the

Ravenglass & Eskdale Railway (page 222). Camping facilities are nothing to shout about – there's a toilet block, laundry and boot-drying room and you can buy logs for campfires.

Low Wray Campsite

Nr Ambleside, T015394-32810, ntlakescampsites.org.uk. Easter-Oct, £4.50-5.50/adult, £2-2.50/child, £11-13.50/family, £3-3.50/vehicle.

🅐 🄾 🄾 🅑 🄾 🄾

A beautiful site on the quiet western shore of Windermere, Low Wray offers the ultimate Lakeland camping idyll – your tent pitched next to a lake, canoes hauled up on a beach, and glorious views across fell and water. It's worth paying the £5 premium for a lakeside site and arriving at Reception promptly at 1200 when pitches are allocated on a first-come, first-served basis. And be sure to spend another £5 on midge repellent. If the nippers get too persistent, take refuge in the Drunken Duck Inn, one of the Lake District's best pubs, a 10-minute drive away.

Park Cliffe Camping and Caravanning Estate

Windermere, T015395-31344, parkcliffe.co.uk. Mar-Nov, £18.75-26.50/pitch (2 people), £5/extra adult, £2/extra child (5-17).

🅐 🄾 😊 🄾 🄾 🅑 🄾 🄾 🆆🄲 🄸 😊

Combining fell-side camping with a few home comforts, Park Cliffe is well equipped for family

camping. A mixture of touring pitches and holiday caravans, the site has a restaurant, shop and immaculate washrooms – you can even hire a private bathroom for £13/night. There are plenty of walks right on the doorstep, although kids will be happy enough messing about in the shallow beck that flows through the campsite.

Low Wray is one of a trio of National Trust campsites in the Lake District. The others are **Great Langdale** (near The Old Dungeon Ghyll Hotel) and **Wasdale** (at Wasdale Head).

Syke Farm Campsite

Buttermere, T017687-70222. Year round, £6/person.

🅐 🄾

Feeling intrepid? Good, because you won't find much in the way of mod-cons at this wonderfully wild-and-woolly site. Wild because it's surrounded by the brooding peaks of Buttermere Fell, and woolly because you'll be sharing it with sheep. Rocky and undulating, it's not the best place to pitch up with an 8-berth super-tent. You also need to carry all gear from the car park across a beck. In return, you'll get a stone hut with toilets and a couple of hot showers (50p a go), cold water for washing up and a picnic shelter. Family camping disaster in-the-making? Not if you like the no-frills approach with superb walking around Buttermere and Crummock Water thrown into the bargain. And as added incentives, the Fish Hotel and a farmhouse café serving cakes, scones and ice cream is just a short stroll away.

Also recommended
Seacote Park St Bees, T01946-822777, seacote.com.

Waterside House Campsite
Pooley Bridge, T017684-86332, watersidefarm-campsite.co.uk.

Yearning for a yurt? **Full Circle** (T07975-671928, lake-district-yurts.co.uk) has a select group at Rydal in the heart of the Lakes. Sleeping up to six, each authentic Mongolian ger has a wood-burning stove, lanterns, rugs and comfortable beds. There's an excellent adventure playground, plus nature's very own version in the form of streams, woods and waterfalls. Rates start at £260/week for a five-day mid-week break. If tipis are more your thing, try **Four Winds** (T01539-821227, 4windslakelandtipis.co.uk) which operates from Low Wray Campsite (see left); rates from £190/week for a tipi sleeping six.

Syke Farm Campsite.

Northumberland

Abucket and spade, miles of sand and a good pinch of imagination. That's all you really need on Northumberland's no-frills beaches. Some have the added bonus of a castle looming above the dunes – a handy reference when adding the finishing touches to your golden-sand replica.

If it's windy, which it often is on this wild and pristine shore, you'll also need a good, strong kite. Beach cricket knows no boundaries on Northumberland's coast and you can really let rip with a frisbee once low tide has revealed acre upon acre of rippled sands.

From stalking the strandline for shells and mermaid's purses to building a dam in fevered,

yet futile defiance of the tide, beachlife in Northumberland is a year-round, all-weather pastime. Not that there's nothing else to do. Far from it. Northumberland's vivid history has endowed the county with a rich legacy of fascinating days out – from exploring the great castles of Alnwick and Bamburgh to marching in the shadow of Hadrian's Wall. No visit is complete without a pilgrimage across the causeway to Lindisfarne (Holy Island) or a wildlife odyssey to the Farne Islands in search of seals and puffins.

Stretching from Hadrian's Wall to the Cheviot Hills, Northumberland National Park lures walkers, cyclists or those simply in search of a quiet picnic, while Kielder Water & Forest Park is awash with outdoor activities.

Best beaches

The **Northumberland Coast Area of Outstanding Natural Beauty** (northumberlandcoastaonb.org) adorns 39 miles of stunning shore between Berwick and the Coquet Estuary, taking in the saltmarshes of Lindisfarne and Budle Bay, the craggy whinstone bluff of Bamburgh (which extends offshore to emerge as the Farne Islands) and a glorious succession of long, sweeping bays. From north to south, these include:

Bamburgh Beach A vast swathe of sand beneath the imposing ramparts of Bamburgh Castle, this magnificent beach also has great views of the Farne Islands. The pretty village of Bamburgh has tea rooms and gift shops, while the small car park in the lee of the dunes (follow the sign to The Wynding) is often frequented by an ice cream van. There's a lovely stream flowing across the beach here – perfect for littl'uns to paddle in – while nearby you'll find good shell-collecting and rock-pooling. Bamburgh is also a great surfing beach (just be wary of currents) and you won't find a better place for sandcastles or kite flying.

Seahouses Better known as the departure point for boat trips to the Farne Islands (see page 235), the fishing village of Seahouses also has a large sandy bay.

Beadnell Bay A popular holiday base, Beadnell has a fascinating old harbour and a sandy, horseshoe-shaped beach, backed by sand dunes. Watersports include diving, sailing, windsurfing and sea kayaking.

Newton Haven Sheltered by offshore reefs, this beautiful sandy bay is close to the 18th-century fishing hamlet of Low Newton. There's good rock-pooling at low tide, while a buggy-friendly trail leads to a birdwatching hide overlooking Newton Pool – a nature reserve tucked away in the dunes. Nip around the low headland and you'll get fine views of skeletal Dunstanburgh Castle presiding over the spectacular scimitar curve of Embleton Bay – a popular surf spot.

Warkworth Beach Another rampant swathe of sand, dune-backed Warkworth Beach stretches from Birling Carrs (good for rock pools) all the way to Amble Breakwater, but is often overlooked by visitors sidetracked by the castle in the nearby village of Warkworth. You might even get the beach to yourself.

Amble Links There's a small bay between the pier and promenade at Amble, but it's not a patch on Amble Links – a huge beach between the town and Low Hauxley, with extensive dunes and the odd rock pool.

Great escapes Northumberland

Get your bearings

Northumberland is easily reached by road, either using the A1, which flirts with the coast, or the A69 which strikes east from the M6, passing just north of Hexham before being engulfed by Newcastle. Rail links are good, too, with the East Coast Mainline connecting Morpeth, Alnmouth and Berwick-upon-Tweed. Services are operated by **National Express East Coast** (nationalexpresseastcoast.com), **Cross Country Trains** (crosscountrytrains.co.uk) and **Northern Rail** (northernrail.org).

Tourist information centres are found in most major towns, including **Alnwick** (The Shambles, T01665-511333), **Amble** (Queen Street, T01665-712313), **Berwick-upon-Tweed** (Marygate, T01289-330733), **Hexham** (Wentworth Car Park, T01434-652220, hadrianswallcountry.org) and **Seahouses** (Seafield Car Park, T01665-720884).

For information on Northumberland National Park, visitor centres are located at **Ingram** (T01665-578890), **Once Brewed** (T01434-344396) and **Rothbury** (T01669-620887).

Springhill Farm.

Pitch your tent

Many families aim for the section of coast between Seahouses and Holy Island for endless beaches and a rich vein of attractions, from castles to boat trips. Not surprisingly, there are several campsites in the area.

Hunkered down in the dunes behind Goswick Sands, **Beachcomber Campsite** (Goswick, T01289-381217, year round, £16/pitch) is just a 2-mile stroll along the coast path to the Holy Island causeway. It's a wild and windy site – a tad bleak when the weather closes in – but a real find for those in search of a simple beach retreat. Kids can scurry straight from their tents onto the beach, and even have a crack at horse riding across the firm sands. Beachcomber Stables offer rides for children as young as five for £14/hr.

Two miles south of Seahouses, **Beadnell Bay Campsite** (Beadnell, T01665-720586, campingandcaravanningclub.co.uk, Apr-Sep, £4.75-7.50/adult, £2.35-2.45/child, plus £6.46 non-member fee per pitch) also enjoys a wonderful beachfront location – although a minor road does run between the camping field and the dunes.

A short distance inland, **Springhill Farm Campsite** (Seahouses, T01665-721820, springhill-farm.co.uk, Mar-Oct, £14-20/pitch) just about sneaks a peak at the sea, and some of the pitches have distant views of Bamburgh Castle. It's a small, level site with the kind of lush, springy grass that turns cows green with envy – they can often be found crowding the fence, gazing at the verdant pasture you're about to flatten with your groundsheet. Facilities include a decent washblock (with family bathroom), a playing field and a walking/cycling track to Seahouses.

For softies (or perhaps those who are wise to the winds of Northumbria), Springhill also offers three luxury barn conversions. If that sounds too pampered, though, try **Pot-a-Doodle Do Wigwam Village** (Borewell, nr Spittal, T01289-307107, northumbrianwigwams.com, Apr-Oct, £18.50/adult, £10.50/child, yurts and tipis from £50/night) where at least the tents have been pitched for you. Actually, 12 of the 'wigwams' are wooden and sleep up to five in fully-insulated luxury. There are also four canvas tipis, three yurts and a dinky little Finnish barbecue hut. Pot-a-Doodle Do is renowned for its art centre where kids can paint ceramics and make mosaics. There's also a gift shop, restuarant, play area and quad biking (minimum age 8).

Away from the coast, prime pitches include the Camping and Caravanning Club Sites at **Bellingham** (T01434-220175) in Northumberland National Park, and **Haltwhistle** (T01434-320106) just 4 miles from Hadrian's Wall.

One of the best holiday parks in the region, **Haggerston Castle** (Beal, nr Berwick-upon-Tweed, T01289-381333, havenholidays.com, check

Knights in armour – for sale at a Northumbrian castle near you; Springhill Farm Campsite; St Cuthbert's Chapel and Arctic tern on Inner Farne; Bamburgh Castle; shell-seekers' treasure; tipis at Pot-a-Doodle Do.

Great escapes Northumberland

website for offers) has a boating lake, nine-hole golf course, indoor and outdoor swimming pools, and a luxury spa.

Cottage rental is available through **Dales Holiday Cottages** (T0844-576 2545, dalesholcot. com), **Northumbria Byways** (T01697-746777, northumbria-byways.com) and **Northumbria Coast & Country Cottages** (T01665-830783, northumbria-cottages.co.uk).

Explore the great outdoors

Kielder Water & Forest Park (visitkielder.com) combines England's largest forest (a 250-square-mile mantle that's home to three-quarters of the country's red squirrels) with the shimmering expanse of Kielder Water, a haven for ospreys and otters. This verdant patch of Northumberland's 'wild west' makes a superb natural break, with activities ranging from hiking and cycling to sailing and wildlife watching.

Get your bearings at one of two visitor centres. Kielder Castle Visitor Centre (T01434-250209, Easter-Oct, daily, plus weekends Nov-Dec) is close to The Bike Place cycle hire shop (T01434-250457), a campsite, youth hostel and the start of the forest drive. Tower Knowe Visitor Centre, meanwhile, has a boarding point for the Osprey ferry, a 74-seat motor cruiser that calls at Leaplish, Tower Knowe, Belvedere and Mirage.

One of the park's best bases for families, Leaplish Waterside Park (T0870-2403549, nwl.co.uk, Easter-Oct) has everything from mini golf, boat hire and an indoor heated swimming pool to a play garden and Kielder Water Birds of Prey Centre (T01434-250400, daily 1000-1700). You can stay at the caravan park or rent a luxury self-catering forest lodge (sleeping 4-6, from around £280-960/wk), while food is available at the Boat Inn Restaurant & Bar (T01434-250294).

Ideal for gentle cycling or walking, the Lakeside Way, a muti-purpose trail encircling Kielder Water, passes through Leaplish Waterside Park. More challenging mountain-biking trails link Kielder Castle with the Deadwater Fells. Dinghy sailing lessons are available at Kielder Water Sailing Club and you can hire various craft at the Hawkhirst Adventure Camp.

Kielder's busy programme of annual events includes a wildlife month in May, featuring deer safaris, red squirrel walks and owl nights.

Stock up on local food

Offering a tasty spread of seasonal produce, from lamb to fresh mussels and strawberries, **Alnwick Farmers' Market** (alnwickmarkets.co.uk) takes place on the last Friday of every month. You can also find a wide variety of homegrown food at **Brocksbushes Farm Shop** (Corbridge, T01434-633100, brocksbushes.co.uk) and **Wallington House Farm Shop** (T01670-773600, nationaltrust. org.uk). **Chain Bridge Honey Farm** (Horncliffe, nr Berwick upon Tweed, T01289-386362, chainbridgehoney.co.uk) has honey to sample in various guises, from mustard to ice cream, while **The Northumberland Cheese Company** (Blagdon, T01670-789798, northumberlandcheese. co.uk) can cut you a slice of its award-winning Coquetdale cheese.

Bamburgh Castle

Plan a big day out

After seal- and puffin-watching in the **Farne Islands** (see right), castles come a close second on most children's holiday wishlists in Northumberland. And if they're Harry Potter fans, **Alnwick Castle** (see page 237) will inevitably reign supreme – it was, after all, where the young wizard first learnt how to fly.

Northumberland's other castles, however, have different tricks up their sleeves. **Bamburgh Castle** (T01668-214515, bamburghcastle.com, Mar-Nov, daily 1000-1700, £7.50/adult, £3.50/child, under 5s free) not only has a magical beach on its doorstep, but also takes children on a mesmerizing tour of vaulted halls and stone passageways. Lying at the heart of the medieval fortress, the Keep has spooky suits of armour standing guard in shadowy recesses and a huge iron chain that was once used for salvaging ships wrecked off the coast. Outside, kids can watch archaeologists at work (there's evidence of habitation at Bamburgh from as early as 7000 years ago) and have a go at digging for artefacts in their own excavation pit. A quiz trail and aviation museum, not to mention the cannon-studded battlements, help to keep interest levels high – until, that is, the beach proves irresistible.

There's less for kids to do at **Lindisfarne Castle** (T01289-389244, nationaltrust.org.uk, Feb-Nov, times vary, £6.30/adult, £3.10/child, £15.70/family). However, this 16th-century miniature fort (converted by Sir Edward Lutyens into an Edwardian holiday home) is just one facet of a day on Holy Island which starts with an exciting crossing of the tidal causeway (check lindisfarne.org.uk for times). The castle has a children's quiz and a walled garden planned by Gertrude Jekyll. Founded by St Aidan in AD635, the nearby ruins of **Lindisfarne Priory** (T01289-389200, english-heritage.org.uk, £4.20/adult, £2.10/child, year round, times vary) are fun to explore and there's also a museum that reveals the story of Northumberland's great holy man, St Cuthbert. At the **Lindisfarne Centre** (T01289-389004, lindisfarne-centre.com) there are electronic versions of the exquisite Lindisfarne Gospels and an exhibit on the altogether less refined vikings who attacked Holy Island in AD793.

A short distance inland from Lindisfarne (assuming you make it safely back across the causeway), **Heatherslaw Visitor Centre** (T01890-820338, ford-and-etal.co.uk, Mar-Oct, daily 1000-1700) makes a good starting point for exploring the 16,500-acre Ford & Etal Estates. Highlights include Etal Castle, Heatherslaw Light Railway, Fenton Bird of Prey Centre and Lady Waterford Hall. You can also hire bikes at the centre.

A refreshing antidote to Northumberland's historical 'heaviness', **Alnwick Garden** (T01665-511350, alnwickgarden.com, year round, daily from 1000, £10/adult, £0.01/child) is a contemporary wonderland with dancing fountains, a bamboo labyrinth and a huge treehouse complete with wobbly rope bridge. The garden's centrepiece is the Grand Cascade where kids can dodge squirting jets of water. Another change of clothes may be required after visiting the Serpent

Spot a seal

Home to one of Europe's largest grey seal colonies, the **Farne Islands** (nationaltrust.org.uk) also provide sanctuary for 100,000 pairs of nesting seabirds, such as puffins, kittiwakes, guillemots and terns. Boat trips operate from Seahouses and usually feature shore time on Inner Farne or Staple. As a guide, allow £12/adult, £8/child for the boat fare and £5.80/adult, £2.90/child for landing fees. Remember your hat if visiting Inner Farne from May-Jul as territorial arctic terns tend to dive-bomb visitors. Before your visit, download the excellent Inner Farne I-Spy sheets from the National Trust website. As well as wildlife, they highlight the island's rich heritage, including St Cutherbert's Chapel and the daring exploits of Grace Darling.

Ditch the car

Running between Newcastle and Carlisle, the **Hadrian's Wall Country Bus AD122** (hadrians-wall.org, Easter-Oct) connects all the main Roman sites along the World Heritage Site, has an on-board guide during peak times and even carries bikes. The full-day Maximus Trip leaves Newcastle at 0900 (or Hexham at 1000), stopping at Chesters Fort, with its amazing baths and gateways, before continuing through Northumberland National Park to Vindolanda, where you can explore full-scale replicas of houses, temples and shops. After lunch, hop back on the bus to Birdoswald Fort for views of the longest stretch of Hadrian's Wall still standing. The late afternoon bus leaves for Hexham at around 1715. See also page 195.

Garden with its interactive water sculptures. The geometrically designed Ornamental Gardens are riddled with pathways and secret corners (cue for a game of hide-and-seek) and if you still have the energy, there's a woodland walk with views of the River Aln and Alnwick Castle.

Treat yourself to dinner

The **Treehouse** restaurant at Alnwick Gardens (see above) is a wonderfully quirky place for a meal. Local seafood and regional dishes always feature on the menu, and you can book a table for lunch or dinner (T01665-511852) without having to buy a ticket for the gardens. Lunch is served daily, 1130-1445, while à la carte evening meals are available Thu-Sat from 1830. Dishes include local sausages and mash (£8.50) and pan-fried fillet of North Sea halibut (£18.95).

Overlooking the dunes and saltmarshes of Lindisfarne National Nature Reserve, **The Barn at Beal** (T01289-381477, barnatbeal.com, Feb-Dec, daily 1000-1600, plus Sat 1900-2300) is not only a lovely spot to take in the views and sample local food at the restaurant, but it also has a free visitor centre where you can investigate the links between the seasons, farming and food. For starters, try the crayfish and avocado salad (£6.45) and continue the seafood theme with a delicious main course of Lindisfarne fishcakes (£8.95). Traditional Sunday roasts are also available, along with a range of light bites. Afterwards, you can join a guided wildlife walk at Beal Farm or watch a falconry demonstration. In fact, why not spend the night? The campsite at Beal Farm has views of Lindisfarne and costs just £5/pitch, plus £2/person.

Essential websites

Tourist information visitnorthumberland.com, visitnortheastengland.com.
Forestry Commission forestry.gov.uk.
Northumberland National Park northumberlandnationalpark.org.uk.

Don't miss

Belsay Hall, Castle and Gardens
Nr Ponteland, T01661-881636, english-heritage.org.uk.
Chillingham Castle
T01668-215359, chillingham-castle.com.
Cragside House and Gardens
Rothbury, T01669-620333, nationaltrust.org.uk.
Dunstanburgh Castle
T01665-576231, nationaltrust.org.uk.
Highland Cattle Centre
Stocksfield, T07968-865591, thehighlandcattlecentre.co.uk.
RNLI Grace Darling Museum
Bamburgh, T01668-214910, rnli.org.uk.
Sanctuary Wildlife Care Centre
Ulgham, nr Morpeth, T01670-791778, wildlife-sanctuary.co.uk.
Warkworth Castle
T01665-711423, english-heritage.org.uk.
Whitehouse Farm Centre
Nr Morpeth, T01670-789998, whitehousefarmcentre.co.uk.

Anyone for Quidditch?

The Windsor of the North, **Alnwick Castle** (T01665-510777, alnwickcastle.com, year round, daily 1000-1800, £11.95/adult, £4.95/child, £29.95/family) is one of the largest inhabited castles in England and has starred in *Blackadder*, *Elizabeth* and as Hogwarts School of Wizardry in the Harry Potter films. Harry received his first lessons in broomstick flying in the castle grounds and crash-landed a flying Ford Anglia in its inner bailey. There are plenty of Potter-themed events held at the castle, while other treats for kids include themed tours, story-telling, magic shows, archery lessons for the over 11s and birds of prey demonstrations. In Knight's Quest, children can dress up as knights and ladies of the realm and experience what life was like in medieval times.

After seal- and puffin-watching in the Farne Islands, castles come a close second on most children's holiday wishlists in Northumberland.

Alnwick Castle – home of the Duke and Duchess of Northumberland.

Contents

240 Map

242 Pembrokeshire
244 Fun & free
246 Best beaches
248 Action stations
252 Big days out
254 Sleeping
257 Eating
259 Essentials

260 Gower Peninsula

268 Snowdonia
270 Fun & free
272 Best beaches
274 Action stations
276 Big days out
278 Sleeping
280 Eating
281 Essentials

Wales

Rhossili

Big days out...

1 Caldey Island
2 Castell Henllys
3 Folly Farm
4 Oakwood Theme Park
5 Carew Castle
6 The Dinosaur Park
7 Heatherton Country Park
8 Pembroke Castle
9 Picton Castle
10 Greenwood Forest Park
11 Snowdon Mountain Railway
12 Bodnant Garden
13 Electric Mountain
14 King Arthur's Labyrinth
15 Portmeirion

Motorway
Primary route
A Road
✈ Airports
⛴ Ferries

Irish Sea

Holyhead
Anglesey
Llangoed
⬇10 Llandudno   Prestatyn
Rhyl
Bangor   Conwy   Colwyn Bay   Denbigh   Mold
Caernarfon   ⬇12   Ruthin
⬇13   A5   A470   A55
⬇11   A487   *Yr Wyddfa (Snowdon)* ▲   Betws-y-Coed   Wrexham
Porthmadog   A470   Llangollen
Llŷn Peninsula   A470   Y Bala
⬇15   A470   A494
Barmouth   A470   A494   Welshpool
Dolgellau   A458
⬇14   Newtown
Cardigan Bay   Machynlleth   A489
A487   A44
Aberystwyth   **ENGLAND**
A470
New Quay   *Cambrian Mountains*   Llandrindod Wells
⬇2   Llanddewi-Brefi   A483   Builth Wells
Cardigan   Llandysul   Llandovery   A438
Newport   A487   A470   A479
Fishguard   ⬇4 ⬇5   A40   A40   Brecon   Felindre   A40   A465
St David's   ⬇3   Carmarthen   A40   A483   Merthyr Tydfil   Abergavenny
Haverfordwest   A40   A48   Ammanford   A465
St Brides Bay   ⬇9   A4076   A477   Llanelli   A465   A4042   A449   M48
Milford Haven   Tenby   Swansea   M4   M4
Pembroke Dock   *Carmarthen Bay*   Porthcawl   Bridgend   Newport
⬇8   ⬇7 ⬇6 ⬇1   *Gower Peninsula*   M4   **Cardiff**

Bristol Channel

N

20 km
20 miles

Kitesurfing at Newgale Sands, Pembrokeshire; Caernarfon Castle; camping in Snowdonia; Cardigan Bay; coastline near Fishguard; lifeguard on Gower Peninsula; Mt Snowdon.

Newgale Sands.

Pembrokeshire

Beautiful beaches come naturally to this southwest tip of Wales. No other county in Britain flies more Blue Flags – and none boast a national park that is almost all coast. But it's the huge potential, from bucket-and-spade to island escapade, that makes Pembrokeshire's seaside such a 'shore thing' for kids.

Pembrokeshire could almost have coined the term, 'multi-activity'. If you thought a beach holiday was pretty full-on if you managed to squeeze in some surfing, a rock-pooling expedition and a sandcastle or two, try an action-packed day of kayaking and coasteering (clambering around cliffs, in and out of the sea like a lemming that can't make up its mind).

Then there are Pembrokeshire's five fabulous offshore islands – each one a contender for your big holiday treat. If you're visiting in spring, the puffins on **Skomer** and **Skokholm** are hard to resist; **Grassholm** has gazillions of gannets all summer, while **Ramsey** has spectacular arches and sea caves that are always thrilling when you're hurtling past them in a RIB (a glorified rubber dinghy with large outboard engine). **Caldey**, as you'd expect from a holy island, offers an altogether more refined experience.

Departure point for Caldey Island boat trips, **Tenby** is Pembrokeshire's favourite harbour pin-up. It also has a handsome bevy of beaches, but none that quite match the golden-sand perfection of bays like Manorbier or Barafundle further west. North of Tenby, **Saundersfoot** is a popular family resort, while **Dale**, near the entrance to Milford Haven, attracts the sailing crowd. St Brides Bay has some of Pembrokeshire's most enigmatic beaches, with **Newgale** topping the leader board for surfers and kite-flyers.

St David's (a delightful, pocket-sized city with a must-see cathedral) is the gateway to Ramsey Island and Whitesands Bay. The coast feels more remote and secluded as you follow its ins and outs towards Strumble Head. Beyond lies **Fishguard**, **Newport** and the great sweep of Cardigan Bay.

Delve inland and most roads lead to the market town of **Haverfordwest**. But just because you've left the coast don't imagine you're in for a quiet time. Cycling, sailing, horse riding and dressing up as a Celtic warrior are just some of Pembrokeshire's non-beachy highlights at places like Preseli Hills, Teifi Marshes, Llys-y-Fran Country Park and Castell Henllys Iron Age Fort.

You must

- Catch a wave at Newgale Sands or Whitesands Bay.

- Time-travel to the Iron Age at Castell Henllys.

- Stroll at least some of the coast path.

- Have a go at coasteering or sea kayaking.

- Take a high-speed RIB ride around Ramsey.

- Cycle to the Welsh Wildlife Centre.

- See Skomer's puffins and Grassholm's gannets.

- Picnic at Barafundle Bay.

- Camp on a clifftop with views of the sea.

Out & about Pembrokeshire

Barafundle Bay

Pembrokeshire's coastline is so varied and beautiful that over 60 miles of it is cared for by the National Trust – a big comfort when you first set eyes on the pristine golden sands of Barafundle Bay. Tucked into the crinkle-cut coast south of Pembroke, it requires a bit of an effort to reach. The half-mile walk over the cliffs from a car park at Stackpole Quay (where you'll also find the nearest toilets and café) has no doubt helped to preserve the special, secluded quality of Barafundle. Backed by dunes and woodland, this is a true hidden gem with squeaky-clean sand, gorgeous swimming and all the makings of one of Britain's best beach-picnic spots.

Broad Haven

Low tide reveals acres of sand at this sheltered beach with its thriving seafront of shops, cafés and holiday homes. Keep an eye on the tide and you can even walk around the headland to Little Haven, a smaller cove with a slipway for dinghies and a trio of pubs right by the sea.

Broad Haven South

The next beach along from Barafundle, Broad Haven South is not to be confused with the much busier Broad Haven on St Brides Bay. This is an altogether more remote and romantic beach with a mile-long walk from Bosherton village that weaves through lily ponds to the dune-backed bay. The soft sand at Broad Haven South should satisfy castle-builders, but swimmers need to be wary of strong offshore currents. The stream that flows from the ponds is a safer bet for littl'uns to splash around in.

Caerfai

A small, sandy cove wedged between cliffs about a mile south of St David's, Caerfai has rock pools, caves and decent surf. Access is steep, however, and the only facilities are a clifftop car park and the farm shop at nearby Caerfai Bay Campsite (page 254).

Dale

Dale has a mainly pebble beach with some sand at low tide. But it's sailing, not sandcastles, that lures families to this busy beach. There isn't a better place in Pembrokeshire to learn the ropes – see page 251 for details.

East Angle Bay

A little-visited swathe of sand and mudflats opposite Milford Haven, where curlews and other waders outnumber windbreaks.

Freshwater East

Popular with watersports enthusiasts, Freshwater East has plenty of sand at low tide when a series of 'mini bays' emerge beneath low cliffs at the eastern end of the beach. Beloved of surfers, nearby Freshwater West is strafed by vicious rip currents.

Marloes Sands

Just round the coast from Martin's Haven (the departure point for boat trips to Skomer and Skokholm – see pages 248-249), Marloes Sands can vanish at high tide. Arrive when the tide is ebbing, however, and you can steadily colonize a broad sweep of sand, delve in rock pools and discover the (albeit subtle) remains of a 19th-century paddle steamer wrecked on adjacent Albion Sands. Parking is available at the National Trust car park half a mile from the beach, while Marloes village has a pub, restaurant and café.

Newgale

Pembrokeshire's answer to Woolacombe Sands in North Devon or Watergate Bay in Cornwall, Newgale is a fabulous beach for surfing and kitesurfing or simply revelling in 2 miles of Atlantic-washed sands. Clamber over the curious pebble ridge (formed during a huge storm in 1859) and you'll also find no

St Brides Bay, looking north from Broad Haven.

shortage of space for simple pleasures like beach cricket, building sandcastles and flying kites. Shallow streams that flow across the beach at low tide make perfect little rapid-runs for toy boats, while the southern end of Newgale has a cave and numerous sheltered bays.

Newport Sands

A broad, sandy beach at the mouth of the River Nevern, Newport Sands is popular with families and watersports lovers. At low tide you can wade across the river to Newport Parrog.

Poppit

Cardigan's local beach, Poppit is lodged in the mouth of the River Teifi where, at low tide, it reveals a rippled tongue of sand extending almost as far as Gwbert on the opposite side of the estuary. Keep a lookout for harbour porpoises at Poppit – but don't take your eye off the tide which races in here.

Saundersfoot

It's easy to see why this is such a popular family resort. Not only is the main beach sandy and spacious, but it nudges up against a lovely little harbour. The adjacent Coppet Beach is the starting point of the old railway tunnel walk towards Wiseman's Bridge, while on the other side of the harbour Glen Beach has rock pools and wooded cliffs.

Tenby

Tenby's beaches are legendary – a sandy quartet that ranges from the mile-and-a-half sweep of Tenby South with its dunes, donkey rides and gently shelving shore, to Castle Beach, hemmed in by Castle Hill and St Catherine's Island and all but consumed at high tide. Easily accessible Harbour Beach, meanwhile, offers a sheltered haven for toddlers, as well as a range of boating options, from Funboats to Caldey Island cruises. You can also hire canoes and sailing dinghies at Tenby North, a safe, well-protected beach wrapped around the harbour at low tide and offering copious seafront facilities. All four beaches can get very busy during the summer holidays, so save time by ditching the car at the park-and-ride and using the free shuttle bus.

Traeth Llyfn

None

The antithesis to Tenby, this beach bolthole on the north coast is reached by steep steps and there are no facilities whatsoever. On the plus side, you'll find a pretty cove, rock pools and few other people.

Whitesands Bay

When the surf's up, Whitesands will be heaving. This dramatic scimitar of sand is swept by excellent surf at its northern end where craggy St David's Head looms above the beach. Surf lessons and board hire are available from the local surf school (see page 251). Consider catching the Celtic Coaster shuttle bus from St David's during the height of summer when parking at Whitesands can be a challenge.

Spot a puffin

Every child's favourite seabird – the dapper little puffin with the pop-art beak and wings that beat like an overwound bath toy – arrives to breed in its thousands on Skomer Island in early April. They take up residence in their nesting burrows, rear their chicks, then leave again in late July – just as the school summer holidays are getting going. It's the same with the razorbills and guillemots that nest on Skomer, a national nature reserve that lies 15 minutes by boat from Martin's Haven. A visit during the May half-term holiday is ideal. Not only will you get close-up views of puffins, but the whole island is ablaze with red campion, bluebells and thrift. Grey seals are seen all year (with pups in September), while other avian highlights include peregrine falcons and short-eared owls. Stay overnight on Skomer (there's basic self-catering accommodation for up to 15 people) and you will be treated to one of Britain's greatest wildlife spectacles when 120,000 pairs of Manx shearwaters return to their nesting burrows under cover of darkness.

Shearwaters, along with puffins and storm petrels, also nest on nearby Skokholm, while further offshore, Grassholm appears dusted with summer snow as 32,000 pairs of gannets settle down to nest.

Boat trips to Grassholm often have the added bonus of porpoise and dolphin sightings. Super pods of up to 500 dolphins are not unheard

The dapper little puffin with the pop-art beak and wings that beat like an overwound bath toy.

Opposite: Posing puffin. Above: Grassholm gannet, surf-swept Skomer, spying seal, Ramsey RIB.

Boat operators

Dale Sailing
Neyland, T01646-603110, dale-sailing.co.uk. Skomer landings Apr-Oct, Tue-Sun, 1000, 1100 and 1200 from Martin's Haven, £10/adult, £7/child (under 16), plus landing fee £6/adult, children free. Sea Safaris (2.5 hr) to either Skomer and Skokholm or Grassholm, daily from Dale, £30/adult, £15/child (height restrictions for under-10s). Phone for details of other cruises.

Thousand Islands Expeditions
St David's, T01437-721721, thousandislands.co.uk, Mar-Oct, Ramsey landings, Mar-Oct, daily 1000 and 1200 from St Justinians, £15/adult, £7.50/child (under 12). Cruise around Ramsey (1.5 hr), daily, £24/adult, £12/child. Jet boat rides, whalewatching and other cruises also available.

Voyages of Discovery
St David's, T0800-854367, ramseyisland.co.uk. Ramsey Island trips (60-90 minutes) Mar-Oct, daily, £24/adult, £12/child (4-16), £5/infant (under 4). Cruises to North Bishops and Grassholm Islands also available, plus offshore whalewatching trips.

Aquaphobia
St David's, T01437-720471, aquaphobia-ramseyisland.co.uk.

Ramsey Island Cruises
St David's, T01437-721423, ramseyislandcruises.net.

Shearwater Safaris
Neyland, T01646-602941, boatrides.co.uk.

Solva Boat Trips
Solva, T01437-721725, solva.net/boattrips.

of, and you might also be lucky enough to glimpse basking sharks, sunfish and minke whales.

Over on the northern edge of St Brides Bay the focus is on Ramsey Island where RIB rides combine wildlife with high-speed thrills.

First you dash across Ramsey Island Sound, keeping an eye out for porpoises and gannets feeding on an ebbing tide, then it's a more tentative approach to The Bitches – a series of maelstrom-molested rocks that have chomped their way through many a shipwreck. Look out for oystercatchers and shags here.

Further around the island, your skipper deftly noses the inflatable craft into giant sea caves or sends it skimming through archways. Kittiwakes, razorbills and guillemots stream from cliff-face rookeries, while grey seals loll about on shingle coves or bob to the surface to watch you pass with large, inquisitive eyes.

>> Several operators run boat trips to Pembrokeshire's wildlife-rich islands (see right). Be sure to choose one that adheres to the Pembrokeshire Marine Code (pembrokeshiremarinecode.org.uk).

Out & about Pembrokeshire

Boat trips
See pages 248-249.

Mackerel fishing trips leave from Saundersfoot, St Justinians, Solva and Tenby.

Cycling: Brunel Trail
Starting at Haverfordwest, this 9-mile, traffic-free trail passes through Bolton Hill Wood and Westfield Pill Nature Reserve before reaching a marina at Brunel Quay, Neyland – once home to Isambard Kingdom Brunel and the terminus of the Great Western Railway.

Mikes Bikes
Haverfordwest, T01437-760068, mikes-bikes.co.uk. Mon-Sat, 0930-1730, adult bike £12/day, child's bike £6/day. Tag-alongs, trailers and child seats also available.

Cycling: Cardi Bach
The mile-long Cardi Bach trail starts at Cardigan Bridge and probes Teifi Marshes where the Welsh Wildlife Centre (page 245) is the perfect spot for a break. Cilgerran Castle is a further 2 miles along a quiet road.

New Image Bicycles
Cardigan, T01239-621275. bikebikebike.co.uk. Mon-Sat from 0930, bikes from £17.63/day.

Cycling: Llys y Fran
Hire bikes from the visitor centre and cycle around the reservoir at the heart of Llys y Fran Country Park. A shorter 1.5-mile family trail skirts the eastern shore.

Cycling: The Tramway
An easy 2-mile ride along an old railway line meandering through woodland between Stepaside and Saundersfoot Harbour.

Tenby Cycles
Tenby, T01834-845573, tenbycycles. co.uk. Mon-Sat, 0930-1730, adult bike £10/day, child's bike £8/day.

Cycling: Other cycle hire shops
Newport Bike Hire
Newport, T01239-820773.

Re-Cycles Green Bike Hire
Bluestones, T01437-711123.

Kitesurfing
Big Blue Kitesurfing
Newgale, T07816-169359, bigbluekitesurfing.com. One-day beginner's course £95/person. With all that sand, surf and space, Newgale attracts kitesurfers like moths to a lightbulb. Teenagers can learn the basics with Big Blue or try their hand at kiteboarding.

Quad biking
Ritec Valley Quad Bikes
Penally, T01834-843390, ritec-valley. co.uk. 30-minute taster session £21/ adult, £17/child (6-15), £69/family. Practice on a purpose-built quad park, then rev up for an off-road adventure (minimum age 16).

Scuba diving
West Wales Diving Centre
Haverfordwest, T01437-781457, westwalesdivers.co.uk. Bubblemaker £35/child (8-10), Seal Team £125/ child (8-10), Discover Scuba £125/ person (minimum age 10). PADI 5-star centre offering full range of courses, including 3-hour Bubblemaker and full-day Seal Team pool sessions for kids.

Surfing
Newsurf
Newgale, T01437-721398, newsurf. co.uk. Year round, daily, lessons £55/full-day, £35/half-day. Newgale's 2-mile strand is one of Pembrokeshire's best surf spots, with waves to suit all levels of experience. Newsurf runs daily lessons during the school holidays and if it's flat calm, you can always try SUP (Stand Up Paddleboarding) or rent a kayak.

Outer Reef Surf School
Pembroke, T01646-680070,

Saddle up

The Dunes Riding Centre
Narberth, T01834-891398, dunes-riding.co.uk.

Maesgwynne Riding Stables
Fishguard, T01348-872659.

Marros Riding Centre
Pendine, T01994-453777, marros-farm.co.uk.

Nolton Stables
Nolton, T01437-710360, noltonstables.com.

outerreefsurfschool.com. Year round, daily, lessons £45/full-day, £25/half-day.
Surf tuition at Broadhaven, Freshwater West, Manorbier and Newgale beaches.

Whitesands Surf School

St David's, T01437-720433, whitesandssurfschool.co.uk. May-Oct, daily, lessons £25/half-day. Learn to surf at Whitesands Bay, near St David's.

Watersports
West Wales Watersports

Dale, T01646-636642, surfdale.co.uk. Windsurfers £15/hr, £50/day; sit-on kayaks £8/hr, £30/day; Pico dinghy £15/hr, £49/day. Half-day tuition £65/adult, £55/child (8-14).
RYA training centre with windsurfers, sailing dinghies, sea kayaks and powerboats to get to grips with. Surfing is available through Newsurf (see left). You can hire by the hour or enrol on courses lasting from a half-day to a week.

Wildlife safaris
Red Heron

Clynderwen, T017815-166735, redheron.co.uk. £10-15/person. Family wildlife sessions, including badger evenings, bug hunting and seal watching.

Pick up a copy of the free **Coast to Coast** newspaper which has listings of national park events, such as rock-pool rambles, crab catching and bat hunting.

Multi activities

Can't make up your mind what activity to try? Several centres offer a wide choice of outdoor pursuits, often merging two or three into a single, action-packed day. TYF Adventure, for example, combines sea kayaking with coasteering on its Coastal Explorer days (from £95/adult, £70/child under 16). Typically, you can expect to pay around £80/adult and £60/child for a full-day activity or £45/adult and £35/child for a half-day session. The minimum age for most activities is eight, although this does vary. Fforest Outdoor has taken infants as young as three on their guided Heritage Canoe tours (£30/adult, £20/child under 14 or £15/child if booked as a family of four). These gentle paddling expeditions take you along the River Teifi, through Cilgerran Gorge and the Teifi Marshes Nature Reserve.

Fforest Outdoor (FFO) Cardigan, T01239-623633, fforestoutdoor.co.uk.

Morfa Bay Adventure (MBA) Pendine, T01994-453588, morfabay.com.

Pembrokeshire Activity Centre (PAC) Pembroke Dock, T01646-622013, pembrokeshire-activity-centre.co.uk.

Sealyham Activity Centre (SAC) Haverfordwest, T01348-840763, sealyham.com.

TYF Adventure (TYF) St David's, T01437-721611, tyf.com.

	FFO	MBA	PAC	SAC	TYF
Archery		●		●	
Canoeing	●		●	●	
Coasteering	●	●	●	●	●
High-ropes course		●		●	
Hill walking		●	●	●	
Mountain biking		●			
Quad biking		●			
Powerboating			●		
Raft-building		●	●		
Rock climbing	●	●			●
Sailing			●	●	
Sea kayaking	●	●	●	●	●
Surfing		●	●	●	●

Out & about Pembrokeshire

Caldey Island

Off Tenby, T01834-844453, caldey-island.co.uk. Boats depart Tenby Harbour (high tide) or Castle Beach (low tide), Easter-Oct, Mon-Fri, plus Sat (May-Sep). Return tickets from harbour kiosk £10/adult, £5/child, family rates on request.

Caldey is owned by monks of the Cistercian Order, whose monastery overlooks the village green. As befits one of Britain's holy islands, this is a gentle day out where you can peruse the Old Priory before taking a stroll to the lighthouse (check for seals on the rocks below) or relaxing on the beach at Priory Bay. The cutesy village has a tea garden, as well as shops selling locally-made perfume, chocolate and shortbread, while the post office doubles as a museum.

Castell Henllys

Meline, nr Newport, T01239-891319, castellhenllys.com. Easter-Oct, daily 1000-1700, Nov-Easter, daily 1100-1500, £3.50/adult, £2.50/child, £9.50/family. Celtic Fun sessions on selected dates Apr-Oct, £2/child.

Reconstructed on the site of an Iron Age hill fort, Castell Henllys is far more than simply a cluster of thatched roundhouses – it's a time capsule where children are whisked back 2000 years to an age of chieftains, Celtic myths and living off the land. Aimed at kids aged 6-12, Celtic Fun sessions at Castell Henllys are run by actors in authentic garb. They're brilliant at getting your tribe to enter into the spirit of the Iron Age with war chants, hunting forays, face-painting and stories around the hearth, but it's not all fun and games. Celtic kids should expect some hard graft, grinding wheat between stones for making bread, twining sheep's wool into cord and hurling a mixture of mud, horse hair and cow poo onto the willow framework of a new roundhouse.

Folly Farm

Begelly, nr Kilgetty, T01834-812731, folly-farm.co.uk. Mar-Nov, daily from 1000; Nov-Feb, weekends only, plus Feb half term. £7.50/adult, £6.50/child (3-15).

Is it a farm park? Is it a funfair? Or is it a zoo? Well, actually, it's all three – and then some. Folly Farm is a sprawling, six-in-one attraction that represents excellent value for money. Plan your visit carefully, though, because it would certainly be folly to try to cram in everything. If it's raining, focus on the indoor Jolly Farm (pet-handling, bottle-feeding etc), Carousel Woods (slides, tubes, nets and soft play) and the huge undercover funfair with its dodgems, carousel and other classic rides. Outside, a playzone with go-karts, diggers, pedal tractors and jungle gyms, merges with Folly Zoo where lemurs, meerkats and zebras head a cast of fairly

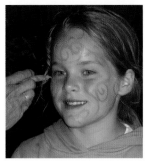

Sign of the times – going Celtic at Castell Henllys Iron Age Fort.

predictable (but imaginatively housed) creatures. Folly Wood, a neighbouring country park with deer, llamas, horses and sheep, can be explored by tractor tour or nature trail.

Oakwood Theme Park

Canaston Bridge, T01834-861889, oakwoodthemepark.co.uk. Apr-Nov, daily from 1000. £16.95/person (10 plus), £13.95/child (3-9), £58/family. 10% discount for online bookings.

If you want to be a bore and upset the kids you could always suggest that Pembrokeshire's coast is nature's very own theme park (why bother with a rollercoaster when you could go coasteering instead?). Chances are, though, that you'll have an insanely good time at Oakwood. The 60-mph Speed coaster has loops, twists and a cheek-pummelling drop that's beyond the vertical. Megaphobia is a rattling-good wooden coaster, while Hydro is Oakwood's big water chute. There are over 30 rides in total, with plenty to keep younger children happy.

More family favourites

Carew Castle

Carew, T01646-651782, carewcastle.com. Mar-Nov, daily, 1000-1700, £3.50/adult, £2.50/child, £9.50/family. A beguiling mix of Norman fort and Elizabethan home, Carew Castle has a dreamy picnic spot by its huge mill pond.

The Dinosaur Park

Gumfreston, T01834-845272, thedinosaurpark.co.uk. Mar-Oct, daily, from 1000, £6.50/adult, £5.50/child (3-15), £22/family. Prehistoric quiz trail through woods populated by fun, but rather clunky-looking, dinosaurs.

Heatherton Country Park

St Florence, T01646-652000, heatherton.co.uk. Pay-as-you-play leisure park with pitch-and-putt, go-karts, bumper boats, archery, paintball, corn maize, fishing and more.

Pembroke Castle

T01646-681510, pembroke-castle.co.uk. Year round, daily from 0930, £3.50/adult, £2.50/child (5-16), £10/family. Mighty fort with lots of tunnels and towers to explore. Kids love the brass-rubbing centre.

Picton Castle

Rhos, T01437-751326, pictoncastle.co.uk. Easter-Sep, Tue-Sun 1030-1700, £5.95/adult, £3/child (under 12). Gardens, maze, woodland trails and adventure playground.

Also recommended

Clerkenhill Adventure Farm

Slebech, T01437-751227, clerkenhilladventurefarm.co.uk.

Dyfed Shires & Leisure Farm

Carnhuan, T01239-891288, leisurefarm.co.uk.

Manor House Wildlife Park

St Florence, T01646-651201, manorhousewildlifepark.co.uk.

Silent World

Tenby, T01834-844498, silentworld.org.uk.

Walk the quests, solve the riddles – that's the cunning plan behind **Pembrokeshire Wizard** (pembrokeshirewizard.co.uk, £19.99 each), a set of five audio CDs that guides you around St David's Peninsula, Strumble Head, Pentre Ifan, Carew Castle, and Skomer Island on walks lasting up to three hours.

Members' perks

Family membership (see page 5) entitles you to free entry to:

National Trust
• Colby Woodland Garden, Amroth.
• Tudor Merchant's House, Tenby.

RSPB
• Ramsey Island (landing only).

Heritage in Wales
Members get free admission to all Cadw sites, T0800-074 3121, cadw.wales.gov.uk, including Lamphey Bishop's Palace near Pembroke.

Rain check

Arts & Crafts
• The Creative Café, Narberth, T01834-861651.
• Pottery Shed Café, Pembroke Dock, T01646-689064, potteryshedcafe.co.uk.
• Wolfscastle Pottery, Wolfscastle, T01437-741609.

Cinemas
• Palace, Haverfordwest, T01437-767675.
• Royal Playhouse, Tenby, T01834-844809.

Indoor play & amusements
• Ocean Commotion, Tenby, T01834-845526, oceancommotion.co.uk.
• Pirate Pete's Adventure Play, Milford Haven, T01646-696531.

Indoor swimming pools
• The Blue Lagoon, Bluestone Holiday Village, T01834-862410, bluelagoonwales.com.
• Pembroke Leisure Centre, T01646-684434.
• Tenby Leisure Centre, T01834-843575

Museums
• County Museum, Scolton Manor, Haverfordwest, T01437-731328.
• Felinwynt Rainforest Centre, nr Cardigan, T01239-810250, butterflycentre.co.uk.
• Haverfordwest Town Museum, T01437-763087, haverfordwest-town-museum.org.uk.
• The Last Invasion Gallery, Town Hall, Fishguard, T01437-776638.
• Milford Haven Heritage & Maritime Museum, The Old Customs House, T01646-694496.
• Museum of Childhood, Pen-ffynnon, T01559-370428.
• Tenby Museum, T01834-842809, tenbymuseum.org.uk.

Sleeping Pembrokeshire

Caerfai Bay Caravan & Tent Park

Caerfai, nr St David's, T01437-720274, caerfaibay.co.uk. Mar-Nov, £10-16/pitch (2 people), plus £4.50/extra adult, £3/extra child (3-12).

One of a pair of campsites just south of St David's, Caerfai Bay has the edge over its neighbour when it comes to family facilities. If you want simpler camping (with no caravans), opt instead for Caerfai Farm – literally across the road. Both sites share fabulous coastal views, easy access to the beach (page 246) and all the culinary delights of the Caerfai Farm Shop. Specialities include cheddar and caerphilly cheese (try the leek and garlic variety), but you'll also find fresh bread and other everyday essentials.

Creampots Touring Caravan & Camping Park

Broadway, T01437-781776, creampots.co.uk. Mar-Oct, £14.75-18.75/pitch (2 people), plus £4.50/extra adult, £3.50/extra child (3-12).

Sheltered, level and perfectly pleasant, Creampots makes a comfortable base a mile or two from the equally family-safe beach at Broad Haven. Caravans dominate at this well-maintained site, but there's still space for 40 tents during the height of summer.

Hendre Farm Campsite

Dinas Head, nr Newport, T01239-820208, hendrefarmholidays.com. £4/person. Cottage also available.

Breezy, basic and blissfully off-the-beaten-track, Hendre Farm perches on Dinas Head and has sweeping views across Newport Bay. The Perkins family, who have been running the sheep farm for 70 years, can rustle up fresh eggs, milk, bread, cakes and ready-meals, while the dark-sand cove of Pwllgwaelod (at the bottom of the steep farm track) has a small, cosy pub.

Newgale Camping Site

Wood Farm, Newgale, T01437-710253, newgalecampingsite.co.uk. Mar-Oct, £5/person.

Location is everything with this campsite. Remove the glorious 2-mile stretch of Newgale Sands from the equation and you're left with a large, exposed field, a basic wash block and the Newsurf beach shop. There's a road between the beach and campsite, so you also need to take care with children. Niggles aside, though, this is the perfect basecamp for beach lovers – particularly if you've enrolled on a few days of surf lessons.

Pencarnan Farm

St David's, T01437-720580, pembrokeshire-camping.co.uk. Year round, £8-15/adult, £4-6/child (6-16).

Breezy, basic and blissfully off-the-beaten track, Hendre Farm has sweeping views across Newport Bay.

Overlooking Whitesands Bay, this cliff-top site has 60 privately-owned static caravans, plus pitches for a further 60 tents. It never feels too crowded, though, thanks mainly to the owner's enlightened policy of not arranging the caravans in ugly, serried ranks. Instead, both the statics and tents are restricted to field margins, leaving ample space for kids to run around. The facilities at Pencarnan are nothing to shout about (a basic shop and washroom and that's it), but what you do get is Porthsele – a sandy cove nuzzled against cliffs right below the campsite. Wriggle from your sleeping bag first thing in the morning and you could be rock-pooling or sea kayaking before breakfast. A short walk north along the coast

Two tipis, two yurts and five camping pitches. Tucked away in a tranquil corner of North Pembrokeshire, **Trellyn Woodland Campsite** (Abercastle, T01348-837762, trellyn.co.uk, May-Sep) is all about low-impact, back-to-nature camping. Each pitch (from £170/wk) has its own picnic table and campfire, while the tipis (£510/wk) come with rugs, futons and a separate campfire kitchen. Upping the 'glamping' stakes, the yurts (£640/wk) have cushion-strewn interiors with a wood-burning stove and double bed.

Also recommended

Gwaun Vale Touring Park
Llanychaer, T01348-874698, gwaunvale.co.uk.

Lleithyr Farm
Whitesands Bay, nr St David's, T01437-720245, lleithyrfarm.co.uk.

Redlands Camping Park
Hasguard Cross, nr Little Haven, T01437-781300, redlandstouring.co.uk.

Ty Parke Farm Campsite
Llanreithan, T01348-837384, typarke.co.uk.

Well Park Camping Site
Tenby, T01834-842179, wellparkcaravans.co.uk.

West Hook Farm
Marloes, T01646-636424.

path leads you to Whitesands Bay where you can hire surf boards and wetsuits and enjoy a snack at the café. Head south from Pencarnan and you soon reach the lifeboat station at St Justinians (see page 244) – departure point for boat trips to Ramsey Island (page 249).

Trefalun
St Florence, T01646-651514, trefalunpark.co.uk. Easter-Oct, £11-22/pitch; 3-bed holiday homes £170-580/week.

A relaxed, friendly site with an enclosed playground and pets to pamper and feed, Trefalun is ideal for young families. Heatherton, the sporty country park (see page 253), is within walking distance, while Tenby is just a few minute's drive away.

Holiday parks

Amroth Castle
Amroth, T01834-813217, amrothcastle.co.uk.
Luxury cottages and caravans in the grounds of an 18th-century castle, yards from Amroth Beach.

Bluestone
See page 256.

Cenarth Falls Holiday Park
Cenarth, T01239-710345, cenarth-holipark.co.uk.

Fishguard Holiday Park
Greenacres, Fishguard, T01348-872462, howellsleisure.co.uk.

Kiln Park Holiday Centre
Tenby, T01834-844121, haven.com.
Indoor and outdoor pools, lively entertainment and direct access to Tenby's South Beach.

Llwyngwair Manor Holiday Park
Newport, T01239-820498, llwyngwairmanor.co.uk.

Lydstep Beach Village
Lydstep Haven, nr Tenby, T01834-871871, haven.com.

Manorbier Country Park
Manorbier, T08704-606607, countrypark.co.uk.

Pendeilo Leisure Park
Amroth, T01834-831259, pendeilo.co.uk.

Sunnyvale Holiday Park
Saundersfoot, T01834-814404, sunnyvaleholidaypark.com.

Swallow Tree Gardens
Saundersfoot, T01834-812398, swallowtree.com.

Sleeping Pembrokeshire

Best of the rest

Clydey Country Cottages
Penrallt, T01239-698619,
clydeycottages.co.uk. Year round,
£350-1400/wk.
Superb self-catering cottages
for families, with a host of
thoughtful extras, such as
a grocery delivery service,
babysitting, beauty treatments
and massages. Kids can explore
the woodland nature trail,
collect eggs from the chickens
and help feed the farm animals.
There's also a gym and snazzy
new games room, but pride
of place goes to the stunning
indoor swimming pool with a
sun terrace that overlooks rolling
Pembrokeshire countryside.

Stackpole Estate
Stackpole, T0844-800 2070,
nationaltrust.org.uk/stackpole,
Year round, from £255-907/wk.
Ten lovingly converted farm
buildings (sleeping up to five),
clustered around a courtyard
and close to the gorgeous sandy
beaches at Barafundle and
Broad Haven South.

Timber Hill Lodges
Broad Haven, T08452-306090,
timberhill.co.uk. Feb-Oct,
£320-680/wk.
Well-fitted, three-bedroom
cedarwood lodges scattered
through 130 acres of parkland
and just a 20-minute woodland
walk from Broad Haven.

For great value accommodation
in excellent locations, both the
Manorbier and Marloes Sands
Youth Hostel (yha.org.uk) have
rooms suitable for families.

Warpool Court Hotel
St David's, T01437-720300,
warpoolcourthotel.com. Year round,
from £65/person B&B, plus £20-35/
child sharing with parents.
Pembrokeshire's premier hotel,
the Warpool is a four-star
country manor with elegant
accommodation (including five
family rooms), superb cuisine
and fantastic views across St
David's Peninsula. There's a
heated swimming pool, a field
for kite-flying, frisbee or football
and beautiful terraced gardens
– ideal for pre-dinner croquet.

Also recommended
Clarence House Hotel
Esplanade, Tenby, T01834-844371,
clarencehotel-tenby.co.uk.

Greenhills Country Hotel
St Florence, T01834-871291,
greenhillshotel.co.uk.

Merlewood Hotel
Saundersfoot, T01834-812421,
merlewood.co.uk.

Rosemoor Walwyn's Castle,
T01437-781326, rosemoor.com.

Cottage agents

Coastal Cottages
T01437-765765,
coastalcottages.co.uk.

Coast & Country Cottages
T01239-881397,
welsh-cottages.co.uk.

FBM Holidays
T01834-845000,
fbmholidays.co.uk.

Jordanston Holiday Cottages
T01834-871583, jordanston
holidaycottages.co.uk.

Nolton Haven Quality Cottages
T01437-710263,
noltonhaven.com.

Quality Cottages
T01348-837871,
qualitycottages.co.uk.

St Brides Bay Cottages
T01437-720027, sbbc.co.uk.

St David's Holidays
T01348-872266,
stdavidsholidays.co.uk.

Opened in 2008, **Bluestone** (Canaston Wood, Narberth, T01834-
862400, bluestonewales.com, £367-£2608/wk) has taken a few tips
from Center Parcs with its superb Blue Lagoon water park (with lazy
river ride, water flumes and wave machine) and 500-acre landscaped
park dotted with luxury timber lodges, studios and cottages
(sleeping up to eight). Onsite children's activities range from teddy
bears' picnics to bushcraft workshops, archery and off-road safaris.
There's also a Junior Rangers programme where kids aged 5-9 are
kept busy with nature trails, bug-hunting, craft activities and mini-
Olympics, while parents are pampered in the well-being spa.

Eating Pembrokeshire

Local goodies

Glasshouse Café
Welsh Wildlife Centre, Cilgerran, T01239-621600, welshwildlife.org. Mar-Dec, daily, 1030-1700.
Located at treetop level in the impressive Welsh Wildlife Centre (see page 245), the Glasshouse Café serves wholesome, organic dishes, including soups, smoked fish and vegetarian paté. With any luck, Welsh lamb casserole or Cardigan crab salad will be on the specials board – and you can't come here without sampling the Welsh cakes and deliciously succulent Bara Brith.

Priory Farm Shop
New Hedges, nr Tenby, T01834-844662. Summer, daily from 0800; winter, daily from 0900.
Perk up your picnics at this excellent farm shop, renowned for its home-made cakes, but also selling a good range of Welsh cheeses, plus local honey, jam and chutney.

Quayside Tearoom
Lawrenny, T01646-651574. Easter-Sep, daily 1100-1700.
Hidden away in the heart of Pembrokeshire, this peaceful tearoom is right at the water's edge on Daugleddau estuary. The crab sandwiches and freshly-baked baguettes are always a sound choice, as is the house special – Quayside Welsh rarebit. Leave room for homemade cakes and puds.

The Refectory
St David's Cathedral, T01437-72176, stdavidscathedral.org.uk. Year round, daily from 1000.
A light and airy café in the newly renovated medieval cloisters of St David's Cathedral, The Refectory offers home-made food using fresh, local ingredients. The lunch menu always includes sandwiches and cakes, while suppers (summer only) feature fish and meat dishes, as well as some tasty vegetarian options.

A Taste of the County
Bethesda Cross, Saundersfoot, T01834-842540. Daily, 0800-1900.
Huge range of local food, from fruit and bread to smoked fish.

Yerbeston Gate Farm Shop
Yerbeston, nr Kilgetty, T01834-891637, farmshopfood.co.uk. Mon-Sat, 0900-1800, Sun 0900-1200.
This is the place to stock up for your barbecue. You won't find better quality burgers or bangers. Special selections start at £5, but for the ultimate sizzling feast go for the Gold Barbecue Pack (£24.95) which contains a meaty medley of Welsh Black steaks, pork loin kievs, chicken pieces, beef burgers and pork sausages – all from locally-reared sources. There's also a great deli here, and you can even pre-order food packs to be delivered to your self-catering accommodation anywhere in Pembrokeshire.

Fun with food
Pembrokeshire folk certainly know how to make a song and dance over local, fresh produce. No less than three culinary festivals take place in the region each summer. **Pembrokeshire Fish Week** (pembrokeshirefishweek.co.uk, usually late Jun-early Jul) features harbourside mackerel barbecues, cookery classes and fishing contests, plus crab-catching, harbour fun days, snorkel safaris and seaside crafts for the kids. In St David's, **The Really Wild Food Festival** (reallywildfestival. co.uk, late Aug or early Sep) celebrates countryside traditions with wild-food cooking, wildlife walks and craft workshops, while the **Narberth Food Festival** (narberthfoodfestival.co.uk, late Sep) has celebrity chefs, street entertainers and craft activities.

Market days
Fishguard, Farmers' market, Town Hall, alternate Sat.
Haverfordwest, Riverside Quay, Fri.
Manorbier Village Hall, Wed.
Narberth Queens Hall, Thu.
Pembroke Town Hall, Thu.
St David's Memorial Hall, Thu.
Tenby St John's Church Hall, Fri.

Fish & chips
The top three chippies are **Fecci & Sons** (Lower Frog St, Tenby, T01834-842484), **Marina** (The Harbour, Saundersfoot, T01834-813598) and **Something's Cooking** (The Square, Letterston, T01348-840621) where it's a toss-up between home-made crab cakes (£7.50) and good-old haddock and chips (£6.50).

Eating Pembrokeshire

The Clock House Café

Marloes, T01646-636527,
clockhousemarloes.co.uk.
Easter-Sep, Tue-Sun, 1130-1630.
It's tempting to order baguettes
here simply to see them arrive
in a seaside bucket, but other
goodies on the menu include
seafood triangles, ciabattas,
salads and cream teas. Children
are very welcome – there's
even a carved statue of a puffin
(called Scaggamuffin) waiting
to greet them on the patio. An
evening menu specialises in
local seafood dishes such as St
Brides Bay crab and mackerel.

Sands Café

Newgale, T01437-729222. Daily.
Located next to Newsurf (see
page 250), this is just the place
to wash the taste of seawater
from your mouth after a surfing
session. Sands Café serves fresh
coffee, Gianni's ice cream and a
range of light snacks, including a
tasty mackerel paté.

The Sloop Inn

Porthgain, T01348-831449, sloop.
co.uk. Year round, daily, 0930-2300;
breakfast 0930-1100, lunch 1200-
1430, dinner 1800-2130.
Porthgain is a curious place
– part cutesy fishing village,
part industrial ruin. It's well
worth picking up a walking-
trail leaflet to explore the
legacy of slate-quarrying and
brick-making that went on here

between 1850 and 1931. An
enduring feature of the village
through all the rock-blasting
and harbour building, The
Sloop Inn dates from 1743 and
is festooned with memorabilia
and old photographs. The
menu boasts the 'Best burger
in Pembrokeshire', and there's
no denying that the £8-Angry
Dog (6 oz of organic mince) is
good to get your teeth into, but
there are other equally tempting
dishes – particularly the cod,
chips and mushy peas with
tartare sauce (£9.60) and the
trio of sausages with mash and
onion gravy (£8.50). Kids' meals
(from £3.60) include scampi,
chicken goujons, fishcakes,
lasagne and sausages.

Also recommended

The Mulberry Restaurant

Saundersfoot, T01834-811313,
themulberryrestaurant.co.uk. Daily.
Popular family eatery located
near the seafront.

The Riverbend Café

Nant y Coy Watermill, Treffgarne
Gorge, T01437-741671, nantycoy.
co.uk. Mar-Dec, daily, 1030-1800.
Organic dishes and homemade
puds served in a renovated mill
with art gallery and nature trail.

The Stackpole Inn

Stackpole, T01646-672324,
stackpoleinn.co.uk. Daily during
summer from 1200.
Award-winning pub with top-
notch menu and lovely gardens.

Ocean Restaurant

Tenby, T01834-844536, tenby-
oceanrestaurant.co.uk. Mon-Sat,
1000-2130, Sun 1000-1600.
There's no shortage of decent
places to eat in Tenby, but
few have views like the Ocean
Restaurant. Book a window
table upstairs and you can
watch the boats in the harbour
below, while navigating a varied
à la carte menu that includes
seabass with fresh local mussels
in a sage-scented broth (£16.25)
and braised fillet of Welsh lamb
served on a bed of bubble and
squeak potatoes (£15.75). The
lunch menu has some choice
light-bites, such as crayfish
salad (£5.50) and salmon and
cod fishcakes (£9.95). Kids get
a shot at the fishcakes on their
own special menu which also
features pasta, grilled chicken
and pizza dishes (from £3.50).

Also recommended

The Cartwheel Restaurant

Amroth, T01834-812100.
Daily from 0900.
Seafront location, local meat
and seafood meals, plus popular
Sunday lunches.

The Old Pharmacy

Main St, Solva, T01437-720005,
theoldpharmacy.co.uk. Daily for
evening meals; Easter-Oct, 1200-
1430 for lunch.
A real treat for seafood lovers, try
the superb bouillabaisse.

Essentials Pembrokeshire

Getting there

By train First Great Western (firstgreatwestern.co.uk) runs as far as Carmarthen, where you need to change to Arriva (arrivatrainswales.co.uk) for routes to either Fishguard or Milford Haven (via Haverfordwest), or to Tenby and Pembroke Dock.

By coach National Express (nationalexpress.com) has services to Fishguard, Haverfordwest, Pembroke and Tenby.

Getting around

By train Greenways Day Ranger tickets allow unlimited train travel in South Pembrokeshire with Arriva Trains Wales (see above).

By bus For unlimited travel on any bus service within Pembrokeshire, purchase a West Wales Rover ticket (£6.60/adult, £3.30/child). The Pembrokeshire Coastal Bus (pembrokeshire.gov.uk/coastbus) provides excellent access to walks, beaches and local attractions. Services include the 315 Puffin Shuttle (Haverfordwest–Marloes, the 387 Coastal Cruiser (Pembroke Dock–Angle–Bosherston–Stackpole), the 400/315 Puffin Shuttle (St David's–Milford Haven), the 403 Celtic Coaster (St David's Peninsula), the 404 Strumble Shuttle (St David's–Fishguard) and the 405 Poppit Rocket (Cardigan–Newport). The Day Tripper Bus is a summer service from Tenby to nearby attractions. For further information, contact Greenways (pembrokeshiregreenways.co.uk), a sustainable transport initiative.

Maps

Ordnance Survey Explorer OL35 (North Pembrokeshire) and OL36 (South Pembrokeshire).

Tourist Information Centres

Pembrokeshire Tourist Board, visitpembrokeshire.com. Opening hours for TICs are generally Apr-Oct, Mon-Sat 0930-1700, Sun 1000-1600; Nov-Mar, Mon-Sat 1000-1600. Fishguard Harbour and St David's are open daily in winter, while Milford Haven is only open during the summer.

Fishguard Harbour Ocean Lab, Goodwick, T01348-872037.

Fishguard Town Market Square, T01437-776636.

Haverfordwest Old Bridge, T01437-763110.

Milford Haven Charles St, T01646-690866.

Pembroke Commons Road, T01437-776499.

St David's T01437-720392.

Saundersfoot The Harbour, T01834-813672.

Tenby Upper Park Road, T01834-842402.

Further Information

Pembrokeshire Coast National Park Authority, Llanion Park, Pembroke Dock, T0845-345 7275, pembrokeshirecoast.org.uk. National Trust Visitor Centre, High St, St David's, T01437-720385, nationaltrust.org.uk.

Hospital

Withybush General, Haverfordwest, T01437-764545.

Pharmacies

Fishguard Boots, Market Square.
Haverfordwest Noott's, Main St.
Pembroke Mendus, Main St.
St David's Co-op, Market Square.
Saundersfoot Patel, The Strand.
Tenby Seafront, High St.

Supermarkets

Fishguard CK, Somerfield.
Haverfordwest Kwik Save, Morrisons, Tesco.
Milford Haven Tesco.
Pembroke Somerfield.
Pembroke Dock Asda, Tesco.
St David's CK.
Tenby Somerfield.

Other shops

Camping supplies Millets, Bridge St, Haverfordwest; Morris Brothers, High St, Tenby.
Surf & watersports shops Haven Sports, Broad Haven; Seaweed Surf Shop, Quay St, Haverfordwest.
Toys & beach gear Clarice Toy Shop, Upper Frog St, Tenby.

Environmental groups

The Wildlife Trust of South and West Wales, T01656-724100, welshwildlife.org.

Major Events

May Milford Haven Maritime Heritage Week.
Jun Pembroke Dock Festival.
Jul High Tide Festival, Manorbier.
Jul & Aug Tenby Summer Spectacular.
Aug Saundersfoot Carnival.
Aug Whitesands Beach Annual Sand Church Competition.

Gower Peninsula

Dangling from South Wales and measuring just 16 miles from tip to toe, the Gower might strike you as more of an appendix than a peninsula. Blockaded by Swansea and neatly sidestepped by the M4 (which seems intent on sweeping you west towards Pembrokeshire) it's all too easily overlooked. Who would have imagined that some 50 beaches and bays are packed into this little snub of land, or that the Gower was declared Britain's first Area of Outstanding Natural Beauty in 1956? And the accolades don't end there.

Not only is the Gower Peninsula one of Britain's finest surfing locations, but four of its beaches have Blue Flag awards – five if you include Swansea Marina. From waterfront city to wild Rhossili, the Gower powers ahead on the seaside-beauty stakes, with three-quarters of the peninsula protected by The National Trust.

Local girl and opera star, Katherine Jenkins sang the praises of Three Cliffs Bay in ITV's *Britain's Favourite View* in 2007. Dylan Thomas, hailing from Swansea, described the Gower as 'one of the loveliest sea-coast stretches in the whole of Britain'. The peninsula even gets a sprinkle of Hollywood stardust from local celebrity, Catherine Zeta-Jones who has a house overlooking Langland Bay where she spent many a childhood summer.

Get your bearings
Once you've reached Swansea, you're at the threshold of the Gower Peninsula – drive there via the M4 or catch the train (First Great Western services link London Paddington with Swansea

via Reading and Bristol Parkway, while Arriva makes tracks from Gloucester, North Wales and Manchester). In many ways, though, Swansea should be seen as an intrinsic part of a holiday in the Gower, rather than a mere transit centre. The city has several family attractions, including an exciting new leisure complex (see page 266), while a nifty bus service – the Gower Explorer – makes it a breeze to get from Swansea to and around the peninsula (see right for route details).

A few miles along Swansea Bay, The Mumbles snags the majority of visitors to the Gower Peninsula. Liberally sprinkled with cafés, restaurants, fashion boutiques and ice cream parlours, its Victorian seafront is rounded off by Mumbles Pier – an 1898 classic with a lifeboat station, amusement arcade, ten-pin bowling, ice skating and fish and chips.

Ditch the car

The Gower Explorer bus network not only offers freedom from your car, but also links walking trails and beaches. Choose the Gower Day Explorer for unlimited travel from Swansea; the Gower Coast Explorer for unlimited travel within the peninsula and the First Day Swansea Bay for travel from Swansea to The Mumbles and Caswell Bay.

14/114 Swansea–Pennard Cliffs.
2/3/37 Swansea–Oystermouth–Newton–Limeslade (and 2A to Caswell Bay during summer).
117/118/119 Swansea–Killay–Oxwich–Horton– Port Eynon–Rhossili.
115/116/119 Swansea–Killay–Llanrhidian– Llanmadoc–Llangennith.
116/119 Swansea–Killay–Gowerton–Llanrhidian.
115/117/118/119 Llanmadoc and Llangennith– Horton and Port Eynon.

Not only is the Gower Peninsula one of Britain's finest surfing locations, but four of its beaches have Blue Flag awards.

The white stuff – surf's up on the Gower Peninsula.

Great escapes Gower Peninsula

Steps lead from the base of the pier to a small cove of sand and pebbles, while just beyond Mumbles Head lie Bracelet Bay, Limeslade Bay and Langland Bay. The latter has the best sand and facilities, but none are a patch on the glorious beaches that lie further west. You only have to nip around the headland between Langland Bay and Caswell Bay to sense the suburban trappings of The Mumbles fall away. Continue west to Three Cliffs Bay, Oxwich Bay and Port Eynon Bay and you're swept into an altogether wilder, more beautiful Gower, culminating in one of Britain's most consummate coastal finales – the 3-mile crescent of Rhossili Bay.

There's no denying that the south coast of the Gower Peninsula steals the show. By contrast, the north has a slightly eerie shoreline of vast sand flats, salt marshes, dunes and cockle beds. No vibrant surfing beaches here. Still, it's worth a look – if only from the vantage of Arthur's Stone, a Neolithic burial chamber with far-reaching views from Gower's rugged spine.

Carreglwyd.

Pitch your tent

The Gower Peninsula has several fine campsites. One of the most family-friendly is the **Carreglwyd Camping & Caravan Park** (T01792-390795, carreglwyd.com, year round, from £18/tent and two people, plus £8/extra adult, £1-2/extra child). It's right on the beach at Port Eynon where a smattering of cottages, a couple of pubs, a chippie, beach shop and grocers' lie at the end of the A4118 from Swansea. For the best views across the bay, pitch your tent near the top of one of the gently sloping camping fields.

If it's views you're after, though, you really ought to pitch up at **Three Cliffs Bay Holiday Park** (Penmaen, T01792-371218, threecliffsbay. com, Apr-Oct, £18-20/family tent). Smothered in media gush for 'best view in Wales' and 'perfect pitch with a view', this clifftop site more than

lives up to the hype. After Catherine Zeta-Jones and Katherine Jenkins, Three Cliffs Bay (see page 264) is the Gower's favourite pin-up. Not only does this well-maintained campsite (with farm shop, modern toilet block and family room) enjoy grandstand views, but you can also put yourself in the picture by following a path down to the beach. Of course, fame has its price – the campsite is crowded in summer and only a lucky few get the prime pitches nearest the bay.

A good alternative, **Nicholaston Farm Caravan & Camping** (T01792-371209, nicholastonfarm.co.uk, Mar-Oct, £17/family tent) overlooks Tor Bay, just to the west of Three Cliffs. There's a footpath from the campsite down to the beach, while the farm has pick-your-own fruit and a farm shop/café.

Out towards Rhossili, **Pitton Cross Caravan Park** (T01792-390593, pittoncross.co.uk, year round, £16-20/family tent) has six level camping paddocks, including a families-only area, as well as a shop selling camping essentials, beach gear, fishing bait and kites. It's about a mile from Rhossili, but if you want something closer to the beach, **Hillend Caravan & Camping Park** (Llangennith, T01792-386204, Apr-Oct, from £12-18/tent) is right behind the dunes near the northern end of the bay. The Welsh Surfing Federation Surf School is based here (see page 265), while other facilities include a smart new shower block, a shop and Eddy's café.

Can't camp won't camp

Home from Home (T01792-360624, homefromhome. com) has the most extensive range of self-catering properties on the Gower Peninsula. Mumbles has guest houses galore, while Swansea has modern hotels, such as the **Marriot** (marriot.co.uk) with its bayside location and indoor pool. Holiday parks include **Summercliffe Chalet Park** (Caswell Bay, T01792-233599, gower-holidays.com) and **Gower Holiday Village** (Scurlage, T01792-390431, gowerholidayvillage.co.uk).

Beach shack, hermit crab and sandcastles at Rhossili;
kayaking at Mumbles Head, rock climbing at Caswell Bay.

Great escapes Gower Peninsula

Hit the beach

You're never far from a fabulous beach on the Gower. Blue-Flag **Caswell Bay** is one of the most family-friendly. You can park right behind it and there's a café, beach shop, showers and toilets, as well as a lifeguard patrol during summer. Best of all, the beach has a winning combination of sand, rock pools and surf. If you can tear the kids away from the sea, there's a lovely walk through Bishops Wood Nature Reserve that backs onto the bay, while a 1.5-mile cliff path leads to adjacent **Langland Bay** – another popular beach spot with good facilities.

Bisected by the sinuous curves of the River Pennard Pill and hemmed in by dragon-back cliffs and steep dunes, **Three Cliffs Bay** is the Gower's iconic beauty spot. Waves lend a delicate filigree to an almost circular disc of golden sand that's best viewed from the crumbling remains of Pennard Castle. To reach the beach itself, you have three options – walk through the woods from Parkmill; take the sloping pathway from Penmaen and cross the stepping stones over the river, or walk from adjacent Pobbles Bay at low tide (check

tide tables beforehand). There's no denying that Three Cliffs is more 'epic escapade' than 'bucket and spade'. Families with older children will love the sense of adventure (there are sea caves and rock pools at the base of the cliffs), but you should be aware that the bay is strafed by rip currents – swimming is particularly dangerous at high tide.

Separated from Three Cliffs Bay by the Great Tor headland, **Tor Bay** is accessed by a mile-long footpath from Penmaen or from the campsite at Nicholaston Farm (page 262). It sweeps west to **Oxwich Bay**, a 2.5-mile swathe of sand with a car park next to the beach at Oxwich Bay Hotel. A café, shop, watersports and lifeguard make this a popular choice for families. Behind the beach, Oxwich National Nature Reserve protects a large area of dunes and marsh – home to orchids, butterflies, dragonflies and common lizards that can be glimpsed from paths and boardwalks. Out on the wooded headland stands Oxwich Castle (actually a grand Tudor mansion). Like Oxwich, **Port Eynon Bay** (a mixture of sand, shingle and rocks) has good access and plenty of facilities.

West of Port Eynon Point, Gower gets all rugged and stand-offish, with cliffs running virtually all the way to the end of the peninsula. **Gower Coast Adventures** (T07866-250440, gowercoastadventures.co.uk) operates two-hour jet-boat trips from Port Eynon along this dramatic section of coast (May-Sep, £28/adult, £20/child under 14) – a great opportunity to spot seals and other wildlife around the spectacular tidal island of Worms Head.

You can also walk to Worms Head from **Rhossili**, setting out from the National Trust visitor centre and shop (T01792-390707, daily from 1030) for an easy, half-mile stroll to the coastguard lookout. Here you can check tide charts before venturing across the rock-pool-riddled causeway to Worms Head. Chances are, however, that once your kids have glimpsed the grand curve of Rhossili Bay from the visitor centre, they'll be dragging you down the steps to the beach. Stop at Sam's Surf Shack for bodyboards (£10/day) and any other last-minute beach gear. Once you reach the beach, there's nothing except miles of gorgeous sand, raked by surf. Rhossili is the ultimate run-wild-and-free beach: play cricket, fly a kite, build a sandy rampart against the tide and scrawl your name in house-size letters.

Hillend, near Llangennith, provides access to Rhossili Bay further along the beach. This is where you will find the **Welsh Surfing Federation Surf School** (T01792-386426, wsfsurfschool.co.uk, daily (Jul-Aug), weekends (Apr-Jun, Sep-Oct) which offers two-hour lessons for £25 (minimum age eight). Also known as Progress Surf, **Gower & Swansea Surf School** (T08707-772489, swanseasurfing.com) offers lessons at Llangennith, as well as Caswell Bay, from £30/half-day and £55/day, including wetsuit and board hire.

Rhossili is the ultimate run-wild-and-free beach: play cricket, fly a kite, build a sandy rampart against the tide and scrawl your name in house-size letters.

Sail away

Euphoria Sailing (Oxwich Bay, T01792-234502, euphoriasailing.com) runs RYA sailing courses for £50/half-day taster or £90/day Stage 1 Youth Scheme. Sailing dinghies can be rented from £30/hr, kayaks £10-20/hr.

Looking towards Worms Head from Rhossili.

Great escapes Gower Peninsula

Sit-on kayaking.

Do something different
You can't visit the Gower and not go surfing. And the clifftop paths promise some exhilarating coastal walks. But how about some quad biking, windsurfing, kitesurfing, gorge walking, mountain biking, horse riding, abseiling, indoor climbing, canoeing or archery? All are available from **Great Gower Outdoors** (Clyne Farm Centre, T01792-403333, greatgoweroutdoors. co.uk). The minimum age for most activities is eight (12 for quad biking), with prices ranging from £12 for an hour-long indoor climbing session to £50 for half a day of abseiling, canoeing or quad biking. Horse-riding lessons cost from £18/hour, while surfing lessons can be arranged for £35. If you relish the idea of getting seriously dirty, sign up for Challenge Valley (£22), a cross between an assault course and a hippo wallow.

Gap Activities (Swansea, T01792-516031, gapactivities.co.uk) offers a choice of surfing, canoeing, coasteering, sit-on kayaking, hill walking and gorge walking, from £35/person.

A 19th-century hunting lodge in 70 acres of woodland near Parkmill, **Parc le Breos** (T01792-371636, parclebreos.co.uk) offers pony trekking on the Gower's big sandy beaches for £42/day or £30/half-day. The minimum age is 10, but younger children can enrol on 20-minute paddock rides (on a lead rein) for £12. The lodge also offers family accommodation, with bed and breakfast costing £34/adult and £17-22.50/child. For a rather less pampered experience in Parc le Breos, contact **Dryad Bushcraft** (T01792-547213, dryadbushcraft.co.uk, phone for prices) which runs family wilderness-survival weekends in which your tribe learn how to build shelters, light fires and forage along the coast.

At **Perriswood Archery & Falconry Centre** (Penmaen, T01792-371661, perriswoodarchery. co.uk) you can let arrows fly (from £5/15-minute lesson) or let raptors fly to your hand during a half-

day falconry session (£50/person, minimum age 12). For a taster of archery, a bird of prey display and tea and cakes, sign up for the two-hour Arrows, Talons and Tea (summer only, £10/person).

Treat yourself to dinner
One of the best pubs on the Gower is the **King Arthur Hotel** (Reynoldston, T01792-390775 kingarthurhotel.co.uk) which serves seasonal game, Welsh beef, locally caught fish and vegetarian dishes in its restaurant, family room, main bar and outside on the green when it's warm and dry. In Mumbles, treat yourself to delicious pizza, pasta and ice cream at **Verdi's** (Knab Rock, T01792-369135, verdis-cafe.co.uk).

Swan around Swansea
The **National Waterfront Museum** (T01792-638950, waterfrontmuseum.co.uk, daily 1000-1700, free) uses the latest interactive technology to tell the story of industry and innovation in Wales over the last 300 years. **Plantasia** (T01792-474555, plantasia.org, daily 1000-1700, £3.80/adult, £2.80/child) brings a touch of the tropics to the city with chameleons, pythons, parrots and a colony of cotton-top tamarin monkeys housed in a giant, climate-controlled indoor garden. **The Chocolate Factory** (T01792-561617, thechocfactory.com, £8/adult, £6/child) offers tours and workshops.

Bay city rollers
Know simply as **LC** (T01792-466500, daily during holidays 0900-2100), Swansea's new waterpark has one of the UK's first indoor surfing pools, as well as a rollercoaster-style water ride, high-speed flumes, lazy river, wave machine and an interactive pool for littl'uns.

Essential websites
Swansea Tourist Information visitswanseabay.com.
Mumbles Tourist Information enjoygower.com.
Gower Holidays the-gower.com.

Get rural

The Gower Heritage Centre (Parkmill, T01792-371206, gowerheritagecentre.co.uk, daily 1000-1700, £4.95/adult, £3.95/child, £16/family, half-price if you arrive by Gower Explorer bus) is a gentle, family-friendly blend of rural life museum, farm animals, play areas and craft activities. Based around a working 12th-century watermill, the centre has a busy calendar of events, featuring pottery, puppet and jewellery workshops. There's also a tractor play area, fish pond and eco arts centre, tearoom, countryside walks and a display about the history of the Gower's wool industry.

Dabbling toes near the Gower Heritage Centre.

Northeast Snowdonia.

Snowdonia

These are quite possibly the world's most family-friendly mountains: wild, austere and unforgiving, yet tamed by cheerful little steam trains and fringed by long sandy beaches. From flip-flops to hiking boots, Snowdonia's blend of mountain and sea appeals to souls (and soles) of all persuasions.

That's not an excuse, though, to spend your entire holiday lazing about on the beach. The region's crowning glory, 1085-m **Mt Snowdon**, should loom large in every itinerary – particularly now that the Hafod Eryri summit visitor centre has been completed. Your bid for the top will involve copious huff-and-puff, whether you hike one of the six trails or catch the Snowdon Mountain Railway from the lakeside town of **Llanberis**.

Other popular centres for peak pursuits include the former slate-quarrying village of **Bethesda**, **Capel Curig** (home of the action-packed National Mountain Centre) and **Betws y Coed** – everyone's favourite Welsh mountain resort with its exquisite Swallow Falls, walks galore and no shortage of outdoor and craft shops to exercise your wallet.

Don't overlook the forests of Snowdonia. They might be less compelling than the peaks, but the vast green cloaks of **Coed y Brenin**, **Gwydyr** and **Beddgelert** conceal a multitude of child-friendly adventures – from nature trails and orienteering to hiking and mountain biking. Lakes, like **Bala**, meanwhile, offer watersports such as canoeing, sailing and windsurfing. And for the ultimate in wet 'n' wild, brace yourself for the rapids on the **Tryweryn River** – one of Britain's most reliable whitewater rafting locations.

Snowdonia's 200-mile coastline is no damp squib when it comes to adventure – try surfing on the gorgeous **Llŷn Peninsula** (a region so remote your mobile phone might send you a message saying 'Welcome to Ireland') or hop on a high-speed RIB in **Aberdyfi** for a dolphin-spotting voyage across Cardigan Bay. From the fortified towns of **Caernarfon** and **Conwy** to popular seaside resorts like **Barmouth**, **Criccieth**, **Llandudno** and **Pwllheli**, Snowdonia's coast has history, scenery and good old seaside fun by the bucketload. You'll find Blue Flag beauties, bustling marinas, peaceful estuaries and wild, surf-gnawed sands that stretch for miles. And when the mountains cast their spell again, head inland to gateway towns like **Blaenau Ffestiniog** and **Dolgellau** – but don't forget to take your flip-flops off first.

You must

- Go rock-pooling at Whistling Sands on the Llŷn Peninsula.

- See the Glaslyn ospreys.

- Take a boat trip in Cardigan Bay.

- Raft the rapids of the Tryweryn River.

- Ride a steam train to the summit of Snowdon.

- Explore a castle.

- Cycle the Mawddach Trail from Dolgellau to Barmouth.

- Try something new, like rock climbing or gorge scrambling.

Out & about Snowdonia

Head for the hills

You can't visit Snowdonia and not take a hike. Even with babies or toddlers you can backpack or buggy them along easy-access trails – for inspiration get hold of a copy of *All-Terrain Pushchair Walks: Snowdonia* (Stobart Davies, 2009). Older children will naturally set their sights on Snowdon. Of the six routes to the summit, the 5-mile Llanberis Path is the longest, but easiest. If the six-hour return hike sounds too arduous, consider travelling one way on the Snowdon Mountain Railway (page 276). A selection of six walks (mostly on easy paths), in areas ranging from the Llŷn Peninsula to the foothills of Snowdon, can be downloaded from Gwynedd Council's website, gwynedd.gov.uk. For any kind of mountain walk, make sure you're properly kitted out with walking boots or shoes, waterproof jackets, spare sweaters, map, compass, whistle, torch, spare food and first aid kit. For maps see page 281.

Check out the happy family

The only pair of breeding ospreys in Wales has been setting up nest in the Glaslyn Valley since 2004. The male usually arrives on, or around, the 26th March, closely followed by his mate. Two or three eggs are laid in their huge twiggy nest a fortnight later, after which there's a six-week incubation period before the full-time job of feeding chicks begins. The fluff balls fledge within seven weeks, before the young osprey family up-sticks and migrates back to Africa. You can witness the entire drama from a hide at the RSPB's Glaslyn Osprey Project (rspb.org.uk/wales) where there's a choice of binoculars, telescopes and live nestcam footage. Open mid-March-early September, daily 1000-1800, the viewpoint is located on the B4410 between Prenteg and Llanfrothen.

Marvel at marine life

Mountains may steal the show, but Snowdonia's coastline is so rich and diverse that parts of it have been designated a Special Area of Conservation (SAC). The Pen Llŷn a'r Sarnau SAC extends north from the Dyfi estuary, encompassing three rocky reefs in Cardigan Bay as well as the head of the Llŷn Peninsula. Boat trips (see page 274) are a great way to witness the area's seabirds and dolphins, but you only have to peek into a rock pool on the Llŷn Peninsula or go beachcombing on Shell Island to appreciate the wealth of wildlife in these seas (see pages 272-273).

Mine of information – National Slate Museum.

Become a rock fan

Located in Padarn Country Park, Llanberis, the National Slate Museum (T01286-870630, museumwales.ac.uk, daily from 1000, closed Sat during winter) occupies the Victorian workshops that once serviced Dinorwig quarry, chiselled out of of Elidir mountain. You'll discover the gritty reality of what life was like in the quarry, foundry, forges and loco shed. Britain's largest waterwheel still does the rounds here, while craftsmen split slate before your eyes. There's also a children's trail, play area and café. Combine your visit to the museum with a walk in Padarn Country Park. You can choose from a nature trail, a circular lakeside walk or a stroll through ancient oak woodland. Other activities include canoeing, sailing and a high ropes course – see page 274 for operators.

Explore the woods

Beddgelert Forest
From Beddgelert village take the A4085 towards Caernarfon for 2.5 miles; park at Pont Cae'r Gors.

Coed y Brenin Forest
Located east of the A470 between Ganllwyd and Trawsfynydd and around 8 miles north of Dolgellau. Follow the brown tourist signs. Visitor Centre, T01341-440747, daily 0930-1630. Café, Mon-Fri 1000-1600, Sat-Sun 0900-1700. Beics Brenin bicycle hire centre, see page 275.

Dyfi Forest
Take the A487 north of Machynlleth.

Gwydyr Forest
Various access points are located off the A5 between Capel Curig and Betws y Coed.

Forestry Commission Wales, forestry.gov.uk/wales.

Snowdonia's forests are mysterious, magical places – green with moss, ripe for adventure.

Snowdonia's forests are riddled with waymarked walking paths, bridleways and mountain biking trails. In Gwydyr, old miners' tracks probe a Tolkienesque world of shadowy glades and tumbling streams, while Beddgelert has a wonderful campsite (page 278) with views of Snowdon itself.

It's Coed y Brenin, however, that's a cut above the others when it comes to keeping children happy. Bisected by four rivers (many with spectacular waterfalls) this vast, 9000-hectare forest has long been a Mecca to mountain bikers (see page 275), but the addition of an eco-friendly visitor centre at Dolgefeilliau has made it equally appealing to families. A wooden roundhouse peeping from the trees, the centre has an imaginative children's play area and a café with stunning views. In the Forest Garden you can learn about trees and folklore, while the easy-access, mile-long Afon Eden Trail leads to a riverside picnic area. Another gentle option, the 45-minute Cefndeuddwr Trail weaves through mixed woodland to a viewpoint and picnic tables. Orienteering trails, including an easy one for beginners, also start at the visitor centre. Remember to keep an eye out for forest critters, such as wood warblers, pied flycatchers, goshawks and fallow deer.

Out & about Snowdonia

Aberdyfi & Tywyn

😊 🚣 🐚 🚤 🐬 🏄 🅿️

Aberdyfi offers good sailing from the slipway or sandy beach. You can also hire canoes or join a wildlife-watching boat trip with Dyfi Discoveries (see page 274). A few miles north at the popular family resort of Tywyn you might glimpse dolphins from shore. Westerly swells also lure surfers – lessons are available with Dragon Surf (T07788-723536, dragonsurfs.com).

Barmouth & Fairbourne

😊 🚣 🐚 🐟 🐬 🏄 🅿️

With donkey rides on the beach and a land train prowling the prom, Barmouth is nothing if not traditional. But adventure lurks nearby. From the quayside you can catch a ferry across the Mawddach Estuary to connect with a steam railway (T01341-250362, fairbournerailway.com, £7.60/adult, £6/child return) which runs alongside the beach at Fairbourne. To add even more puff to your day, start by cycling to Barmouth along the Mawddach Trail (see page 275). Alternatively, stick to shore and roam north of Barmouth where the vast, sandy beaches of Llanaber and Bennar, white-ribbed with surf, sweep for miles along Cardigan Bay.

Conwy Bay & Llandudno

😊 🚣 🐚 🐟 🐬 🏄 🐟 🅿️

West of Conwy, the Victorian resorts of Llanfairfechan and Penmaenmawr have plenty of traditional seaside trimmings, from Punch and Judy to cafés on the prom, but there are natural treats here too. Both have rock pools at low tide, while Llanfairfechan has a nature reserve with bird hides and a picnic site. For traditional Welsh seaside at its best look no further than lively Llandudno.

Harlech & Shell Island

🚣 🐚 🐟 🅿️

The battlements of 13th-century Harlech Castle loom above the town's gorgeous beach, reached by following a path through a golf course and across some of Britain's finest dunes. At low tide, the strand reaches north towards Glaslyn Estuary and south towards Shell Island (shellisland.co.uk). This privately-owned 'island' is connected to the mainland by a tidal causeway (£5/car) as well as the long stretch of beach that extends south to Barmouth. It's not only a shell-seeker's paradise, but a great spot for botanising, birdwatching and messing about in boats on the estuary. Shell Island also has one of Europe's largest campsites (see page 278). Just to the north, Landanwg has a sandy beach with a curious 13th-century church hidden in the dunes.

Main pic: Squeaky clean Whistling Sands near the tip of the Llŷn Peninsula.
Above: Llŷn rockpools are like mermaid's jewellery boxes.

When the mountains of Snowdonia brood under heavy cloud, try the Llŷn Peninsula for sun, sand and surf.

Top 8 Llŷn Peninsula beaches

Abersoch

A trendy, lively resort with boutiques, bistros and a thriving watersports scene, Abersoch has a beautiful, broad sandy beach.

Black Rock Sands

Black Rock Sands has rock pools and caves to explore at low tide when it's also possible to walk to the neighbouring beach at Criccieth.

Dinas Dinlle

West of Caernarfon, pebbly Dinas Dinlle reveals a large expanse of sand at low tide. It's a popular beach for watersports, while local attractions include an Iron Age fort.

Llanbedrog

Sheltered swimming from a sandy cove backed by colourful beach huts.

Nefyn

Two miles of sandy bay linking Morfa Nefyn and Porth Dinllaen.

Porth Ceiriad

Well worth the steep walk down the cliffs, this secluded, sandy beach has good surf and snorkelling.

Porth Neigwl (Hell's Mouth)

Catching the brunt of south-westerly swells, this 4-mile arc of pebbles and sand is popular with surfers.

Porth Oer (Whistling Sands)

Dry sand above the high-tide mark might squeak when you walk on it, but that's not the only reason for making a song and dance over this gorgeous bay, nestling like azure between pincer headlands. With sand the texture of fluffy cake mixture, good surf and a National Trust beach café selling everything from pizza and ice cream to buckets and spades, Porth Oer is perfect for families. At low tide, shallow lagoons create perfect paddling pools for toddlers, while older children explore the exquisite rock pools – festooned with pink coralline algae – at either end of the beach. Snorkelling is also excellent, but watch out for waves and currents.

Out & about Snowdonia

Action stations

Boat trips
Dyfi Discoveries
Aberdyfi, T01654-767676,
dyfidiscoveries.co.uk. Year round,
one-hour trips £20/adult, £9/child
(5-12), £54/family.
RIB rides to Cardigan Bay's
wildlife-rich sarns (or reefs).

Enlli Charter
Pwllheli, T07836-293146, enllicharter.
co.uk. Daily departures at 0845, 1000
& 1100, from £25/adult, £10/child
(5-16), £60/family.
Voyages to Bardsey Island off
the tip of the Llŷn Peninsula,
departing from Pwllheli (with
the added bonus of spotting
seals at St Tudwal's Islands)
or Porth Meudwy – a shorter,
20-minute crossing to Bardsey.
Dolphins, puffins, gannets and
shearwaters are often seen.

RIB Menai Ventures
Victoria Dock, Caernarfon, T0791-
404 0001, ribride.co.uk. Year round,
one-hour trips £20/adult, £15/child.
Zip along the Menai Strait at 50
mph, dicing with wicked tides
and whirlpools.

Climbing
Beacon Climbing Centre
Ceunant, nr Caernarfon, T01286-
650045, beaconclimbing.com. Year
round, Mon-Fri from 1100, Sat-Sun
from 1000, from £6/1.5 hr session.
Indoor and outdoor climbing
courses, including an excellent
range of holiday clubs for kids.

Horse riding
Snowdonia Riding Stables
Waunfawr, T01286-650342,
snowdonia2000.fsnet.co.uk. Year
round, introductory ride £17/hr.
Riding for all abilities on traffic-
free bridleways in the beautiful
Gwyrfai Valley. Half- and full-day
mountain hacks also available.

Whitewater rafting
Canolfan Tryweryn
The National Whitewater Centre,
Frongoch, Bala, T01678-521083,
ukrafting.co.uk. £31/person (40-
minute taster), £60/person (2-hr
session), minimum age 12.
As a dam-released river, the
Tryweryn is often in full flow
when other rivers are mere
trickles, so you're almost
guaranteed a white-knuckle
ride on the 20-minute stretch of
grade 3-4 rapids (1 is like bath
water, 6 is commercial suicide).

Woodland adventures
Ropes and Ladders
Padarn Country Park, Llanberis,
T01286-872310, ropesandladders.
co.uk. School holidays 0900-1700,
£20/adult, £16/child (8-16).
High ropes course with giant
swing and zip wire, plus a low-
level course for kids (£8).

Treetop Adventure
Nr Betws y Coed, T01690-710914,
ttadventure.co.uk. Daily from 0900,
£20/adult, £15/child (under 16),
minimum height 1.3 m.
Tackle 28 challenges, including
rope bridges and zip wires.

Multi activities

Bala Adventure & Watersports
Bala, T01678-521059,
balawatersports.com.
Canoeing, gorge scrambling,
kayaking, sailing, whitewater
rafting and windsurfing.

Boulder Adventures
Padarn Country Park,
Llanberis, T01286-870556,
boulderadventures.co.uk.
Abseiling, canoeing, climbing,
gorge scrambling, kayaking, raft
building and mountain walking.

Get Wet Adventure Company
Bala, T07909-768950,
get-wet.co.uk.
Canoeing, high ropes, mountain
biking and paintballing.

National Mountain Centre
Plas y Brenin, Capel Curig,
T01690-720214, pyb.co.uk.
Abseiling, canoeing, dry-slope
skiing, mountain walking,
orienteering and rock climbing.

National Watersports Centre
Plas Menai, Caernarfon, T01248-
673943, plasmenai.co.uk.
Canoeing, climbing, dinghy
sailing, mountain biking,
powerboating and windsurfing.

Surf Lines
Y Glyn, nr Llanberis, T01286-
879001, surf-lines.co.uk.
Canoeing, coasteering, kayaking
and rock climbing.

Booking agents

Adventure North Wales
T0870-365 4265, adventure-
northwales.com.

iTry T0844-902 2970,
itry-snowdonia.com.

Mawddach Trail.

Cycle the flat bits

Beics Brenin
Coed y Brenin Visitor Ctr, Ganllwyd,
T01341-440728, beicsbrenin.co.uk.
Year round, Mon-Fri 1000-1700,
Sat-Sun 0930-1700,
closed Tue & Wed from Dec-Feb.
Bikes from £25-50/day.

Beics Menai Cycles
Caernarfon, T01286-676804,
beicsmenai.co.uk. Daily from 0930.
Adult bike £19/day, £12/2 hr;
child's bike £11/day, £8/2 hr;
trailer £11/day, child seat £5/day.

Dolgellau Cycles
Dolgellau, T01341-423332,
dolgellaucycles.co.uk.
Dollgellau, daily 0930-1700.
Adult bike £20/day, £13/half-day;
child's bike £12/day, £7/half-day.

Coed y Brenin Forest Park

The Coed y Brenin Forest Park (see also page 271) separates the free-wheelers from the full-on mountain bikers. It offers some of Britain's most exhilarating and demanding rides on rough rocky trails. Beics Brenin rents everything from 24-inch children's bikes to full suspension trail-bashers for adults. The best route for families is the 7-mile Yr Afon Trail which follows some of the gentler forest roads and passes waterfalls on the Gain and Mawddach rivers.

Lonydd Glas

Established along disused railway lines, Gwynedd's five recreational routes (known as Lonydd Glas) are ideal for traffic-free cycling. One of the most family-friendly of the Lonydd Glas, the 9-mile **Mawddach Trail** links Dolgellau and Barmouth along a level track through woods and alongside the estuary. There's a liberal scattering of picnic tables along the way, as well as interpretation boards describing the area's wildlife and history. The more demanding **Cregennen Lakes Trail** follows quiet mountain lanes from Dolgellau to link up with the Mawddach Trail shortly before it crosses the estuary on Barmouth's foot/rail bridge.

The 12-mile **Lôn Eifion** route takes you from the shadow of Caernarfon Castle to the rural village of Bryncir. It's possible to travel one way on the Welsh Highland Railway (see page 276) and cycle back. **Lôn Las Menai** traces 4 miles of the Menai Straits between Caernarfon and the village of Y Felinheli, while **Lôn Las Ogwen** runs from Porth Penrhyn to Tregarth, crossing the Glasinfryn Viaduct en route. Finally, **Lôn Las Peris** covers an easy mile from Llanberis, following the shoreline of Llyn Padarn until it connects with roads that lead to the villages of Cwm y Glo and Llanrug.

Out & about Snowdonia

Greenwood Forest Park

Nr Caernarfon, T01248-670076, greenwoodforestpark.co.uk. Daily, Mar-Nov, 1000-1730, from £6.85/adult, £5.75/child, £22.50/family. It's strange how some kids will run the equivalent of a double marathon at an adventure park like Greenwood, but drag their feet at the mere mention of a hike on Cader Idris. But if you need an action-packed day-out in Snowdonia this is the place to go. Greenwood has everything from giant bouncing pillows, and treetop walkways to an eco-friendly rollercoaster.

Snowdon Mountain Railway

Llanberis, T0871-720 0033, snowdonrailway.co.uk. Mar-Nov, daily; Summit Station usually open early May-late Oct, otherwise trains terminate at Clogwyn or Rocky Valley. Llanberis Ticket Office daily during season from 0815; first departure 0900. Llanberis–Summit return fare £23/adult, £16/child; single fare £16/adult, £13/child, discounts available for advance booking of 0900 departure.

A marvel of engineering, Britain's highest rack railway is just the ticket for preventing blisters and whingeing children. Return trips to Snowdon's 1085-m summit take two and a half hours, including a 30-minute stop at the new Hafod Eryri Visitor Centre. Setting off from Llanberis, the plucky little steam train crosses viaducts and skirts a waterfall cascading though ancient oak woodland before emerging on treeless, boulder-strewn slopes with panoramic views as far as Ireland. The innovative summit visitor centre (with its curved granite roof and non-reflective windows) has a café, toilets and shop, as well as live weather information for those planning to walk back down the mountain.

On the right track at Llanberis Lake.

In addition to the Snowdon Mountain Railway (left), train rides are available with:

Bala Lake Railway

Llanuwchllyn, T01678-540666, bala-lake-railway.co.uk

Fairbourne Steam Railway

See page 272.

Ffestiniog & Welsh Highland Railways

Porthmadog, T01766-516000, festrail.co.uk.

Llanberis Lake Railway

T01286-870549, lake-railway.co.uk.

Welsh Highland Heritage Railway

Porthmadog, T01766-513402, whr.co.uk.

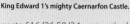
King Edward 1's mighty Caernarfon Castle.

Save money on entry to the 'Big 4' castles in North Wales (Beaumaris, Caernarfon, Conwy and Harlech) with a **World Heritage Explorer Pass** from Cadw (cadw.wales.gov.uk). A three-day pass costs £11/adult or child (under 16), £17.50/two adults or two children and £25/family. A seven-day pass costs £16/26.50/34 respectively. Each castle has plenty to keep kids entertained, from scaling the mighty ramparts of Conwy to climbing Caernarfon's Eagle Tower. Other castles in the Snowdonia region include Criccieth – a wonderful spot for a picnic by the sea.

Members' perks

Family membership (see page 5) entitles you to free entry to:

National Trust
• Bodnant Garden, Tal-y-Cafn.
• Conwy Suspension Bridge.

RSPB
• Conwy Nature Reserve.

Heritage in Wales
Members get free admission to all Cadw sites, T0800-0743121, cadw.wales.gov.uk. See also box, left.

More family favourites

Bodnant Garden

Tal-y-Cafn, T01492-650460, bodnant-garden.co.uk. Feb-Nov, daily from 1000, £7.50/adult, £3.75/child. Boasting huge Italianate terraces and a wild wooded valley, Bodnant has a family trail, plus activity packs for budding artists, bug-hunters and fairy-spotters.

Electric Mountain

Llanberis, T01286-870636, electricmountain.co.uk. Year round, daily from 0930. Free entry to visitor centre. Power station tours, Easter-Oct, daily, £7.50/adult, £3.75/child (4-15), £21.50/family. Minimum age 4. Feel the force during an hour-long tour of Europe's largest man-made cavern where buses transport you around the huge power station that lies within Elidir Mountain. The visitor centre has a café and children's soft-play area (see box, right).

King Arthur's Labyrinth

Corris, T01654-761584, kingarthurslabyrinth.com. Mar-Nov, daily 1000-1700, £6.95/adult, £4.95/child.
Electric Mountain (above) will certainly give you a buzz, but this subterranean adventure is supercharged with suspense as you explore Arthurian legends and tales of dragons, giants and treachery – brought to life through cunning light and sound effects. For an additional charge, Bard's Quest challenges

you to search a maze (above ground) for lost Welsh myths. There's also a craft centre, playground and picnic area.

Portmeirion

T01766-770000, portmeirion-village.com. Year round, daily from 0930, £7.50/adult, £4/child (5-16), £19/family.
Sitting pretty on its own private peninsula, Clough Williams-Ellis' model village is mostly hotel or self-catering accommodation, but day visitors can still browse the shops and explore 70 acres of sub-tropical gardens. Caffi Glas, an Italian restaurant in the village centre, is a good choice for families, assuming you can get the kids past the Cadwaladers Ice Cream Café.

Also recommended
Conwy Butterfly Jungle

Conwy, T01492-593149, conwy-butterfly.co.uk.

Gypsy Wood

Bontnewydd, nr Caernarfon, T01286-673133, gypsywood.co.uk.

Llechwedd Slate Caverns

Blaenau Ffestiniog, T01766-830306, llechwedd-slate-caverns.co.uk.

Sygun Copper Mine

Beddgelert, T01766-890595, syguncoppermine.co.uk.

Welsh Mountain Zoo

Colwyn Bay, T01492-532938, welshmountainzoo.org.

Caves & mines
See left for Electric Mountain, King Arthur's Labyrinth, Llechwedd Slate Caverns and Sygun Copper Mine.

Cinemas
• Cineworld, Conwy, T0871-200 2000.
• Coliseum, Porthmadog, T01766-512108.

Indoor play
• Yr Hwylfan, The Fun Centre, Caernarfon, T01286-671911, thefuncentre.co.uk.
• Glasfryn Parc, Pwllheli, T01766-810202, glasfryn.co.uk.
• The Den, Electric Mountain, Llanberis, T01286-873050, yden.co.uk.

Indoor swimming pools
• Arfon Leisure Centre, Caernarfon, T01286-676451.
• Bangor Swimming Pool, T01248-370600.
• Dwyfor Leisure Centre, Pwllheli, T01758-613437.
• Glaslyn Leisure Centre, Porthmadog, T01766-512711.
• Rhyl Sun Centre, T01745-344433, rhylsuncentre.co.uk.

Museums
• Airworld, Caernarfon, T01286-830800, air-world.co.uk.
• Centre for Alternative Technology, Machynlleth, T01654-705950, cat.org.uk.
• Cywain Centre, Bala, T01678-520920, cywain.co.uk.
• Gwynedd Museum and Art Gallery, Bangor, T01248-353368.
• Maritime Museum, Porthmadog, T01766-513 736.
• National Centre for Welsh Folk Music, Dolgellau, T01341-421800, tysiamas.com.

Sleeping Snowdonia

Beddgelert Campsite

T 01766-890288, forestholidays.co.uk. Year round, £8-14/pitch (2 people), plus £4.25-6.25/extra adult, £1.75-3.25/extra child, £1 family discount.

Well-run, forested site offering canoeing and pony trekking.

Eisteddfa

Nr Criccieth, T 01766-522696, eisteddfapark.co.uk. Mar-Oct, £12.50-18/pitch.

Secluded site close to beaches, with tipi available for hire.

Shell Island

Llanbedr, T 01341-241453, shellisland.co.uk. Mar-Oct, £6-7/adult, £2.50-3/child (3-15yrs).

Although it's technically a peninsula (see page 272), Shell Island still captures something of the magic of a remote outpost – particularly out of season when the vast expanse of dunes and rolling fields are less crowded with campers. Bag a prime spot next to the sandy beach and your kids will be in heaven. Facilities include a couple of useful stores, a restaurant and a café.

Ty'n yr Onnen Caravan & Camping Park

Waunfawr, T 01286-650281, tyn-yr-onnen.co.uk. Apr-Oct, £12-17/pitch (2 people), plus £5/extra adult, £3/extra child (3-14).

This is a relaxed family site, where you're more likely to see children hurling frisbees than hardened hillwalkers lacing up for an assault on Snowdon (although there is a path to the mountain from the campsite). Connoisseurs of the molten marshmallow will appreciate the liberal policy on campfires, while various cute-and-cuddlies (donkeys, lambs etc) will keep children of all ages happy. Ty'n yr Onnen is ideally located between Snowdon and sea, with both Llanberis and Caernarfon less than 6 miles away.

Also recommended

Black Rock Sands Camping Park Morfa Bychan, T 01766-513919.

Bwch-yn-uchaf

Llanuwchllyn, nr Bala, T 01978-812179, bwch-yn-uchaf.co.uk.

Hendre Mynach Touring Park

Barmouth, T 01341-280262, hendremynach.co.uk.

Snowdonia Park

Waunfawr, T 01286-650409, snowdonia-park.co.uk.

Trawsdir Llanaber, nr Barmouth,

T 01341-280999, trawsdir.co.uk.

Bring on the marshmallows – Ty'n yr Onnen campsite on the western flanks of Snowdonia.

Best of the rest

Gwynfryn

Pwllheli, T01758-612536, northwales-countryholidays.com. Year round, 8-person cottage £400-1070/wk, 4-person cottages £240-815/wk.

The glorious beaches of the Llŷn Peninsula are right on the doorstep of this organic dairy farm, which has a choice of 11 four- or five-star self-catering cottages sleeping up to eight. The farmer is always grateful for a helping hand feeding calves, pigs, goats, lambs and chickens – but the farm menagerie has stiff competition from the plethora of indoor and outdoor facilities, ranging from pool, gym and playroom to tennis court and family bikes.

Trefeddian Hotel

Aberdyfi, T01654-767213, trefwales. com. Year round, nightly rates including dinner, bed and breakfast £55-102/adult, £12-42/child when sharing with parents.

A long-established family favourite, 'Tref' has welcomed generations of holidaymakers to this choice spot overlooking Cardigan Bay near the lovely old fishing village of Aberdyfi. A sandy beach is just a short stroll through the dunes, while hotel facilities include family rooms, a children's playroom and an indoor heated swimming pool. Outside, there's a putting green and tennis court. Dining is a treat with an excellent children's supper served from 1715-1745.

Tyddyn Mawr Farm Cottages

Rowen, nr Conwy, T01492-650302, snowdonia-farm-cottages.co.uk. Feb-Dec, £250-650/wk.

The five self-catering stone cottages at Tyddyn Mawr sleep up to six and have been fitted to a high standard. But it's the fabulous setting of this 400-acre beef and sheep farm (tucked into Snowdonia National Park, but just a few miles from Conwy) that makes it especially appealing. The cottages are close to a string of wildlife-rich lakes, while paths probe woodland and lead for miles across unspoilt countryside. A great choice for an authentic Welsh hill-farm experience.

Also recommended
Bodwi Farm Holidays

Abersoch, T01758-713631, abersoch-holidays.co.uk.

Bryn Sion Farm

Dinas Mawddwy, Machynlleth, T01650-531251, brynsion.co.uk.

Cefn Coed Holiday Cottages

Chwilog, Pwllheli, T01766-810259, cefncoedholidays.co.uk.

Llŷn Peninsula Farm Holidays

T01758-712570, happyhols.com.

Mid Wales Farm Holidays

Tywyn, T01654-711703, midwalesholidays.co.uk.

Holiday parks

Abererch Sands Holiday Centre
Nr Pwllheli, T01758-612327,
abererch-sands.co.uk.
Great location for exploring the beaches of the Llŷn Peninsula.

Caernarfon Bay Caravan Park
Dinas Dinlle, T01286-830492,
caernarfonbaycaravanpark.com.
Short stroll from Blue Flag beach.

Glan-y-Borth Holiday Village
Llanrwst, T01492-641543,
glanyborth.co.uk.
Twenty holiday bungalows on the banks of the River Conwy.

Greenacres
Morfa Bychan, T01766-512781,
greenacres-park.co.uk.
Short walk from Black Rock Sands.

Hendwr Scandinavian Lodges
Nr Bala, T01490-440210,
hendwr-lodge.cymru1.net.
Well-equipped cabins on the edge of Snowdonia National Park.

Plas-y-Bryn Chalet Park
Bontnewydd, nr Caernarfon,
T01286-672811, plasybryn.co.uk.
Chalet park close to Caernarfon.

Sarnfaen Holiday Park
Talybont, nr Barmouth, T01341-247241, sarnfaen.co.uk.
Excellent facilities and a stone's throw from Talybont beach.

Cottage agents

North Wales Holiday Cottages
T01492-582492, northwales holidaycottages.co.uk.

Sea & Mountain Cottages
Porthmadog, T01766-513829,
sts-holidays.co.uk.

Eating Snowdonia

Local Goodies

Caban Café
Nr Llanberis, T01286-685500, caban-cyf.org. Daily 0900-1600.
Located in Brynrefail near the base of Snowdon, Caban Café is a co-operative established to boost local rural economies – something it does with culinary flair thanks to creative home cooking using local organic produce. Choose from a full range of breakfast and lunch dishes, including kids' specials like penne pasta with basil and tomato sauce (£2.55).

Cadwaladers Ice Cream
Castle St, Criccieth, T01766-523665, cadwaladersicecream.co.uk. Mar-Oct, plus weekends and holidays during winter.
Cadwaladers began selling ice cream in Criccieth back in 1927. Now it also has cafés in Betws y Coed, Llandudno, Porthmadog, Portmeirion and Pwllheli. Vanilla is still its flagship flavour, but chances are you will be mightily tempted by an exotic range of sundaes, smoothies and shakes.

Fish & chips
Close to the beach, **The Mermaid** (Barmouth, T01341-280614) has been frying fish since 1964, while **Spinnaker**, (Abersoch, T01758-713557) is another top chippie. Also try **Tegfan Fish & Chip Shop**, (Caernarfon, T01286-678282) and **Castle Fish & Chips** (Criccieth, T01766 -522081).

Glasfryn Farm Shop
Y Ffôr, Pwllheli, T01766-810 044 siop-glasfryn.com.
Huge choice of local produce, plus homemade ready meals, chocolates, biscuits and snacks.

Also recommended
Edwards of Conwy
High St, Conwy, T01492-592443, edwardsofconwy.co.uk.
Award-winning master butcher.

The Quarry Shop & Café
Centre for Alternative Technology, Machynlleth, T01654-702624, cat.org.uk, Mon-Sat from 0900.
Vegetarian café, plus shop selling local seasonal produce.

Quick & Simple

Esther's Cuisine Café
Electric Mountain, see page 281.
Good range of dishes, plus a garden area for eating outside.

Glaslyn Ices & Glandwr Café
Beddgelert, T01766-890339, glaslynices.co.uk.
Relaxed café renowned for pizza (from £5.95), but also serving

Market days
Bala Mon (summer).
Barmouth Thu, Sun (summer).
Blaenau Ffestiniog Tue.
Caernarfon Sat, Mon (summer).
Conwy 4th Wed.
Dolgellau Mon.
Llanrwst Tue, 3rd Sat.
Porthmadog Fri (summer).
Pwllheli Wed, 2nd Sun.

jacket spuds, fish & chips etc. Leave room for the delicious ice cream or the Holy Grail of puds – chocolate pizza (£6.95).

Oriel Fach Café
Abersoch, T01758-713158.
Popular tearoom with outdoor seating area – perfect spot for a light lunch or Welsh cream tea.

Also recommended
Poachers Restaurant
High St, Criccieth, T01766-522512, poachersrestaurant.co.uk.
Good value home cooking.

Tebot Bach
Castle St, Caernarfon, T01286-678444.
Tearoom serving tasty snacks.

Ysgethin Inn
Tal y Bont, nr Barmouth, T01341-247578, ysgethin-inn.com.
Riverside pub, full of character.

Posh Nosh

Porth Tocyn Hotel
Abersoch, T01758-713303, porth-tocyn-hotel.co.uk.
Dinner is for adults only, but the relaxed lunches – especially the huge buffets on Sundays – are ideal for families.

Also recommended
The Celtic Royal Hotel
Caernarfon, T01286-674477, celtic-royal.co.uk.

Trefeddian Hotel
See page 279.

Essentials Snowdonia

Getting there

By train Arriva Trains Wales
(T0870-900 0773, arrivatrainswales.
co.uk) runs from Manchester to
Llandudno, where the Conwy
Valley Line (conwyvalleyrailway.
co.uk) heads south to Betws y
Coed and Blaenau Ffestiniog.
Arriva also runs from Birmingham
to Machynlleth, via Shrewsbury,
with connections to the Cambrian
Line (thecambrianline.co.uk)
which links Aberdyfi, Barmouth,
Porthmadog and Pwllheli.
By coach National Express
(T0871-781 8181, nationalexpress.
com) services run to Llandudno,
Bangor, Caernarfon, Porthmadog
and Pwllheli.

Getting around

By train For £10, a discount card
from Great Little Trains of Wales
(greatlittletrainsofwales.co.uk)
entitles you to 20% off return fares
on Bala Lake, Ffestiniog, Llanberis
Lake, Snowdon Mountain and
Welsh Highland lines. See page
276 for contact details.
By bus The Snowdon Sherpa
(snowdoniagreenkey.co.uk)
provides an excellent bus service
around northern Snowdonia. A
day ticket (£4/adult, £2/child)
allows you to hop on and off as
many times as you like. Sherpa
routes are S1 (Llanberis–Pen y
Pass), S2 (Llandudno–Betws y
Coed–Pen y Pass), S4 (Caernarfon–
Beddgelert), S6 (Bangor–Betws
y Coed) and S97 (Porthmadog–
Beddgelert–Pen y Pass). Some
routes use open-top buses.

Maps

For walking and other activities,
choose from Ordnance Survey
Explorer OL17 (Snowdon), OL18
(Harlech, Porthmadog & Y Bala),
OL23 (Cadair Idris & Bala Lake)
and 253/254 (Llŷn Peninsula). For
more general touring, consider
Landranger 115 (Snowdon),
123 (Llŷn Peninsula) or 124
(Porthmadog & Dolgellau).

Tourist Information Centres

General tourist information can
be found at visitsnowdonia.info
and gwynedd.gov.uk. Snowdonia's
network of TICs includes:
Aberdyfi The Wharf Gardens,
T01654-767321.
Bala Pensarn Rd, T01678-521021.
Barmouth Station Rd,
T01341-280787.
Betws y Coed Royal Oak Stables,
T01690-710426.
Caernarfon Stryd y Castell (Castle
St), T01286-672232.
Conwy Castle Buildings,
T01492-592248.
Llanberis Stryd Fawr (High St),
T01286-870765.
Llandudno Mostyn St,
T01492-577577.
Porthmadog Stryd Fawr (High St),
T01766-512981.
Pwllheli Min y Don,
T01758-613000.

Further Information

Snowdonia National Park
Authority, T01766-770274,
snowdonia-npa.gov.uk.
Countryside Council for Wales,
ccw.gov.uk.

Hospital

Dolgellau Dolgellau & Barmouth
District Community Hospital,
T01341-422479.

Pharmacies

Barmouth Rowlands, High St.
Caernarfon Castle, Bridge St.
Llanberis Rowlands, High St.
Llanrwst Alliance, Denbigh St.
Porthmadog Rowlands, High St.
Pwllheli Rowlands, High St.

Supermarkets

Bala Somerfield.
Caernarfon Kwik Save, Morrison.
Conwy Asda.
Dolgellau Somerfield.
Llanberis Costcutter.
Llanrwst Somerfield.
Porthmadog Tesco.
Pwllheli Asda.

Other shops

Baby supplies Mothercare,
Victoria Centre, Llandudno.
Camping supplies Cotswold
Outdoor, Holyhead Rd, Betws y
Coed; Ellis Brigham, Capel Curig.
Toys & beach gear Aladdin's Cave,
Aberdyfi; R A Jones & Son, High St,
Caernarfon.

Environmental groups

North Wales Wildlife Trust,
T01248-351541, wildlifetrust.org.
uk/northwales.

Major Events

Jul Gwyl Caernarfon Festival.
Aug Abersoch Regatta (featuring
crabbing and sandcastle contests).
Aug Conwy River Festival.

Contents

284 Map

286 Glasgow
287 Edinburgh

288 The Cairngorms
290 Fun & free
292 Action stations
295 Big days out
297 Fort William & Lochaber
297 Loch Lomond & the Trossachs
298 Sleeping
300 Eating
301 Essentials

302 Isle of Mull
309 Isle of Arran
309 Isle of Skye

Scotland

One morerock for
the cairn on Cairn Gorm.

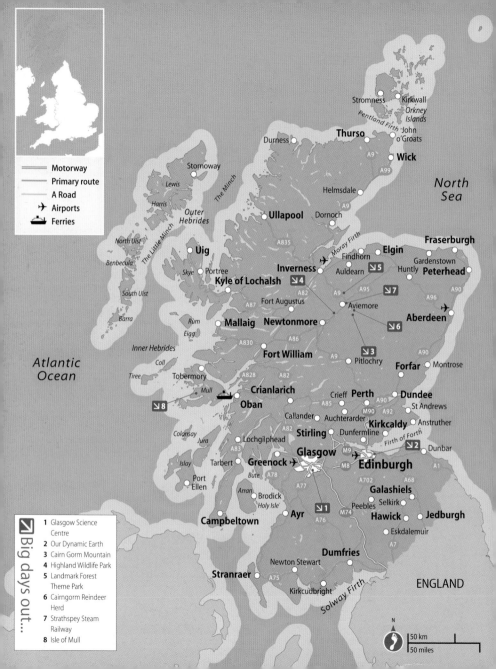

Motorway
Primary route
A Road
✈ Airports
⛴ Ferries

Big days out...

1 Glasgow Science Centre
2 Our Dynamic Earth
3 Cairn Gorm Mountain
4 Highland Wildlife Park
5 Landmark Forest Theme Park
6 Cairngorm Reindeer Herd
7 Strathspey Steam Railway
8 Isle of Mull

North Sea

Atlantic Ocean

ENGLAND

Orkney Islands
Stromness
Kirkwall
Pentland Firth
John o'Groats
Thurso
Wick
Durness
Helmsdale
A9
A99
Dornoch
Ullapool
A835
Moray Firth
Findhorn
Elgin
Fraserburgh
Gardenstown
Stornoway
Lewis
Harris
Outer Hebrides
The Minch
North Uist
The Little Minch
Benbecula
South Uist
Barra
Uig
Portree
Skye
Kyle of Lochalsh
Inverness
Auldearn
Huntly
Peterhead
A96
A90
Aberdeen
Aviemore
A95
A9
A87
Fort Augustus
A82
Mallaig
Newtonmore
A830
A86
Fort William
Rum
Eigg
Inner Hebrides
Coll
Tiree
Tobermory
Mull
A828
A82
Crianlarich
Oban
Callander
A85
Crieff
Perth
Forfar
Montrose
Pitlochry
A9
A90
Colonsay
Jura
Lochgilphead
A83
Islay
Tarbert
Bute
Port Ellen
Arran
Brodick
Holy Isle
Stirling
Dunfermline
Auchterarder
M90
A92
Dundee
St Andrews
Anstruther
Kirkcaldy
Firth of Forth
Dunbar
A1
Glasgow
Greenock
M9
M8
Edinburgh
A78
A77
Ayr
A76
Peebles
M74
Galashiels
Selkirk
A68
Hawick
Jedburgh
Eskdalemuir
A7
Campbeltown
Dumfries
Newton Stewart
A75
Stranraer
Kirkcudbright
Solway Firth

N
50 km
50 miles

⊠8
⊠4
⊠5
⊠7
⊠6
⊠3
⊠2
⊠1

Cycling in Rothiemurchus Estate; heather in close-up; whalewatching in the Hebrides; the Cairngorms from Loch Morlich; Edinburgh Castle; sailing in Tobermory harbour; the Trossachs.

Great escapes

Glasgow

Unlike Edinburgh (see right), there are no iconic landmarks in Glasgow, but what this modern-thinking city lacks in the way of volcanoes and castles it more than compensates for with a lively cultural scene and several superb museums. By far the best for kids, the **Kelvingrove Art Gallery and Museum** (glasgowmuseums.com) has everything from Egyptian mummies to a Second World War Spitfire. Children under five get their own hands-on Mini Museum, while older kids can learn about wildlife, history and art at various discovery centres. Don't miss the webcam link to the Loch Ness Monster, the 14-ft Ceratosaur skeleton or the impressive collection of paintings which includes Salvador Dali's *Christ*.

Highlights at the nearby **Museum of Transport** (glasgowmuseums.com) include locomotives from the Caledonian and Highland Railways and a collection of 250 model ships. Nip down to the north bank of the River Clyde and you'll find the 19th-century, three-masted *SS Glenlee*, otherwise known as **The Tall Ship at Glasgow Harbour** (glenlee.co.uk). On the opposite bank, Pacific Quay is the location of the excellent **Glasgow Science Centre** (gsc.org.uk) – a technological treasure house where kids can tinker with hundreds of interactive exhibits, join workshops to build hot-air balloons and rockets, and go goggle-eyed in the planetarium and IMAX cinema. East of the city centre, but still on the Clyde, **People's Palace and Winter Gardens** (glasgowmuseums.com) reveals Glasgow's social history, while less than an hour's drive southeast of Glasgow, **New Lanark World Heritage Site** (newlanark.org) is a beautifully restored 18th-century village where kids can discover what life was like in a Victorian cotton mill.

>> seeglasgow.com

Magnificent flying machines and wonders of nature at Kelvingrove Art Gallery and Museum.

Edinburgh

Plenty of cities have castles, but not many have a castle perched on an extinct volcano – a double whammy for child-friendly Edinburgh. A fun way to get an overview of this bonny World-Heritage-listed city is to take a ride through the medieval Old Town and Georgian New Town with **Edinburgh Bus Tours** (edinburghtour.com). Next, visit **Edinburgh Castle** (historic-scotland.gov.uk) to see Scotland's Crown Jewels and the Stone of Destiny. Listen out for the One O'Clock Gun and visit the dungeons to see the Prisons of War exhibition.

Just below the castle, **West Princes Street Gardens** is ideal for letting youngsters burn off energy, although teenagers will probably prefer to exercise their wallets along adjacent Princes Street. Alternatively, head east from Castle Hill along the **Royal Mile** – once the main thoroughfare of medieval Edinburgh, linking the castle to the Royal Family's **Palace of Holyroodhouse** (royal.gov.uk). Flanked by impressive buildings like St Giles Cathedral and Parliament House, it's the **Museum of Childhood** (edinburgh.gov.uk) – crammed with toys past and present – that will appeal most to kids.

On nearby Holyrood Road, **Our Dynamic Earth** (dynamicearth.co.uk) takes you on a ground-shaking journey through the planet's history, from Big Bang to global warming. Don't miss FutureDome where you can help decide Earth's fate. Rearing up behind this ultra-modern science centre, you can scramble over the ancient lava flows of **Arthur's Seat**, a volcano that blew its top between 350 and 400 million years ago.

A rainy-day favourite, the **Brass Rubbing Centre** is located opposite the Museum of Childhood, while the excellent **Edinburgh Zoo** (edinburghzoo.org.uk) is always a hit, whatever the weather.

Edinburgh's most notorious ghost tour, City of the Dead, is hosted nightly by **Blackhart Entertainment** (blackhart.uk.com) – but be warned: a possible encounter with the MacKenzie Poltergeist is not for the faint-hearted. The Secret City Tour is suitable for all ages and features a quirky mixture of Harry Potter, Frankenstein's monster and the origins of Christmas.

For a city escape, head east towards North Berwick, taking in 12th-century **Dirleton Castle** (historic-scotland.gov.uk) and the **Scottish Seabird Centre** (seabird.org) where you can watch footage beamed live from Bass Rock, 3 miles offshore and smothered in over 100,000 gannets between January and October. There are also several fine beaches close to Edinburgh, including the popular surf spot of Gullane Bents and wildlife-rich Longniddry Bents.

>> edinburgh.org

It's only when you hand-feed a reindeer that you realise just how soft and velvety their muzzles are.

Reindeers – running free and wild in the Cairngorms.

The Cairngorms

What child could resist a rendezvous with a real-life Rudolf? Roaming with reindeers is just one of the family perks in Britain's largest national park, where mountain, loch, river and forest conspire to form the ultimate adventure playground. There's simply no better place for kids to experience the Highlands.

On the face of it, the Cairngorms should be about as child-friendly as the moon. Not only does the national park cover an area of nearly 1500 square miles (40% more than the Lake District), but it also has four of Scotland's five highest peaks and the largest tract of arctic mountain terrain in Britain.

Most of the central part of the Cairngorms remains an austere wilderness. It's only around the edges – especially where the Spey and the Dee have carved inroads – that the national park softens sufficiently for 16,000 human inhabitants and a thriving tourism industry.

Two major roads flirt with the Cairngorms. The A93, between Perth and Aberdeen, loops through the southeast of the park, passing the Glenshee Ski Area before joining the Dee at **Braemar**, a popular centre for walkers and the site of the annual Braemar Gathering. It continues east, past **Balmoral**, to the village of **Ballater** where it seems that every shop, from florist to chemist, displays a royal warrant. South of Ballater, a single-track road probes Glen Muick, a fine spot for loch-side walks beneath mighty Lochnagar.

On the western fringes of the Cairngorms National Park, the A9 Pitlochry–Inverness road passes **Dalwhinnie** (home to Scotland's highest distillery) before dipping alongside the River Spey near **Newtonmore** and **Kingussie** where you'll find the fascinating Highland Folk Museum. Further north, near **Kincraig**, Loch Insh has a superb watersports centre, but it's nearby **Aviemore** that's the undisputed adventure capital of the Cairngorms. Although the town itself makes an ideal base for exploring the mountains, the road west to Rothiemurchus Estate, Loch Morlich and Glenmore Forest combines the very best of family-friendly accommodation and activities in the national park – from camping in the Caledonian Forest and cycling around tranquil lochs to visiting the free-roaming reindeer herd and hiking to the summit of mighty Cairn Gorm itself. Aviemore is also the western terminus of the Strathspey Steam Railway which runs to **Boat of Garten** with its famous osprey centre.

You must

- Get afloat on a canoe or sailing dinghy.
- Feed the reindeer.
- Conquer Cairn Gorm.
- Bike and hike through Caledonian pine forest.
- Spot an osprey, red squirrel and golden eagle.
- Get 'multi-active' at Rothiemurchus Estate.
- Eat a clootie.
- Ride the Strathspey Steam Railway.
- Climb, slide and leap at the Landmark Forest Park.
- Join a ranger walk.

Out & about The Cairngorms

Roam with a ranger

There are several Ranger Bases in the Cairngorms (see page 301 for contact details), each one providing a wealth of information on activities, the environment and how to experience the national park in a safe and responsible way. Rangers also run an annual programme of free events, including outdoor activities, guided walks and talks. There are free visitor centres at Balmoral Estate (Loch Muick), Glenlivet Estate (Tomintoul), Glenmore Forest Park (near Aviemore) and Glen Tanar Estate (Braelonie). Also free to enter, the Explore Abernethy Centre (Nethy Bridge, T01479-821565, exploreabernethy.co.uk, Easter-Oct, Sat-Wed 1100-1600) has hands-on exhibits and an Explore Club where children aged 7-11 can find out about wildlife and history on ranger-led events during the school holidays.

Hit the beach

Emerging from the conifer woods surrounding Loch Insh or Loch Morlich, you step abruptly from a carpet of pine needles to soft, golden sand – ideal for digging canals or making sandcastles. Those brave of heart may even feel inclined to go for a paddle or swim in the lake. Both lochs have excellent watersports centres (see page 294) with cafés overlooking the beach, while Loch Insh has the added bonus of three children's adventure play areas.

Take a hike

There are numerous walking trails suitable for families in the Cairngorms National Park. Even the 1244-m summit of Cairn Gorm itself is within reach of outward-going children thanks to the steep, but well-marked Coire Cas Trail that snakes up the mountain from the base station of the funicular railway (see page 295). And, of course, the big incentive for tackling this mighty munro on foot is that you can take the mountain train back down again. Cairn Gorm is the crowning glory of many families' hiking escapades in the national park, but there are other less lofty options, weaving through forests or looping around lochs. Call in at a visitor centre (see page 301) where rangers can advise you on the most appropriate trail.

Pedal in the park

The Cairngorms have plenty of steep, scree-ridden, boulder-hopping trails for hardened mountain bikers, but families will also find plenty of less teeth-rattling options – many on wide, gently undulating gravel tracks that double as cross-country skiing trails in winter. Some of the best child-friendly cycle paths are in Inshriach Forest, Glenmore Forest Park and Rothiemurchus

Visit The Highland Folk Museum

Why? This fascinating museum uses historic buildings and costumed actors to portray 200 years of Highland rural life, from the early 1700s to the mid 1900s. It includes a reconstruction of part of the medieval township of Easter Raitts with its turf-walled, heather-thatched dwellings. A 1930s farm features a wartime kitchen where children can learn about rationing, while other buildings include a railway halt, post office, shepherd's bothy, clockmaker's workshop and saw mill – all linked by a vintage bus ride. Don't forget to enrol the kids for a 1930s-style lesson at the tin-wall school. A summer events programme includes activities such as baking and weaving. The museum has picnic sites and a café, plus a play area, gift shop and red-squirrel feeders.

How? Open Easter-Oct, daily. Apr-Aug 1030-1730, Sep-Oct 1100-1630.

Contact Highland Folk Museum, Newtonmore, nr Kingussie, T01540-661307, highlandfolk.com.

Estate. At Inshriach, head off across the Moor of Feshie or follow one of the routes from the Feshiebridge car park. In Rothiemurchus Estate, there's superb offroad biking to Loch an Eilein and an excellent cycle path to the visitor centre in Glenmore Forest Park. From here, you can set off on an hour-long circuit of Loch Morlich, weaving through pine forest and across heather-clad slopes, crossing tea-coloured streams and pausing for breaks at hidden sandy coves. Perhaps the finest route of all, though, is the one that follows a stunning valley of Caledonian pine from the visitor centre to Green Loch. For details of bike-hire centres and other good cycling spots, see page 292.

The Cairngorms National Park is home to a quarter of the UK's threatened bird, animal and plant species. Red squirrels are lured to feeders at visitor centres, while ospreys nest at Loch Garten (Boat of Garten, T01479-831476, Apr-Aug, daily 1000-1800). See if you can also spot a golden eagle soaring over the mountains, or woodland birds such as the capercaillie, crested tit and crossbill. Out on the moors keep your eyes peeled for red deer and black grouse. Bonus points for the forest-skulking pine marten and bonus-points-with-bells-on for wildcat.

Picnic perfect

If the idea of a picnic in the Scottish Highlands conjures images of huddling next to a boulder on a bleak mountainside while gale-force winds do their best to dismantle your ham salad sarnies, think again. The Cairngorms National Park is studded with sheltered lochs where you'll find sandy beaches caressed by limpid waters and fringed by shady forests. Some are right by the roadside, but it's far more fun to pack a picnic, hop on some bikes and cycle to somewhere a bit more off the beaten track, like Green Loch pictured here.

Green Loch, Glenmore Forest Park.

Out & about The Cairngorms

Action stations

Cycling
Bothy Bikes

Rothiemurchus, nr Aviemore,
T01479-810111, bothybikes.co.uk.
Year round, daily 0900-1730, adult
bike £20/day, £15/half-day; child's
bike £8/day, £6/half-day. Helmets
tool kits and maps included.
With off-road trails leading
straight from the shop, Bothy

Bikes offers access to several
easy routes in the spectacular
Rothiemurchus Estate (see
pages 294 and 298). The 6-mile
Loch an Eilein trail is rewarded
by the sight of a ruined castle
rising from an island in the
middle of the loch, while the 10-
mile Ancient Forest route probes
beautiful Caledonian pine forest,
rich in wildlife. You can combine
both routes or link up with trails

to the Glenmore Forest Park
region. See also pages 290-291.

Cycle Highlands

Ballater, T013397-55864,
cyclehighlands.com. Year round,
daily from 0900, adult bike £15/day,
£10/half-day; child's bike £7-9/day,
£5-7/half-day. Tag-alongs, child seats
and tandems also available. Helmets,
tool kits and maps included.
Ballater is surrounded by a

network of bike trails, including family-friendly options such as the Old Deeside Railway Cycle Route (with tearooms and riverside views), the Bike Safari Route (where you stand a good chance of spotting red squirrels and Highland cattle) and the more challenging Glen Muick to Glen Girnock Route. Guided rides lasting from two hours to a full day are also available.

Cyclelife Aviemore

Aviemore, T01479-810478. Year round, Mon-Sat from 0930, Sun (Apr-Oct) from 1200, adult bike £20/day, £12/half-day, child's bike £10/day, £8/half-day, tag-along £5, trailer £7. A town-centre bike shop a short ride from the family-friendly trails in Rothiemurchus Estate.

Glenmore Campsite

See page 298.

Loch Insh Watersports

See page 294.

Horse riding
Alvie Stables

Alvie, nr Aviemore, T07831-495397. Year round. Phone for rates. Superb riding on well-schooled horses and ponies in the Alvie Estate, with lessons for children as young as four, and hacks for the more experienced.

Boats to go

The watersports centres at Loch Insh and Loch Morlich (see page 294) can get you afloat by the hour or by the day.

Single kayaks from £8/hr, £22/day.
Double kayaks from £12/hr, £27/day.
Canadian canoes from £16/hr, £35/day.
Rowing boats from £15/hr, £45/day.
Windsurfers from £16/hr, £45/day.
Sailing dinghies (ie Optimist or Funboat) from £10/hr, £25/day.
Sailing instruction from £19/hr.
One-day RYA sailing course from £51/adult, £44/child (8-14).
Learn to Sail weekend course for families from £160.

Falling head over keels for Loch Morlich

Out & about The Cairngorms

Carrbridge Pony Trekking Ctr
Ellan Bridge Stables, Carrbridge, T01479-841602. May-Oct. Phone for rates.
A chance for the whole family to saddle up, the Carrbridge Pony Trekking Centre offers escorted one- and two-hour treks with children under 12 led on reins.

Tomintoul Riding Centre
St Bridget Farm, Tomintoul, T01807-580210, highlandhooves.co.uk. May-Oct. Rides £70/day, £38/half-day, £25/hr. Family discounts available. Escorted horse riding on Glenlivet Estate.

A great opportunity to spot ospreys, boat tours around Loch Insh, the Insh Marshes and River Spey depart Apr-Oct, daily, from the Loch Insh Watersports Centre (see below).

Woodland adventures
See Landmark Forest Adventure Park, page 296.

Wildlife safaris
Land Rover safaris are available from the following operators:

Braemar Highland Safaris
Braemar, T013397-41420, braemarhighlandsafaris.co.uk.

Glenlivet Wildlife
Tomnavoulin, T01807-590241, glenlivet-wildlife.co.uk.

Highland Wildlife Safaris
Aviemore, T01479-811169, highlandwildlifesafaris.co.uk.

Multi activities

Ace Adventures (AA)
Aviemore, T07792-034291, aceadventures.co.uk.

Active Outdoor Pursuits (AOP)
Newtonmore, T01540-673319, activeoutdoorpursuits.com.

Boots 'n' Paddles (BP)
Kirkhill, T0845-612 5567, boots-n-paddles.co.uk.

Full On Adventure (FOA)
Aviemore, T07885-835838, fullonadventure.com.

G2 Outdoor (G2O)
Aviemore, T01479-811008, g2outdoor.co.uk.

Loch Insh Watersports Centre (LIW)
Kincraig, T01540-651272, lochinsh.com.

Loch Morlich Watersports (LMW)
Glenmore Forest Park, T01479-861221, lochmorlich.com.

Rothiemurchus Centre (RC)
Nr Aviemore, T01479-812345, rothiemurchus.net.

There's an extraordinary range of year-round activities available in the Cairngorms region, from family rafting on the Spey (minimum age 8, from £45/person) to canyoning (minimum age 6, from £35/person) and weaseling (scrambling under boulders). You can also learn to sail or rent a canoe (see page 293).

	AA	AOP	BP	FOA	G2O	LIW	LMW	RC
Archery			●			●		●
Canoeing/kayaking	●	●	●	●	●	●	●	●
Canyoning			●	●	●			●
Hill walking	●		●	●			●	
Mountain biking	●		●	●	●		●	●
Quad biking	●							●
Raft building			●	●				
Rock climbing/abseiling	●		●	●	●			●
Sailing						●	●	
Snow sports	●			●	●			●
White water rafting	●	●			●			●
Windsurfing						●	●	
Weaseling			●					

Big days out

Cairn Gorm Mountain

CairnGorm Mountain Railway, nr Aviemore, T01479-861261, cairngormmountain.org. Dec-Apr, daily 0900-1630, May-Nov, daily 1000-1700, trains run every 15-20 minutes, first train up 1000, last train down 1630-1700. Day tickets £9.50/adult, £6/child (5-16), £28/family; down-only tickets £7/adult, £4.50/child, £20.50/family. Check website for winter sports packages.

It takes about 90 minutes to hike from the Coire Cas car park to the Top Station – an altitude gain of about 630 m as you follow a wide, well-marked path on the flank of Britain's 6th highest mountain. Every half-hour or so, a bright purple funicular train glides effortlessly past, but the reason you're slogging up 1244-m Cairn Gorm on foot is that people who catch the train are not permitted to leave the Top Station to go out onto the mountain. They'll still get the fabulous views, but the magical, rarified beauty of this mighty munro is that it guards a vast, yet fragile, upland plateau that's a refuge for arctic flora and fauna (you'd have to travel 2000 miles to northern Norway to see anything similar). To experience this extraordinary habitat, a roped-off path leads

Cairn Gorm – the only way is up.

from the Top Station to the summit (an extra 20 minutes of puff) where you can add a rock to the cairn and, if you're lucky, share your on-top-of-the-world moment with a herd of reindeer – an unforgettable sight as they stream like smoke across the rock-shattered summit.

You can reward your efforts with a meal at the Top Station's Ptarmigan Restaurant (see page 300) or catch the train down to the Base Station where a café serves hot chocolate crowned with mountains of thick cream and marshmallows.

Remember to plan your mountain hike with care. Take warm clothes, water, snacks and sun protection and make sure everyone has shoes or boots with good grip and ankle support. If it all sounds too daunting, restrict your walk to the easy-access trail from the

Base Station which takes in the Wild Mountain Garden – a kind of Cairn Gorm in miniature.

Highland Wildlife Park

Kincraig, T01540-651270, highlandwildlifepark.org. Year round, daily from 1000, £11.50/adult, £8.75/child (4-15), £37/family. Your very own Highlands safari, part of this excellent zoo is a drive-through reserve where you can spot European bison, yak, Tibetan wild ass, mouflon and red deer from the comfort of your car. Then it's on foot to see more mountain wildlife, ranging from red pandas and Japanese macaques to wolves and the highly endangered Amur tiger.

Cry wolf at the Highland Wildlife park.

Out & about The Cairngorms

Landmark Forest Theme Park

Carrbridge, T01479-841613, landmark-centre.co.uk. Year round, daily from 1000, £10.55/adult, £8.25/child (4-14), 5% discount for families, reduced rates during winter.

There's nothing gimmicky about this theme park. It's got a woody, back-to-nature feel, where a red squirrel trail (with buggy-friendly treetop board walk) and a steam-powered sawmill hold their own against thrill rides like the triple water chutes (with sit-on inflatables) and simulated sky-dive tower jump. Adventureland is the hub of activity where, in addition to the tower jump, you'll find a high-wire challenge course (minimum height 1.5 m), rock-climbing wall, maze, slides and undercover play area. Don't miss the fire tower (105 steps to the top) or a chance to meet Lex the soppy great Clydesdale horse.

More family favourites

Cairngorm Reindeer Herd

Glenmore, T01479-861228, reindeer-company.demon.co.uk. Year round, daily hill visits 1100, plus 1430 (May-Sep), £9/adult, £4.50/child (6-16), £27/family.

It's only when you hand-feed a reindeer that you realise just how soft and velvety their muzzles are. The Cairngorm herd numbers around 150

and the opportunity to feed and pet them is a dream come true for most children. Like Christmas in reverse, you help carry sacks of (edible) goodies out onto the mountainside where the main herd lives year-round.

Strathspey Steam Railway

Aviemore Station, T01479-810725, strathspeyrailway.co.uk. Standard service Apr-Oct. Round-trip fares £10.50/adult, £5.25/child (5-15), £26/family.

The round trip from Aviemore to Broomhill takes approximately 90 minutes. Take your bikes on the train and stop off at Boat of Garten for the 3-mile cycle to the RSPB's osprey viewpoint at Loch Garten.

Also recommended
Balmoral Castle

Ballater, T01339-742534, balmoralcastle.com.

Blair Castle

Blair Atholl, Pitlochry, T01796-481487, blair-castle.co.uk.

Watch a Highland shepherd and his border collies run rings around sheep at **Leault Farm** (Kincraig, T01540-651310, year round, Sun-Fri 1600, £4/adult, £2/child). Depending on the time of year, you will also be able to bottle-feed lambs or see a traditional sheep-shearing demonstration. And if you're really lucky, there may even be collie pups to cuddle.

Rain check

Cinemas
• Eden Court, Inverness, T01463-234234.
• Vue, Inverness, T0871-224 0240.

Indoor play & amusements
• Aviemore Indoor Climbing Wall, Extreme Dream, T01479-812466, extreme-dream.com.
• The Fun House, Hilton Coylumbridge, nr Aviemore, T01479-813081. Mini golf, soft play, arcade, ten-pin bowling, outdoor discovery adventure park and American diner.
• Waltzing Waltzers, Newtonmore, T01540-673752, waltzingwaters.co.uk. Dancing fountain show, Daily, 1000-1600, £4.25/adult, £2.50/child.

Indoor swimming pools
• Inverness Leisure, Bught Park, Inverness, T01463-667500.
• Leisure Arena, Macdonald Aviemore Highland Resort, T01479-815275.

Museums
• Grantown Museum, Grantown-on-Spey, T01479-872478, grantownmuseum.co.uk.

Best of the rest Scottish Highlands

The Cairngorms National Park is a natural choice for adventurous family holidays – nowhere in the Scottish Highlands will you find a more child-friendly range of accommodation, activities and attractions. That's not to say, however, that the rest of the Highlands are out of bounds. Both of the following locations have plenty to keep families happy.

Fort William and Lochaber

Covering a vast wedge of Scotland, from Loch Ness and Rannoch Moor in the east to Mallaig and Ardnamurchan in the west, Lochaber has one foot in the mountains, the other in the sea. No surprise, then, that Fort William, at the region's hub, has declared itself the UK's Outdoor Capital (outdoorcapital.co.uk).

Despite the town's plethora of adventure opportunities, Ben Nevis still reigns supreme in most visitors' plans. Even if you don't intend climbing Britain's highest mountain (1343 m), the **Nevis Range Mountain Gondola** (T01397-705825, nevisrange.co.uk) can whisk you effortlessly to 655 m on the north face of neighbouring Aonach Mor where easy walking trails lead to breathtaking viewpoints of Ben Nevis and the Great Glen. On the lower slopes of Aonach Mor, Leanachan Forest has over 25 miles of cycle tracks, including family trails. For cycle hire, contact **Off Beat Bikes** (T01397-704008, offbeatbikes.co.uk).

Just south of Fort William, the **Glencoe Visitor Centre** (T01855-811302, glencoe-nts.org.uk) provides a family-friendly gateway to one of the Highland's most spectacular glens. Inside you'll find interactive displays and activities on the landscape, wildlife and history of Glencoe, a café serving homebaked food and all the advice you need for

forays in the great outdoors.

At nearby Kinlochleven, **Ice Factor** (T01855-831100, ice-factor.co.uk) offers special family sessions on its ice-climbing wall (minimum boot size 4) and can arrange multi-activity days combining rock- or ice-climbing with canyoning or white water rafting. Other operators offering multi activities in the Fort William area include **Highland Activities** (T0845-094 5513, highlandactivities.co.uk), and **Snowgoose Mountain Centre** (T01397-772467, highland-mountain-guides.co.uk).

Fort William is also the departure point for two contrasting Highland journeys – **Crannog Cruises** (T01397-700714, crannog.net) operates 90-minute voyages in search of seals on Loch Linnhe, while **The Jacobite Steam Train** (T01524-732100, steamtrain.info) chuffs 42 miles to the coast, crossing the 21-arch Glenfinnan viaduct of Harry Potter fame before reaching the fishing village of Mallaig where ferries run to Rum, Eigg and Muck.

Loch Lomond & The Trossachs National Park

Just 20 miles north of Glasgow (see page 286) Loch Lomond & The Trossachs National Park (lochlomond-trossachs.org) is one of the most accessible chunks of the Scottish Highlands – you could easily sample it on a day-out from the city. Far better, though, to immerse yourself in this beautiful swathe of forest, loch and mountain.

To get your bearings, start at Balloch where **Loch Lomond Shores** (T01389-751035 lochlomondshores.com) merges shopping, eating and leisure under one convenient, if rather commercial, roof. It's not only the location of the Gateway Centre, where rangers can advise

Autumn in the Trossachs.

on activities and walks (such as the easy-access Woodland Trail behind the centre), but it's also home to Can You Experience (for canoe, kayak and bike hire), Sweeney's Cruises, the Loch Lomond Aquarium and a ceramics painting studio.

Aberfoyle, meanwhile, is on the fringes of **Queen Elizabeth Forest Park** (forestry.gov.uk) where the David Marshall Lodge Visitor Centre lies at the heart of a network of walking and cycling trails. The centre also has a play area, Go Ape high-wire adventure course and live footage of ospreys and red squirrels.

Some of the Trossach's best scenery can be experienced from the **SS Sir Walter Scott** (T01877-332000 lochkatrine.com), a classic steamship that plies the waters of Loch Katrine from Trossachs Pier. Make a day of it by hiring bikes at the pier from **Katrinewheelz** (T01877-376316), taking them on board for the morning cruise to Stronachlachar and then cycling back along the shores of the loch.

North of Callander, the A84 skirts the slender whisp of Loch Lubnaig where **Forest Holidays** (T0845-130 8223, forestholidays.co.uk) operates one of its cabin sites (see page 19).

Head west, towards Stirling and you'll find **Doune Castle** (T01786-841742, historic-scotland.gov.uk) and the **Blair Drummond Safari and Adventure Park** (T01786-841456, blairdrummond.com).

Sleeping The Cairngorms

Pick of the pitches

Glenmore Caravan Park and Campsite

Glenmore Forest, T01479-861271, forestholidays.co.uk. Year round, £11-19/pitch (two people), plus £5.25-8.25/extra adult, £2.75-4.25/extra child. £1 discount for families.

⛺ 🏕️ 🚿 🔥 🅿️ 🎒 🐕 🛒 🍴 🚲 ♿

A superb family campsite right in the heart of the Cairngorms, Glenmore has 220 pitches scattered through pine forest next to Loch Morlich. It's a popular site, so don't expect a Highland wilderness experience with just the red squirrels for company. Instead, you'll find a bustling community with children zipping around on bikes (available for hire from £10-12/day), washrooms with piped-in radio and a host of onsite activities. Choose from forest safaris, orienteering, birdwatching, minibeast hunts and bat forays – all from around £5/adult, £4/child or £15/family (purchase a Forest Experience Card and you'll receive a discount on these and other local activities and attractions). Children's activity books (£2) and Young Explorers' Club packs (£8) are available from reception.

Opposite the entrance to the campsite, the Glenmore Forest Park Visitor Centre has a ranger station, shop and café (see page 300). Loch Morlich Watersports (page 294) and the Cairngorm Reindeer Herd centre (page 296) are also within walking distance. Just before the entrance to the campsite (on the road from Aviemore), you'll find a great little café serving breakfasts (a godsend if you emerge from your tent to find the midges are bad), as well as snacks, soups and legendary apple strudel – all with picture-window views of a red-squirrel feeding station. Next door, a shop sells groceries and outdoor gear.

Rothiemurchus Camp and Caravan Park

Coylumbridge, nr Aviemore, T01479-812800, rothiemurchus.net. Year round, from £7/adult, £2/child (5-16).

⛺ 🏕️ 🚿 🅿️ 🚲 ♿

Like Glenmore, above, the campsite at Rothiemurchus Estate is pitch-perfect for active families. In addition to an activity line-up that almost spans the entire alphabet (from archery to white water rafting), the estate's adventure centre (page 294) offers various jollies tailor-made for families. These include gorge walks (minimum age six), rafting on the Spey (eight-plus) and daily feeding sessions at Kenapole Deer Farm. But it's River Raiders that will really get kids' pulses thumping. Featured on none other than *Raven* (the BBC children's programme that had every parent coining the phrase, "Let the challenge begin"), this unique adventure course sees your little darlings zip-sliding, abseiling, rock climbing and grappling with all kinds of obstacles above the mighty River Findhorn (minimum age seven).

Back at the campsite – nestled in a blissfully peaceful glade of Caledonian pines – there's an excellent farm shop and deli (see page 300), as well as a restaurant/café serving fresh, local produce.

Also recommended
Dalraddy Holiday Park

Dalraddy Estate, nr Aviemore, T01479-810330, alvie-estate.co.uk.

Invercauld Caravan Club Site

Braemar, T01339-741373, caravanclub.co.uk.

Glenmore Caravan and Camping Site.

Lazy Duck
Nethy Bridge, T01479-821642, lazyduck.co.uk. May-Oct, hostel £13/person; campsite £9/pitch (one person), £4/extra person.
There are 22 hostels scattered throughout the Cairngorms. (cairngormshostels.co.uk) and this is one of the smallest and, as the name suggests, the most relaxed. The snug little bunkhouse sleeps eight and has a wood-burning stove and covered garden area with barbecue. You can chill out in a hammock with views across heather moorland and Caledonian pine forest to the Cairngorms beyond, or really chill out under the solar-powered outdoor shower. A tiny campsite has space for just four small tents. And, yes, there are ducks – lazy Aylesbury ones – plus more active red squirrels, deer and capercaillie.

Best of the rest

Great North Lodges
Aviemore, T01479-812266, greatnorthlodges.co.uk. Year round, £279-4799/wk.
Luxury lodges in and around the Aviemore region, ranging from the cosy Twa Hoots holiday cabin (sleeping four) to the imposing Mountain Bear Lodge with room for 16 and nice little extras like a sauna and hot tub.

Hilton Coylumbridge
Nr Aviemore, T01479-810661, hilton.co.uk/coylumbridge. Check online for latest offers. Children under 10 stay and eat for free when sharing a room with an adult.

It's not exactly the rustic mountain experience you might be looking for, but there's no denying the family appeal of this swish hotel with its pool, sauna, family rooms and babysitting service. The Hilton's Fun House (see page 296) is the region's most popular wet-weather bolt-hole, while the outdoor adventure park has a dry ski slope and climbing wall.

Macdonald Aviemore Highland Resort
Aviemore, T0844-879 9152, macdonaldhotels.co.uk. Year round, Highland Lodges from around £1100/wk; check online for offers.
With no fewer than four hotels,

18 luxury self-catering lodges (sleeping six), plus half a dozen restaurants, this large resort caters for most budgets. Its big drawcard for kids is the Leisure Arena which boasts an indoor pool with water flumes and a wave machine. There's also a Fun Factory with inflatable slides, tunnels and bouncy castles.

Wigwam Holidays
Grantown-on-Spey, T01479-872474, wigwamholidays.com. Year round, from around £12.50/person.
More like wooden chunks of Toblerone than wigwams, these quirky, but cosy, cabins sleep up to five and come equipped with mattresses, seating and heating.

Eating The Cairngorms

Local goodies

Clootie Dumpling Restaurant
Speyside Heather Garden, Dulnain Bridge, T01479-851359, heathercentre.com. Year round, Mon-Sat 0900-1730, Sun 1000-1700.
A fruity suet dumpling, traditionally wrapped in a cloth (or *cloot*) and cooked in a pot over an open fire, clooties are tasty on their own or with a wee bit o' butter. But Granny Clootie serves them here in no less than 21 gooey guises – try ice cream and chocolate, heather honey and cream or butterscotch sauce and flaked almonds.

Rothiemurchus Farm Shop
Coylumbridge, nr Aviemore, T01479-812345, rothiemurchus.net. Year round, daily 0930-1730.
This fabulous farm shop sells organic beef reared on the Rothiemurchus Estate, fresh or smoked rainbow trout and wild venison, plus other local produce like Highland Blue cheese and heather honey.

Spey Valley Smokehouse
Achnagonalin, Grantown-on-Spey, T01479-873078, speyvalleysmokedsalmon.com.

Market days
Aviemore Myrtlefield Centre, 2nd Sun (Jun, Aug, Oct).
Grantown-on-Spey The Square, 1st Sun (May, Jul. Sep).
cairngorms-farmers-market.com.

Year round, Mon-Fri 0900-1700, plus Sat 1000-1400 during summer.
Witness the time-honoured process of curing, hanging and smoking prime Scottish salmon.

Quick & simple

The Boathouse Restaurant
Loch Insh Watersports Centre, Kincraig, T01540-651394, lochinsh.com. Year round, breakfast 0800-1800, dinner 1830-2100.
This popular restaurant on the shores of Loch Insh has a good view of the action going on at the watersports centre – especially from the sheltered, glass-sided balcony. Light bites include toasted sandwiches and jacket potatoes (from £4), haggis with mash (£5.85) and haddock, chips and salad (£7.30). The dinner menu features plenty of local flavour. Try the braised shank of Highland lamb (£11.95) or the Speyside salmon with prawn and mango salsa (£11.50).

Glenmore Forest Visitor Ctr
Glenmore Forest Park, T01463-791575, forestry.gov.uk. Year round, daily 0900-1700.
Pick up some information on local walks, then treat yourself to a Belgian waffle with syrup and cream (£2.75). Savoury dishes include soup with oatcakes (£3.60) and haggis on toast (£3).

Gordon's Restaurant
Braemar, T01339-741247, gordonsbraemar.com. Year round,

Mon-Fri 1000-1700, Sat-Sun 1000-1600, 1800-2000.
Traditional home-cooking with a fine steak pie (£8.25) and sticky toffee pudding (£3.50).

La Taverna
Aviemore, T01479-810683, highrange.co.uk. Year round, daily.
Atmospheric pizzeria with an eat-as-much-as-you-like buffet of stone-baked pizzas, pasta dishes and salads from £12.95/adult and £6.95/child.

Also recommended
Happy Haggis Fish and Chips
Grampian Road, Aviemore, T01479-810430. Year round.

Posh nosh

The Ptarmigan Restaurant
CairnGorm Mountain, T01479-861341, cairngormmountain.org. year round, daily, summer 1000-1700, winter 0900-1620.
Britain's highest restaurant (1097 m) serves daytime snacks, but the hottest tickets in the Highlands are its summer evening ceilidhs (Jul-Aug, Thu), where a three-course buffet with dancing costs from £23/adult, £16/under-12s and £60/family, including travel on the funicular railway.

Also recommended
Mountview Hotel
Nethybridge, T01479-821248, mountviewhotel.co.uk. Evening meals from 1800, plus Sunday lunch.

Essentials The Cairngorms

Getting there

By air Scheduled flights operate between Inverness (the main gateway to the Highlands) and Belfast, Birmingham, Bristol, Dublin, East Midlands, Edinburgh, Gatwick, Luton, Manchester, and Southampton. Car hire is available at the airport from Avis (T01667-464070, avis.co.uk) or Hertz (T01667-462652, hertz.co.uk).

By train National Express East Coast (nationalexpresseastcoast.com) and ScotRail (scotrail.co.uk) operate services between Edinburgh or Glasgow to Inverness, via Newtonmore, Kingussie and Aviemore in the Cairngorms. ScotRail also runs Caledonian Sleeper Trains between London Euston and Scotland. National Express East Coast trains run from London King's Cross to Edinburgh, via Peterborough, York and Newcastle, while Virgin Trains (virgintrains.co.uk) operate along the west coast from Euston via Crewe and Carlisle to Glasgow. Virgin also runs a direct service from Birmingham to both Edinburgh and Glagow, while First TransPennine Express (tpexpress.co.uk) operates direct services to Edinburgh and Glasgow from Manchester Airport. CrossCountry (crosscountrytrains.co.uk) links Cardiff, Penzance and Brighton with Glasgow and Edinburgh, via Birmingham.

By coach National Express (T0871-781 8181, nationalexpress.com) operates services to Aviemore and Kingussie.

Getting around

By train See Strathspey Steam Railway, page 298.

By bus Operated by Stagecoach (stagecoachbus.com) the Heather Hopper 501 summer bus service connects Ballater and Grantown-on-Spey, running twice daily through the Cairngorms. The 34 service runs between Grantown and Cairn Gorm, via Boat of Garten, Aviemore and Glenmore.

Maps

Ordnance Survey Explorer 387 (Glen Shee & Braemar), 403 (Cairn Gorm & Aviemore), 404 (Braemar & Glen Avon) and Landranger 36 (Grantown & Aviemore).

Tourist Information Centres

On the A9 near Newtonmore, the Highland Gateway Visitor Centre has tourist info, a picnic area and woodland walk, as well as the Ralia Café. Useful websites include visitcairngorms.com, visitaviemore.com and visithighlands.com, while tourist information centres can be found in several towns, including:
Aviemore Grampian Rd, T08452-255121. Jun-Sep, Mon-Sat 0900-1800, Sun 1000-1700; Oct-May, Mon-Sat 0900-1700, Sun 1000-1600.
Ballater Old Royal Station, T01339-755306. Jun-Sep, daily 0900-1800, Oct-May, daily 1000-1700.
Braemar Mar Rd, T01339-741600.
Grantown-on-Spey High St, T08452-255121.
Tomintoul The Square, T01807-580285.

Further information

Cairngorms National Park, T01479-873535, cairngorms.co.uk.

Ranger Bases

Coylumbridge Rothiemurchus Visitor Centre, T01479-812345.
Nethy Bridge Explore Abernethy Visitor Centre, T01479-821565.
Glenmore Glenmore Forest Visitor Centre, T01479-861565.
Tomintoul Glenlivet Estate Office, T01479-870070.

Hospital

Raigmore Hospital, Old Perth Road, Inverness, T01463-704000.

Pharmacies

Aviemore Aviemore Pharmacy, Grampian Rd.
Ballater Davidsons, Bridge St.
Grantown-on-Spey Lloyds, High St.
Kingussie P Grant, High St.

Supermarkets

Aviemore Tesco.

Other shops

Camping supplies Ellis Brigham, Grampian Rd, Aviemore.
Toys & beach gear The Toy Shop, Bridge St, Ballater.

Environmental groups

Scottish Natural Heritage, T01479-810477, snh.org.uk.
Scottish Wildlife Trust, T0131-312 7765, swt.org.uk.

Major Events

May Cairngorms Walking Festival.
Sep Braemar Gathering.

Great escapes

Isle of Mull

What's the story in Balamory? Well, they stopped filming the cult children's television programme on Mull years ago and, although wide-eyed toddlers can still join a tour to see the colourful homes of Miss Hoolie, Josie Jump, Spencer and PC Plum (not forgetting, of course, Edie McCredie's garage), this Hebridean gem has a new cast of less garish celebrities – namely the otters, golden eagles, sea eagles, whales and dolphins that inhabit its spectacular coast and mountains.

From CBeebies to safaris, Mull has become a firm family favourite. Third largest of the Hebridean islands, it's easy to reach (with regular ferries from Oban), has a good range of reasonably priced accommodation, some wild and beautiful beaches and plenty to keep you occupied when it rains – which it does fairly frequently.

Get your bearings
In a child's mind, one of the big thrills of a holiday on Mull is the journey there.

The voyage between Oban and Craignure may only last 46 minutes, but it's tinged with all the excitement of a mini-cruise as the ferry (complete with cafés, restaurant, play area and shop) noses its way through the Sound of Mull. As you approach the eastern tip of the island, you'll see Duart and then Torosay Castle. Keep your eyes peeled for harbour porpoises which are often sighted in the Sound. For ferry bookings, contact **Caledonian MacBrayne** (T08000-665000, calmac.co.uk) which operates daily crossings between Oban and Craignure from £4.45/person and £39.50/car one-way or £7.55/person and £54/car for a five-day saver return.

At Craignure there's a tourist information centre (T01680-812377) and CalMac office opposite the jetty, as well as a supermarket, pub and craft shop. Craignure lies roughly halfway along the A849, the island's main road which heads west along the Ross of Mull to Fionnphort (departure point for ferries to the monastic Isle of Iona) or north, skirting the Sound of Mull to Tobermory.

The Balamory theme tune is bound to infiltrate your mind as you enter this picture-postcard village with its brightly-painted buildings framing a harbour filled with

From CBeebies to safaris, Mull has become a firm family favourite.

Waiting for the ferry

If you've got time to kill in Oban before cruising to Mull, walk past the ferry terminal into town. On the way, you'll pass stalls selling fresh seafood straight off the fishing boats tied up against the quay. Harbourfront George St is usually heaving in summer, but you can escape the crowds by continuing along the Esplanade towards the ruins of seventh-century Dunollie Castle and nearby Ganavan Sands, a safe, sandy beach about 1.5 miles north of the town. With more time, you could travel inland to the **Scottish Sea Life Sanctuary** (Barcaldine, T0871-423 2110, sealsanctuary.co.uk) where rescued seal pups receive expert medical care before being released back to the wild. This friendly little centre, on the shores of Loch Creran, also has resident otters and seals, as well as aquariums teeming with life found in the lochs of the West Highlands – including sea horses, sharks and rays.

Hebridean idyll – camping and canoeing on the shores of the Sound of Mull.

Great escapes Isle of Mull

trawlers and yachts. Balamory tours, including a visit to a children's farm are available from **Mull & Iona Taxi** (T01681-700507, mullionataxi.co.uk, £27.50/adult, £20/child). The tourist information centre (T01688-302182) is at the far end of Main Street by the pier. You can catch ferries from here to Kilchoan on the Ardnamurchan peninsula.

Sheilings.

Pitch your tent
On an island renowned for its wildness, where kelp runs riot on rocky shores and clouds skulk amongst forbidding mountains, there is something rather comforting about the immaculate campsite run by **Sheiling Holidays** (T01680-812496, shielingholidays.co.uk, Mar-Nov, £16/pitch for two people, plus £5/extra adult, £2.50/extra child). With wonderful views over the Sound of Mull and across Loch Linnhe towards Ben Nevis, this grassy site is located a few hundred metres from the ferry pier at Craignure. Ninety pitches are split between two levels. The lower one is next to a shingle cove and children's playground, and has hardstandings for caravans and motorhomes, while the upper one is a gently sloping camping field – more exposed to the elements, but with better views. Facilities are excellent, with hot showers, kitchen, common room and canvas awnings to dry towels and wet clothes beneath. You can watch the CalMac ferry coming and going and listen out for the whistle of the narrow-gauge steam train that trundles back and forth between Craignure and Torosay Castle. There's even the possibility of glimpsing seals, porpoises and otters from your tent. What really sets this campsite apart from others on Mull, however, are its shielings. Named after the summer cottages of Highland shepherds, these white-canvas tents bring a touch of 'glamping' to the island with their carpets, wood-burning stoves, *real* beds (up to six) and self-contained bathrooms and kitchens. All you need to bring is bedding,

cooking and eating utensils – or you can hire them from the campsite. Each sheiling costs from £30/night for two people (minimum stay two nights), plus £12/extra adult and £8.50/extra child.

Located in beautiful countryside with woods and a burn, **Tobermory Campsite** (T01688-302624, tobermory-campsite.co.uk, Mar-Oct, £6/adult, £3/child aged 5-11) is just a 20-minute walk from the town and has good facilities, including hot showers and electric hook-up.

More far-flung and basic – but with a location to die for – **Fidden Farm Camping** (T01681-700427, £4/adult, £2/child) enables you to pitch your tent behind Fidden Beach at the very tip of the Ross of Mull (see page 307). Mod-cons amount to little more than showers and toilets in a farmyard portacabin and you'll need a sturdy tent to withstand such an exposed location. In return, however, you get to crawl straight from your tent onto pristine sands and to round off days with beach barbecues overlooking the Sound of Iona.

Check-in to something more weatherproof
Numerous farmhouses and cottages offer self-catering accommodation on Mull. In the northwest of the island, **Treshnish Farm** (nr Calgary, T0845-458 1971, treshnish.co.uk, year round, £225-560/wk) has eight cottages sleeping up to four. The Treshnish cottages are clustered near the farmstead, while the Haunn cottages include three converted blackhouses tucked away down a farm track with views across the Sound of Coll.

Scoor House (Scoor, T01681-700105, scoorhouse.co.uk, year round, £150-440/wk) is another holiday hideaway, this time in the southwest of Mull. Its six properties sleep up to eight and are within easy walking distance of several sandy beaches on the Ross of Mull.

Isle of Mull Holidays (T01681-700260, isleofmullholidays.com) also offers self-catering accommodation on the Ross of Mull. For something less rural, the **Tobermory Youth Hostel** (T0870-004 1151, syha.org.uk, Mar-Oct, from

Peering at plankton on a Sea Life Surveys cruise in the Sound of Mull; Tobermory harbour; seals hauled out on Calve Island near Tobermory; lobster pots, buoy and a salad of seaweeds.

Great escapes Isle of Mull

£13.25/adult, £9.25/child) and **The Tobermory Hotel** (T01688-302091, thetobermoryhotel.com, year round, from £49/adult B&B and £8-24.50/child) both have family rooms.

Calgary Bay.

Explore the north

Don't try and squeeze Mull into a day – the island might only be 26 miles east to west and 24 miles north to south, but the roads are slow, convoluted and jammed with excuses to stop, get out and explore. At the very least, divide Mull into two day tours – one looping around the island's northern third, the other striking west along the Ross of Mull (see opposite).

Tobermory is the most obvious starting point for exploring the north of Mull. The B8073 toils inland past the Mishnish Lochs before unwinding in a dramatic series of twists and turns to **Dervaig** with its pencil-spire church and **Old Byre Heritage Centre** (Apr-Oct, T01688-400229, old-byre.co.uk) where exhibitions and short films depict the history and wildlife of Mull and Iona. There's also a tearoom here serving cakes, crofters soup and hot clootie dumplings with cream.

Five miles west of Dervaig, **Calgary Bay** is one of the most beautiful Hebridean beaches – a sweeping arc of silver-white sand backed by flower-speckled machair and woodland. It's the perfect spot for a picnic (or overnight stay if you're prepared for self-sufficient wild camping). There are footpaths along the edge of the bay, but don't miss the fabulous sculpture trail through Calgary Woods to the beach which has been developed by **Calgary Art in Nature** (T01688-400535, calgaryartinnature.co.uk).

For something more bracing drive a couple of miles south to a car park located in an old quarry near the entrance to Treshnish Farm (page 304). Here you'll find the starting point of a fairly challenging 4-mile walk skirting the dramatic **Treshnish Headland**. As well as spectacular views

of the Treshnish Isles, you might spot seals and sea eagles, while the latter stages of the hike pass the remains of villages abandoned during a typhoid epidemic in the mid-1800s.

A short distance south along the B8073, near the head of Loch Tuath, **Eas Fors** is a series of waterfalls, culminating in a horse-tail plume that plunges 100 ft into a sea pool. The ferry slipway for crossings to the **Isle of Ulva** (ulva.mull.com) is just down the road, but you'll need at least a half-day to do justice to this little beauty – if only to fully appreciate the oysters, salmon and other local delicacies served at The Boathouse.

From Ulva, the road turns east, hugging the shore of Loch na Keal before straddling Mull's pinched waist to reach the pretty village of **Salen**. A mile north you'll find the ruins of 14th-century **Aros Castle**, once a stronghold of the Lords of the Isles. Look out for common seals basking on rocks nearby, then continue north to Tobermory.

Duart Castle.

Castles, trains & raptors

There are several attractions close to Craignure, including **Torosay Castle** (T01680-812421, torosay.com, Apr-Oct, gardens year round, £6.50/adult, £3.75/child, £16.50/family) where, in addition, to the baronial-style Victorian family home, there are 12 acres of gardens to explore, plus an adventure playground and café. You can reach Torosay on the narrow-gauge steam train operated by **Mull Rail** (T01680-812494, mullrail.co.uk, return tickets £4.50/adult, £3/child, £13/family) which rattles along a mile and a quarter of track between Craignure and the castle. A 3-mile footpath links Torosay with **Duart Castle** (T01680-812309, duartcastle.com, Apr-Oct, £5.30/adult, £2.65/child). You can also drive to the ancestral home of the Clan Maclean, but there is something undeniably epic about approaching this magnificent clifftop castle on foot. Save some energy for exploring the state rooms, dungeons and keep. Nearby, **Wings over Mull** (T01680-812594, wingsovermull.com, Apr-Oct, £4.50/adult, £1.50/child, £10/family) has over 40 birds of prey with flying displays (indoors or out) and information on Mull's wild raptors.

Ben More.

Explore the Ross of Mull

From Craignure, the A849 loops south through forest before ascending rugged Glen More. Just before you climb into the mountains, though, a left turn tempts you south to Lochbuie and the remote sweep of **Laggan Sands**. As well as exploring the wild and beautiful beach, you can visit Moy Castle and an ancient stone circle.

Back on the main road, the mountains beckon. Surrounded by Mull's highest peaks, including 3170-ft Ben More, **Glen More** is arguably the best place in the world to spot a golden eagle. Three territories converge on the glen and it's worth pulling over in one of the parking spaces to scan the ridges of Beinn Talaidh and Ben Buie for the telltale silhouettes of eagles soaring on broad, finger-tipped wings held in a flat v-shape. You're almost guaranteed to see other birds of prey, such as buzzards, kestrels and, with luck, short-eared owls. To stand a chance of sighting Mull's largest raptor, however, drive on towards **Loch Scridain**.

Here, in the shadow of Ben More, you might glimpse a sea eagle – even larger than a golden eagle and characterised by huge broad wings, a short white tail and heavy hooked bill. These magnificent birds once bred throughout north and west Britain with at least 100 eyries recorded in the early 19th century. Shooting, trapping and poisoning, however, decimated the population and in 1916 the last two were shot on Skye. In 1975, however, a reintroduction programme helped them regain their former Scottish haunts, with Mull becoming a major stronghold.

As you continue west along the southern shore

Safari so good

A rising tide nuzzles rocks drizzled with honey-coloured seaweed. Each rhythmic swell chuckles through heaped piles of kelp, massaging them to life until they are twitching, swirling and cavorting with the sea – playing otter-tricks with your mind.

You can always tell a seal from an otter by the way the latter flicks its tail in the air before diving underwater. And otter prints have four pad marks, whereas dogs have five. Or is it the other way round? The best way to be sure is to join an organised wildlife safari where local experts will take you to all the best spots on Mull for sighting otters, eagles, buzzards, hen harriers, short-eared owls, seals and red deer. Expect a full day travelling in a minibus (usually with ardent birdwatchers), stopping often to spend long periods scouring lochs and mountains through binoculars – fine for a budding Bill Oddie, but not something for very young children prone to fidgeting or whingeing. Expect to pay around £30-40/person.

Discover Mull T01688-400415, discovermull.co.uk. **Island Encounter** T01680-300441, mullwildlife.co.uk. **Isle of Mull Wildlife Expeditions** T01688-500121, torrbuan.com. **Mull Wildlife Tours** T01680-812440, mullwildlifetours.co.uk **Wild About Mull** T01681-704229, wildaboutmull.co.uk.

Spot an otter, bag a buzzard.

Great escapes Isle of Mull

of Loch Scridain, keep your eyes peeled for otters and seals. At **Pennyghael**, there are superb views across the loch towards the pyramidal peak of Ben More. The hamlet also has a small shop for picnic snacks. Seven miles on, a track branches south from **Bunessan** to sandy **Uisken Beach** which has views out to Colonsay and the Paps of Jura. Neighbouring **Ardalanish Bay** is another of Mull's white-sand beauties.

From Bunessan it's a further five miles to **Fionnphort** and the road's end – or rather the slipway for ferries to **Iona**, lying just a mile offshore. Banished from Ireland, St Columba made landfall here in 563 and the abbey that he founded is one of Scotland's most celebrated Christian centres. Caledonian MacBrayne (see page 303) operates ferries to the island, while Historic Scotland (T0131-668 8800, historic-scotland.gov. uk) manages both **Iona Abbey** (year round, daily, £4.70/adult, £2.35/child) and the **Columba Centre** (Apr-Oct, Tue-Thu 1030-1730, free), next to the slipway at Fionnphort.

The cove at Fionnphort is sandy and has a curious boulder split down the middle, but there are other more exciting beaches nearby. South of the village, **Fidden Beach** might just scoop the prize for Mull's best beach. A swathe of soft sand with pink-granite outcrops and pockets of pebbles, speckled like birds' eggs, anything goes at Fidden – from sandcastles and rock-pooling to paddling in startlingly turquoise inlets.

North of Fionnphort, meanwhile, a winding track fizzles out at **Kintra** where white-washed cottages (some available to rent) huddle around a small rocky bay. There's not much sand here, but the rock-pooling and crab-hunting are excellent.

Join a boat trip

Sea Life Surveys (Tobermory, T01688-302916, sealifesurveys.com) offers the best choice of wildlife cruises for families on Mull. A pricey treat, the four-hour Wildlife Adventure cruise (£45/adult, £35/child, £144/family) takes you from Tobermory along the Sound of Mull in search of harbour porpoise and basking shark, visiting a salmon farm, a seal colony, trawling for plankton and listening out for dolphins using a hydrophone. The eight-hour Whalewatch Explorer (£75/adult) is not recommended for children under 14, but does venture further offshore where you are more likely to see dolphins and minke whales. For slightly more affordable options, the two-hour Ecocruz (£27/adult, £22/child, £88/family) is a shorter version of the Wildlife Adventure trip, while the Seal Cruise (£12/adult, £6/child) nips across to Calve Island to see some common seals.

Turus Mara (T01688-400242, turusmara. com) operates boat trips from Ulva Ferry to the Treshnish Isles where you get two hours ashore in the company of nesting puffins (mid-Apr-early Aug). The six-hour cruise (£45/adult, £22.50/child, £120/family) also includes a landing on Staffa where you can clamber about the extraordinary basalt columns of Fingal's Cave.

Tobermory treats

Walk from the car park towards the pier and take your pick of the following colour-coded highlights:
Chocolate Co (dark blue) Handmade chocs, plus café.
Fish and chips (silver trailer on the jetty) Mon-Sat from 1230, king scallops £5, fish and chips from £4.60.
Hebridean Whale & Dolphin Trust (pink) Cetacean-themed gift shop and conservation centre.
Bakery (pink) Orkney ice cream, £1.50/scoop.
Mull Museum (brown and cream) Easter-Oct, Mon-Sat from 1000. Find out about the mysterious shipwreck of the Spanish galleon in Tobermory harbour.
Togs & Toys (yellow) Sailing boats, buckets and spades.
Corner Shop (red) Balamory clothes and gifts.
The Mishnish (dark grey) Iconic pub with a great menu featuring local meat and seafood dishes.

Essential websites

Tourist information visitscottishheartlands.com.
Holiday Mull & Iona holidaymull.co.uk.

Best of the rest Scottish Islands

Isle of Arran

With mountains in the north and lowland forest in the south, Arran (ayrshire-arran.com) is 'Scotland in miniature'. It's popular with day-trippers, but spend a night or two to make the most of its attractions.

The main ferry route to the island is between Ardrossan and Brodick. If you're camping, **Seal Shore** (Kildonan, T01770-820320, campingarran.com, Mar-Oct, £6/adult, £3/child, £1-4/tent) is a quiet, beach-side family site 12 miles south of Brodick Pier. It's run by a local crab and lobster fisherman, has great rock-pooling and – with a bit of luck – a steady, midge-ridding sea breeze. If canvas is out of the question, however, head to the north of the island where **Lochranza Youth Hostel** (T0870-004 1140, syha.org.uk, Mar-Oct, from £12.50) makes a wonderful base for walking and cycling.

For organised activities, contact **Arran Adventure** (Brodick, T01770-302244, arranadventure.com) which offers everything from mountain biking and sailing to sea kayaking and abseiling. The Isle of Arran Outdoor and Walking Festival takes place in September, while the annual wildlife festival (with safaris, guided walks and workshops) is usually held in May.

Historical highlights on Arran include **Brodick Castle** (nts.org.uk) and **Lochranza Castle** (historic-scotland. gov.uk), but if you're on a culture-quest don't miss the **Isle of Arran Heritage Museum** (T01770-302636, arranmuseum.co.uk, Mar-Oct, daily from 1030) which has old farm tractors and an activities shed for the kids. Next door, the Rosaburn Café serves Arran oat cakes, ice cream and other local goodies.

Raining? Make a dash to **Balmichael Farm & Visitor Centre** (Shiskine, T01770-860596, balmichael.com) which offers indoor archery and laser shooting, pottery painting, local crafts and a coffee shop.

Isle of Skye

You can drive to Skye (isleofskye.com) across the bridge from Kyle of Lochalsh to Kyleakin or take the ferry from Mallaig to Armadale, looking out for dolphins en route.

The mountain scenery on Skye is legendary. So, too, are the midges and the rain – and you get all three in abundance at **Sligachan Campsite** (T07786-435294, sligachan.co.uk, Apr-Oct, £5/adult, £3/child). Gaze down on this modest campsite from the surrounding peaks of the Cuillins and the tents resemble flakes of confetti. For something more substantial, Sligachan Hotel (which manages the campsite) has family rooms, as well as self-catering cottages and a bunkhouse with dorms. There are also hostels at Broadford and Uig (syha.org.uk), plus numerous cottages available to rent on the island.

Skye is a paradise for walkers and, although many routes are demanding, several are suitable for mini-trekkers. Try the Fairy Glen, near Uig, where a surreal landscape of cone-shaped mounds, gullies and burns is crying out to be explored. Or, for a bit of a challenge, hike the 3.5-mile trail along the Trotternish escarpment to the striking rock formations of the Quiraing.

Back at sea level, trade boots for boats and take a three-hour cruise on the *Bella Jane* (Elgol, T0800-731 3089, bellajane.co.uk, Apr-Oct, £20/adult, £8/child) to see the seals in Loch Coruisk.

In Portree, the weatherproof **Aros Centre** (T01478-613649, aros.co.uk) has exhibitions about Skye, as well as an indoor play area, cinema, gift shop, art gallery and café. Other attractions on the island include **Armadale Castle and Gardens** (Sleat, T01471-844305, clandonald. com, Apr-Oct, £6/adult, £4.40/child), **Glendale Toy Museum** (T01470-511240, toy-museum.co.uk, year round, £3/adult, £1/child), **The Skye Museum of Island Life** (Kilmuir, T01470-552206, skyemuseum.co.uk, Apr-Oct, £2.50/adult, £0.50/child) and **Skye Serpentarium Reptile World** (Broadford, T01471-822209, skyeserpentarium.org.uk, Mar-Oct, £3/adult, £2/child).

Caledonian MacBrayne

Ferry trails – CalMac ferries ply routes throughout the Hebrides.

Information for overseas travellers

When to go
Britain has a mild climate with summer temperatures ranging from 14-30°C. The high season runs from April until October when most attractions are open. School holidays (most of July and August) are very busy, especially at the most popular tourist destinations such as The Lakes, Devon and Cornwall, the Scottish Highlands, Cotswolds and the Pembrokeshire coast.

Getting there
One of the busiest airports in the world, London Heathrow (heathrowairport.com) is served by most major international airports. London has three other main airports (Gatwick, Stansted and Luton), while regional airports include Edinburgh, Glasgow, Cardiff and Manchester. The national carrier is British Airways (ba.com), while low-cost airlines include easyJet (easyjet.com), Flybe (flybe.com) and Ryanair (ryanair.com). Ferries operate along 33 routes to England and Wales, arriving at ports on the south, east and west coasts, including Dover, Newhaven, Portsmouth, Harwich, Hull, Liverpool, Fishguard and Holyhead. Prices vary enormously according to season: check ferrycrossings-uk.co.uk or contact operators such as Brittany Ferries (brittanyferries.com). The only option that doesn't involve travel to Britain by air or sea is to use the Channel Tunnel (eurotunnel.com) from mainland Europe.

Getting around
Its compact size and excellent infrastructure make Britain easy to get around. Self-drive is a flexible option; roads and motorways are well maintained, but bear in mind that major tourist routes can become heavily congested in peak periods and fuel is expensive. All the major car rental companies can be found at airports. For coach travel try National Express (nationalexpress. com) and Scottish Citylink (citylink. co.uk). For rail travel, Britrail (britrail. com) provides an online booking service for overseas visitors.

The **Great British Heritage Pass** (britishheritagepass.com) offers free entry to more than 580 of Britain's most popular heritage sights, including Stonehenge and Shakespeare's Birthplace. Family passes (two adults and up to three children under 15) cost from £72 (4 days) to £180 (30 days).

Accommodation
There is no shortage of places to stay in Britain and Ireland: everything from hiring your own private castle to pitching a tent is on offer. Hotels can often be expensive, with family rooms costing upwards of £150/night. Popular family choices include self-catering cottages, farm stays (farmstayuk.co.uk) and family-friendly hotels and guesthouses. Holiday villages have been popular in Britain for decades, ranging from traditional favourites like Butlins (butlins.com) to climate-controlled Center Parcs (see page 16). Another great British institution, B&Bs can be found everywhere, while the Youth Hostel Association (yha. org.uk) and Scottish Youth Hostel Association (syha.org.uk) provide excellent value accommodation at hundreds of locations throughout Britain. Bridge Street Worldwide (bridgestreet.co.uk) offers serviced apartments in all major UK cities.

Health and safety
No vaccinations are required for entry. Citizens of EU countries are entitled to free medical treatment at National Health Service (NHS) hospitals on production of a European Health Insurance Card (EHIC). For details see nhs.uk. Australia, New Zealand and several other non-European countries have reciprocal health-care arrangements with Britain. Citizens of other countries will have to pay for all medical services, except accident and emergency care given at Accident and Emergency (A&E) Units at most (but not all) NHS hospitals. Health insurance is therefore strongly advised for citizens of non-EU countries.

Fast facts
Time GMT
Language English, Welsh, Scottish
Money GB pound (sterling)
International dialling code +44
Tourist info visitbritain.com
Visas ukvisas.gov.uk
Plug adaptor Three-square pin

Index

A

Abbey Gardens 72
Abbotsbury Swannery 82
Aberdyfi 269, 272
Abersoch 273
Alnwick Castle 24, 234, 237
Alnwick Garden 235-236
Alton Towers 27
Alum Bay 47, 50, 55
Animal Farm Park 73
Amazon World Zoo Park 56
aMazing Hedge Puzzle 163
Amble Links 231
Animal Ark 184
Aquarium of the Lakes 222
Arlington Court 106
Arreton Barns Craft Village 56
Arundel 35
    Wetland Centre 36, 41
Ashdown Forest Centre 36
Aviemore 289
Avon Dam 93
Avon River 73

B

Bala 269, 276
Ballater 289
Balmoral 289
Bamburgh Beach 231
Bamburgh Castle 234
Bantham 90, 97
Barafundle Bay 246
Barmouth 269, 272
Barnstaple 89, 99
Barricane Bay 90, 94
Battle 35, 41
Bath 73
Beachy Head 36
Beadnell Bay 231
Beaulieu 66
Becky Falls 106
Beddgelert Forest 271
Bedruthan Steps 124
Beer 75, 78
Beesands 96
Bembridge 47, 48, 50
Bempton Cliffs 197, 206
Bentley Wildfowl Museum 41
Berney Marshes Reserve 177
Berry Head 90
Betws y Coed 269
BeWILDerwood 182
Bibury 155
Bicton Park Gardens 83
Bideford 89, 98, 99
Bigbury-on-Sea 96

The Big Sheep 102
Blackberry Farm 41
Blackgang Chine 55
Blackpool 27, 97, 194
Black Rock Sands 273
Blakeney 175, 185
Blenheim Palace 155
Bluebell Railway 40
Blue Reef Aquarium 138
Boat of Garten 289
Bodiam Castle 34, 40
Bodmin 119, 123, 138
Bodnant Garden 277
Bognor Regis 38
Boscastle 119, 123
Bossiney Haven 124
Bracklesham Bay 35, 36
Brading Marshes Reserve 56
Brading Roman Villa 56
Braemar 289
Brancaster 175, 178
Branscombe 75
Bridlington 197, 200
Bridport 75, 76
Brighstone Village Museum 56
Brighton 35, 38, 39
Bristol 73
British Museum 32
Brixham 96
Broad Haven 246
Broad Haven South 246
The Broads 23, 175, 180-181
Brook Bay 46, 50
Bryher 73
Buckfastleigh 89
Buckland Abbey 106
Buckler's Hard 66
Bude 119, 126
Budleigh Salterton 75, 78
Bure Valley Railway 184
Buttermere 216

C

Caerfai 246
Caernarfon 269, 276
Cairn Gorm 290, 295
Cairngorm Reindeer Herd 296
Calbourne Water Mill 56
Caldey Island 243, 252
Caldecott Horse Sanct 176
Caldicote Castle 163
Calgary Bay 306
Camber Sands 35, 38
Camel Trail 132
Canonteign Falls 106
Cardigan Bay 270

Cardinham Woods 122
Carew Castle 253
Carisbrooke Castle 54
Cars of the Stars 223
Castle Drogo 106
Castle Howard 204
Castell Henllys 252
Castlerigg Stones 219
Caswell Bay 264
Challaborough 96
Charlestown 119, 138
Charmouth 77, 78
Chessington World of
    Adventures 27
Chester Zoo 195
Cheddar Caves & Gorge 73
Chipping Campden 155
Clearwell Caves 162
Cley 177, 178
Clovelly 106
Coed y Brenin Forest 269,
    271, 275
Colliford Lake Park 138
Colwell Bay 50
Compton Bay 50
Combe Martin Bay 94
Coniston 215
Conkers 169
Constantine Bay 127, 133
Conwy 272
Corfe Castle 83
Cornish Birds of Prey Ctr 138
Cotehele 138
Cotswold Water Park 155
Cotswold Way 155
Cotswold Wildlife Park 155
Court Farm Country Park 73
Cowes 47, 50
Crackington Haven 124
Craignure 303
Crealy 102, 134
Criccieth 269
Crich Tramway Village 194
Cromer 175, 178
Crooklet's Beach 126
Croyde 89, 92, 94, 101
Cuckmere Valley 37, 39
Cumberland Pencil
    Museum 222

D

Dairyland 138
Dalby Forest 197, 203
Dale 243, 246
Danby 197, 199
Dart Estuary 91

Dartington Crystal 106
Dartmeet 93
Dartmoor 93
Dartmouth 89, 91, 98, 106
Dawlish Warren 96
Daymer Bay 124
Dean Forest Railway 162
Dean Heritage Centre 162
The Deep 204
Dervaig 306
Dick Whittington Farm 162
The Dig 205
Diggerland 106
Dinas Dinlle 273
Dinosaur Adventure 182
Dinosaur Coast 198
Dinosaur Isle 54
The Dinosaur Park 253
Donkey Sanctuary 76
Drayton Manor 27
Drusillas Park 35, 40
Duart Castle 306
Durham 195

E

East Angle Bay 246
Eastbourne 35, 38, 39
East Portlemouth 96
Eden Camp 206
The Eden Project 135
Edinburgh 287
Electric Mountain 277
Elizabethan House Museum
    184
Elterwater 215
Escot Gardens 82
Eureka! 204-205
Exbury Gardens 67
Exmoor National Park 73
Exmoor Zoo 106
Exmouth 75, 78, 100
Explore-at-Bristol 73

F

Fal Estuary 119
Falmouth 119, 123, 128,
    130, 132, 133
Family Cycle Trail 158
Farne Islands 235
Ferrers Centre 173
Fidden Beach 308
Fionnphort 308
Filey 197, 200
First & Last Trail 132
Fishguard 243
Fistral 126

Folly Farm 252
Fort William 297
Fountains Abbey 206
Flambards 134
Flamingo Land 27, 205
Fleet Air Arm Museum 73
The Forbidden Corner 205
Fowey 119, 128, 130, 132, 133
Freshwater 47, 50
Freshwater East 246
Friston Forest 36
FutureWorld @ Goonhilly 134

G

Geevor Tin Mine 138
Glasgow 286
Glencoe 297
Glenfinnan Viaduct 24, 297
Glen More 307
Glenmore Forest 290, 291, 298
Gloucester Cathedral 24
The Gnome Reserve 105
Goodrich Castle 163
Grassholm 243, 249
Great Mattiscombe Sands 92
Great Yarmouth 178, 184
Greenwich 32
Greenwood Forest Park 276
Gressenhall Farm 184
Gwithian 123, 126

H

Hadrian's Wall 195, 235
Harewood House 206-207
Hartland Point 92
Hastings 38
Harbour Park 35
Harlyn Bay 127
Hartfield 35, 36
Haverfordwest 243
Hawker's Cove 124
Hayle Estuary Reserve 123
Hayle Sands 124
Heatherton Country Park 253
Heights of Abraham 194
Hele Bay 94
Helford Estuary 119
Helford Passage 128, 130
Herstmonceux Castle 41
Hickling Broad Reserve 177
Hidcote Manor Gardens 155
Hidden Valley Discovery 139
Highland Folk Museum 290
Highland Wildlife Park 295
Holkham 175, 178
Holy Island – see Lindisfarne
Holywell Bay 124
Honistor Slate Mine 222
Hope Cove 97

Hornsea 200
Hove 35, 38, 39
Howletts & Port Lympne
  Wild Animal Parks 26
Hull 197, 198
Hunstanton 175, 178, 182

I

Ilam Park 194
Ilfracombe 89, 95, 98, 107
Iona 308
Ironbridge Gorge 154
Isle of Arran 309
Isle of Skye 309
Isle of Ulva 306
Isle of Wight Donkey
  Sanctuary 56
Isle of Wight Railway 56
Isle of Wight Zoo 56
Isle of Wight Model Village 56
Isles of Scilly 72-73

J

Jorvik Viking Centre 205

K

Kelvingrove Art Gallery &
  Museum 286
Kennack Sands 128
Keswick 215
Kielder Water & Forest
  Park 234
Kimmeridge Bay 76, 78
King Arthur's Labyrinth 277
Kingsbridge 91, 98
Kynance Cove 128

L

Lacock Abbey 24
Lake District Visitor Ctr 218
Laggan Sands 307
Lakeside & Haverthwaite
  Railway 222
Landmark Forest Theme
  Park 296
Land's End 120-121, 136
Langdale Valley 216
Langland Bay 264
Lanhydrock 134
Lannacombe 96
Lappa Valley Railway 139
Launceston Railway 139
Leault Farm 296
Lee Bay 94
Legoland 27
Lepe Country Park 66
Lindisfarne 235
Littlehampton 35, 38
Liverpool 195

Living Coasts 107
Lizard Peninsula 119
Llanbedrog 273
Llanberis 269, 270, 276
Llandudno 272
Llyn Peninsula 269, 272-273
Loch Insh 290
Loch Lomond & The
  Trossachs 297
Loch Morlich 290
Loch Scridian 307
London 32-33
  Aquarium 32
  Dungeon 32
  Eye 32
  Science Museum 33
  Zoo 33
Longdown Activity Farm 67
Longleat 73
Looe 119, 128
Lost Gardens of Heligan 134
Lulworth Cove 77, 78
Lundy Island 103
Lyme Regis 75, 77, 78
Lyndhurst 64
Lynmouth 89, 91, 94, 98
Lynton 89

M

Manchester 195
Marazion 128
Marloes Sands 246
Mawddach Trail 275
Mawgan Porth 124
Mevagissey 119
Mid-Yare Valley Reserve 177
The Milky Way 107
Mill Bay 97
Mineral Tramway Trail 133
Miniature Pony Centre 107
Mirehouse 222
Monkey World 82
Monmouth Beach 77
Moors Valley Country
  Park 66
Morston 175
Mother Ivey's Bay 124
Mottistone Manor Garden 57
Mousehole 119, 122
Mullion Cove 128
Muncaster 222
Mundesley 175, 178
Murton Park 207

N

National Gallery 32
National Forest Maize Maze 173
National Lobster Hatchery 139
National Marine Aquarium 102

National Maritime Museum
  135
National Railway Museum 198
National Seal Sanctuary 139
Natural History Museum 32
The Needles 47, 55, 57
Nefyn 273
Nevis Range Mountain
  Gondola 297
Newcastle 195
New Forest Centre 64
New Forest National
  Park 65
Newgale 243, 246
New Lanark World Heritage
  Site 286
Newport (Isle of Wight) 47
Newport (Pembrokeshire) 243
  Sands 247
Newquay 119, 126, 132, 139
Newton Haven 231
Newtonmore 289
Niton Maze 57
Norfolk Lavendar 176
North Norfolk Railway 184
North York Moors Moors
  National Park 24, 197, 198,
  199, 203
North Yorkshire Moors
  Railway 206

O

Oakwood Theme Park 252
Oban 303
Osborne House 54
Otter Estuary Reserve 76
Otter, Owl & Wildlife Park 67
Owl & Falconry Centre 57
Oxford 24, 146, 154
Oxwich Bay 264

P

Padarn Country Park 270
Padstow 119, 130, 132
Paignton 96, 107
Paradise Park 139
Parkhurst Forest 48
Paultons 66
Peak Cavern 194
Peak District National Park 194
Pecorama 83
Pembroke Castle 253
Pembrokeshire Coast Path 243
Pendennis Castle 139
Pennywell Farm 103
Penrith 215
Pensthorpe 183
Pentewan Valley Trail 133
Penzance 119, 130

People's Palace & Winter
   Gardens 286
Perranporth 119, 126, 133
Perrygrove Railway 162
Philpot Museum 78
Pickering 197
Picton Castle 253
Pitt Rivers Museum 154
Plymouth 89, 92, 96, 100
Polzeath 119, 126
Poppit 247
Porth Ceiriad 273
Porthcothan 125
Porthcurno 128-129
Porthgwidden 125
Porthmeor Beach
Porthminster Beach 125
Porth Neigwl 273
Porth Oer – see *Whistling
   Sands*
Porthtowan 119, 126
Port Isaac 125
Portsmouth 33
Pooh Sticks Bridge 36
Port Eynon Bay 264
Portmeirion 277
Port Quin 119, 132, 133
Powderham Castle 107
Praa Sands 129
Prickly Ball Farm 107
Purbeck Marine Reserve 76
Pulborough Brooks 36, 35
Puzzlewood 162
Pwllheli 269

Q
Queen Elizabeth Forest
   Park 297

R
Ramsey Island 243, 249
Ranworth Broad Reserve 177
Ravenglass & Eskdale
   Railway 222
Rhossili 238, 265
River Wye 161
Roald Dahl Museum 26
Robin Hill Countryside
   Adventure Park 55
Robin Hood's Bay 197, 200
Rock 65, 133
Roman Baths 73
RHS Garden Rosemoor 107
Roseland Peninsula 119, 129
Rosliston Forestry Centre 172
Ross-on-Wye 157
Rothiemurchus Estate 298
Runswick Bay 201
Ryde 47, 50

S
St Agnes 73
St Aldhelm's Head 77
St Austell 119, 129
St Barbe Museum 67
St Bees 218
St David's 243, 244, 245
St George's Cove 125
St Ives 119, 126, 132
St Martins 73
St Mary's 72
St Mawes 119
St Michael's Mount 136
Salcombe 89, 96, 98, 100
Salthouse 175
Sandown 47, 51
Sandsend 201
Saundersfoot 243, 247
Saunton 90, 94, 101
Scarborough 197, 206, 207
Scottish Sea Life Sanct 303
The Sculpture Trail 158
Seaford 35
Seagrove Bay 51
Seahouses 231
Sea Palling 175, 178
Seaton 75, 76
Seaton Tramway 83
Seaton Marshes Reserve 76
Seatown 78
Seaview Wildlife Encounter 57
Sence Valley Forest Park 169
Sennen Cove 120-121, 126
Seven Sisters Country Park
   36, 37, 39
Shakespeare Birthplace 154
Shanklin 47
Sheffield Park 35, 40
Shell Island 272
Sheringham 175, 178, 184
Sherwood Forest 154
Sidmouth 75, 78
Skokholm 243, 248-249
Skomer 243, 248-249
Slapton Sands 96
Snettisham Park 183
Snettisham Reserve 177
Snibston Discovery
   Museum 172
Snowdon 269
   Mountain Railway 276
Snowshill Manor 155
Soar Mill Cove 97
South Devon AONB 92
South Downs National Park
   35, 36
South Devon Railway 103
South Downs Way 36
South Hams 97

Southport 195
South West Coast Path 92
South West Lakes Trust 122
Speedwell Cavern 194
Staithes 201
Start Bay 92
Start Point 92, 105
SS Great Britain 73
Steephill Cove 51
Stonehenge 73
Strathspey Railway 296
Strumble Head 244
Studland Bay 77, 79
Summerleaze 126
Sundown Adventure Park 154
Swanage 75, 79
Swanage Railway 83
Symonds Yat Rock 157, 159

T
Tarka Trail 99
Tarn Hows 216-217
Tate St Ives 123, 136
Teifi Marshes 245, 250
Tenby 243, 247
Thanet Coast Project 33
Thornton-le-Dale 197
Thorpe Park 27
Three Cliffs Bay 264
Thurlestone 96
Time & Tide Museum 184
Tintagel 119, 136
Tintern Abbey 163
Titchwell 175, 177
Tobermory 303
Tor Bay 264
Torosay Castle 306
Torquay 89, 96
Totland Bay 51
Totnes 98
Traeth Llyfn 247
Treak Cliff Cavern 194
Trebah Gardens 139
Trebarwith Strand 127
Tresco 72
Trevaunance Cove 125
Trevone 127
Trevose Head 119, 127
Treyarnon Bay 125
Trotters World of Animals 223
Tunnels Beaches 95
Twycross Zoo 173

U
Undercliffs Nature Reserve 76
Upper & Lower Tamar
   Lakes 90

V
Ventnor 47, 51
   Botanic Gardens 48

W
Wadebridge 119
Walsingham 175
Warwick Castle 154
Warkworth Beach 231
Watergate Bay 123, 126
Weald & Downland
   Open Air Museum 41
Wells & Walsingham
   Railway 184
Wells-next-the-Sea 175, 178
Welney Wetland Centre 184
Welsh Wildlife Centre 245
Wembury Marine Centre 90
West Bay 79
Westbury Court Gardens 163
Westonbirt Arboretum 155
Westward Ho! 95, 101
West Wittering 35, 38
Weymouth 75, 79, 83
Whinlatter Forest Park 218
Whistling Sands 273
Whitby 197, 201
Whitesand Bay (Cornwall)
   119, 120-121, 126
Whitesands Bay
   (Pembrokeshire) 247
Widemouth Bay 126
Wiggonholt Common 36
Wilderness Wood 41
Wildlife and Dinosaur Park 104
The Wildlife Park at Cricket
   St Thomas 73
Windermere 215, 216
Withernsea 201
Wonwell 96
Woodlands Leisure Park 104
Woody Bay 94
Wookey Hole Caves 73
Woolacombe 89, 90, 95, 101
World of Beatrix Potter 223
World of Country Life 83
Wye Valley Butterfly Zoo 163

Y
Yarmouth 47, 48, 49, 51, 52
Yaverland 51
York 197, 205
Yorkshire Dales National
   Park 197

Z
Zennor 122

Mineral Tramways
Network of Trails– Mid-Cornwall

MINERAL TRAMWAYS

60km of predominantly off-road, flat trails.
Ideal for beginners, novices and families.
Cycle coast to coast in just a few hours and explore a whole network of trails. Enjoy stunning scenery and discover Cornwall's rich mining heritage along the way.
Various picnic areas and refreshment stops en route.

For more information go to
www.cornwall.gov.uk/mineral-tramways
or call **01872 322000**

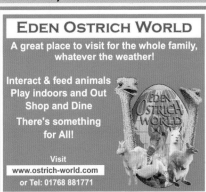
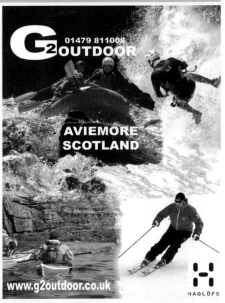

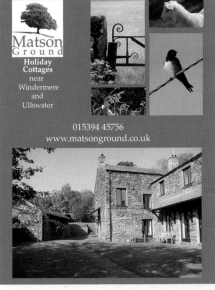